THE LAND-GRANT COLLEGES AND THE RESHAPING OF AMERICAN HIGHER EDUCATION

THE LAND-GRANT COLLEGES AND THE RESHAPING OF AMERICAN HIGHER EDUCATION

ROGER L. GEIGER AND NATHAN M. SORBER, EDITORS

PERSPECTIVES ON THE HISTORY OF HIGHER EDUCATION

VOLUME THIRTY, 2013

PENNSTATE
1855

Transaction Publishers
New Brunswick (U.S.A.) and London (U.K.)

Library of Congress Catalog Number: 2012029404
ISBN: 978-1-4128-5147-3
Printed in the United States of America

Library of Congress Cataloging-in-Publication Data

The land-grant colleges and the reshaping of American higher education / Roger L. Geiger and Nathan M. Sorber, editors.
    p. cm. — (Perspectives on the history of higher education ; 30)
    ISBN 978-1-4128-5147-3
    1. State universities and colleges—United States—History.
2. Education, Higher--United States—History. I. Geiger, Roger L., 1943- II. Sorber, Nathan M.
LB2329.5.L33 2013
378'.0530973—dc23
                                                                    2012029404

Contents

Preface

The higher education community has recognized major anniversaries of the Morrill Act of 1862 with commemorations, public celebrations, and scholarly publications. This special volume of *Perspectives on the History of Higher Education* includes a collection of articles that were originally presented at a symposium to mark 150 years since the passage of the act. Such remembrances are warranted by the significant contributions that land-grant colleges have made over the generations. However, in this celebratory spirit, in both histories and public rites, there has been a tendency to romanticize the origins and evolution of land-grant colleges. Land-grant college leaders often wax eloquently about expanding access to previously underserved populations, growing state economies, becoming engines of research and technological development, advancing agriculture to meet the needs of a modern economy, and providing support and educational opportunities to rural communities. The higher education community looks with nostalgia on Morrill's great achievement, when democracy created people's colleges.

The articles in *The Land-Grant Colleges and the Reshaping of American Higher Education* provide a critical reexamination of such traditional and often romantic narratives. The authors highlight the achievements of the movement, but avoid crafting a hagiography of the land-grant actors and institutions. The intention is not the displacement of land-grant colleges, which serves as a laudatory example of the value of partnerships between higher education and the state. Instead, the objective is to present a more accurate depiction of the founding and evolution of land-grant colleges, based on empirical investigations and attention to new departures in historiography. It has been five decades since Earle Ross wrote *Democracy's College,* arguing that expansion of democratic participation and demands for higher education reforms motivated the movement. However, despite challenges by Eldon Johnson,

Roger Williams, and other revisionists, the image of land-grant colleges persists as an inevitable, popular retort to aristocratic classical colleges. This volume presents a more nuanced assessment of the origin and development of land-grant colleges and universities.

On July 2, 1862, President Abraham Lincoln signed the Land-Grant College Act of 1862, "An Act Donating public lands to the several States and [Territories] which may provide colleges for the benefit of agriculture and the mechanic arts." Although it was an instance of forward-looking statecraft to expand the educational attainment of the people, which was made possible by the secession of southern opposition from the Congress, the premise was also to advance the economic competitiveness of the nation and enhance the scientific understanding and practice of agriculture. It provided federal land to each state and territory that was to be sold for the purpose of maintaining

> . . . at least one college where the leading object shall be, without excluding other scientific and classical studies, and including military tactics, to teach such branches of learning as are related to agriculture and the mechanic arts . . . in order to promote the liberal and professional education of the industrial classes in the several pursuits and professions of life.

Justin Morrill defended his bill to the Congress by invoking four objectives. First, he intended to open educational opportunities for the "industrial classes." Since colleges mostly prepared students for various professions and were patronized by the professional class, Morrill envisioned a college in each state: "accessible to all, but especially to the sons of toil"—the "thousand willing and expecting to work their way through the world by the sweat of their brow." Second, to provide instruction in the "practical avocations of life," the Act specifically mentioned agriculture and the mechanic arts as being the leading objects. The third aim was to teach the practical arts alongside "other scientific and classical studies." Morrill's purpose was simultaneously cultural—to elevate these studies and students to the same social standing as A.B. degrees—and functional—to advance these subjects through a connection with the higher learning. The fourth goal was to encourage what nowadays would be called *economic development through research*. A large part of Morrill's speech advocating his bill described the declining productivity of American agriculture, which was in contrast with European countries in which agriculture was studied in a scientific manner. Modern sciences, he presciently argued, "are more or less related to agriculture or the mechanic arts." He specifically envisioned professors of agriculture at the land-grant colleges who would apply scientific knowledge to reverse the curse of falling farm productivity.

This volume divides the long, complex story of the land-grant movement into five Parts. The introduction to each Part provides an overview of the developments in that era; the twelve individual articles provide closer examinations of representative developments. In Part I, Adam Nelson and Nathan Sorber explore the key factors underlying the origins of the act. Several aspects of the legislation did not originate with Justin Morrill: Similar educational schemes had been tried or proposed at agricultural colleges and polytechnics. The unique feature was offering the largess of the federal government, through its ample supply of public land, to assist in creating a perpetual endowment. The Act received passing mentions in the press, more as a federal land policy than as an educational innovation. The legislation was initially opposed in the West and South, and was not the product of popular demand for higher education reform. Farmers and workers remained on the sideline, skeptical of the value of "book learning." Gentlemen farmers from agricultural societies, scientists trained in German universities, and statesmen with interests in stimulating the economy instigated and supported the land-grant movement.

In Part II, articles by Peter Moran, Roger Williams, and Susan R. Richardson explore the establishment of land-grant colleges in Pennsylvania and Texas, demonstrating that the Morrill Act did not produce a single institutional form or mission. The responsibility of defining and implementing the land-grant act fell to the states, and regional peculiarities and state political dynamics produced institutional variety in the nineteenth century.

The promise of useful education in agriculture and the mechanical arts for the industrial classes would keep the land-grant colleges yoked to what contemporaries called the *industrial class*. However, as Frederick Rudolph argued years ago in *The American College and University*, "dirt farmers" were largely uninvolved in instigating the land-grant movement. In his study, Greg Behle demonstrates that few "sons of toil" enrolled in the early years. The principal issue facing the first generation of land-grant colleges was whether they were intended to be agricultural colleges, primarily serving the farming community, or full academic institutions, teaching "scientific and classical studies" in addition to agriculture.

Part III explains the first phase of this conflict during the last decades of the nineteenth century. By the 1870s, farmers had developed a proprietary attitude toward land-grant colleges, and launched a prolonged campaign to remove land-grant funds from full universities or force agricultural colleges to do more with the aim of aiding farmers. The aims of the populist movement, described by Scott Gelber, typified this campaign. Populists used newfound power in state legislatures to attune land-grant college programs, admission standards, and curricula in order to meet the needs of farmers. In six states, the land grants were moved from original designees to new institutions that entirely focused on the farmers' interpretations of useful knowledge. However, the greatest victory of agriculture occurred in the Congress. Commencing with the Hatch Act of 1887, creating agricultural experiment stations, a series of enactments provided a dedicated stream of federal funding for agricultural research and, ultimately, extension. Colleges of agriculture became insular units within universities with separate funding and a broad mission to serve the agricultural community through research, extension, short courses, and outreach.

At the same time, engineering developed spontaneously and became the largest field of study at land-grant institutions. The Massachusetts Institute of Technology pioneered the new engineering education, but it did not take off until the 1880s. Then, as Gregory Zieren explains, Robert Thurston overcame the obstacles to teaching mechanical engineering and led the expansion of this field of study. Arguably, more than any other field, engineering was the first to fulfill the Morrill mandate of integrating practical and scientific studies.

By 1900, it was increasingly apparent that full-fledged universities were the dominant institutions of American higher education. However, only a handful of institutions possessed the scale and scope to offer a full range of disciplinary and professional studies with credible programs for graduate education and research. In 1910, fourteen institutions were christened the *Great American Universities*, with just five of them being given land grants, including private Cornell. Before 1900, in fact, public land-grant universities lagged far behind the leading privates in doctoral education. Afterward, they rapidly strengthened their university credentials, led by the universities of Wisconsin, California, and Illinois. The University of Illinois, under the presidency of Edmund James (1903–1920), was the late starter of this group, and it well represents the transformation of the first generation of land grants into public research universities. Part IV examines the second generation of land grants in the rise of Pennsylvania State College, led by President Ralph Hetzel (1926–1947), to university status during the interwar years. What amounted to a third generation of land-grant universities made this transition after World War II. The evolution of American universities, land grants and otherwise, toward a common model raises the question of what remained of the land-grant tradition.

Part V clearly shows that the land-grant mission is alive and well in university colleges of agriculture and, in fact, is inherent to their identity. A key element in this mission has been the agricultural extension agents, who provide the tangible link between university expertise and state farmers. The critical role played by agents during the New Deal is explored here by Christopher Loss. This mission has also inspired visions and actual efforts to transpose it to other kinds of social problems. Ethan Schrum examines the attempt to shape the new branch of the University of California at Irvine into a resource for applied social science that is capable of using academic expertise to solve the problems of American cities. Finally, Scott Peters reminds readers of two important truths: The land-grant tradition has always spawned more comprehensive interpretations—called *metanarratives*—that encompass facts, values, and hopes; second, this tradition has also been contested by metanarratives which emphasize the negative consequences of the progress driven by land-grant agricultural technologies.

These papers were prepared for and presented on June 22–24, 2011, at a Conference at the Pennsylvania State University called "The Legacy and the Promise: 150 Years of Land-Grant Universities." The authors would like to thank the following offices that supported this conference: The Penn State Alumni Association, the Office of the Provost, Penn State Outreach, the College of Agricultural Sciences and the College of Education, the Center for the Study of Higher Education, and former president Graham Spanier. As a commemoration of the 1862 Morrill Act, these papers do not address the historically black land-grant colleges and universities, most of which were created in response to the Second Morrill Act of 1890. However, material on these institutions is included in Volume Twenty-Nine of *Perspectives on the History of Higher Education: Higher Education for African Americans before the Civil Rights Era, 1900–1964* (2012).

A longitudinal view of 150 years of land-grant history provides a more nuanced and more accurate depiction of the legacy of the 1862 Morrill Act. The new institutions were built on some existing foundations, but they initially had to decide whether they were a part of American higher education or an alternative to it. The former position carried the day with the emergence of American universities. In *The Uses of the University*,

Clark Kerr identified the land-grant tradition as the homegrown, American component of the amalgam that comprised our twentieth-century universities. However, as is obvious in Part V, agriculture and its federal partnership retain a unique umbilical cord to the original Morrill Act. The editors hope that the following studies contribute toward an appreciation of the depth, complexity, and continuing value of the land-grant tradition.

Roger L. Geiger
Pennsylvania State University

Nathan M. Sorber
West Virginia University

Part I

Scientific and Social Foundations

Introduction

Nathan M. Sorber

The Morrill Land-Grant Act of 1862 created institutions that were known by various names: People's Colleges, Agricultural and Mechanical Colleges, and Industrial Colleges. The monikers highlighted the legislation's aims of expanding higher education access to the so-called *industrial classes*, and of providing instruction in the "useful subjects" of agriculture and mechanical arts. Historians have depicted the land-grant colleges as a reaction to the elite and aloof classical colleges, and a response to popular demand for expanded opportunity and utility in higher education. Land-grant college histories are often framed within the social milieu of Jacksonian Democracy, and the origins of the movement are represented as an outgrowth of increasing participation and influence of the "common man" on American education, politics, and culture. Most notable and lasting is Earle Ross' *Democracy's College,* which views land-grant colleges as products of a burgeoning industrial education movement that is premised on displacing the old collegiate order with practical education suited to the industrial classes. Major land-grant histories follow Ross' lead (i.e., Edward Eddy, Allan Nevins, and J. G. Edmonds), but this consensus was due for revision after Eldon Johnson and Roger Williams found little evidence of a popular movement demanding or supporting land-grant colleges in the early years. In the aftermath of the revisionists' critique, the popular demand thesis was scuttled, but no new consensus emerged. The articles in this first section contribute to a new framework for understanding the origins of the Morrill Act and the land-grant colleges.[1]

Perspectives on the History of Higher Education 30 (2013): 3–12
© 2013. ISBN: 978-1-4128-5147-3

In the first two articles, Adam Nelson and I explore Morrill Act antecedents besides those premised on the "common man" awakening to the benefits of higher education. In doing so, we highlight how the growth of science, economic development, and international competition served as impetuses of the land-grant movement. Expanding the context beyond the intellectual strictures of Jacksonian Democratic thought, these works consider the influence of Whig and Proto-Republican political and economic philosophies on the development of the land-grant idea. Adam Nelson's "Institutionalizing Agricultural Research in the Early American Republic" and my "Creating Colleges of Science, Industry, and National Advancement" align the Morrill Act with those reformers who viewed public higher education investment as a means to expand the economic and political influence of the United States. The core political beliefs of Whigs such as Justin Morrill included support for internal improvements: bridges, canals, and turnpikes to aid commerce and communication; tariffs to protect and nurture fledgling industries; and investment in science and higher education to spur growth in technology, develop new industries, and create scientists, engineers, and skilled laborers. Nelson uncovers an embryonic stage of this state-higher-education symbiosis, finding public investment in higher education five decades before the Morrill Act. He argues that legislatures, colleges, and agricultural societies partnered to institutionalize the plant sciences in higher education with the hope of advancing agricultural science and practice. I find similar developments, albeit on a wider scale, surrounding the land-grant activities of the 1860s. The Morrill Act was the culmination of a growing state interest to develop the nation's scientific capabilities, especially in the areas of agricultural and industrial science, and to enhance the productivity and profitability of American agriculture and industry.[2]

A major theme that pervades these articles, as well as recent scholarship on Morrill Act origins, is that the land-grant colleges joined an eclectic higher education landscape at mid-century. As opposed to being an original event that separates premodern and modern higher education, the land-grant colleges were an institutional expression of a remarkably innovative zeitgeist. This period witnessed a host of educational ventures that experimented with scientific and applied studies, including scientific schools, agricultural schools and colleges, polytechnic institutes, and multipurpose colleges.[3]

One of the most fertile areas for new educational departures was agriculture, thanks to the influence and leadership of state and local agricultural societies. As Nelson and I discuss in our articles, agricultural societies were the domain not of farmers who tilled the field for their livelihood, but of scientifically minded professionals, merchants, or public officials, including Justin Morrill. In order to improve agriculture, these gentlemen farmers experimented on their farms and gardens, hosted state and county fairs, and published agriculture journals. In addition, they wanted to introduce science into higher education. Robert Gardiner's lyceum in Maine (f. 1821), for example, became the nation's first institution to "teach those branches of natural philosophy and chemistry which are calculated to make scientific farmers and mechanics." Other private ventures followed, most notably the Farmers College in Cincinnati, Ohio (f. 1846). While ultimately ceasing collegiate-level instruction in 1866, the Farmers' College initially succeeded by offering a traditional classical program, short courses in practical agriculture, and a scientific course encompassing agriculture, engineering, and surveying. More lasting contributions of the agricultural societies were the founding of state agricultural colleges. In concert with financial support from state governments, society members played a leading role in inaugurating the Michigan State Agricultural College, the Maryland Agricultural College, the New York Agricultural College, and the Pennsylvania Farmers' High School in the decade before the Morrill Act. With the exception of New York (which would follow a different path after the intersession of Ezra Cornell), each state made these institutions its land-grant college.[4]

As agricultural science gained a foothold in higher education, the mechanical arts and engineering were finding homes in military academies, polytechnics, and some "classical colleges." Surveying and civil engineering were first, with West Point offering instruction as early as 1817. Most attempts by antebellum colleges at civil engineering were short lived, but the pioneering Union College managed to organize a regular course in the subject in 1845. Engineering penetrated higher education in a much more permanent way by mid-century, as collegiate programs displaced the mechanics institutes where artisans gave manual instruction in "shop-culture." In 1851, Rensselaer Polytechnic (f. 1824) became the nation's first, full-fledged engineering college that offered a degree in civil engineering. It was soon followed by polytechnics in Philadelphia in 1853 and Brooklyn in 1854, and William Barton Rogers was perfecting his scheme for the Massachusetts Institute of Technology in 1860. MIT was to provide "systematic training in the applied sciences . . . [and] to give to the industrial classes sure mastery over the materials and processes over which they are concerned." When it opened in 1865, it set a new standard for applied science education and research.[5]

Although these higher education enterprises emerged throughout the first half of the nineteenth century, traditional literary colleges remained popular for professional preparation and cultural refinement. Stable enrollments and the specter of the Yale Reports of 1828 kept leading institutions from straying too far from their classical fare. However, as Adam Nelson's article suggests, there was plenty of room for innovation on the margins of the classical curricula at Columbia, the University of Pennsylvania, and Harvard. Nelson notes that historians tend to view colleges of this era as denominational schools while emphasizing strictly classical education," but he concludes that "such a characterization obscures not only the role of the state but also the role of science—and scientific research—in these institutions."[6]

One way in which colleges such as Yale and Harvard could participate (and lead) in this movement for the applied sciences, while preserving their traditional clientele and programs, was by establishing separate scientific schools. As depicted in my article, the earliest incarnation of Yale's Sheffield Scientific School, the Department of Philosophy and Arts, began instruction to students who had not enrolled in Yale's academic program in 1846. The curriculum initially included courses in analytical chemistry, agricultural chemistry, botany, and vegetable physiology, and after becoming a scientific school in 1856, it offered courses in engineering, metallurgy, and organic and industrial chemistry. The new institution was to serve as a refuge for those "students of science" who wanted to engage in original inquiries in college laboratories or on model farms, and those with desires to enter the "higher practical occupations." The latter referred to those who were interested in joining a new middle-class workforce as engineers, scientists, and business managers. Harvard's Lawrence Scientific School (1847) focused on basic science and individual study after having recruited famed Swiss scientist Louis Agassiz, but neglected instruction in applied sciences such as engineering. The Chandler Scientific School at Dartmouth attempted a three-year engineering program, but young and ill-prepared students diminished hopes of creating a scientific outpost in New Hampshire. The Sheffield Scientific School was at the vanguard of applied science education and research when it was named "Connecticut's land-grant college" in 1863. It was celebrated for its degree programs in chemistry and engineering, graduate study, and faculty who were trained in leading European universities. Justin Morrill and "National Schools of Science" advocate Daniel Coit Gilman regularly praised the Sheffield Scientific School as the ideal land-grant college.[7]

Growing attentiveness to expanding scientific knowledge, developing the American industry, and competing with international economies led to the rise of agricultural colleges, polytechnics, schools of science, and, ultimately, land-grant colleges. The explanation for the introduction of scientific study is manifold. Agricultural societies worked to connect scientific discoveries to farm practices in agricultural colleges; European universities, expatriate scholars, and the rapid expansion in chemical knowledge influenced the development of America's "schools of science"; multipurpose, denominational colleges experimented with irregular applied science offerings to meet the demands of local constituents; and polytechnics fulfilled the skilled manpower needs of urban industries. Although the expansion of science in higher education was impressive, for some, it was not progressing quickly enough. Educational reformers at the state level, usually led by agricultural society members, called on state legislatures to fund initiatives that would expand scientific research and education. They argued that state partnerships were essential for developing a scientific understanding of agriculture, improving farm practices, and increasing the profitability of the state's agriculture industry.[8]

Adam Nelson argues that the state-higher education collaboration for expanding scientific knowledge has roots stretching back to the early years of the republic. By tracing the contributions of four leading botanists, he explains how agricultural society members and plant scientists worked to institutionalize their scientific subjects within higher education. In addition to serving as early faculty in botany, agriculture, and materia medica, they pressed for botanical gardens and herbaria at their respective institutions. By 1815, all of them had contributed personal collections and lobbied state leaders for financial support to expand their scientific holdings. Benjamin Smith Barton, a University of Edinburgh graduate, brought his own herbarium of 5,000 plant species to his post as professor of botany at the University of Pennsylvania, which supplemented his lectures on applied botany. Samuel Latham Mitchill was a New York state legislator, a leader of the state agricultural society, and a lecturer on botanical subjects at Columbia College. Holding membership in the government, society, and college domains made Mitchill a natural spokesman for investing state resources to advance scientific studies in higher education. His campaign at Columbia was joined by David Hosak, who contributed an extensive herbarium and botanical library, and in 1795, he was named professor of botany and materia medica at the medical school. Nelson concludes by discussing the establishment of a professorship of natural history at Harvard in 1805. The Massachusetts Society for Promoting Agriculture led a campaign that solicited more than $31,000 to fund the new faculty chair (a large portion of the sum came from a state land grant). Alumnus William Dandridge Peck, a member of the Massachusetts Agricultural Society, was appointed to the post and immediately sent to Europe to "acquaint himself with the object and the manner of instruction" from the world's leading botanical scientists. He returned to Cambridge with deeper insights of the science, as well as numerous specimens and books.[9]

My article explains that the land-grant act was a federal extension of decades of disparate state efforts to advance science in higher education, progressing toward the ultimate purpose of "elevat[ing] American capital and labor to best international competitors." In 1861 and 1862, Whig Senator Justin Morrill's Tariff Act and Land-Grant Act were consistent "American System" policies of government intervention to nurture the rise of a developing economy. The aim of the former was to protect fledgling industries from competition; the latter held the promise of creating profitable new technologies and practices, and of developing skilled human capital to implement science-based processes within a modern economy. In 1862, the most critical industry was agriculture, where the French and English were besting the Americans in crop yields, exports, and profits. Morrill's intentions were revealed on the Senate floor: "Should no effort be made to arrest the deterioration and spoliation of the soil in America, while all Europe is wisely striving to teach her agriculturalists the best means of hording up capital . . . we are doomed to be dwarfed in national importance."[10]

Soon after the Morrill Act had been passed, the narrow-term "agricultural college" was commonly used as shorthand for the land grants, obfuscating the broad intentions of the act. Michigan Agricultural College, the state land-grant recipient, became the progenitor of a land-grant vision that is best described as "vocational agricultural education." The "Michigan Plan" of manual labor, subcollegiate curricula, and modest admission standards was embraced by several Midwestern and Western land-grant institutions as being the best scheme for providing practical education to rural youth and returning them to the farm.

Daniel Coit Gilman penned his treatise "Our National Schools of Science" to counter the ideas in the Michigan Plan by reasserting the primacy of scientific research in land-grant colleges. Land-grant colleges should not "train young men to go back and labor with the hoe or the anvil . . . [but] rather train men by scientific courses of study for the higher avocations of life . . . to be leading scientific men," he argued. Although Gilman reported that only his Sheffield Scientific School had achieved the high aim of postgraduate study and the pursuit of science for its own sake, several land-grant colleges—most notably in the Northeast—followed a portion of his "National School of Science" prescription and made the scientific study of practical problems the hallmark of original curricula. Professors at these colleges included scientists who had often pursued advanced study in German universities, who were quite different from the practicing farmers who tended to staff the agricultural colleges of the West. Land-grant colleges that followed Gilman's line included the likes of Evan Pugh, Samuel Johnson, and Andrew Dickson White—scholars not farmers—and they wanted an alternative to the literary colleges, not an institution below collegiate grade. The rigorous study of chemistry, botany, mathematics, and engineering was to be supplemented, not diminished, by instruction on a farm, in a laboratory, or in a workshop.[11]

A fairly rigorous scientific curriculum was present at the Illinois Industrial University at its founding, and as such, it is not surprising that in the final article in this section, "Educating the Toiling Peoples: Students at the Illinois Industrial University, spring 1868," J. Gregory Behle ununcovers few "children of toil" of humble circumstance. Behle argues that the original course of study at Illinois' land-grant college combined a replica of Union College's scientific course, the engineering program at West Point, and the traditional liberal arts. The institution was quite generous in admitting students with varying degrees of preparation, yet those who were not privately fitted or academy trained likely struggled, as the college had no remediation or preparatory classes. The less wealthy students could not afford the luxury of private preparation, and this may have contributed to only 16 percent of the original seventy-seven students remaining to graduate.[12]

Not only did the challenges of collegiate coursework deter poorer students from applying or persisting, but apparently so did the cost. Let us consider Behle's examples of the average income for the following industrial class workers according to the 1870 census: the Illinois farm laborer making $200 a year, the unskilled factory worker at $200 a year, the skilled machinist at $700 a year, or the college janitor at $480 a year. Annual tuition, room and board, and ancillary expenses could run nearly $160 a year, and Behle concludes, the cost "consumed more of a family's annual income than could be tolerated for those in a lower economic position."[13] Indeed, the author finds a dearth of students enrolling from such backgrounds. In contrast, the students in the inaugural class at Illinois' land-grant college were the sons of professionals, merchants, and, most often, prosperous farmers. In 1870, the average family wealth for students (property value + personal assets) was nearly $20,000; it was more than the college president could claim and double the average wealth of the college faculty. Although it is difficult to ascertain annual income figures from wealth data for farmers (as figures are skewed by large, nonliquid property holdings), the modal student was connected to a large farm that was five times the acreage and value of the state's average 160-acre family farm. It is likely that these large farm enterprises produced enough annual income for fathers to forgo the labor of a working-age child and to fund a college education instead.

The findings from Behle's in-depth assessment of the first class at the Illinois Industrial University are consistent with his previous article on the social origins of students at the university between 1868 and 1894. In that case, a random sample revealed the typical student coming from a well-to-do agricultural background. The average wealth of student families in the sample was again more than $10,000, and nearly ten times that of the average people of the Illinois Prairie. This phenomenon was not confined to Illinois, as a similar demographic profile has been found in the northeastern United States. At Maine's land-grant college, the average family wealth of graduates from the first three graduating classes (1872–1875) was $10,402 compared with a state mean of $1,333, and at Massachusetts Agricultural College, the student family wealth of $10,150 was twice the state average. Finally, Cornell University attracted wealthy students from across the country, and the average family wealth of the class of 1878 was $31,000. Although the sample is slightly misleading due to the presence of a few progeny of extremely wealthy farmers and industrialists, the median wealth of New York's land-grant students was still nearly twenty times that of the state's average family.[14]

Land-grant colleges were introduced, in part, to elevate science and advance America's economic prowess. The implementation of such a scheme required scientific curricula and high academic standards; a costly plan that likely deterred the poorer members of the industrial class. Since original land-grant college promoters wanted to produce human capital and advance scientific knowledge, new voices arrived in the 1870s that embraced the ideas of the "Michigan Plan"—an alternative model which viewed the land-grant colleges as a means of resisting and criticizing the social changes accompanying a modernizing economy. As farmers faced financial ruin after the banking crash of 1873 and its resulting depression, they joined populist movements and demanded that land-grant colleges improve the profitability of agriculture and keep their sons from leaving the farm. Through organizations such as the Grange, farmers agitated for extension services and rural community outreach, modest admission standards and free tuition, and vocational programs to train future farmers. They hoped their version of the Michigan Plan would help elevate farming's waning status in an increasingly urban-based, nonagricultural economy. Populists and the patrons of science would contest the central values of land-grant education during this period, an era that is discussed in Part III of this volume.

Notes

1. The traditional canon of land-grant college history has advanced a democratization thesis for the origins of the movement and includes the following: Earl D. Ross, *Democracy's College: The Land-Grant Movement in the Formative Stage* (Ames, IA: Iowa State University Press, 1942); Edward Eddy, *Colleges for Our Land and Time: The Land-Grant Idea in American Education* (New York: Harper Brothers, 1956); Allan Nevins, *The State Universities and Democracy* (Ames, IA: Iowa State University Press, 1962); and J. G. Edmonds, *The Magnificent Charter: The Origin and Role of the Morrill Land-Grant Colleges and Universities* (Hicksville, NY: Exposition Press, 1978). For the revisionist who found little evidence of popular demand for land-grant colleges in the early years, see Eldon L. Johnson, "Misconceptions about the Early Land-Grant Colleges," *The Journal of Higher Education* 52, no. 4 (July 1981); Roger L. Williams, *George W. Atherton and the Origins of Federal Support for Higher Education* (State College, PA: The Pennsylvania State University Press, 1991).
2. On the evolution of the Whig philosophy of internal improvement policies, see John Lauritz Larson, *Internal Improvements: National Public Works and the Promise of Popular Government in the Early United States* (Chapel Hill: The University of North Carolina Press, 2001). For a sweeping overview of Whig politics and ideology, see Michael F. Holt, *The Rise and Fall of the American Whig Party: Jacksonian Politics at the Eve of the Civil War* (New York, NY: Oxford University Press, 1999). For the major work that influenced Justin Morrill's political economy philosophy, see Henry Charles Carey, *Principles of Political Economy* (Philadelphia, PA: Carey, Lea, & Blanchard, 1837). For the emerging Republican philosophy and its Whig antecedents, see Eric Foner, *Free Soil, Free Labor, Free Men: The Ideology of the Republican Party Before the Civil War* (New York, NY: Oxford University Press, 1995).
3. Roger L. Geiger, "The Rise and Fall of Useful Knowledge," in *The American College in the Nineteenth Century*, ed. Roger L. Geiger (Nashville, TN: Vanderbilt University Press, 2000), 153–68. For a discussion of how the historiography has changed on this question, see the editor's introduction of Roger L. Geiger in *The American College in the Nineteenth Century* (Nashville, TN: Vanderbilt University, 2000), 1–36.
4. Alfred C. True, *A History of Agricultural Education in the United States, 1785–1925* (New York, NY: Arno Press, 1969), quote on 35–36; Julianna Chaszar, "Leading and

Losing in the Agricultural Education Movement: Freeman G. Cary and Farmers' College, 1846–1884," *History of Higher Educational Annual* 18 (1998): 25–46; Carl Becker, *Cornell University: Founders and the Founding* (Ithaca, NY: Cornell University Press, 1943).

5. Geiger, "Rise and Fall," 153–68; A. J. Angulo, *William Barton Rogers and the Idea of MIT* (Baltimore, MD: The John Hopkins Press, 2009), 86–123; quote on 93–94; Julius A. Stratton and Loretta H. Mannix, *Mind and Hand: The Birth of MIT* (Cambridge, MA: Massachusetts Institute of Technology Press, 2005).

6. On the Yale Reports and the popularity of the traditional curricula, see David B. Potts, *Liberal Education for a Land of Colleges: Yale's "Reports" of 1828* (New York: Palgrave Macmillan, 2010); "Curriculum and Enrollment: Assessing the Popularity of Antebellum Colleges," in *The American College in the Nineteenth Century*, 37–45. Nelson quote, p. 14.

7. Russell H. Chittenden, *History of the Sheffield Scientific School of Yale University, Vol. 1* (New Haven, CT: Yale University Press, 1928); Geiger, "Rise and Fall," 153–68; Daniel Coit Gilman, "Our National Schools of Science," *North American Review* (October 1867). Quote is from *Proposed Plan for a Complete Organization of the School of Science, Connected with Yale College* (New Haven, CT: Ezekiel Hayes, 1856).

8. See Nathan M. Sorber, "Farmers, Scientists, and Officers of Industry: The Formation and Reformation of Land-Grant Colleges in the Northeastern United States, 1862–1905" (diss., The Pennsylvania State University, 2011).

9. Nelson, p. 26.

10. Sorber quote, p. 56; For Morrill's speech quote, see Justin S. Morrill, "Agricultural Colleges: Speech of Hon. Justin S. Morrill, of Vermont in the House of Representatives," June 6, 1862, The University of Vermont Special Collections, Congressional Speeches, Vermont, No. 19, E415.7 .C66, 123.

11. For an interesting discussion of how the name "agricultural college" came into usage, and was detested by Morrill, see Williams, *Origins of Federal Support*; Gilman, "Our National Schools of Science," quote on 27.

12. Behle, "Educating the Toiling Peoples: Students at the Illinois Industrial University, Spring 1868," *The Land-Grant Colleges and the Reshaping of American Higher Education (Perspectives on the History of Higher Education)*

13. Behle, quote on p. 82.

14. J. Gregory Behle and William Edgar Maxwell, "The Social Origins of Students at the Illinois Industrial University, 1868–1894," *History of Higher Education Annual* 18 (1998): 93–110. For the data on the northeast, see Sorber, *Farmers, Scientists*, 162, 176, and 187.

Institutionalizing Agricultural Research in the Early American Republic: An International Perspective

Adam R. Nelson

I. Introduction

Ours is a time of significant debate—some would say deep concern—about the future of state support for public higher education. Perhaps nowhere is the debate more vigorous, or the concern greater, than it is in the nation's land-grant universities, which have been long considered pillars of US higher education and research. To set contemporary debates in a broader context, this article provides a few thoughts about the long history of the land-grant idea. In particular, it examines the links between higher education, scientific research, and state investment before the Morrill Act of 1862. Rather than seeing the Morrill Act as the start of something "new" in American higher education, it is cast as the culmination of ideas stretching all the way back to the early republic. In a sense, the Morrill Act rediscovered and reframed ideas that had been around for a very long time.

In the decades before the US Supreme Court decision in the Dartmouth case (1819), a decision often noted for severing the states' control over the original colonial colleges, American colleges received various forms of financial assistance from their states. Institutions such as Harvard, Yale, Columbia, and the University of Pennsylvania were, in effect, "semi-public" colleges with important connections to their respective

Perspectives on the History of Higher Education 30 (2013): 13–39
© 2013. ISBN: 978-1-4128-5147-3

state legislatures. While some historians characterize the colleges of this era as denominational schools emphasizing strictly classical education, such a characterization obscures not only the role of the state but also the role of science—and scientific research—in these institutions. In the early republic, colleges supported by their states were often dynamic engines of scientific research and, in turn, economic development.

To see this scientific dynamism, colleges must be placed in relation to other learned institutions. In many cases, the faculty in the nation's colleges were also the leaders of influential learned societies (and, sometimes, as this article will show, they were also state legislators). Thus, the college, the learned society, and the state went hand in hand. Indeed, these links should not surprise us. They were inherited from Europe, where, in this period, "teaching" and "research" were typically pursued in separate institutions—the university on the one hand, the scientific society on the other—and it was the state's role to bridge their separate activities. The idea of a modern "research university" was all but unknown in this period, that is, until the University of Berlin combined teaching and research into one institution in 1810 . . . near the end of the period addressed in this article.

To find the roots of state investment in higher education and research, it is, therefore, necessary to look back to an earlier era. It is also important to broaden our inquiry to include not only domestic but also, as my reference to the University of Berlin suggests, foreign influences on the development of American higher education. State investment in colleges was (then, as now) driven not only by local and national interests but also by international forces and, specifically, by a desire to bolster the international competitiveness of the United States. Americans expected scholarly institutions, both colleges and learned societies, to advance their economic interests in a globally competitive marketplace. One can hardly examine the history of higher education in this period without being struck by the international networks that aided its development. To build the state (including the national state), American scholars cultivated international connections.

Such connections were clearly evident in the field of agricultural research, a field that was integral to subsequent debates over the Morrill Act. In this field, three northern states took an early lead: Pennsylvania, New York, and Massachusetts. While various states in the south—Virginia and South Carolina, for example—had numerous local agricultural societies and other institutions to promote scientific work, southerners in the early republic generally eschewed state aid to research.

Later, the South initiated the first state-funded geological surveys to assess soil conditions and locate mineral-based fertilizers (gypsum, etc.), but it took the post–Civil War transformation of the plantation economy to inspire southerners to accept—or even seek—state aid for systematic agricultural research. Northern states were far more active. However even in the North, states had to be persuaded to support agricultural science.[1]

In Pennsylvania, New York, and Massachusetts, the institutionalization of agricultural science relied on well-placed scholars, state legislators, and learned societies. Between 1785 and 1815, four scholars' activities demonstrate not only the scientific cooperation that occurred between colleges, learned societies, and the state but also the role of international competition in the institutionalization of state-funded agricultural research. Benjamin Smith Barton at the University of Pennsylvania, Samuel Latham Mitchill and David Hosack at Columbia, and William Dandridge Peck at Harvard were leaders in the plant sciences. All four cultivated international connections; all four helped persuade state legislatures to invest in scientific innovation; and by 1815, three of these four had secured some measure of public aid for college-based botanic gardens to promote agricultural education and research.

The cooperation between colleges, learned societies, and the state in the institutionalization of agricultural science in the early republic was noted more than a century ago by the great agriculturalist Liberty Hyde Bailey, dean of agriculture at Cornell (and a graduate of Michigan Agricultural College), in his four-volume *Cyclopedia of American Agriculture*, published between 1907 and 1909 (as he led the National Commission on Country Life). Bailey explained: "the desire for education in terms of agriculture had become widespread long before the middle of the last century. The difficulty of founding and maintaining effective institutions naturally led to a demand for state and federal aid. The subject was widely discussed in societies, so much so that we may say that from agricultural societies has come the foundation of the state agricultural colleges. It is in these organizations that the ideas crystallize; and they finally make their demands upon the legislatures."[2]

Bailey astutely focused his analysis on individual leaders in states such as Pennsylvania and New York: "The movements begin, of course, with individuals," he wrote—those "who looked into the future and who insisted on the soundness of their views." From these individuals came learned societies, and from the learned societies came appeals for state support. "At first," Bailey noted, "it was proposed that the societies themselves . . . should support the schools; but the idea of government support gradually grew, and finally controlled." He added that the establishment of the land-grant colleges was "an event of such unusual importance to the American nation and to the world that its full record should some time be collected and a connected history written." The present volume takes a step toward realizing Bailey's hope for a history of the land-grant colleges, and this article fills a gap in our understanding of their early roots.[3]

II. Early Roots in Pennsylvania and New York

In 1785, as Congress in Philadelphia debated the first Northwest Ordinance, a group of wealthy gentlemen farmers and scholars met to establish a Society for the Promotion of Agriculture and Agricultural Reform. The society aimed "to promote the greater increase of the products of the land within the American states," and it saw the nation's colleges as its allies in the institutionalization of agricultural science. Not long after its creation, its members named a committee to plan a statewide "society for the promotion of agriculture, connecting with it the education of youth in the knowledge of that most important art while they are acquiring other useful knowledge suitable for the agricultural citizens of the state." The proposal called on state legislators to fund new "professorships to be annexed to the University of Pennsylvania and the College of Carlisle [Dickinson College] . . . for the purpose of teaching the chemical philosophy and elementary parts of the theory of agriculture."[4]

Even before the submission of this proposal, the University of Pennsylvania had acted on its own. In 1789, it appointed a new professor of botany—an alumnus named Benjamin Smith Barton—who had recently finished his medical studies at the University of Edinburgh. Barton was well equipped for the job. While abroad, he had acquired a large herbarium (a collection of dried plants used for taxonomic purposes) that was later employed in his teaching. Among his specimens were plants from Australia (provided by the naturalist who had accompanied the first convict settlers to Sydney in 1788) and South Asia (shipped to him from the Royal Botanic Garden in Calcutta), as well as plants from South Africa (supplied by the Swedish botanist Carl Thunberg, who had collected specimens in Japan, Java, and Sri Lanka on his way to Cape Town) and more than one hundred from South America (presented by Julius von Röhr, a Danish botanist who visited Philadelphia in 1791 on his way back to Europe from Suriname and Brazil).[5]

Altogether, Barton's herbarium of more than 5,000 species covered six continents, and it formed the centerpiece of his lectures on applied botany at the university and its medical school. However, the University of Pennsylvania was not the only school that expanded its offerings in botanical science during this period. In 1791, an association of scholars and farmers in New York founded their own Society for the Promotion of Agriculture, Arts, and Manufactures, which, the next year, persuaded New York's legislature to create a new professorship in natural history, chemistry, agriculture, and economics at Columbia. Meanwhile, the college's medical school established a separate professorship in botany, to which it appointed a recent Edinburgh graduate named Richard Kissam. When professor Kissam left the college a year later, both new professorships passed to a young farmer and state legislator—and eventually US congressman—named Samuel Latham Mitchill.[6]

Mitchill, yet another product of the medical school at Edinburgh, vigorously supported the use of botanical science to aid New York farmers. Shortly after his appointment at Columbia, he addressed this subject in an oration before the quasi-masonic Society of Black Friars in New York City: "Hear how the poet describes the condition of an American farmer," he began, citing a few stanzas from Connecticut Wit Timothy Dwight, whose poems had lauded "fair Columbia . . . where all things bloom." Contrasting the freedoms of American farmers with "the tithe-paying, rack-rented, tax-oppressed, poverty-stricken peasantry throughout the greater part of Europe," he saw tremendous opportunities for agricultural expansion in the American republic. "Compare this with any other region," he told his audience, "and rejoice that your better fortune has given you a substantial interest in such a soil as this."[7]

To realize the nation's agricultural potential, Mitchill called for more botanical research. Two years after taking up his post at Columbia, he outlined the "state of learning" at the college, including his own course in botany and agriculture. "Botany is here a distinct branch of study," he noted in 1794. "In this course, besides the discussion of the Linnaean, or sexual, system, the explanation of terms and phrases, and the arrangement or classification of the vegetable species, an attempt is made by the professor—who is a practical farmer—to elucidate and explain the economy of plants, their affinity to animals, and the organization, excitability, . . . life, diseases, and death of both classes of beings. The physiology of plants, including their food, nourishment, growth, respiration, perspiration, germination, and etc., is therefore particularly enlarged upon, as connected with GARDENING and FARMING."[8]

Of course, each of these subjects interested Mitchill's patron organization, the New York Society for the Promotion of Agriculture, Arts, and Manufactures, to which he devoted much of his time. Among the members of the society were his fellow state legislators Robert Livingston and Simeon DeWitt, both of whom advocated state aid to scientific development. Livingston, a successful farmer in his own right, read papers at society meetings on topics such as the botany of forage grasses, the cultivation of fruit trees, the use of manures, and the care of Merino sheep (as well as the best methods for training wild elk to serve as draft animals). DeWitt, the state's surveyor general, called repeatedly for public investment in internal improvements. Meanwhile, state legislator and revolutionary war hero Ezra L'Hommedieu, who was another member of the society, delivered papers on varied subjects such as the use of shells and seaweed as fertilizers and the advantages of clover in restoring soil nutrients (as well as the joy of raising daisies).[9]

Mitchill and his contacts in the New York Society for Promoting Agriculture, Arts, and Manufactures pressed the state to invest in agricultural research. In 1794, shortly after delivering his first lectures, Mitchill and his friends led a campaign to build a botanic garden at Columbia—a garden to be jointly financed by the society, the college, and the state. "A garden is nearly connected with a professorship of botany," he asserted. "Lectures must always be lame and defective without a garden." Noting that virtually every university in Europe had a botanic garden, he added that a garden would teach students how to cultivate the widest variety of plants. "A botanical garden," he argued, "is not only the most useful and most important of public improvements, but it also comprises within a small compass the history of the vegetable species of our own country; and, by the introduction of exotics, makes us acquainted with the plants of the most distant parts of the earth." To grow "exotics" domestically was, of course, to reduce the need for imports.[10]

Mitchill stressed the benefits of a college-based botanic garden for statewide agricultural development. He wrote, "by facilitating experiments upon plants at this time when a true theory of nutrition and manures is such a desideratum, a botanic garden may be considered one of the means of affording substantial help to the labors of the Agricultural Society, and be conducive to the improvement of modern husbandry." It was clear, Mitchill held, that a garden, located at the college and funded by the society and the state, would advance the state's long-term economic interests. In his words, "it can scarcely be doubted that a botanic garden under the direction of the society, or of the college, with a view to further agricultural interest, will be set on foot and supported by legislative provision to the end that young minds be early imbued with proper ideas on this important subject."[11]

III. David Hosack at Columbia

Mitchill was not alone in his appeal for a botanic garden at Columbia. Joining him in this effort was a young colleague named David Hosack, a man destined to have an even more lasting effect on American botany than Mitchill himself. As a student, Hosack attended both Columbia and Princeton and spent two years in the medical school at the University of Pennsylvania before deciding that his education would not be complete until he studied abroad. He later recalled: "the distinction which our citizens at that time made between physicians who had been educated at home and those who had had additional instruction from the universities in Europe made study abroad necessary if one would succeed." Arriving in Edinburgh in 1792 (just as Mitchill took up his post at Columbia), Hosack immediately felt his weakness in botany. "I was mortified by my ignorance of botany," he wrote, and "resolved . . ., whenever an opportunity might offer, to acquire a knowledge of that department of science."[12]

And so he did. He quickly departed Edinburgh for London to hear the lectures of James Edward Smith, the owner of Linnaeus' personal herbarium. "I spent several hours daily for four months examining the various genera and the most important species contained in that extensive collection," Hosack wrote. He also met other botanists, including Joseph Banks, president of the Royal Society; Thomas Martyn, Regius Professor of Botany at Cambridge; and William Curtis, author of *Flora Londinensis* and editor of the *Botanical Magazine* whose garden at Brompton had recently opened. Curtis' vast garden, Hosack observed, "was arranged in such a manner as to render it most instructive to those desirous of becoming acquainted with this ornamental and useful branch of medical education." So delighted was Hosack with Curtis' botanic garden that he visited the establishment nearly every day.[13]

With help from Curtis, young Hosack acquired a large herbarium and bought thousands of books. His library was "probably the most complete of the kind in America," according to contemporaries. "Such a collection can only be made by watching the sales of private libraries; and many of the books, descriptive of American, Russian, Swedish, Italian, and Indian plants, are rare, even in England." Hosack's library and herbarium were exceptional for their day, but neither would be useful, he believed, unless complemented by a botanic garden. He maintained that in Europe, no one studied botany without access to a well-equipped garden. As he put it: "an abstract account of the principles of these sciences as taught by books, colored engravings, or even with the advantages of an herbarium, must necessarily be very imperfect and unsatisfactory when compared with the examination of living plants, growing in their proper soils."[14]

It was, therefore, no surprise when Hosack, on his return to New York in 1794, joined Mitchill's campaign to win state aid for a botanic garden at Columbia. A year later, in 1795, he became professor of botany and materia medica at Columbia's medical school, and he used his position to advance the campaign for a garden. Progress, however, was slow. Two years later, he was still writing to ask whether his professorship could "be endowed with a certain annual salary sufficient to defray the necessary expenses of a small garden . . . where such plants as furnish the most valuable medicines and are most necessary and valuable for medical instruction" might be cultivated. Yet, aid from the college was not forthcoming. As his biographer Christine Chapman Robbins explains, Columbia's board of trustees "expressed sympathy but finally replied that, for want of sufficient funds, they could not comply with Hosack's request."[15]

Gradually, Hosack and Mitchill reframed their garden plan as a contribution not only to American agriculture but also to American agricultural competitiveness. A sense of international rivalry was a key motive behind the institutionalization of plant science in this period. The rivalry was particularly strong between the United States and Great Britain. In 1794 (the year Mitchill issued his first appeal for a garden), the English Board of Agriculture had dispatched one of its members to examine the progress of American farms and, specifically, to see whether they could supply Britain's growing need for imported grains. By the early 1790s, Britain was no longer a self-sufficient producer of cereals; two decades of poor harvests, combined with the outbreak of military conflict with France, had depleted food reserves in London, and the need for imports was clear. Could the United States supply Britain's market? What, if anything, could British farmers learn from their American counterparts?[16]

The English Board had commissioned William Strickland to examine American farms in New York, New Jersey, Pennsylvania, Maryland, and Virginia. He investigated the cultivation of American cereals, especially wheat, but was intensely critical of American agricultural methods. Claiming that Europeans produced at least two or three times more wheat per acre, he attributed low yields in America not to insects or soil deficiencies (the culprits identified by most scientific societies) but rather to political culture, or, in his words, to "the present constitutions of the states and the manners of the people." In republican America, he wrote, land was badly managed, "for the poor and ignorant must unavoidably wear it out." He went on: "The mass of those we should call planters or farmers [in the United States] are ignorant, uneducated, poor, and indolent; . . . he boasts of his independence, and enjoys inaction." Scarcely concealing his aristocratic prejudices, Strickland had little regard for America's republican farmers.[17]

According to Strickland, the only bright spot in American farming was New York. As historian Melvin Herndon notes, "He proclaimed New York the granary of America and added that, if America was to become the granary of Europe, 'this must be the part that must do it.'" However, his review of New York was hardly better than his review of other states. He blasted New York farmers for sowing wheat and corn side by side in the same field. "With such a mode of agriculture," Strickland declared, "it is not to be wondered that the produce of wheat should be so small." Herdon writes, "Since the English gentlemen consumed neither corn bread nor corn whiskey, he condemned the most universally grown American staple by declaring, 'Maize is everywhere a losing crop, and has been destructive to America.'" In the end, Strickland found almost nothing to admire in American agriculture.[18]

In 1796, Strickland returned to London to work on his *Observations on the Agriculture of America*. Even before it was published, this work provoked a reaction. As Simeon Dewitt told the New York Society for the Promotion of Agriculture, Arts, and Manufactures in 1799: "This state, it must be confessed, does not unfold to the philosophical world a much admired feature in the portrait of America. . . . A university, colleges, and academies we have, it is true; they serve to save us from the shame of not following the fashion of nations. [But] Nothing extraordinary can be placed to our credit on their account. What more have we to boast of?" It was left to the New York Society, he asserted, to redeem the state's reputation at home and abroad. Surely one way the society could do so was by promoting the study of agriculture in the nation's colleges, and one way to do this was by supporting the construction of a botanic garden at Columbia.[19]

IV. Institutionalizing Agricultural Research

In 1800, frustrated by the lack of progress on a botanic garden at Columbia, David Hosack asked the state for a five-year appropriation to fund this project. When the legislature once again failed to act, Hosack moved forward on his own. In 1801, he purchased a twenty-acre plot three miles north of the college. On this site, he built an impressive greenhouse (sixty-two-feet long, twenty-three-feet wide, and twenty-feet high) complete with temperature controls. He then laid out a garden organized by genus and species and encircled it with a diverse collection of trees. Not limiting his project to native specimens, he gathered plants and seeds from all over the world. "My collection of plants is yet small," he admitted to friends a few months after starting, but "I have written to my friends in Europe and the East and West Indies for the plants. I will also collect the native productions of North and South America." Within five years, he was able to boast more than 2,000 species.[20]

New York governor DeWitt Clinton praised his work as a service to the state. "The first institution in the United States established as a repository of the native vegetable productions of this country and for the purpose of naturalizing such foreign plants as are distinguished by their utility, either in medicine, agriculture, or the arts, was the Elgin Botanic Garden founded in 1801 by Dr. David Hosack, at that time professor of botany and materia medica in Columbia College," Clinton wrote. "The buildings, which are erected on the most recent plan adopted in institutions of this kind, consist of three large and well-constructed houses. . . . The greater part of the ground is brought in a state of the highest cultivation and divided into various compartments, calculated for the instruction of the student of botany and medicine and made subservient to agriculture and the arts."[21]

Certainly, Hosack had built an impressive garden, but his repeated appeals for financial assistance went unanswered. He built his garden with no aid from the college, the state, or the New York Society for the Promotion of Agriculture, Arts, and Manufactures. Indeed, an entire decade would pass before he received any external aid—and then, only after other states acted. Pennsylvania was first. In 1806, Benjamin Smith Barton (who had just received a commission from President Thomas Jefferson to catalog the plants of the Lewis and Clark expedition) asked the Pennsylvania state legislature for aid to build a botanic garden. The next year, the state gave the University of Pennsylvania $3,000 "for the purpose of enabling them to establish a garden." The sum was far less than Hosack had spent on his garden at Columbia, and it was only a one-time contribution, but it set other activities in motion.[22]

In 1806, the year he requested state aid for a botanic garden, Barton was elected founding president of the American Botanical Society (later renamed the American Linnaean Society to mark its connection with its London counterpart). Half the members of the new society had been Barton's students at the University of Pennsylvania. In 1807, he addressed the new society with *A Discourse on Some of the Principal Desiderata in Natural History, and on the Best Means of Promoting the Study of This Science in the United States*. A wide-ranging oration on the need to institutionalize natural history as an applied science, the *Discourse* emphasized "those subjects in the investigation of which we, as Americans, are especially interested." Barton noted, in particular, the practical applications of botany, calling for a more scientific approach to agriculture in the United States.[23]

Barton predicted that future research would help American farmers grow more crops in more diverse locations. "If I do not greatly mistake," he asserted, "some of our native *Convolvuli* (perhaps *Convolvulus panduratus*, called Yams and Hog-potato) might be used as substitutes for the Sweet-Potato (*Convolvulus Batatas*). Some measures ought to be taken to preserve that large subterranean Tuber which is called Tuck-a-hoe in Virginia in other parts of the Union." He went on: "The Indians made bread of this vegetable production, and I am assured that a most delicious cake is prepared by mixing with the farinacious matter of the Tuck-a-hoe a portion of rice-meal. The natural history of this vegetable, together with its chemical analysis, would be well received by the public." Barton proceeded to show how local tribes used indigenous plants to make a wide variety of dishes and drinks.[24]

Barton similarly pointed to forage plants that had been ignored by American farmers: "On the rich hills of Virginia, the *Collinsonia Canadensis*, which is there called 'Rich-weed,' affords a most excellent pasture for the horses. . . . It is much to be wished that some intelligent and industrious naturalist . . . would furnish us with a set of tables of the wild plants of our country, pointing out the places of their growth and . . . noticing, in connecting with these circumstances, what plants are eaten, and which are rejected, by the domesticated animals, especially the horse, the ox, and the sheep." Barton pointed out that such tables had been published abroad, to great effect. "The *Pan Suecus* of Linneaus is one of the most important specimens of the kind," he wrote, adding, "Never will the agriculture of our country be properly understood, or economically attended to, until something on this plan is attempted in the United States."[25]

Barton saw botanical science as a contribution to national development. Reflecting on Lewis and Clark's journey, he noted: "When we consider the great extent of the United States, even excluding the country beyond the Mississippi, I presume it may be stated, at a moderate calculation, that at least one-eighth part of our native vegetables is entirely unknown, certainly to the botanists of Europe, and, with respect to the regions between the Mississippi and the ocean, the botany is still more imperfect. . . . this vast region will, unquestionably, afford much for the gratification of the botanist. In its higher latitudes, we may expect to find many of the vegetables of the north and east of Asia; as we have already found, in those latitudes, many of the animals of Asia; and in the lower latitudes we shall, in all probability, meet with many of the plants of China, and Japan, and Cochin-China, Hindoostan, and other regions of the old world."[26]

The implication was clear: the United States might well possess within its borders untold botanical riches—plants with agricultural value that would otherwise have to be imported from abroad. If such plants could be cultivated domestically and scientifically, then any investment in botanical research promised to be repaid many times over. "We are the inhabitants of a country peculiarly blessed by the all-wise and benevolent Creator of the universe," Barton wrote. "He has given us an abundance of valuable esculent herbs, and roots, and fruits, of various kinds, and our soil and climate are admirably adapted to the growth of many others, which are not indigenous." As far as Barton was concerned, the Great West might well serve as a nursery for commercially viable foreign plants, thus contributing to the nation's agricultural self-sufficiency (and avoiding the import dependency of countries such as Britain).[27]

V. William Dandridge Peck at Harvard

In the field of botanical education for the sake of agricultural development, Columbia and the University of Pennsylvania had taken an early lead, but Harvard was not far behind. As early as 1802, Harvard began raising funds for a new professorship in natural history. During that year, James Jackson, a professor at Harvard Medical School, wrote to a friend in Salem: "You probably may hear that the subscription has commenced for the establishment of a Professorship of Natural History at Cambridge. . . . You must exert your eloquence in Salem, as you have opportunity, in favor of the new establishment. . . . It is useful to have it made a subject of conversation and to have it appear that all men of learning approve the design. It must be believed that it will go, that it is a rising sun, and that all golden men who value their reputation must worship it. If I were not busied in other things, I would immediately begin the study of natural history—and particularly botany—that I might seem learned to the many who will talk on these subjects."[28]

Spearheading the campaign to endow the new professorship was John Lowell, a member of Harvard's board of visitors and, simultaneously, president of the Massachusetts Society for Promoting Agriculture. Established in Boston in 1792 (a year after the New York Society for the Promotion of Agriculture, Arts, and Manufactures), the Massachusetts Society was—along with the American Academy of Arts and Sciences— the state's primary agency for applied scientific research. Indeed, the Massachusetts Society received an annual appropriation from the legislature to fund premiums for successful experiments in practical farming. (In its first year, for example, the society awarded two premiums: $50 for "the most satisfactory account of the natural history of the canker-worm" and $100 for the cheapest and most effective method of eradicating this crop-destroying pest.)[29]

With a membership that included John Adams, John Hancock, Samuel Adams, Timothy Pickering, Charles Bulfinch, and Josiah Quincy (all Harvard alumni), the Massachusetts Society was an influential organization, and when fifty-nine-year-old Lowell died shortly after launching his campaign for a natural history professorship at Harvard, its members picked up where he left off. Appealing for state assistance, they cited recent European gains in agricultural education and research made possible by government aid to universities. Here again, the idea of international competitiveness pervaded requests for state aid: "The European world has long experienced the multiple benefits of such institutions," they noted in one solicitation, adding that "Establishments which are there fostered by the care and bounty of government cannot, in this country, be created and maintained without the liberal contributions of public-spirited individuals."[30]

Pledging to build a botanic garden in connection with the new professorship, Harvard's board insisted that, by the early nineteenth century, the advantages of agricultural research and education had become indisputable. "To those intelligent men whose contributions are invited," they held, it was "unnecessary to state how commerce, agriculture, medicine, and the arts would be aided and promoted by a zealous, well-directed, and extensive cultivation of those branches of science." The appeal worked. More than 150 donors contributed more than $31,000 to establish the so-called "Massachusetts Professorship in Natural History" at Harvard in 1805. A major portion of this sum came from a land grant from the state. Legislators "voted a township of wild land in Maine (part of Massachusetts until 1820) to the trustees of the Massachusetts Society for Promoting Agriculture for the benefit of the new professorship."[31]

To fill its new professorship, the college selected Harvard alumnus William Dandridge Peck, a nephew of Harvard medical professor James Jackson (who had won the society's first premium for the best essay on the cankerworm). Immediately after his appointment, Peck was sent to Europe to prepare for his teaching responsibilities. The college allotted $1,250 for his voyage, plus $700 for books and $300 for botanical equipment. He was urged "to acquaint himself with the object and the manner of instruction as it is given in the seminaries where the knowledge of nature has been cultivated with the greatest ability and effect." With regard to botanical studies, in particular, he was asked to steer "his inquiries and observations . . . to the situation, form, size, contents, arrangement, and expense of botanic gardens; the methods in which they are supplied with plants, cultivated, and managed; and whatever else may serve for determining their respective merits and defects."[32]

Harvard's leaders were clear about the aims of Peck's mission. "The subserviency of this institution to the promotion of the arts and agriculture of our country being among the principal objects of its founders, and entitled to the solicitous care of the board, the Professor, in the course of his travels, will endeavor to enlarge his knowledge of the means by which this desirable end may be obtained," they wrote. He was "to learn in what methods, and to what extent, botanical institutions are capable of being conducted with special reference to the interests of husbandry, medicine, and manufactures." Further, using the funds at his disposal, he was "to possess himself of a valuable collection of seeds and plants for the garden and of drawings, herbaria, and various articles belonging to the vegetable, animal, and mineral kingdoms, worthy of being deposited in the cabinet." If possible, he was also to find a professional gardener to aid him in his work.[33]

Peck's travels brought him to Sweden, Germany, France, and England. In each place, he met distinguished botanists. In Sweden, he spent most of his time at the University of Uppsala, where he met Carl Thunberg, the successor to Linneaus whose extraordinary botanical travels were known far and wide. "The good old man received me with great politeness and affection," Peck noted. "The herbarium of Professor Thunberg is the richest in Europe in the plants of Japan, collected by himself." Thunberg's associate, Adam Afzelius, brought Peck to see the university's botanic garden (recently donated by the king). Peck described the eight-acre garden in a letter to his friends at Harvard: "The annual expense of this garden—including the salary of the gardener, the wages of laborers, and seeds—is 500 dollars. Seeds, however, demand but a very small sum, as there is an annual interchange with gardens in other countries."[34]

Everywhere he went, Peck took detailed notes on botanic gardens. From Sweden, it was on to Germany and the University of Kiel, where professors Friedrich Weber and Daniel Matthias Heinrich Mohr showed him the university's garden. "The botanic garden was begun about three years before I visited it and contained at that time about 9,000 plants," he marveled."The sum of 1,000 dollars is annually devoted to the expense of this garden for paying laborers, furnishing manure, seeds, etc. The gardener's salary is 250 dollars. The herbaria of Professor Weber and Dr. Mohr—particularly the carpological collection of the former and the marine plants of the latter—arrested my attention." Peck stopped briefly to see the garden at the University of Leyden before going to Amsterdam to visit its "medical garden, which was once the most respected in Europe, when the extensive commerce of Holland brought to it the most valuable plants from all quarters of the globe." Who could fail to admire the benefits of government aid to botanic gardens?[35]

VI. Model Gardens in France and England

From the Netherlands, he proceeded to France, which was arguably the epicenter of European plant science. In Paris, he visited the sixty-acre Jardin des Plants—a mecca for botanists everywhere—which occupied him for nearly a year. He called the Jardin des Plantes "a magnificent institution where every branch of natural history is taught." For anyone endeavoring to establish a garden, the Jardin des Plantes was the model par excellence. "The botanic school, or that portion of the garden devoted to instruction in botany, is rich in plants from various climes, descending to the cultivation of the lowest order of plants," Peck reported."The collection of fruits and seeds, and specimens of different woods from all climes, is very interesting." All the plants were classified according to the natural method of Antoine Laurent de Jussieu—a method that had been introduced twenty years earlier as an alternative to the Linnaean method of sexual classification.[36]

After France, Peck visited England and, in particular, Sir Joseph Banks, who had served as Captain James Cook's botanist on his first voyage around the world. "This munificent patron promotes with unexampled liberality the advancement of natural science," Peck told his friends at Harvard after meeting the renowned Banks. "His herbarium and library are always open to persons who are properly introduced and who wish to consult them. The former consists of the botanic treasures which he amassed in his circumnavigatory voyage, several original herbaria, and the rich contributions which are poured into it by his friends and correspondents in all parts of the world." Banks' collection, summarized in a five-volume catalog, was nothing less than a revelation: "An establishment like this is of unspeakable advantage to natural science," Peck wrote, as well as "a benefit to his country."[37]

Visiting the small garden at Banks' country estate, Spring Grove, Peck noticed several American species: "The *Tizania aquatica*, an indigenous American grass from the [Great] Lakes, which produces a grain called Canada Wild Rice, grows perfectly well at Spring Grove. I was favored with some seeds of it, which I transmitted to New York, begging Dr. Hosack to raise the plant in the hope that, at a future day, I might be able to introduce it [in Massachusetts]. It may grow in our ponds without requiring any culture and be, sometime or other, worth attending to." In addition to his time with Banks, Peck also sought out Dr. James Edward Smith and Linneaus' herbarium, as well as the famed entomologist William Kirby, an expert on bees and a member of the Linnaean Society of London (which Smith had founded). All counseled him on the best way to institutionalize botanical science at Harvard.[38]

In Oxford and Cambridge, young Peck took time to examine the universities' extensive gardens. He was particularly amazed by the network of heated greenhouses at Cambridge, where he counted 10,000 species, including "the mahogany tree, the passion flower, the night-blowing Cereus, and the Indian banana and bamboo." From this collection, the gardener gave him seeds to send back to Harvard, care of John Lowell, Jr. It seems that Harvard was very much on Peck's mind while he was in Cambridge. After his visit, he wrote in his travel diary that Harvard could easily match Cambridge's botanical accomplishments as soon as the college had a garden of its own. "Nothing but money is wanting to give us botanical gardens in America. And, indeed, after the first establishment, the annual expense would be no very serious affair," he wrote. The question was: could Harvard find the money for such an endeavor?[39]

The chief obstacle facing American botany, he asserted, was a preoccupation with short-term gains. Peck argued, "The commercial spirit which pervades our country either overlooks or despises the interests of science and sees no advantages in a well-informed mind and a control gained over nature by physical researches which can at all compare with the more immediate benefits of insurance shares and bank stock. I have often been chagrined when conversing with commercial men to find that friendship, science, and all other considerations are immediately brought to the touchstone of loss and gain, and when I have watched the workings of their minds as manifested by casual remarks—even on subjects apparently unconnected with trade—I have often been mortified to find that this sordid spirit was everywhere uppermost." He concluded, "We have, in truth, the ability to accomplish much more than we are likely soon to attempt."[40]

Peck wondered how to persuade legislators to support long-term scientific investments. He noted, "when a mind unfurnished with materials for thought and conversation derived from a good early education becomes devoted to the acquisition of money as the great business of life, and especially when the means of acquiring [wealth] are not conducive to the improvement of the understanding and the cultivation of good moral affections, it is wonderful how soon this 'sacra fames auri' acquiesces the complete dominion of the man and lives and breathes and speaks and acts in all he does." He added (perhaps referring to himself), "the man who has spent his youth and diminished his resources in forming his mind to the highest standard of intellectual dignity will still find—with grief and indignation—that the world cares not a groat for him and all he knows and will most feelingly realize the truth of that comprehensive motto which Smallett has prefixed to the life of Roderick Random: 'Et genus and virtus nisi cum re vilior alga est [without substance, honor and valor are more worthless than seaweed].'"[41]

Despite the fact that Harvard, with help from the Massachusetts Society for Promoting Agriculture, had raised significant resources for plant science, and despite the fact that Peck himself enjoyed more generous support than most other American botanists, he, nevertheless, sensed that his efforts would be assessed not in terms of his contributions to scientific research but chiefly in terms of his contribution to economic development. His professorship, sponsored by commercially minded donors, framed botany as a practical art that was designed to promote financial gain. Peck feared that a narrow focus on short-term interests might jeopardize the United States' prospects for more fundamental discoveries, but he saw few alternatives. "Money," he observed, "will always go for more than talents, knowledge, taste, and the noblest moral qualities" (though it seems he still hoped to reconcile these seemingly divergent ends).[42]

In 1808, Peck returned to Harvard, bringing with him a gardener from Yorkshire to assist in the construction of a botanic garden that would support his teaching. Historian Jeanette E. Graustein has described his seven-acre plot: "The grounds were enclosed by a high, close fence and carefully laid out on two levels 'with the formal lines of smaller London establishments used as a model.' In the lower part, a pool for aquatic plants formed the center of a series of concentric beds. A great variety of trees and shrubs, native and exotic, were promptly planted. . . . On the higher ground, a conservatory, placed in line with the pool below, was linked . . . by a wide gravel walk and wooden (later granite) steps. To the northeast, concealed by a fine hedge of European beech, was a working area of seed-plots, cold frames, and hotbeds." In his garden, it seems, Peck tried to balance the scientific, economic, and aesthetic aspects of the botanic art.[43]

VII. The Role of the State

Peck's garden at Harvard was larger than Barton's at the University of Pennsylvania, but it was considerably smaller than Hosack's at Columbia. Everyone knew that professor Hosack had the most extensive garden of the day. It covered more ground and had more specimens than any other. It also cost more than any other college garden—more than Hosack's personal budget could sustain. By the fall of 1809, Hosack had run out of money. He needed someone to buy his garden and make it a permanent feature of Columbia's scientific apparatus. The medical faculty was unanimous in its view that a botanical garden was essential for its work but could not afford to operate the garden on its own. When it became clear that his medical colleagues were unable to buy him out, Hosack sought aid from the state. Governor DeWitt Clinton, a long-time advocate of Hosack's work, brought the matter to the legislature.

Clinton endorsed Hosack's proposal for state ownership of his botanical garden: "The expense requisite to effect [sic] these several purposes far exceeding the calculations the proprietor had originally formed, and being desirous of perpetuating the institution, he was induced to offer the whole establishment for sale to the state. An almost entire unanimity prevailing among the medical faculty relative to the advantage to be derived from an institution of the kind as highly necessary to complete a system of medical instruction, and similar sentiments being entertained by many others who felt an interest in the literary reputation of the state, application was made to the legislature . . . for the purchase of the botanic garden." Petitions from the city council as well as several county agricultural boards finally persuaded the legislature to act. On March 12, 1810, Hosack's botanic garden "became the property of the state."[44]

The high value placed on Hosack's garden was reflected in the price the state paid for it: $74,268.75 (in adjusted dollars, this price would amount to more than $1 million today). Obviously, the state recognized the usefulness of a botanical garden. Clinton, for one, was delighted by the purchase and looked forward to further state aid to science. He wrote, "it is ardently hoped that an institution so honourable to the individual by whom it was originally projected, and by whose care and munificence it has been eminently conducive to the promotion of the science of botany, may not be impaired in its character or usefulness through any want of public support, and it is respectfully suggested that nothing could more effectually secure the important objects of this institution than some permanent provision made by the legislature and the annexation to the establishment of a botanical professorship."[45]

Four years after it purchased Hosack's garden, the state returned control of the property to the college (in the interim, the management of the garden had been turned over to the New York College of Physicians and Surgeons—founded in 1807 and merged with Columbia in 1814—of which Hosack was a member). Simultaneously, New York's legislature increased its investment in higher education. It authorized statewide lotteries to generate $20,000 for Columbia for scientific equipment and library materials, plus $30,000 to cancel outstanding debts. It also directed $40,000 to Hamilton College for expenses and $100,000 to Union College for a new campus. Between 1810 and 1814, state legislators invested more than $250,000 in higher-education infrastructure—at a time when total federal revenues amounted to less than $12 million a year. This was only the beginning. In 1818, Governor Clinton asked the state for resources to establish a state board of agriculture, as well as a school of agriculture to be linked to the University of the State of New York (at that time a supervisory body). It was time, he argued, for the state to institutionalize agricultural education and research.[46]

Clinton wrote, "If not the exclusive duty, it is certainly the peculiar province of the state governments to superintend and advance the interests of agriculture." To this end, he asked the state to create "a board, composed of the most experienced and best-informed agriculturalists and to render it their duty to diffuse agricultural knowledge." Board members would correspond with local agricultural societies and "introduce useful seeds, plants, trees, and animals, implements of husbandry, and labor-saving machines." Moreover, he suggested, "a professorship of agriculture connected with the board or attached to the university might also be constituted, embracing the kindred sciences of chemistry and geology, mineralogy, botany, and the other departments of natural history." Such a professorship would fulfill the plan outlined for Columbia two decades earlier by the New York Society for the Promotion of Agriculture, Arts, and Manufactures.[47]

In April 1819, the New York state legislature appropriated $10,000 to create a state board of agriculture. During the same year, state-surveyor Simeon DeWitt, the governor's cousin, published his *Considerations on the Necessity of Establishing an Agricultural College*. Observing that the legislation establishing the state board of agriculture had not funded any professorships, DeWitt argued that agricultural education was urgently needed throughout the United States. In Europe, he asserted, the landed gentry could "afford to make experiments" and disseminate their findings widely. "Thus," he explained, "every landlord's farm becomes, to a certain degree, a school of practical agriculture, where experiments are constantly made by wealthy, scientific, and practical men, to ascertain the best methods of profitable culture; where the knowledge of it is transmitted as a family inheritance and sheds its meliorating influence." However, in republican America, with no aristocracy, it was the state's responsibility to foster agricultural development.[48]

Turning the earlier criticism of William Strickland on its head, DeWitt linked the virtues of republican citizenship to the idea of state aid to agricultural science. "We have no landlords, and fewer still of that class who turn their attention to farming," he asserted. "It is the glory of our country that, with such rare exceptions, every farmer is the absolute, independent lord of his own territory (little as it may be) and works it with his own hands." He conceded, however, that "the mediocrity of [the average farmer's] circumstances and his habitual prudence will not permit him to hazard experiments for improvements. What he knows of it—as practiced by his father—will be known by his children, and they will probably . . . follow in his track without deviation. Under such circumstances, agriculture must remain at a stand." Making American farms scientific was the responsibility of the state and, in turn, the aim of DeWitt's Agricultural College of the State of New York.[49]

VIII. Conclusion

Neither Clinton's School of Agriculture nor DeWitt's Agricultural College of the State of New York came to fruition. The Panic of 1819, the worst economic recession the nation had seen to date, undermined their plans. The downturn—which derived in part from rampant speculation in agricultural land—lasted five years, and state aid to internal improvements, with the exception of the Erie Canal, ground to a halt. When the crisis ended, however, efforts resumed. In 1824, Stephen Van Renssalear, chair of the board of agriculture (the state's largest private landholder), founded the Renssalear School under the direction of botanist and geologist Amos Eaton, and, two years later, Lieutenant Governor James Tallmadge called for broader access to agricultural education. Within a decade, legislators had passed "An Act to Incorporate the New York State Agricultural School."[50]

We often associate the Morrill Act with the beginning of a new era in American higher education—the dawn of state aid for applied research in agriculture and other practical arts with the expressed aim of advancing both state and national economic development. In many ways, the Morrill Act did launch a new era, but it was not the first era of state aid for university-based research in the practical sciences. The idea of state aid for applied research in agriculture and other practical arts was as old as the nation itself. This idea emerged in the early republic, when semi-public institutions such as Harvard, Columbia, and the University of Pennsylvania received financial support from their respective state legislatures. In this era, when the notion of a "modern research university" was but a twinkle in the nation's eye, states brought together the strengths of colleges and learned societies to promote a wide array of useful arts.

Foremost among these arts was the art of agriculture, which played a central role in the nation's economic development and, ultimately, its global competitiveness. With the help of internationally connected scholars such as Benjamin Smith Barton at Pennsylvania, Samuel Latham Mitchill and David Hosack at Columbia, and William Dandridge Peck at Harvard, various states made a start—a modest start, to be sure, but a start nonetheless—toward the institutionalization of agricultural science, which played a central role in the nation's economic growth. One might even say that agricultural research later conducted in the land-grant universities would not have been possible without the institutional foundations laid by Barton, Mitchill, Hosack, Peck, and others during the early republic. The path to later breakthroughs was paved by an infrastructure constructed in this era with state support.[51]

In closing, I offer a few words about the period between the 1820s and the Morrill Act in the 1860s. Historians often associate this period between the 1820s and the Morrill Act with the expansion and democratization of higher education in the United States, but this era also saw new forms of research specialization and professionalization and the beginning of a mass academic migration to Europe (particularly Germany). Over time, new forms of specialization and professionalization gave the university a more elite character—despite growing access—as well as an increasing reputation for pursuing abstract over applied research. It was this elite character and reputation for "esoteric" study that Congressman Justin Morrill sought to address, in part, through his land-grant act. By emphasizing public support for scientific education with an economic focus, the Morrill Act rediscovered long-standing ideas about the purpose of American higher education. In a sense, Morrill reframed a set of institutional values that had been around since the early years of the republic.

Today's discussions about the future of state support for public universities may signal another moment of "rediscovering" and "reframing" core institutional values. If so, those who believe in the idea of state investment in public higher education can be confident that such values have been around for a long time—indeed, perhaps even longer than the land-grant universities themselves. They can also be confident that, when it comes to soliciting and securing the aid of the state, economic priorities are nearly always likely to predominate. William Dandridge Peck, who observed remarkably similar priorities more than two centuries ago, wrote perceptively: "I could name several commercial gentlemen who form most honorable exceptions to this general fact and, without being less attentive to business or less successful in it, believe that money is not the only valuable thing," but such individuals were indeed "exceptions." When the state invested in higher education and research, he concluded, it expected a rapid economic return.[52]

Notes

1.   On state geological surveys in the South, see James X. Corgan, ed., *The Geological Sciences in the Antebellum South* (Birmingham: University of Alabama Press, 1982). See also G. Melvin Herndon, "The Impact of the American Revolution on Agriculture and Agrarian Leadership in the South: An Interpretation," *Louisiana Studies* 15, no. 3 (1976) 279–86.
2.   Liberty Hyde Bailey, ed., *Cyclopedia of American Agriculture: A Popular Survey of Agricultural Conditions, Practices, and Ideals in the United States and Canada*, vol. 4 (New York: Macmillan, 1909), 386. On the period after 1815, see especially Peter D. McClelland, *Sowing Modernity: America's First Agricultural Revolution* (Ithaca, NY: Cornell University Press, 1997); Margaret Rossiter, *The Emergence of Agricultural Science: Justus Liebig and the Americans, 1840–1880* (New Haven, CT: Yale University Press, 1975); and "The Organization of Agricultural Sciences," in *The Organization of Knowledge in Modern America, 1860–1920*, ed. Alexandra

Oleseon and John Voss (Baltimore, MD: Johns Hopkins University Press, 1976), 211−48. See also Alan I. Marcus, *Agricultural Science and the Quest for Legitimacy: Farmers, Agricultural Colleges, and Experiment Stations, 1870–1890* (Ames: Iowa State University Press, 1985).

3. Bailey, *Cyclopedia of American Agriculture*, 386.

4. On the membership of the agricultural societies, see Stevenson Whitcomb Fletcher, *The Philadelphia Society for Promoting Agriculture, 1785–1955*, 2nd ed. (Philadelphia, PA: Philadelphia Society for Promoting Agriculture, 1976), 17–18; Simon Baatz, *"Venerate the Plough": A History of the Philadelphia Society for Promoting Agriculture, 1785–1985* (Philadelphia, PA: Philadelphia Society for Promoting Agriculture, 1976), 6. See "Outlines of a Plan for Establishing a State Society of Agriculture in Pennsylvania" (1794), reprinted in the *Memoirs of the Philadelphia Society for Promoting Agriculture, Containing Communications on Various Subjects in Husbandry and Rural Affairs*, vol. 1 (Philadelphia, PA: Johnson and Warner, 1815), xvii, xx, quoted in Benjamin Marshall Davis, "Agricultural Education: Agricultural Societies," *The Elementary School Teacher* 11, no. 5 (January 1911): 266–77. See also Lucius F. Ellsworth, "The Philadelphia Society for the Promotion of Agriculture and Agricultural Reform, 1785–1793," *Agricultural History* 42, no. 3 (July 1968): 198–99; Whitfield J. Bell, Jr., "The Scientific Environment of Philadelphia, 1775–1790," *Proceedings of the American Philosophical Society* 92, no. 1 (March 1948): 6–14; and M. L. Wilson, "Survey of Scientific Agriculture," *Proceedings of the American Philosophical Society* 86, no. 1 (September 25, 1942): 52–62. For more on the role of learned societies in agricultural research, see Ralph S. Bates, *Scientific Societies in the United States* (New York: J. Wiley and Sons, 1945); Bruce Stone, "The Role of Learned Societies in the Growth of Scientific Boston, 1780–1848" (PhD diss., Boston University, 1974); and Simon Baatz, "Philadelphia Patronage: The Institutional Structure of Natural History in the New Republic, 1800–1833," *Journal of the Early Republic* 8, no. 2 (Summer 1988): 111–38. See also Donald B. Marti, "Agricultural Journalism and the Diffusion of Knowledge: The First Half-Century in America," *Agricultural History* 54, no. 1 (1980): 28–37.

5. Joseph Ewan, "From Calcutta and New Orleans, or, Tales from Barton's Greenhouse," *Proceedings of the American Philosophical Society* 127, no. 3 (June 1983): 125–34. See also Francis W. Pennell, "Benjamin Smith Barton as Naturalist," *Proceedings of the American Philosophical Society* 86, no. 1 (September 25, 1942): 108–22; "Historic Botanical Collections of the American Philosophical Society and the Academy of Natural Sciences of Philadelphia," *Proceedings of the American Philosophical Society* 94, no. 2 (April 21, 1950): 137–51. See also Benjamin Smith Barton, *Elements of Botany, Or, Outlines of the Natural History of Vegetables* (Philadelphia, printed for the author, 1803). For more on international and colonial botanical exchange, see, for example, Lucile H. Brockway, *Science and Colonial Expansion: The Role of the British Royal Botanic Gardens* (New York: Academic Press, 1979); F. Nigel Hepper, *Royal Botanic Gardens, Kew: Gardens for Science and Pleasure* (London: Her Majesty's Stationery Office, 1982); and David Mackay, *In the Wake of Cook: Exploration, Science, and Empire, 1780–1801* (London: Croom Helm, 1985).

6. See Courtney Robert Hall, *A Scientist in the Early Republic; Samuel Latham Mitchill, 1764–1831* (1934; repr., 1967, New York: Columbia University Press, 1934).

7. Samuel Latham Mitchill, *An Oration Pronounced Before the Society of Black Friars, at Their Anniversary Festival, in the City of New York, on Monday, the 11th of November, 1793* (New York: Friar M'Lean, 1793), 29–30. See also Timothy Dwight,

"Epistle from Dr. Dwight to Col. Humphreys," *The Miscellaneous Works of Colonel Humphreys* (New York: Hodge, Allen, and Campbell, 1790), 102–10. For a survey of botanical studies of North and South American plants till 1800, see Mitchill, "A Discourse Delivered Before the New York Historical Society at Their Anniversary Meeting, 6th December 1813, Embracing a Concise and Comprehensive Account of the Writings Which Illustrate the Botanical History of North and South America," *Collections of the New York Historical Society* II (New York: Van Winkle and Wiley, 1814), 149–215. See also Frederick Brendel, "Historical Sketch of the Science of Botany in North America from 1635 to 1840," *The American Naturalist* 13, no. 12 (December 1879): 754–71; and John C. Greene, "American Science Comes of Age, 1780–1820," *Journal of American History* 55, no. 1 (June 1968): 22–41.

8. Samuel Latham Mitchill, *The Present State of Learning in the College of New York* (New York: T. and J. Swords, 1794), 11–12. See also Mitchill, *Outline of the Doctrines in Natural History, Chemistry, and Economics, Which, under the Patronage of the State, Are Now Delivering in the College of New York* (New York: Childs and Swain, 1792). Mitchill's *Outline* was divided into six sections: geology, meteorology, hydrography, mineralogy, botany, and zoology. The botany lectures covered Vegetable Poisons, Farinaceous Matter of Plants, Coloring Material of Plants, Fibrous Parts of Plants, Saccharine Substance of Plants, Saline Parts of Plants, Product of Vegetables by Fermentation, Astringent Parts of Plants, and Agriculture, or Cultivation of Plants (including Soils, Manures, Food, and Diseases).

9. Donald B. Marti, "Early Agricultural Societies in New York: The Foundations of Improvement," *New York History* 48, no. 4 (1967): 313–31.

10. Samuel Latham Mitchill to the New York Society for the Promotion of Agriculture, Arts, and Manufactures, published in its *Transactions* (1794), *xxxiv*, quoted in Christine Chapman Robbins, *David Hosack: Citizen of New York* (Philadelphia, PA: American Philosophical Society, 1964), 52–53. As early as 1791, Samuel Bard, a founding member of the New York Society for the Promotion of Agriculture, Arts, and Manufactures and later president of the New York College of Physicians and Surgeons (founded in 1807), may have built a two-square-block garden on the grounds of the New York hospital between Broadway and Duane, Worth, and Church Streets. See Robbins, "David Hosack's Herbarium and Its Linnaean Specimens," *Proceedings of the American Philosophical Society* 104, no. 3 (June 1960): 298n24: "Samuel Bard had received botanical instruction from Jane Colden at Coldenham, New York, and from John Hope [keeper of the University of Edinburgh botanic garden] at Edinburgh. . . . In New York he was influential in founding the Society for the Promotion of Agriculture, Manufactures, and Useful Arts [*sic*]. The society (1794) went on record as favoring a botanical garden under their direction or that of the college. Bard was sympathetic with Hosack's views and Hosack's attempt to gain financial support for the botanic (Elgin) garden he eventually established at his own expense."

11. Samuel Latham Mitchill to the New York Society for the Promotion of Agriculture, Arts, and Manufactures. In 1797, Mitchill founded *The Medical Repository*, which included articles on botany. See also U. P. Hedrick, *A History of Horticulture in America to 1860* (New York: New York University Press, 1950); James L. Reveal, *Gentle Conquest: The Botanical Discovery of North America with Illustrations from the Library of Congress* (Washington, DC: Starwood, 1992); and Therese O'Malley "'Your Garden Must be a Museum to You': Early American Botanic Gardens," *The Huntington Library Quarterly* 59, no. 2/3 (1996): 212.

12. Quoted in Robbins, *David Hosack*, 23, 24.

13. Quoted in Ibid., 27, 28. See also William Curtis, *Subscription Catalogue of the Brompton Botanical Garden for Year 1792 . . . and a Catalogue of the Books Contained in the Library of the Garden* (London: W. Curtis, 1792); and Samuel Curtis, *Lectures on Botany as Delivered to His Pupils* (London: William Phillips, 1803). See also A. Hunter Dupree, "Nationalism and Science—Sir Joseph Banks and the Wars with France," in *A Festschrift for Frederick B. Artz*, ed. David H. Pinkney and Theodore Ropp (Durham, NC: Duke University Press, 1964), 37–51.

14. First quotation from Robbins, "David Hosack's Herbarium," 299; second quotation from Robbins, *David Hosack*, 60.

15. Quoted in Robbins, *David Hosack*, 61. See also David Hosack, *Syllabus of a Course of Lectures on Botany Delivered in Columbia College* (New York: John Childs, 1795; repr., *American Medical and Philosophical Register* 4 [1814]: 460–75); and *An Introductory Lecture on Medical Education Delivered at the Commencement of the Course of Lectures on Botany and Materia Medica* (New York, 1800).

16. See G. Melvin Herndon, "Agriculture in America in the 1790s: An Englishman's View," *Agricultural History* 49, no. :3 (1975): 505–16. See also Rodney C. Loehr, "The Influence of English Agriculture on American Agriculture, 1775–1825," *Agricultural History* 11, no. 1 (January 1937): 3–15; and Hubert G. Schmidt, "Some Post-Revolutionary Views of American Agriculture in the English Midlands," *Agricultural History* 32, no. 3 (1958): 166–75.

17. Quoted in Herndon, "Agriculture in America in the 1790s," 512. See also William Tatham, *Communications Concerning the Agriculture and Commerce of America* (London: S. Gosnell, 1800).

18. Herndon, "Agriculture in America in the 1790s," 510. Strickland was less critical of German farmers, Herndon notes, "He did, however, exempt the Germans in Pennsylvania from the 'usual lamentable state of ignorant cultivation.' 'This industrious people,' he continued, were fortunate in possessing some of the finest lands in American and 'have, either from superior knowledge when they arrived in the country, or superior attention to the nature of the soil and the climate, brought the cultivation of their country to a degree of excellence, which may vie with that of the old countries.' Their wheat crops averaged about eighteen bushels per acre and they frequently produced as much as twenty-five or thirty, which raised the average for the entire four-state area to eight bushels. Strickland was also impressed with their buildings, meadows, and pastures, which bore 'a style of neatness and perfection unknown in other parts of America.' He concluded his praise of the Pennsylvania Germans by saying that they 'ought certainly to be given the credit of introducing irrigation into this part of America, and, I believe, the knowledge of gypsum in every part of it'" (Herndon, "Agriculture in America in the 1790s," 510–11).

19. Simeon DeWitt, quoted in John C. Greene and John G. Burke, *The Science of Minerals in the Age of Jefferson* (Philadelphia, PA: American Philosophical Society, 1978), 44n1. See also William Strickland, *Observations on the Agriculture of the United States of America* (London: W. Bulmer, 1800).

20. David Hosack to Thomas Parke (July 25, 1803), quoted in Robbins, *David Hosack*, 65. See also David Hosack, *Catalogue of Plants Contained in the Botanic Garden at Elgin in the Vicinity of New York* (New York: T. and J. Swords, 1806; repr., *The Medical Repository* 10 [1807]: 209); "Description of the Elgin Garden, Property of David Hosack," *Portfolio* and *Boston Anthology* (January 1810); *A Statement of Facts Relative to the Establishment and Progress of the Elgin Botanic Garden, and Subsequent Disposal of the Same to the State of New York* (New York: C.S. Van Winkle, 1811); and *Hortus Elginensis, Or a Catalogue of Plants Indigenous*

and Exotic Cultivated in the Elgin Botanic Garden (New York: T. and J. Swords, 1811).

21. DeWitt Clinton, "An Inaugural Discourse delivered before the Literary and Philosophical Society of New York on the Fourth of May, 1814" (New York: David Longworth, 1815), 41.

22. Ewan, "From Calcutta and New Orleans, Or, Tales from Barton's Greenhouse," 126. See also Robert C. Baron, ed., *Thomas Jefferson: The Garden and Farm Books* (Golden, CO: Fulcrum, 1991); Edwin Morris Betts, *Thomas Jefferson's Garden Books, 1766–1824* (Philadelphia, PA: American Philosophical Society, 1944); and *Thomas Jefferson's Farm Book, with Commentary and Relevant Extracts from His Other Writings* (Philadelphia, PA: American Philosophical Society, 1953). For more on Jefferson, science, and science policy, see Silvio A. Bedini, *Jefferson and Science* (Charlottesville, VA.: Thomas Jefferson Foundation, 2002).

23. Benjamin Smith Barton, *A Discourse on Some of the Principal Desiderata in Natural History and on the Best Means of Promoting the Study of This Science in the United States, Read Before the Philadelphia Linnaean Society, on the 10th of June, 1807* (Philadelphia, PA: Denham and Town, 1807), 15. See also Baatz, "Philadelphia Patronage," 112–16.

24. Ibid., 46.

25. Ibid., 49.

26. Ibid., 41.

27. Ibid., 45.

28. James Jackson to John Pickering (April 3, 1802), quoted in Mary Orne Pickering, *Life of John Pickering* (1887; printed for private distribution), 213.

29. "Massachusetts Society for Promoting Agriculture Records, 1764–1963: Guide to the Collection,"http://www.masshist.org/findingaids/doc.cfm?fa=fa0245 (accessed August 8, 2007). In its first decade, the Massachusetts Society offered sizable premiums for "the cultivation of wheat and other grains; the improvement of land, including the reclamation of salt marshes; the raising of trees; the greatest stock maintained on the least land; the best vegetable food for wintering stock; the most and best wool from a given number of sheep; the best process for making cider, maple sugar, butter, cheese, flax, and salted provisions; and for the best farm journals, manures, tree plantations, advances in ploughs and ploughing techniques, and farms in general."

30. See also Harvard University, *Foundation of the Massachusetts Professorship of Natural History, at Harvard College, in Cambridge, with Documents, Relative to Its Establishment* (1805), Harvard University Archives (UAI 15.1076), 19. See also Benjamin Waterhouse, *The Botanist: Being the Botanical Part of a Course of Lectures on Natural History, Delivered in the University at Cambridge* (Boston, MA: Joseph T. Buckinham, 1811), vii–viii.

31. Ibid.

32. Instructions to William Dandridge Peck from the Harvard Corporation's subcommittee "chosen to consider the expediency of the Professor's visiting Europe, prior to his entering on the duties of his office, for the purpose of obtaining knowledge of the best and most economical means of affecting the objects of this Institution and also the probable expense attending this measure, and report at the adjournment." Papers of William Dandridge Peck, Harvard University Archives (HUG 1677.xx).

33. Ibid.

34. William Dandridge Peck to the Hon. The President of the Board of Visitors (June 11, 1808), unpaginated letter, Papers of William Dandridge Peck, Harvard University Archives.

35. Ibid.
36. Ibid.
37. Ibid.
38. Ibid.
39. Ibid.
40. Ibid.
41. Ibid.
42. Ibid.
43. Jeannette E. Graustein, "Harvard's Only Massachusetts Professor of Natural History: Establishing Harvard's Botanic Garden and Equipping It with a Director," *Harvard Alumni Bulletin* (December 13, 1958), 243. See also Graustein, 257: "Peck did not start his teaching activities until many months after his return from Europe [in 1808] because Dr. Benjamin Waterhouse of the Harvard Medical School, who had been giving a course in Natural History annually at the College since 1788, was very loath to hand over the work and the fees to anyone else. He had bitterly opposed the establishment of the Massachusetts Professorship, the first incumbent of which was to be elected by the subscribers: in a long Memorial he begged the Corporation not to allow the proposed professorship to deprive him of vested interests rooted in the pioneer work of starting a new subject and building up interest in it under difficulties and discouragements through seventeen years. When Peck arrived in Cambridge from Europe in the spring of 1808 he was too occupied by other business to assume the course in Natural History, and in the spring of 1809 Waterhouse proceeded to meet the class as usual. The Corporation voted to permit him to finish the course but rescinded his rights for the future." For more on Peck at Harvard, including excerpts from his inaugural lecture, see W. M. Smallwood, *Natural History and the American Mind* (New York: Columbia University Press, 1941), 302–3.
44. Clinton, "An Inaugural Discourse," 43.
45. Ibid. For the purchase price of Hosack's garden, see Codman Hislop, *Eliphalet Nott* (Middletown, CT: Wesleyan University Press, 1971), 160.
46. Hislop, *Eliphalet Nott*, 261. See also Don Conger Sowers, *The Financial History of New York State from 1789 to 1912*, vol. 57, no. 2 (New York: Columbia University Press, 1914).
47. DeWitt Clinton, speech to the New York state legislature, January 27, 1818, quoted in Bailey, *Cyclopedia of American Agriculture*, 386.
48. Simeon DeWitt, *Considerations on the Necessity of Establishing an Agricultural College, and Having More of the Children of Wealthy Citizens Educated for the Profession of Farming* (Albany, NY: Webster and Skinners, 1819), quoted in Bailey, *Cyclopedia of American Agriculture*, 388.
49. Ibid.
50. See Bailey, *Cyclopedia of American Agriculture*, 388–90.
51. For similar claims, see Alfred Charles True, *A History of Agricultural Education in the United States, 1785–1925* (New York, NY: Arno Press, 1969), chap. 1.
52. William Dandridge Peck to the Hon. The President of the Board of Visitors (June 11, 1808).

Creating Colleges of Science, Industry, and National Advancement: The Origins of the New England Land-Grant Colleges*

Nathan M. Sorber

It is safe to say that the battle which had been raged between the devotees of science and the proficients in letters are over. The question is settled! Science has won its spurs and achieved its knightly rank.[1]

—Daniel Coit Gilman

Should no effort be made to arrest the deterioration and spoliation of the soil in America, while all Europe is wisely striving to teach her agriculturalists the best means of hoarding up capital in the lands on that side of the Atlantic . . . [then] we are doomed to be dwarfed in national importance. . . .[2]

—Senator Justin Morrill,
Addressing the purposes of his Land-Grant College Bill on June 6, 1862.

Introduction

The origins of the New England land-grant colleges cannot be explained by Earle Ross' thesis in *Democracy's Colleges,* in which he concludes that the "determining influence [of the land-grant movement] was that of popular determination and direction" for the diverse ends of expanded access, vocational training, and social welfare.[3] New England land-grant colleges were created by educational reformers who hoped to advance science and expedite America's economic advance. Agricultural society members and professional scientists trained in European universities jointly lobbied state legislatures and founded the early land-grant

Perspectives on the History of Higher Education 30 (2013): 41–71
© 2013. ISBN: 978-1-4128-5147-3

colleges. The gentlemen farmers, men of affairs, and amateur scientists who populated state agricultural societies wanted to elevate the status and productivity of the farmer by uncovering the scientific principles at the core of agricultural practice.[4] Young scholars returning from abroad sought to use the largess of the federal government to recreate in America places of scientific research and dissemination similar to what they had enjoyed in Europe.[5] Both groups were sympathetic to a land-grant agenda predicated on expanding the study of chemistry, botany, biology, geology, and engineering in a higher education landscape dominated by the classical curriculum.

Daniel Coit Gilman became the intellectual leader and most fervent defender of this bourgeois vision of land-grant colleges that he coined "National Schools of Science."[6] He lauded Yale's Scientific School as an exemplar, as it had the avowed purpose of "instruction and researches in the mathematical, physical, and natural sciences, with reference to the promotion and diffusion of science . . ."[7] Dismissing any notion of using land-grant funds to support manual training schemes that certified practicing farmers, Gilman foresaw land-grant colleges' highest aim as producing "officers of industry."[8] These scientifically trained graduates would fill an increasing number of white-collar positions in the new middle class—engineers, farm managers, chemists, agricultural researchers, or industrial supervisors—overseeing and improving the complex processes driving America's industrialization.[9] Gilman's views were endorsed by Justin Morrill, who argued that the purposes of the land-grant colleges were to advance and disseminate scientific knowledge, prompt agricultural and industrial development, and increase the nation's economic standing.

Gentlemen scientists or agriculturalists are omnipresent in land-grant college foundings, whereas Yankee yeomen, artisans, and the working class are absent. As historian Frederick Rudolph observed,

> All these [land-grant college] activities owed little if anything to the views of dirt farmers and workingmen's associations. They were the work of middle class reformers who were prepared to advance some theoretical and ideological notions of what popular technical education should be.[10]

It was not until the financial crash of 1873, the resulting depression, and the rise of New England state granges in the 1870s and 1880s that farmers took an active interest in higher education and attempted to reform land-grant institutions in their image. As Roger Geiger, Scott Gelber, Alan Marcus, Roy V. Scott, and I have written in different contexts, this second period was epitomized by a tension between farmers and academics for control of land-grant colleges.[11] When farmers became politically engaged through state granges, they worked to align higher education with the needs of rural communities, steering institutions toward the celebrated functions of agricultural extension and outreach.[12] In New England, the rise of the state granges brought dramatic results: It ended the land-grant status of Yale, Brown, and Dartmouth, and ushered in three new land-grant colleges that would become the University of Connecticut, the University of Rhode Island, and the University of New Hampshire, respectively.

Before 1873, this tension was in its infancy, however, as most farmers remained aloof of the land-grant movement. This left land-grant colleges in the hands of the de facto leadership of agricultural societies, university-trained scientists, and economically minded statesmen. Original curricula, faculty, and students reflected their values. Academic programs maintained fairly stringent admission standards, curricula rich in scientific subjects, and theoretical instruction in lieu of manual training. Students hailed from middle to upper-middle class families, and although many had wealthy farmer fathers, only a few made careers in farming after graduation. As Gilman had envisioned, most students pursued new middle-class lives in the "specialist" vocations within science, engineering, or business. This article chronicles the antecedents of land-grant education and the political and intellectual leadership of the New England movement during this understudied, origination era. It is a history which suggests that the first land-grants should not be conceived of as *Democracy's Colleges*, but perhaps *Science's Colleges* or *Industry's Colleges*.

Agricultural Societies and the Scientific Spirit

Ezekiel Holmes left his home in Kingston, Massachusetts, at sixteen years of age for Brown University. The year was 1817, and Holmes had completed his college preparations at the hand of a local minister.[13] His first two years at Brown were filled with Greek and Latin grammar, readings from Cicero, Homer, Euclid, and the Greek Testament, the study of Hedge's Logic and Roman Antiquities, arithmetic, and geography.[14] One student described his professors as follows: "portly men, going on sixty. Sitting crossed legged in an arm-chair . . . They would insist on you giving them the exact words of Blair, or of Kames, and of Stewart and Hedge . . . there was nothing . . . but translating, and parsing . . ."[15] As an escape from mundane coursework, students joined one of the two rival literary societies, where they enjoyed private libraries, debates, declamations, and socials. The *Philermenian Society* was the older of the two and embraced an aristocratic, Federalist heritage, whereas the *United Brothers* had Republican leanings.[16] The young Ezekiel Holmes had little interest in literary clubs or politics; so, in 1818, he and his likeminded classmates established the *Philophysian Society:* a group that was devoted to his budding interest in scientific research.[17]

A scientific spirit had entered the halls of Brown during Ezekiel Holmes' tenure at the instigation of chemistry professor John D'Wolf and botany lecturer Dr. Solomon Drowne. D'Wolf had attended Brown but did not take a degree and received the bulk of his training from nationally renowned chemist Dr. Robert Hare.[18] Student testimonials extolled the teaching abilities of the young D'Wolf: "He opened to the eyes of the young student . . . the wonders of a new and brilliant science . . . Sometimes in drawing practical deductions from the science he was teaching . . ."[19] Dr. Drowne was a much older man (b. 1753), having graduated from Brown at the dawn of the revolution and serving in the continental army before matriculating to the University of Pennsylvania Medical School and European study. Even though advanced in years, he was remembered as a man "full of enthusiasm," who had honed his craft by giving public lectures in Philadelphia and Providence. Drowne cultivated his own botanical garden, supplementing the paucity of material available in the scientific texts.[20]

Starting in his junior year, Ezekiel Holmes took courses in the natural sciences and was awed by D'Wolf and Drowne.[21] The *Philophysian Society* students were inspired to undertake their own scientific inquiries, "searching for plants and minerals during . . . leisure hours . . . [and through] experiments in chemistry conducted by means of simple private apparatus [that Holmes] had purchased himself."[22] One of Holmes' scientific explorations resulted in the discovery of what would be called the Mt. Mica Quarry in Paris, Maine. He had unearthed the most remarkable deposits of tourmaline in the United States, which would produce the world's first rose quartz crystals and remain a profitable gem mine right into the twenty-first century.[23]

In the days before the Brown commencement of 1821, the members of the *Philophysian Society* gathered for an address titled "Utility of Philosophy to a Nation," by Ezekiel Holmes. The speaker reminded society members of their responsibility to the world they would inherit:

It is our duty to peruse the great volume of Nature which [God] has spread . . . to increase the talent he has given us . . . to investigate the objects about us, to learn their uses, and apply them for the benefit of the community.[24]

Holmes declared that throughout history, men tried to pass along indefatigable truths to future generations, but a Philophysian was skeptical of such claims. For he said, "Experience answers, adhere strictly to the truth . . . admit nothing certain until it has undergone the most severe scrutiny of the senses . . ."[25] His final words reveal a confidence that scientific men would not only bring progress to the people, but also become celebrated leaders of the nation: "Go on by your researches . . . until every nation on the Globe which reveres the name of an American will also bow with respect to that of a *Philophysian*."[26]

The scientific society ended in 1827, but Ezekiel Holmes and his compatriots persisted in leading the lives of Philophysians. After taking a medical degree from Bowdoin College in 1824, Holmes settled in Gardiner, Maine, to practice medicine.[27] He was soon recruited to teach natural sciences at the Gardiner Lyceum, where he set on collecting minerals, insects, and plant life to share with his students.[28] In 1829, Holmes was promoted to the position of principal, but he endured a pittance in salary and a constant lack of funding for apparatus and supplies. In a letter to the trustees, he pleaded, "something must be done to save the reputation of the institution . . . The public [has] been disappointed and they in turn will and do disappoint you in their patronage."[29] The beleaguered principal proposed the enlargement of the model farm, the building of a workshop, and an expansion of the boarding house. No additional funds came, and progress was allusive.[30] In 1832, disheartened, he left Gardiner, and embarked on a host of new ventures: writing for agricultural journals, agitating for the state's first geological survey, introducing new livestock breeds to the state, and writing the founding constitution of the Maine State Agricultural Society.[31] Holmes' editorship of the *Maine Farmer*—the state's leading agricultural journal—would leave a legacy on land-grant education in Maine. In 1864, when Bowdoin College was poised to become the state's land-grant college, the editor warned fellow agricultural society members that attachment to a classical college would mean the subjugation of scientific studies.[32] For, as envisioned as a student in 1820, he wanted colleges to be established with the purpose of "holding out encouragement to those who are desirous of knowledge . . . [where] the humble admirer of Nature may roam at his pleasure."[33] Remembering the challenges at Gardiner, he rallied support among his agricultural society brethren for a perpetual federal fund that could permanently sustain scientific studies. His successful advocacy for an independent land-grant college for Maine was premised on making scientific studies the equal of literary pursuits, and giving a place for aspiring and established Philophysians to uncover scientific truths and promote human progress.

Ezekiel Holmes is representative of the cohort of college-educated, science-minded individuals who left an indelible mark on higher education in the mid-nineteenth century. Similar to how members of the revolutionary generation joined philosophical societies, amateur and professional scientists of the 1830s, 1840s, and 1850s formed agricultural societies to advance knowledge of those branches related to farming, mining, and mechanics—botany, chemistry, geology, physics, and animal physiology.[34] In Jacksonian America, farming dominated not only the economy but also the social and cultural milieu, and scientists were interested in improving all aspects of the national vocation.[35] Agricultural society members held primary careers as doctors, lawyers, merchants, or public officials, and devoted their free hours to experimentation with the crops and animals on their farm laboratories.[36] The agricultural society movement spawned agricultural fairs, agricultural journals, state agricultural boards, and experiment stations that served as sites for sharing new discoveries, discussing theories, and debating the future of agricultural science and farming practice.[37]

In the 1850s, agricultural society members turned to educational reform, calling for agricultural colleges to advance the science of farming.[38] One Pennsylvania agriculturalist argued that "books, periodicals, and agricultural exhibitions" were no longer sufficient to teach "so profound a science as agriculture . . . [which] is susceptible of more rapid progression than any other pursuit." He argued that neither individual experimenters nor agricultural societies "possess[ed] the means . . . to make experiments . . . on an extensive and reliable scale.". If state agricultural colleges were established, the author continued, "liberally endowed, provided with competent professors and tutors, and a farm of sufficient extent," then farmers would be afforded the opportunity ". . . of becoming acquainted with the physical sciences."[39] Charles Plumb, an agricultural scientist from the Northeast, noted that agricultural colleges would not only advance the science of agriculture but also produce individuals who could lead the vocation's advances. He imagined agricultural college graduates improving the industry by "advising and directing [farmers and by] exercising a progressive, intelligent influence over the work of husbandman."[40]

Massachusetts witnessed the strongest movement for an independent agricultural college in New England before the Morrill Act, thanks to the efforts of an upstart classical college with lofty ambitions. Amherst College, a small college that was just two decades old, came under the capable leadership of one of the most fervent supporters of agricultural and scientific education in Massachusetts in 1845. President Edward Hitchcock, an active member of the scientific community, was a member of the local agricultural society, a chemistry and natural history professor at Amherst, the state geologist, and the prime investigator on the first scientific survey of Western Massachusetts.[41] In addition to chemistry, he taught courses in botany, geology, zoology, astronomy, and anatomy.[42] Hitchcock's mentor was Benjamin Silliman of Yale College, the leading science professor of the day and founder of the *American Journal of Science and the Arts*. As Frederick Rudolph attests, "Silliman was a magnet for young men with scientific aspirations... [who] won fame as a popularizer of the scientific outlook."[43] After having completed a scientific survey of the region, Hitchcock was convinced that Amherst could be structured to improve Massachusetts agriculture. In 1845, speaking directly to agricultural education naysayers in the state, he said, "The day had gone by ... when we reject and treat contemptuously what has been called book farming."[44] The president was joined by Amherst professor Dr. Charles Shephard, who gave several lectures to students and agricultural societies alike on scientific agriculture. Shephard issued his own dire warning to farmers: "Either participate in the movement or else see [your] sons leaving their homes ... daughters entering the cotton mills... and farms sliding from under [you] into more enterprising hands."[45]

In 1847, the Amherst trustees petitioned the legislature for a state agricultural college—an institution with "an experimental farm, botanical gardens... and other needed apparatus."[46] A charter was issued by the state, as was a pledge of $15,000 under the condition that the institution could raise $15,000 on its own. Popular support for an agricultural college proved wanting, and the fundraising campaign fell flat. However, when a new hope for agricultural education arrived in the form of the Morrill Act of 1862, a tried and tested agricultural science coalition—centered and led from Amherst—seized the opportunity to implement the agricultural society's vision.

Americans in Europe

The scientists and gentlemen farmers who populated agricultural societies were often educated in basic sciences in a classical college or self-taught,[47] whereas New England reformers Samuel Johnson, Ezekiel Dimond, William Clark, and John Pitkin Norton pursued advanced scientific studies in the universities of Europe. At these universities, they encountered new discoveries in chemistry, botany, geology, and engineering, and were propelled into New England's land-grant leadership. Norton and Johnson were leading lights at Yale's Sheffield Scientific School; Dimond, at the New Hampshire Agricultural and Mechanical College; and Clark, at the Massachusetts Agricultural College.[48] Although a smattering of American students studied in Europe between 1820 and 1850, the trickle became a steady stream in the 1850s.[49] On returning home, these students were zealous missionaries for expanding scientific studies and for linking science with practice in American higher education.[50]

The pace of scientific discovery in Europe in the first half of the nineteenth century was truly remarkable, especially in the areas of chemistry and geology.[51] This rich intellectual landscape attracted American students who wished to share in this European enlightenment. Two institutions proved especially attractive: the University of Gießen and the University of Göttingen. The most renowned chemist of the era and intellectual forefather of agricultural science was Justus von Liebig at the University of Gießen. Some of New England's earliest and most celebrated agricultural chemists studied under Liebig: John Pitkin Norton, the first professor of the Yale Sheffield Scientific School; Norton's successor John A. Porter;[52] and William Brewster, the first agricultural professor at the New York State Agricultural College in Ovid and Sheffield faculty.[53] America's scientific education was also invigorated by the colony of students who encamped at the University of Göttingen in the 1850s and 1860s, including future New England land-grant leaders William Clark, Samuel Johnson, George Caldwell, J. P. Kimball, and Ezekiel Dimond.[54] The New England contingent joined future land-grant leaders from other regions, most notably agricultural chemist Evan Pugh, the founding president of the Pennsylvania State Agricultural College and a close companion of Samuel Johnson.[55] The formative experience in Germany resulted in intellectual growth and credentials, membership in an international fraternity of scientists and scholars, and commitment to the scholarly values of academic professionalism. As historian Charles Rosenberg eloquently explains,

[T]he German experience gave to American students a particular body of techniques and concepts, knowledge which at once justified and, in a sense, constituted the peculiar status of the man of learning . . . Once he had accepted the values of the world of academic science, the American scholar could measure achievement primarily in terms of acceptance as a creative scholar by his disciplinary peers . . . American chemists returned to their native land not only with a reformer's zeal, but with a blueprint to guide them.[56]

As these expatriates returned stateside, they sought to instill these same academic values in the institutions they would build, orienting the land-grant colleges toward original research and scientific education of a high intellectual grade.

Creating National Schools of Science

Scientific education and research in America was drastically different from what it was Europe, but it was a situation that returning students hoped to alter. The return of one expatriate—John Pitkin Norton—began the slow but steady process of building a school of science in New England. Norton was the product of both reform influences: the agricultural society movement and advanced scientific studies in Europe. He was the son of wealthy Connecticut businessman and gentleman farmer John Treadwell Norton. After becoming independently wealthy, Norton, Sr. spent time at his mansion and expansive farm where he collaborated with a fellow gentleman from the state agricultural society.[57] It was here that Norton, Jr. became fascinated with the study of nature and the science of agriculture. His father recognized this budding passion and encouraged (and financed) him to become an "educated farmer."[58] The young Norton received a strong preparatory education at a New York academy, but there were few options for advanced scientific education in agriculture, and so, he crafted his own educational program from multiple sources. Between 1838 and 1840, he spent winters under the tutelage of Dr. Theodore Dwight of Brooklyn, studying classical subjects and mineralogy, geology, and chemistry.[59] Summers were spent on New York farms, including one of the state's largest agricultural operations, observing scientifically trained Scottish agriculturalists. Between 1841 and 1843, Norton attended lectures on chemistry, mineralogy, and natural philosophy in New Haven and Boston, and although not a Yale student, he was a private pupil in Benjamin Silliman's laboratory for three years.[60]

In 1844, John Pitkin Norton informed his father that he intended to be a professor of agricultural chemistry, and sailed across the

Atlantic for advanced studies.[61] He came under the mentorship of famed agricultural chemist James F. Johnston and worked in his experiment station in Edinburgh.[62] Norton found Johnston to be "very pleasant indeed and just the man for a good instructor," and appreciated his willingness to take excursions across Scotland and explain the best methods of scientific cultivation.[63] Under his mentor's guidance, Norton produced two scientific papers that were read at Cambridge. One, a complete analysis of "Oats . . . the husk, the chaff & the straw of different varieties," won him £50 from the Highland Agricultural Society.[64] *On the Analysis of the Oat* (1845) not only brought the promising scholar recognition as a leading agricultural chemist in Britain, but also garnered considerable attention from former associates at Yale College.[65]

In the spring of 1846, John Pitkin Norton returned to New Haven to visit Benjamin Silliman. An anonymous donation was made to Yale that proposed "to give five thousand dollars for the endowment of a professorship of agricultural chemistry and of animal and vegetable physiology," and Silliman wanted Norton for the post.[66] The ageing Silliman argued that failing to recruit Norton, a man of impeccable credentials and unlimited promise, would be assuredly regretted. The corporation assented, appointing Norton as professor of agricultural chemistry. At the same meeting, Benjamin Silliman, Jr. (for many years assistant to his father) was named professor of practical chemistry. In 1847, Norton and Silliman, Jr. became the founding faculty of the School of Chemistry within the newly established Department of Philosophy and the Arts.[67] The aim of the department was to provide the opportunity to study science for its own sake and to prepare students for "the 'higher' practical occupations of life . . . such as engineering, architecture, agriculture, mining, and manufacturing . . . [and as] teachers of natural science."[68] It was reserved for "graduates . . . and other young men of good moral character," but not for members of Yale's undergraduate class.[69] Students attended lectures on agricultural chemistry, analytical chemistry, vegetable physiology, and botany, and conducted chemical experiments in the laboratory. Included in these first classes were Samuel Johnson, William H. Brewer, and George Brush; all became professors at Yale and renowned scientists in their own right.[70]

The Yale Corporation offered the Department of Philosophy and the Arts little more than the status of the Yale name. Salaries were generated from student fees, the department had to pay rent for classroom and laboratory space, and Silliman, Jr. and Norton drew on their personal finances to buy scientific apparatus.[71] As Yale Professor Thomas Lounsbury explained,

> The college . . . had no money to give, but even if it had, it is more than doubtful that they would have given it. No one . . . ever dreamed of the supreme importance which the natural sciences were soon to assume in every well-devised scheme of education.[72]

Yale's traditional academic program remained one of the most popular courses of study in the country, and the leadership was weary of redirecting resources toward untested educational experiments.[73] The Yale leadership stayed true to the curricular manifesto, *The Yale Reports of 1828*, a defense of the ancient languages and classical texts. Under this traditional scheme, the purpose of higher education was the cultivation of mental discipline and not the accumulation of specific knowledge.[74] Historian David Potts argues that Yale was following a rational strategy, as between 1828 and 1860, the college experienced 60 percent enrollment growth by maintaining a rigid commitment to the classical curriculum.[75] It is for these reasons that the Yale Corporation was careful not to let the new scientific program devalue or compete with its staple product by prohibiting the college's undergraduates from taking courses in the department.

While cautious of rapid innovation, the Yale administration noticed the steady enrollment growth in the School of Chemistry, and created a Bachelor of Philosophy degree for graduates of the Department of Philosophy and the Arts. In 1852, the first class matriculated with this distinction. That same year, the department swelled to forty-six after adding a new course in engineering to its staple of chemistry.[76] The continuation of the department was in serious doubt, however, after the loss of the two founding professors in as many years. In 1850, Benjamin Silliman, Jr. was recruited away by the University of Kentucky as its analytical chemistry professor, and after the first graduation in the spring of 1852, John Pitkin Norton died prematurely at the age of thirty.[77] On his deathbed, Norton bequeathed his books and apparatus and uttered: "I hope it will be kept up."[78] The Yale Corporation had been pleased albeit surprised at the quality and number of students availing themselves of the programs under Norton and Silliman's tutelage, and decided it would be "kept up." Luckily for Yale, qualified scholars became available, thanks to faculty discontent and aborted reforms at neighboring Brown University.

In his 1850 *Report to the Corporation of Brown University on Changes in the System of Collegiate Education,* higher education reformer and Brown University president Francis Wayland proposed a reorganization of the college degree programs. The Bachelor of Arts degree would continue traditional staples of the classical curriculum at Brown, but in addition, students could choose between additional courses in the ancient languages and mathematics, modern languages, or new courses in the applied science fields.[79] Central to Wayland's agenda was the hiring of two science professors: Professor William Augustus Norton in engineering and John A. Porter in agricultural chemistry. Norton had taught at Delaware College[80] and was a graduate of West Point—a seminary that Wayland argued had produced more civil engineers and "done more towards the construction of railroads than all our one hundred and twenty colleges united."[81] Porter had spent the two years before studying advanced agricultural chemistry in Germany with Justus von Liebig, and was hired at the recommendation of his esteemed mentor.[82]

The initial enthusiasm held by the two professors dissipated on arrival. Although they may have expected a European-styled scientific school in Providence, both men discovered that Brown remained beholden to its traditional roots. Porter was upset with Wayland over requirements to manage student behavior. A student rebellion of 1851, including a riot in chapel and "abusive epitaphs towards the President and faculty," was seen by the administration as the result of disagreement amid the faculty over what constituted proper student discipline. Porter and Norton argued that while doing nothing "intentionally" to prompt the student rebellion, they had made it known to students that "police visits" to dormitories were "degrading" to their standing as scholars and scientists. At the end of their first term, both men resigned.[83]

The failure of the Brown University reforms proved to be a blessing to Yale's new scientific department. After underwhelming experiences at Brown, John A. Porter and William Augustus Norton accepted the professorships of analytical chemistry and engineering in Yale's scientific department.[84] Not only had Brown lost the two leading scholars at the core of its reform initiative, but also fifteen engineering students followed Norton from Providence to New Haven.[85] Norton would be the leading force in establishing the School of Engineering at Yale.[86] In 1856, the faculty expanded again when two former graduates of the scientific program—fresh from study in Europe—returned to take positions at their alma mater. George J. Brush had studied at the Royal

Mining School of Freiberg and the Royal School of Mines in London, before becoming Yale's Professor of Metallurgy.[87] After having worked with Liebig, Samuel Johnson became the second alumni hired when he returned from Germany to devote his professional life to agricultural science at Yale, and became the foremost advocate for establishing agricultural experiment stations in America. In 1856–1857, he succeeded John A. Porter as professor of analytical chemistry.[88] Natural History Professor James D. Dana of the regular collegiate department and Benjamin Silliman Jr. (who had returned from Kentucky in 1856 to take a post on the regular academic faculty at Yale) also taught the scientific students, rounding out the department's instructional staff.[89] In 1856, Professor Dana penned the *Proposed Plan for a Complete Organization of the School of Science Connected with Yale College,* explicating the purposes and organization of what was then called the Yale Scientific School.[90]

James Dana's proposal suggests that the Yale Scientific School was to be America's answer to the great European universities. For faculty members such as founder John Pitkin Norton, as well as with the later additions of John A. Porter, Samuel Johnson, and George Brush, the experiment was an opportunity for scientifically minded men to recreate the setting of discovery and dissemination that they experienced abroad. The documents states,

> [Our] country is now ready for the establishment of a school of science . . . The studies pursued in the best institutions of Europe have been carefully considered in reference to our educational establishment and to the wants of our country . . .[91]

The program of study would be of the highest intellectual order, as each student would receive both "good mental discipline and thorough scientific acquirements."[92] Dana argued that students would come with two different aspirations: "students of science" who would "find means for carrying out their investigations of nature" and those preparing "for the higher practical occupations."[93] Graduates would receive their Bachelor of Philosophy Degree after three years of study. Dana's pamphlet was circulated across the region to solicit private donations. The campaign proved its worth when a generous gift was secured from Joseph Sheffield in 1858. The school was renamed in his honor.

Although Yale's Sheffield Scientific School was the first institution in the United States that offered a comprehensive, undergraduate curriculum in the natural and applied sciences, it coexisted with antebellum science reforms at other institutions. Harvard's Lawrence Scientific

School (f. 1847) recruited Louis Agassiz to Cambridge, and under his guidance, the institution became dedicated to pure science inquiry and individualized study.[94] During the 1850s, the science of engineering took root at the military academies at West Point and Annapolis, the Rensselaer Polytechnic Institute, and the innovative Union College.[95] By 1860, William Rogers was planning the Massachusetts Institute of Technology, which would become the national leader in expanding knowledge of engineering and other applied sciences.[96] As previously noted, a coalition of agricultural society members and Amherst faculty was poised to establish a Massachusetts Agricultural College under the auspices of the state agricultural board and society. Society members in Michigan, New York, and Pennsylvania were doing the same in their respective states and each would open an agricultural college before the Morrill Act. Literary institutions remained committed to the dictates of the *Yale Reports of 1828* and to the fixed course in the classics. Yet as Adam Nelson's article in this volume attests, "classical colleges" often dabbled with scientific courses and research, but the failure of the Brown experiment was a warning of the danger of straying too far from tradition. A smattering of denominational colleges attempted to meet local demands for practical instruction, but these usually amounted to irregular courses or lectures supplementing the classical core.[97] Finally, a collection of intermediate grade agricultural schools was established, such as the Gardiner Lyceum in Maine and the Cream Hill School in Connecticut, that attempted to teach scientific agriculture to precollege youth, but most had closed their doors by the 1840s. This was the uneven state of applied science in higher education at the eve of Justin Morrill's Land-Grant Act of 1862.

Schools of Industry and National Advance

In an economy that rewarded inventive new technologies, America's scientific backwardness was seen as a threat to economic competitiveness and national progress. Reformers looked to higher education to increase the nation's agricultural, manufacturing, and industrial output through scientific discoveries, and proposed enhancing the quality of science education to produce a more productive labor force, especially among the emerging technical fields of engineering and scientific agriculture.[98] The Morrill Act was a product of this ideology which was premised on the belief that American higher education could hasten the rise of American capitalism and advance the nation's standing in the world. Justin Morrill's speech in defense of the bill on June 6, 1862 illustrates how the father of the land-grant colleges viewed the proposed colleges as a means of economic development and national progress. In later years, Justin Morrill would regularly comment that his humble roots as a blacksmith's son and a lack of formal education were major impetuses in writing his land-grant bill to provide college access to the industrial classes.[99] However, his speech in 1862 was short on public good and democratic rhetoric, as he framed the issue of student access largely in economic terms.

[E]ach man is trained to bring into action is whole mental and physical force . . . a superior and more valuable labor . . . Science, working unobtrusively, produces larger annual returns and constantly increases fixed capital, where ignorant routine produces exactly the reverse.[100]

After having discussed how the bill could increase the productivity of American labor, Morrill turned to an economic assessment of agriculture. He highlighted the failures of American agricultural production and the need for federal investment to increase output and prevent dependence on European goods. Morrill argued that between 1850 and 1860, the United States had witnessed a decrease in wheat, corn, hay, swine, oxen, and cheese production. The state of agriculture was even more unsettling in the face of European advances in agricultural science and cultivation. Scientific techniques of the English, including the exhausting, restoring, and clearing of crops, allowed each harvest to be more profitable than the last. The investments of Louis Napoleon's government in agricultural education and science led crop production to double and, in some cases, increase fourfold. Without getting into the specific innovations of European universities and scientific schools, Morrill concluded, "It is enough to know that [Europe] seems eager to place their people ahead in the great race for mastery."[101]

Morrill's purposes are best understood in the context of his political values and views on economic development. As a staunch Whig, Morrill followed in the footsteps of party leader Henry Clay in promoting "American System" policies: high tariffs to protect American industries and investment in internal improvements to develop economic infrastructure."[102] Morrill was mentored by economist and social theorist Henry Charles Carey, who penned numerous treatises on protectionism and developmental capitalism. Carey proposed that in a developing economy such as the United States, government intervention into the economy was the only way to ensure industrial expansion, high wages, and international competitiveness.[103] Beholden to these ideas, Morrill became Congress' leading proponent of protectionism policies for American industry, and a year before the Morrill Act debate of 1862, he succeeded in passing the Morrill Tariff of 1861.[104] The tariff bill, while being odious to southerners who produced cheap goods for export, was a boon to the northern industry, especially for the New England staples of wool and cheese. So, when debating the Morrill Act of 1862, it is not surprising that Morrill states, "it is of the highest moment that at this time we make no blunder in the guidance of the industry of the country . . ."[105] For its founder, the policy to create land-grant colleges was at its core an internal improvement program in the Whig tradition; it was a government intervention that guided America's economic development.[106] Agricultural education would lead to scientific cultivation, improved lands, increased valuation of fixed capital, and the creation of educated and productive labor for the new economy. While the Morrill Tariff protected the industry from foreign goods, the Morrill Land-Grant Act aimed at elevating American capital and labor to best international competitors.

Justin Morrill was not alone in his views. The most prolific writer and commentator of this stripe was future Johns Hopkins president Daniel Coit Gilman. After returning from Europe in the 1850s, he became a staunch advocate for linking higher education to America's industrial advances. During Gilman's time abroad, he became convinced that Europe's economic and commercial supremacy was a product of liberal investment in universities and scientific schools. In his 1856 article, he declared that anyone comparing the manufactured products on display at the World's Fair Exhibition of 1851 to American goods would have to conclude: "the productions of our shops and factories are . . . inferior to what are made at a corresponding cost abroad."[107] Gilman posed the following question to the American people,

> Now, to what is the underdeveloped state of our mines, the imperfect character of our agriculture, the inferior quality of our manufactures, and the disappearance of our forests, to be attributed?[108]

It was not because Americans were lazy or unintelligent, but because the nation lacked "the educational means we require . . ." Common schools provided basic education and colleges suited the learned professional, but Gilman asked what about the "specialties" and the training of "specialists."[109] He witnessed European students studying architecture and engineering, mining and metallurgy, mechanical arts, and applied chemistry, and pursuing technical careers that advanced the industries of their countries. Gilman concluded, "In the present condition of our country, it is . . . important that a Scientific School of the highest order should receive a corresponding degree of sympathy and support."[110]

In 1858, Daniel Coit Gilman was working as the Yale librarian when he learned of Justin Morrill's first land-grant bill, and wasted no time in collecting petition signatures in Connecticut on behalf of the legislation.[111] President Buchannan's veto did not quash his passion, and his interest turned to the rapid advance of the recently renamed Sheffield Scientific School. When the second bill was passed in 1862, Gilman was in a new position as Sheffield Scientific School's professor of geography.[112] In December of 1862, the Connecticut legislature agreed to the terms of the Morrill Act and during the next year, Yale's Sheffield Scientific School was designated the state's land-grant institution.[113] Gilman and his faculty colleagues greeted the news with excitement and caution. Of promise was the opportunity to use federal funds to expand the school's faculty, and to these ends, three professorships were added in 1864 in support of agricultural science.[114] Yale hired scientific school graduate William Henry Brewer as professor of agriculture, Daniel Eaton as professor of botany, and Louis Agassiz protégé Addison Verrill as professor of zoology. Notwithstanding the land-grant's role in expanding their ranks, the faculty members were concerned with state legislative debates and newspaper coverage that characterized land-grant colleges as schools of manual or vocational education.[115]

Most troubling to Gilman and the faculty of the Sheffield School was the persistent claim that the land-grant act was meant to create "Agricultural Colleges."[116] Gilman lamented the

inaccurate and incomplete designation 'Agricultural Colleges' [that] continu[ed] to gain favor . . . [and] had already led, in some places, to unpleasant discussions with farmers and their friends, who have claimed all the advantages of the grant . . .[117]

William Brewer, Sheffield's new professor of agriculture, criticized misguided manual education and agricultural college schemes as being incompatible with Yale's scientific aims.[118] However, no consensus on either the scientific or manual approach emerged in the 1860s, and before the opposition gained strength, Gilman wanted to rally supporters behind his vision. The Morrill Act was of great importance, but to Gilman, the momentous legislation was passed abruptly and without "thorough discussion in the periodicals of the day."[119] It was this rapid passage that led to the fragmented understanding of the act's guiding principles, according to Gilman. With a hope of spurring national dialogue, suppressing the tendency toward agricultural or technical school schemes, and building a consensus around his own ideas, Gilman penned an article for the *North American Review* titled "Our National Schools of Science."

Gilman wanted the land-grant funds invested in publically funded institutions for "the study of natural science in its application to industry."[120] These National Schools of Science would promote "those branches of useful knowledge which exhibit the Creator's works in their true aspects, and connect with material advancement and civilization of mankind."[121] For Gilman, it was not enough to develop new scientific knowledge in laboratories or experimental farms; the colleges had to connect those findings to socioeconomic outcomes. He focused his attention on who would be trained, what would be taught, and what students would pursue after graduation. Gilman's problem with agricultural colleges was neither their focus on agricultural science nor the promotion of American agriculture. In fact, Gilman expressed appreciation for the agricultural colleges in Pennsylvania, New York, Michigan, and Illinois for developing "the science of agriculture by investigation and experiments." His fear was that some within the agricultural college movement preferred manual, vocational training of a lower grade for the purpose of graduating practicing farmers.[122] As Roger Geiger writes, Gilman wanted to prepare "mangers not workers," and collegiate instruction of a higher grade was needed to produce the leaders of American industries, including agriculture. Gilman summarized with the following:

> We do not think it likely or desirable that they [land-grant colleges] should train young men to go back and labor with the hoe or the anvil. They are rather to train men by scientific courses of study for the higher avocations of life, and especially to take charge of mines, manufactories, the construction of public works, the conduct of topographical and other scientific surveys,—to be leading scientific men.[123]

Gilman's experiences in Europe and at the Sheffield Scientific School convinced him that "far greater results . . . in the development of national industry" could be obtained by preparing students for the host of middle-class jobs in management or science—"the higher avocations of life."[124] Such a program required land-grant curricula where mathematics, physical, and natural science of a high intellectual grade would provide the basis for an industrial or scientific career. America should mirror France, Gilman argued, where when someone witnessed a great industrial organization in Paris, they invariably asked, "Was the manager of this establishment a pupil of the Ecole Centrale des Arts et Manufactures?"[125] If America followed his lead, then Gilman foresaw the nation's next great industrial advances led by land grant, "National School of Science" graduates.

After the publication of "Our National Schools of Science," Gilman invited Justin Morrill to meet with Sheffield Scientific School faculty to settle questions about the purpose of his legislation. Gilman was confident that the "Sheffield Scientific School [was] just such an institution as was described in the act of Congress," but his faculty colleagues wanted further assurances that their present scientific course and high standards would not run afoul of the land-grant law.[126] Morrill pleased the gathering by declaring that the funds were meant neither for creating agricultural schools, nor institutes of low grade, but were intended to make the useful sciences the equal of literary studies.[127] He expressed hope that talented students would pursue useful careers in industry, science, and business instead of the overcrowded professions.[128] Morrill would deliver the same message time and again, most famously during an address at Massachusetts Agricultural College when he stated, "the design was to open the door to a liberal education for this large class . . . offer something more applicable to the productive employment of life. It would be a mistake to suppose it was intended that every student should become a farmer or mechanic."[129]

The New England Land-Grant Colleges Take Form

Following in the footsteps of Yale's John Pitkin Norton, John A. Porter, Samuel Johnson, and Daniel Coit Gilman, former German university students Ezekiel Dimond and William Clark promoted European-styled scientific education at the new land-grant colleges in New Hampshire and Massachusetts. The quasi-independent New Hampshire College of Agricultural and Mechanical Arts controlled its own finances, curricula, and buildings but was located adjacent to Dartmouth, and the two were "held together by a contract and interlocking board of trustees . . ."[130] As its first faculty member and principal, Dimond charted an independent course at New Hampshire, when he secured an experimental farm and established a makeshift chemistry laboratory that was filled with apparatus and specimens which he had brought from Europe.[131] Committed to the academic standards he nurtured at Göttingen, he denounced using land-grant funds for manual training. Dimond noted that institutions thus designed

> would dwindle into . . . apprentice-shops where boys would be blindly taught the manual arts of agriculture and manufacture, as monkeys are taught to perform antics in order to procure copper for their masters.[132]

He wished to recreate a "National School of Science" in New Hampshire, but it remained a parochial affair in its early years. However, with the much-needed assistance of two $10,000 state grants and a private bequest of $25,000 in 1870, the college was able to construct a new chemical laboratory, classrooms, and a natural history museum. This was followed by appropriations to expand the college farm, and to build a dining hall and dormitory building to accommodate 135 students.[133]

Massachusetts' share of the federal funds appeared headed for Cambridge, when Governor John Andrews proposed attaching the land grant to Harvard University.[134] The Bay State received the largest land-grant scrip in New England, and the governor wanted to combine the proceeds with the recently donated Bussey Estate.[135] In his "Great Plan for Massachusetts," Andrews noted that the opportunity afforded by the federal funds could provide the means for "a university which would be worthy of the dream of her fathers, the history of the state, and the capacity of the people."[136] Andrews was inspired by the great German universities and their commitment to research, science, and learning: "Let us plan to concentrate here the 'gladsome light' of universal science. Let learning be illustrated by her most brilliant luminaries, and the claims of every science be vindicated by its bravest champions."[137] The state board of agriculture campaigned against the governor's plan through its network of agricultural societies and called for an independent agricultural college.[138] The most fervent opposition to Andrews' plan came from Amherst, where the coalition of agriculturalists and scientists plotted to bring the land-grant college to their small village. The legislature ultimately sided with the Amherst coalition and the state agricultural society, agreeing that the traditional educational elites at Harvard would not give ample attention to the applied science of agriculture. A new independent agricultural college in Amherst was created and given two-thirds of the federal grant (the other one-third was given to the Institute of Technology for education in the mechanical arts).[139] The return from Europe of agricultural chemist William Clark to assume the presidency brought a strong scientific leader to the Massachusetts land-grant college and helped solidify a broad-gauge, scientific orientation.

Contrary to the expectations of some in the agricultural press, the new agricultural college did not produce practicing farmers during its first decade.[140] In addition to graduating many leaders of New England industries, the Massachusetts Agricultural College nurtured leaders of agricultural education and science who were critical to the future of the land-grant movement. President Clark's chemistry courses and the research on the college farm and in the laboratory inspired several students to follow in his footsteps. Some notable examples include John Washburn, the first president of the Rhode Island Agricultural College; Charles Flagg, the president of the board of trustees of the Rhode Island Agricultural College; William Brooks, director of the Massachusetts Agricultural Experiment Station; and Horace Stockbridge, the first president of the North Dakota Agricultural College.[141]

In 1863, in Rhode Island and Vermont, the agricultural societies had missed their opportunity to form independent agricultural colleges. Rhode Island received the smallest return from land-grant sales in the region, and the legislature was unwilling to appropriate funds to build a new institution after Brown had signaled its willingness to take on the responsibility for free. A smattering of botany courses did little to calm agricultural society critics who argued that the college was doing little for agricultural science. However, with no alternative institution and no funding to build an agricultural college, Brown persisted as the state land grant until the 1890s.[142]

Vermont agriculturalists were unable to raise a sum of $100,000 that was mandated by the legislature as a condition of founding a state agricultural college.[143] This led the University of Vermont to inherit the state's land-grant college largely by default. Under the leadership of President Matthew Buckham, the university boldly asserted that "the term 'agricultural colleges,' as applied to the national institutions [land-grant colleges], is unofficial and misleading . . . and agriculture was only one of many subjects grouped under a convenient designation."[144] Instead, Buckham declared defiantly that it was only the responsibility of the university to instruct students in the "braches of learning related to agriculture."[145] Experimental farms were unnecessary and wasteful, the administration argued, as a faculty member could simply explain experiments to farmers, and their "results would be more trustworthy because of the variety of soil, location, and climate" throughout Vermont.[146] James R. Angell, Buckham's predecessor, had a broad, "National School of Science" conception of the Morrill Act, hiring chemistry professor Peter Collier and natural history professor George Perkins.[147] It was his intention to pursue a professorship of agricultural chemistry to spearhead agricultural research and education at the university, but the plan lay fallow when Angell accepted the presidency of the University of Michigan.[148] Buckham did not create the position of professor of agriculture until 1886.[149]

The absence of an agricultural professor and a department (not formed until 1888) made scientific courses at Vermont the elective append-ages to the classical core, not a part of a cohesive scientific program. By 1874, sixty-one of the undergraduates were in the classical course; six, in the chemistry course; and none, in agriculture.[150] As a Greek scholar, President Buckham had a great affinity for the classics and wanted to provide a respectable A.B. degree that would lure Vermont-ers away from Harvard, Yale, and, most importantly, Middlebury.[151] In 1873, he reported favorable progress, stating, "We think that our standard of classical attainment will compare favorably with that of any American college . . . and is being steadily raised year by year as fast as we can secure improvement in the style of preparation."[152] Ancient language requirements, high tuition, no model farm, and no agricultural program attracted neither aspiring farmers nor agricultural scientists. The president concluded that if the state wanted the University of Vermont to do more, then it would have to pay for it. He declared that agricultural societies and legislators had numerous education ideas, "but [had] not helped by one acre or one cent."[153] The University of Vermont remained conservative in its traditional orientation toward the classical curriculum, the learned professions, and to literary and cultural education. This reality was quite apparent when its president lectured audiences on the need and utility of ancient languages in speeches such as "The Less Obvious Benefits of a Liberal Education" and "Dead Languages For-sooth!"[154] In the history of land-grant colleges in New England, Matthew Buckham plays the part of Noah Porter.[155] He holds strong to the view that the aim of the college course was "to give power to acquire and to think, rather than to impart special knowledge or special discipline."[156] There were perhaps no stranger bedfellows in all of higher education than a land-grant college and an antiquarian.

The act to establish the Maine State College of Agriculture and Me-chanical Arts was passed in February 1865, but the college would not open until 1868. Even after the death of its leading voice Ezekiel Hol-mes, the state agricultural society and agricultural board were actively involved in shaping the direction of the institution. The legacy of the agricultural scientists and their commitment to agricultural chemistry was apparent in the first catalog:

> Each student will devote three hours a day to Analysis, under the direction of the Professor of Chemistry, thus acquiring facility in conducting experiments, and secur-ing a practical knowledge of the methods employed in chemical investigations.[157]

The influence of the agricultural societies' scientific perspective waned in 1866, when Phinehas T. Barnes replaced Holmes as the most prolific commentator on land-grant education in Maine. His public notoriety advanced his candidacy to the board of trustees, where he became a leading member.[158] He had been a professor of ancient languages at Bowdoin College, but his passion was industrial education.[159] In 1866, Barnes wrote a series of articles in the *Maine Farmer*, in which he declared that an answer was needed to three questions: *Who are to be educated in the industrial college? How are they to be educated? And, to what ends?*[160] His answers to these questions could be summarized as follows: The great working masses would become more productive, self-sustaining, and content laborers if they received an education at the state college of a practical and manual nature. Under Barnes' leadership, the college seemed poised to embrace a narrow-gauge vision below a collegiate grade.[161]

The Morrill Act called for the education of the industrial classes, and to Phinehas T. Barnes, this was a reference to working people who were historically barred due to lack of means. He concluded tuition was not the barrier, but it was subsistence during the college years.[162] Maine should address this problem, he argued, by not only offering free tuition but also providing paid labor. The proposed labor could also serve an educational purpose, as students actively implemented lessons learned in the classroom. Barnes posited that "the mind is best developed, best disciplined and best refined, where there is . . . an equal exercise of the physical powers."[163] This "bodily vigor," according to Barnes, should be gained through laboring in one's future calling not through the trappings of college "boat clubs" or "ball teams."[164] He concluded with a warning that Maine would be wise not to mimic the design of the scientific schools of Yale or Harvard; these colleges were simply expanding the sphere of educated professions to include engineers, chemists, geologists, and managers of labor.[165] Barnes believed that the Maine land grant should not fulfill this role, as there were too few positions of this type in the economy and college graduates would soon "glut the market."[166] Instead, they needed to focus on the 50,000 working young people in the state who would profit from scientific and vocational studies, who on graduation could become the most educated, cultured, and productive mechanics, farmers, and skilled workers anywhere.[167]

Phinehas T. Barnes was offered the presidency and the opportunity to implement his utilitarian vision, but he turned it down.[168] It was a fateful decision that would bring a president who moved Maine away from his industrial education model and toward an emulation of the National Schools of Science. In 1869, Merritt C. Fernald was hired as president.[169] After graduating from Bowdoin College in 1857, Fernald taught in village schools and spent winters in the laboratories of Harvard University's Lawrence School of Science. He was the assistant to Harvard chemist Josiah P. Cooke (author of *The New Chemistry*) and in 1864, managed his laboratory. Fernald retained deep ties with Harvard's Scientific School. He returned to Cambridge during winter breaks to visit the chemistry laboratory and the college observatory.[170] Fernald's legacy was bringing the scientific spirit to Orono, making the laboratory and the college farm places of experimentation instead of manual training.

* * *

The land-grant college in New England originated from a confluence of forces for higher education reform—the advancement of agricultural science, the cultivation and dissemination of American science in the tradition of the European universities, the improvement of agriculture and industry, and the production of graduates to fill emerging careers as "officers of industry" in engineering, mining, industrial management, architecture, and so on. Gentlemen from the agricultural society movement, expatriate European scholars, businessmen philanthropists, and statesmen had different reform motivations, but all were served by elevating science in American higher education. Before 1873, this coalition dominated the land-grant college movement in New England, resulting in the creation of institutions that aspired to the broad gauge, "National School of Science" agenda of Daniel Coit Gilman. However, in their midst, conflicting perspectives were already appearing. Phinehas T. Barnes offered an alternative, seeking to extend the benefits of the Morrill Act to working masses of his state. In the 1860s, little political support or pressure was offered from regular farmers and workers to advance such an agenda.

All this would change after 1873, when the onset of a great depression and the rise of the grange would bring a mass of farmers into debates over land-grant colleges, and cause institutional reformations throughout the region.[171] The grange would offer an alternative, utilitarian vision of land-grant education, hoping that practical studies and broader access would increase the profitability of their vocation and keep sons from leaving the farm, the rural community, and the class.[172] Farming progeny that had graduated from land-grant colleges in the 1860s and 1870s and moved off the farm into new middle-class jobs as scientists, engineers, or businessmen would fuel granger claims in the 1880s and 1890s that the colleges were exacerbating rural outmigration and threatening farmers' survival. The uncontested era of the *Science's Colleges* and *Industry's Colleges* would come to an end as the grange interceded to demand "People's Colleges"—narrow-gauge colleges for the farming masses. It is only with this second phase of land-grant development that we can return to the familiar interpretative confines of Earle Ross' *Democracy's College*.

Notes

*   A version of this article was first presented at "The Legacy and the Promise: One Hundred Fifty Years of Land-Grant Universities," Penn State University, June 23–24, 2011. Special thanks are due to Roger Geiger, Roger Williams, Scott Gelber, Greg Behle, Adam Nelson, and Alan Marcus for their insightful comments on this article. Portions of this article were published in Nathan M. Sorber, *Farmers, Scientists, "Officers of Industry": The Formation and Reformation of Land-Grant Colleges in the Northeastern United States, 1862–1905* (Diss. The Pennsylvania State University, 2011).

1.   Daniel Coit Gilman, "On the growth of American Colleges and Their Present Tendency to the Study of Science." Papers read before the American Institute of Instruction at Fitchburg, MA, July 26, 1871 (Boston, MA: American Institute of Instruction, 1872), 104.

2.   Justin S. Morrill, "Agricultural Colleges: Speech of Hon. Justin S. Morrill, of Vermont in the House of Representatives, June 6, 1862," The University of Vermont Special Collections, Congressional Speeches, Vermont, No. 19, E415.7.C66, 123.

3.   Earle D. Ross, *Democracy's College: The Land-Grant Movement in the Formative Stage* (New York, NY: Arno Press, 1969[1942]), 2.

4.   See Lyman Carrier, "The United States Agricultural Society, 1852–1860: Its Relation to the Origin of the United States Department of Agriculture and the Land-Grant Colleges," *Agricultural History* 11, no. 4 (October 1937): 278–88. On the growth and development of the early state agricultural societies, see Alfred Charles True, *A History of Agricultural Education in the United States, 1785–1925* (New York, NY: Arno Press, 1969), 7–27.

5.   Charles E. Rosenberg, *No Other Gods: On Science and American Social Thought* (Baltimore, MD: The Johns Hopkins University Press, 1997 [1976]), 135–52.

6.   See Daniel Coit Gilman, *Our National Schools of Science* (Reprinted from *North American Review*). (Boston, MA: Ticknor and Fields, 1867), 16.

7.   *Catalogue of the Officers and Students in Yale College* (New Haven, CT: Tuttle, Morehouse, & Taylor Printers, 1875), 63.

8.   This occupational grouping was referred to by many names: the higher avocations of life, specialists, new learned professions, and so on. The term "officers of industry" was coined by Andrew Dickson White, the president of Cornell University, and it described those scientific, technical, and business specialists who would find careers in the emerging industries of the new economy. Occasionally, Daniel Coit Gilman borrowed this terminology.

9.   For the breadth of his vision on this issue, see Gilman, "On the growth of American Colleges"; Gilman, *Our National Schools of Science*; and Daniel Coit Gilman, "The

Sheffield School of Yale University, New Haven," in author, *University Problems in the United States* (New York: The Century Company, 1898), 120–21.

10. Frederick Rudolph, *The American College & University – A History* (Athens: The University of Georgia Press, 1990 [1962]), 249.

11. Geiger, "The Rise and Fall of Useful Knowledge," 153–68; Scott M. Gelber, *Academic Populism: The People's Revolt and Public Higher Education, 1880–1905* (Diss. Harvard University, 2008); Alan Marcus, *Agricultural Science and the Quest for Legitimacy* (Ames, IA: Iowa State University Press, 1985); Roy V. Scott, *The Reluctant Farmer: The Rise of Agricultural Extension to 1914* (Champaign, IL: University of Illinois Press, 1970); and Sorber, *Farmers, Scientists*, 192–260.

12. Scott, *Reluctant Farmer*.

13. N. T. True, "Biographical Sketch of Ezekiel Holmes." *Tenth Annual Report of the Secretary of the Maine Board of Agriculture, 1865* (Augusta, ME: Stevens & Sayward, Printers to the State, 1865), 207–8.

14. Walter C. Bronson, *The History of Brown University, 1764–1914* (Providence: Brown University, 1914), 167.

15. This quote is from Brown University's undergraduate Barnas Sears of the class of 1825, cited in Bronson, *History of Brown University*, 167.

16. Ibid., 180–82.

17. See Samuel L. Boardman, "Ezekiel Holmes, Memorials, Journals, and Correspondence," *The Home Farm*, IV, No. 32, July 19, 1884. University of Maine Archives, Ezekiel Holmes Collection.

18. Bronson, *History of Brown University*, 160–61.

19. Student quote cited in ibid., 161.

20. On Solomon Drowne, see ibid., 160–61.

21. True, "Biographical Sketch of Ezekiel Holmes," 208.

22. Ibid., 208.

23. Ibid., 209.

24. Ezekiel Holmes, "Utility of Philosophy to a Nation," Published in Boardman, "Ezekiel Holmes. Memorials, Journals, and Correspondence," 188.

25. Ibid.

26. Ibid.

27. True, "Biographical Sketch of Ezekiel Holmes," 209–10.

28. Ibid., 210.

29. This is a reprint of Ezekiel Holmes' letter to the Gardiner Lyceum Trustees. Samuel L. Boardman, "Correspondence of 1828–30," in *The Home Farm*, IV, No. 42, August 28, 1884. University of Maine Archives, Ezekiel Holmes Collection, 192.

30. Ibid., 192.

31. True, "Biographical Sketch of Ezekiel Holmes," 212–18; David C. Smith, *The First Century: A History of the University of Maine, 1865–1965* (Orono, ME: University of Maine at Orono Press, 1979), 2–5.

32. Smith, *First Century*, 4–5.

33. Ezekiel Holmes, "Utility of Philosophy to a Nation," 188.

34. Alan Marcus, *Agricultural Science and the Quest for Legitimacy: Farmers, Agricultural Colleges, and Experiment Stations, 1870–1890* (Ames, IA: Iowa State University Press, 1985), 18–20.

35. Ibid., 7–26.

36. For a discussion of the genteel membership of agricultural societies in different contexts, see Gerald L. Prescott, "Farm Gentry vs. the Grangers: Conflict in Rural America," *California Historical Quarterly* 56, no. 4 (Winter, 1977/1978): 328–45; Erik A. Ernst, "John A. Kennicott of the Grove: Physician, Horticulturist, and Journalist in Nineteenth-Century Illinois," *Journal of the Illinois State Historical*

Society 74, no. 2 (Summer, 1981): 109–18; Gerald L. Prescott, "Gentlemen Farmers in the Gilded Age," *The Wisconsin Magazine of History* 55, no. 3 (Spring, 1972): 197–212; Lyman Carrier, "The United States Agricultural Society," 278–88.

37. True, *History of Agricultural Education*, 23–24.
38. See Carrier, "The United States Agricultural Society," 278–88; True, *History of Agricultural Education*, 48–51, 58–60, 67–71.
39. Quotes are from Lewis H. Gause, "Agricultural Colleges," *New England Farmer* 4, no. 10 (October 1852): 475.
40. Cited in Marcus, *Agricultural Science*, 35.
41. True, *History of Agriculture Education*, 78.
42. Edward Hitchcock, *Reminiscences of Amherst College: Historical, Scientific, Biographical, and Autobiographical: Also, of Other and Wider Life Experiences* (Northampton, MA: Bridgman & Childs, 1863).
43. Rudolph, *American College*, 223–24.
44. This quote is from an address delivered by Hitchcock in Northampton, Massachusetts, and is quoted in Harold Whiting Cary, *The University of Massachusetts: A History of One Hundred Years* (Amherst, MA: The University of Massachusetts Press, 1962), 12.
45. Ibid., 12.
46. Ibid., 12–13.
47. For a good background on some of the leading lights of the agricultural society and journal movement, see George F. Lemmer, "Early Agricultural Editors and Their Farm Philosophies," *Agricultural History* 31, no. 4 (October 1957): 3–22.
48. See Rosenberg, *No Other Gods*, 135–52; Robert W. Hill, "John Pitkin Norton's Visit to England, 1844," *Agricultural History* 8, no. 4 (October 1934): 219–22; Jacqueline M. Bloom, *Evan Pugh: The Education of a Scientist, 1828–1858* (M.A. Thesis, Pennsylvania State University, 1960), 20–81; Donald C. Babcock, *History of the University of New Hampshire* (Rochester, NH: The Record Press, 1941), 15–18.
49. Laurence R. Veysey, *The Emergence of the American University* (Chicago, IL: The University of Chicago Press, 1965), 10.
50. Rosenberg, *No Other Gods*, 135–52.
51. Richard Holmes, *The Age of Wonder: The Romantic Generation and the Discovery of the Beauty and Terror of Science* (New York, NY: Random House Digital, 2010).
52. Chittenden, *History of the Sheffield Scientific School.*
53. Ibid.
54. Rosenberg, *No Other Gods*, 135–52.
55. See Sorber, *Farmers, Scientists*, 127–33.
56. Rosenberg, *No Other Gods*, 142.
57. Arthur Brandegee and Eddy N. Smith, *Farmington, Connecticut: The Village of Beautiful Homes* (Farmington, CT: Authors, 1906).
58. William A. Lanard, "John Pitkin Norton," *The New Englander* 10 (November 1852): 613–31.
59. Ibid.
60. Chittenden, *History of the Sheffield Scientific School*, 43–44.
61. Lanard, "John Pitkin Norton," 613–31.
62. Hill, "John Pitkin Norton's Visit to England, 1844," 219–22.
63. Cited in ibid., 219.
64. Ibid.
65. Ibid.
66. The text of this resolution is cited in Lanard, "John Pitkin Norton," 620–21.
67. Chittenden, *History of the Sheffield Scientific School*, 45–48.

68. Combination of two quotes in *Proposed Plan for a Complete Organization of the School of Science, Connected with Yale College* (New Haven, CT: Ezekiel Hayes, 1856), 4, 7.
69. See the department's corporate authorization in Chittenden, *History of the Sheffield Scientific School*, 40–41.
70. Ibid., 48–49.
71. Ibid., 46.
72. Cited in ibid..
73. David B. Potts, *Liberal Education for a Land of Colleges: Yale's "Reports" of 1828.* (New York: Palgrave Macmillan, 2010).
74. *Reports on the Courses of Instruction in Yale College by a Committee of the Corporation and the Academical Faculty* (New Haven, CT: Hezekiah Howe, 1828).
75. David B. Potts, "Curriculum and Enrollment: Assessing the Popularity of Antebellum Colleges," in *The American College in the Nineteenth Century*, ed. Roger L. Geiger (Nashville, TN: Vanderbilt University Press, 2000), 37–45.
76. For enrollment numbers, see Chittenden, *History of the Sheffield Scientific School*, 60–61.
77. Ibid., 54.
78. Cited in Lanard, "John Pitkin Norton."
79. See Bronson, *History of Brown*, 279–83.
80. In the 1850s, Delaware College prolonged its existence by experimenting with courses in agricultural science and engineering. For the quote, see Ross, *Democracy's College*, 20.
81. Wayland, *Report to the Corporation of Brown University*, 18.
82. See biographical entry on John A. Porter in Henry S. Olcott, *Outlines of the First Course of Yale Agricultural Lectures* (New York, NY: C. M. Saxton, Barker, 1860).
83. For an accounting of the student rebellion and faculty conflict that led to Porter's and Norton's resignations, see Bronson, *History of Brown*, 296.
84. Ibid., 287; Chittenden, *History of the Sheffield Scientific School*, 55–62.
85. Chittenden, *History of the Sheffield Scientific School*, 61.
86. Ibid., 57.
87. Ibid., 69–70.
88. Ibid., 64.
89. See Elizabeth Harriet Thomson, *Benjamin Silliman and His Circle* (New York, NY: Science History Publications, 1979).
90. *Proposed Plan for a Complete Organization of the School of Science, Connected with Yale College* (New Haven, CT: Ezekiel Hayes, 1856).
91. Ibid., 5.
92. Ibid., 7.
93. Ibid.
94. Geiger, "Rise and Fall of Useful Knowledge," 153–68.
95. Ibid.
96. See A. J. Angulo, *William Barton Rogers and the Idea of MIT* (Baltimore, MD: The Johns Hopkins Press, 2009).
97. Roger L. Geiger, "The Era of the Multipurpose Colleges in American Higher Education," in *The American College in the Nineteenth Century*, 127–52.
98. Duemer, *Origins of the Morrill Land Grant Act of 1862.* Although Duemer's analysis is quite general, he asserts that macroeconomic changes (which he terms "modernization") were a key influence on the origins of the land-grant movement.

99. Coy F. Cross II, *Justin Smith Morrill: Father of the Land-Grant Colleges* (East Lansing, MI: Michigan State University, 1999), 77–78.
100. "Speech of Honorable Justin S. Morrill of Vermont, In the House of Representatives, June 6, 1862." University of Vermont Archives. No.19: Congressional speeches, 123.
101. Ibid., 121.
102. Michael F. Holt, *The Rise and Fall of the American Whig Party: Jacksonian Politics at the Eve of the Civil War* (New York, NY: Oxford University Press, 1999).
103. Henry Charles Carey, *Principles of Political Economy* (Philadelphia, PA: Carey, Lea, & Blanchard, 1837).
104. Holt, *Rise and Fall*.
105. "Speech of Honorable Justin S. Morrill," 124.
106. Holt, *Rise and Fall*; John Lauritz Larson, *Internal Improvements: National Public Works and the Promise of Popular Government in the Early United States* (Chapel Hill: The University of North Carolina Press, 2001).
107. Daniel Coit Gilman, "Scientific Schools in Europe: Considered in Reference to Their Prevalence, Utility, Scope, and Desirability in America," *Bernard's Journal of Education* (March 1856): 326.
108. Ibid., 323.
109. Ibid.
110. Ibid., 327.
111. Veysey, *Emergence of the American University*, 159.
112. Chittenden, *History of the Sheffield Scientific School*, 84–86.
113. *Acts of the Congress of the United States and of the Legislature of Connecticut Pertaining to the National Grant of Public Lands for the Promotion of Scientific Education* (New Haven, CT: Yale University, 1883). Manuscripts and Archives, Yale University Library, Box 52, No. 574.
114. In *Democracy's College*, Earle Ross writes that Connecticut made "official connection with one of the best developed scientific schools in the country without any expenditure for equipment and maintenance, and the Sheffield Foundation secured essential aid (the federal land grant) at a formative stage" (74).
115. On the Sheffield faculty reaction to the land-grant bill, see True, *History of Agricultural Education*, 106–8.
116. As Roger Williams notes, Justin Morrill himself never conceded to the term "agricultural colleges," which was applied by the legislative clerk. He also states that many land-grant presidents and association leaders were "overwrought" with the public perception that land-grant funds were meant for establishing "agricultural colleges." See Williams, *The Origins of Federal Support for Higher Education* (University Park, PA: Penn State University, 2000), 2.
117. Daniel Coit Gilman, *Our National Schools of Science* [Repr. from *North American Review*] (Boston, MA: Ticknor and Fields, 1867), 16.
118. True, *History of Agricultural Education*, 106.
119. Gilman, "Our National Schools of Science," 6.
120. Ibid., 16.
121. Ibid., 9; Geiger, "Rise and Fall of Useful Knowledge," 160–61.
122. Gilman, "Our National Schools of Science," 27–28.
123. Ibid., 27.
124. Ibid.
125. Ibid., 23.
126. Ibid.
127. This encounter between Morrill and the Sheffield faculty is provided in True, *A History of Agricultural Education*, 107–8.

128. Morrill's remarks were relayed in a letter by Professor Brewer. An excerpt of that letter is provided in ibid., 107–8.

129. Justin Morrill, "Address," Delivered at the Massachusetts Agricultural College, June 21, 1887 (Amherst, MA: J. E. Williams, Book and Job Printer, 1887), 20.

130. Babcock, *History of the University of New Hampshire*, 11.

131. Ibid., 15–16.

132. Quote reprinted in ibid., 20.

133. Ibid., 15–46.

134. Harold Whiting Cary, *The University of Massachusetts*, 23–37.

135. Benjamin Bussey was a prominent Boston merchant and farmer who bequeathed a part of his estate to Harvard University for "instruction in agriculture, horticulture, and related subjects." In time, the proceeds of the gift were used to establish the Bussey Institute, a school that was dedicated to agricultural science and experimentation. For a discussion of the Bussey Institute, see Samuel Eliot Morison, *Three Centuries of Harvard, 1636–1936* (1936, repr. Cambridge, MA: Harvard University Press, 2001).

136. *Acts and Resolves Passed by the General Court of Massachusetts in 1863* (Boston, MA: Wright and Potter State Printers, 1863), 620.

137. Ibid.

138. Ross, *Democracy's College*, 70–71.

139. Cary, *University of Massachusetts*, 23–37. For an excellent discussion of MIT's place in Massachusetts' land-grant history, see Julius A. Stratton and Loretta H. Mannix, *Mind and Hand: The Birth of MIT* (Cambridge, MA: The MIT Press, 2005).

140. *New England Farmer* and *Massachusetts Ploughman* editorials make regular reference to the scientific, practicing farmers who attend and graduate from agricultural colleges. See Sorber, *Farmers, Scientists*, 192–260.

141. *The Catalog of Graduates and Former Students of the Massachusetts Agricultural College* (Amherst, MA: The University of Massachusetts Press, 1913), 1–24.

142. Ibid., 225–50.

143. Robert O. Sinclair, "Agricultural Education and Extension in Vermont," in *The University of Vermont: The First Two Hundred Years*, ed. Robert V. Daniels (Burlington, VT: University of Vermont, 1991), 179–80.

144. *Biennial Report of the Trustees of the University of Vermont and State Agricultural College for 1873–74*, 9. University of Vermont Special Collections. Open Stacks.

145. Ibid., 9–10.

146. Ibid., 11.

147. T. D. Seymour Bassett, "The Classical College, 1833–1895: Growth and Stability," in *The University of Vermont*, 85–86.

148. See "The Natural Science and George Henry Perkins," in *The University of Vermont*, 138–39.

149. Sinclair, "Agricultural Education," 184.

150. *Biennial Report of the Trustees . . . 1874–75*, 4. University of Vermont Special Collections. Open Stacks.

151. See "Vermont Students in Other Colleges," in *Biennial Report of the Trustees of the University of Vermont and State Agricultural College for 1873–74*, 4–5. University of Vermont Special Collections. Open Stacks. For the historical context of the state rivalry between UVM and Middlebury, see P. Jeffrey Potash, "Years of Trial: Religion, Money, War, Fire, and the Competition with Middlebury," in *The University of Vermont*, 34–47.

152. *Biennial Report of the Trustees . . . 1873–74*, 7–8.

153. Ibid.
154. Matthew Buckham, *Dead Languages Forsooth!* (Burlington, VT: Free Press, 1908); Matthew Buckham, "Some of the Less Obvious Benefits of a Liberal Education." This is a handwritten speech delivered at an unknown time and place but is available in the University of Vermont Special Collections. Mathew Buckham Papers.
155. Noah Porter (1811–1892) was a Yale graduate, congregational minister, professor of moral philosophy, and president of Yale from 1871 to 1886. He remained committed to the traditional curriculum, moral education, and mental discipline at Yale, as reformers such as Charles Eliot at Harvard were embracing the emerging university model. He is the archetype of an educational conservative in an era of rapid modernization. See Vesey, *The Emergence of the American University*, 23–25.
156. Noah Porter's quote is reprinted in ibid., 23–24.
157. *Catalogue of the Officers and Students of the State College of Agriculture and Mechanic Arts. Orono, Maine, 1868* (Bangor, ME: Benjamin A. Burr, Printer, 1868), 4.
158. Smith, *First Hundred Years*, 7.
159. Barnes settled on the label "Industrial College," but was hesitant to use the term "college." David Smith argues that the land-grant schools would attempt to emulate traditional colleges, and Barnes proposed institutions with a broader clientele with direct vocational outcomes. See ibid., 6–10.
160. The articles that Phinehas T. Barnes wrote to *The Maine Farmer* were reprinted in Maine Board of Agriculture. *The Eleventh Annual Report of the Secretary of the Maine Board of Agriculture, 1866* (Augusta, ME: Stevens & Seward, Printers for the State, 1866), 199–235.
161. Earle Ross describes the two major land-grant visions as "broad-gauge" and "narrow-gauge" in *Democracy's College*, 88–89. He states, "the national school of science" model was not premised on "training working farmers and mechanics" but for "educating leaders in the sciences." Those who supported this view held a "broad gauge" view of land-grant education. In contrast, those who held a "practical training" or "manual training" view of the land-grant colleges wanted to "reduce higher education to its lowest terms and give it the widest extension."
162. Phinehas T. Barnes, "The Industrial College – No. 5, Questions of Costs," *The Maine Farmer*. Reprinted in Maine Board of Agriculture. *The Eleventh Annual Report*, 225–35.
163. Ibid., 229.
164. Citied in Smith, *First Hundred Years*, 7.
165. See Phinehas T. Barnes, "Scientific Schools," *The Maine Farmer*. Reprinted in Maine Board of Agriculture. *The Eleventh Annual Report*, 210–16. Quote 213.
166. Ibid., 214.
167. Ibid., 210–16.
168. Smith, *First Century*, 9.
169. Ibid., 10–11.
170. For Fernald's personal biography and academic background, see photographed document "Merritt Caldwell Fernald from *History of Penobscot County, 1882*. University of Maine, ORO Special Collections, Box 50, Folder 45.
171. See Scott M. Gelber, *Academic Populism;* Scott, *The Reluctant Farmer;* and Sorber, *Farmers, Scientists*, 192–260.
172. Sorber, *Farmers, Scientists*.

Educating the Toiling Peoples: Students at the Illinois Industrial University, Spring 1868

J. Gregory Behle

Traditional histories of the land-grant college movement have popularized the idea that the Morrill Act democratized higher education by opening access to an under-privileged working class. The Morrill Act stipulated that the beneficiaries of the legislation were to be from the "industrial classes"—sons of working farmers and mechanics who lacked access to traditional higher education and desired a course of study that prepared them for life on the farm or in the machine shop. This investigation explores student backgrounds, course of studies, and postcollegiate attainments of the students who attended the Illinois Industrial University at its opening term in the spring 1868. While demonstrating that these students were the progeny of farmers and mechanics, this paper adds that they were also from homes of wealth and social standing; took courses in traditional college studies; and opted for less labor-intensive careers in the new middle class. Such findings corroborate criticisms of land-grant colleges in the agricultural press of the day and challenge the traditional interpretation that land-grant colleges opened access to and tailored curricula to the working poor—"the toiling peoples."

Introduction

I have heard about the Illinois Industrial College from a friend of mine . . . He was telling me that any young man can pay his way through college who is willing for the sake of an education to practice steadily the virtues of industry & economy. If this is a true assertion, I would on account of reduced circumstances frankly undergo such practice. (Adam Gerlach, son of an Illinois farmer)[1]

Perspectives on the History of Higher Education 30 (2013): 73–94
© 2013. ISBN: 978-1-4128-5147-3

Histories of the land-grant college movement have created and popularized an idea: The Morrill Act democratized higher education by opening access to the industrial classes—to the children of farmers and mechanics who might otherwise find college financially inaccessible or unnecessary for their vocational aspirations. In the fall of 1868, Adam Gerlach issued the above plea to a trustee of the new Illinois Industrial University. A hardworking child of the farm, born of immigrant parents, and apparently struggling due to reduced circumstances, Gerlach appears, at first blush, to be the ideal student for this new type of college funded by federal land grants. Although scholars might point to Gerlach as an example of how the Morrill Act afforded an education to struggling families, what is not apparent in his plea of poverty is that his father owned three farms and was described as a "leading citizen" of his community.[2] Gerlach never enrolled at the university.

Prophesied at Illinois' inaugural exercises, Dr. Newton Bateman cast his vision of the new land-grant university:

> Thank God, monopolies of learning, by privileged classes, are among the discrowned shadows of the past. A new element is henceforth to bear sway in the destinies of these States and of the nation. To the dust must go, and will go, whatever schemes, devices or systems, refuse to affiliate with or set themselves in opposition to, the Lord's redeemed and anointed—the *People*.[3]

Who were *the people* and how were *the people* to be redeemed and anointed? According to literature of the land-grant movement, and reiterated in institutional histories, the industrial class included the sons, and later daughters, of the underprivileged. The aim of the land-grant colleges, so conceived, was to provide access and practical curricula to democratize participation in higher education. The Morrill Act, however, does not define the industrial classes. Jonathan Baldwin Turner, a visionary of industrial university education, offered a definition by utilizing occupational categories. He described society as consisting of "a small class . . . [of leaders] in religion, law, medicine, science, art, and literature; and a much larger class, who are engaged in some form of labor in agriculture, commerce and the arts. . . . We will designate the former the *professional*, and the latter the *industrial classes* [Emphasis added]." Turner reflected,

> Probably in no case would society ever need more than five men out of one hundred in the professional class, leaving ninety-five in every hundred in the industrial; . . . [In summary] we do not really need over one professional man for every hundred, leaving ninety-nine in the industrial.[4]

Early land-grant college advocates identified with the industrial class, even though many were of significant economic means and social standing. These educational reformers focused on changing the purpose and curriculum of higher education to create a more attractive system for the industrial class. They juxtaposed themselves to the elite, professional classes and contrasted the land-grant experiment with the majority of colleges in existence. They critiqued these traditional colleges for being structured to educate the professional class—clergymen, doctors, and lawyers. Mathias Lane Dunlap, an Illinois trustee, widely read agriculturalist, and state leader in industrial education, stated it this way,

> The truth is, we must educate the laboring or industrial classes in that which is useful to them. If one desires to be a preacher or lawyer, or a doctor, educate him accordingly; but do not give the farmer's son who is to be a farmer, the same education; for if you do; he will follow one of these professions, live by office, or become a genteel loafer.[5]

This investigation seeks to clarify several questions that are pivotal to the democratization thesis. Who attended these new universities? Were they sons of toil, children of the underprivileged, as suggested in the historiography? What was their socioeconomic position? Did they study subjects that were relevant to industrial pursuits? What did they do after college? Did they return to follow in their father's livelihood or did they seek opportunities in nonlabor intensive occupations of the new middle class? As the sesquicentennial of the Morrill Act is celebrated, and pronouncements are made regarding its contributions, the land-grant colleges' role in democratizing higher education should be considered in light of the historical data. As the case of Illinois illustrates, early state industrial reformers recognized a tension between the promise and the actual implementation of the Morrill Act and raised an alarm regarding a conflict between legislative intent and institutional direction.

Democracy's Colleges?

The traditional canon of land-grant historiography (i.e., the works of Earl Ross, Allan Nevins, Edward Eddy, and J. B. Edmonds) has embraced the democratization thesis—that the land-grant colleges were in response to popular demand for expanded higher education access and utility—largely without supporting empirical evidence. Eldon Johnson responded that misconceptions exist in the land-grant historiography, including the notion that student demand was a driving motivation for the land-grant college movement.[6] Behle and Maxwell examined a cross section of students attending the University of Illinois between 1868 and 1894 and found that students hailed from families of financial means and social standing in contrast to the assertion that the land-grant colleges served as a gateway for the lower classes.[7] Popular surveys of the land-grant movement and institutional college histories have propagated the democratization idea without attending research support. These individual college histories range from excellent historical analysis to institutional hagiography and self-laudatory rhetoric, thereby adding to the confusion.[8]

The absence of research into who actually attended the land-grant colleges is generally consistent with the absence of students in the history of higher education. As Rudolph noted, "College students constitute the most neglected, least understood element of the American academic community."[9] The Morrill Act stipulated the industrial classes as beneficiaries, but the lack of research regarding student origins precludes forming conclusions on the degree to which land-grant colleges expanded higher education access. The empirical evidence of Maxwell, Behle, and Johnson warrants a re-examination of the conventional wisdom regarding the intent and fulfillment of the Morrill Act.

Scholars have recognized that the Morrill Act and the land-grant universities instituted some reforms which were aimed at meeting the demands of the industrial classes, including: encouraging applied sciences to the practice of agriculture and engineering; a greater emphasis on science as the core and driving force of the curriculum; an emerging role of research to inform and reshape knowledge; the introduction and emphasis on manual labor; and the place of military studies. This brought a new curricular dimension to American higher education that was absent in most colleges and universities at the time.

Beyond the curricular reforms, the central tenet of the democratization thesis is that the Morrill Act opened access to a sector of society that was ignored or excluded from traditional higher education. Language used by contemporary reformers, such as "industrial classes," "the people," "democracy's colleges," and "underprivileged," has been interpreted by scholars to mean that the land-grant movement was intimately connected to concerns with working poor. Historian Allen Nevins noted that

> The central idea behind the land-grant movement was that liberty and equality could not survive unless all men had full opportunity to pursue all occupations at the highest practicable level. No restrictions of class, or fortune, or sex, or geographical position—no restrictions whatsoever—should operate.[10]

He cites Ira Allen, a benefactor of the University of Vermont in Morrill's home state: "It is not the rich man that I am calculating to assist . . . as the poor, the rich may send their sons to what college they please but the poor have it not in their power."[11]

In his oft-cited book, *Democracy's College*, Earle Ross observed, ". . . A. and M. colleges reached a *stratum* [emphasis added] of students for whom higher or even intermediate training would not otherwise have been available."[12] Edward Eddy picked up on this thread: "Ross concludes that the term 'industrial classes' was a general designation for 'all groups of the educationally underprivileged.'"[13] As Mumford summarized,

> It is claimed for the land-grant college that it has democratized education. This democratization of education has been accomplished in two ways: first, it has broadened the curriculum; and second, it has made it possible for students of *limited means* [emphasis added] to profit from higher education. The land-grant college is a direct challenge to the idea that higher education is for the privileged few.[14]

In crafting these conclusions, historians focused on public statements on the meaning of the land-grant act that were advanced during the formative period. Several such declarations were proffered after the death of Justin Morrill, similar to when during a eulogy, fellow Vermont legislator Horace Powers remarked on the democratic significance of the land-grant colleges: "the farmer, the artisan, the wage-earner of whatsoever name is entitled to the same opportunities in the race of life as his more fortunate fellow-citizens."[15]

Ross focused on this historical rhetoric when he proclaimed land-grant colleges as "Democracy's Colleges." The preponderance of public statements was the basis for his assertions, not empirical data evidencing who the students actually were, where they came from, and what they did with their college education. In the absence of supportive data, the degree to which land-grant colleges democratized higher education remains an open question. This analysis of student attendees at one land-grant college, the Illinois Industrial University, seeks to address this question.[16]

In February 1867, the Illinois Industrial University (later, the University of Illinois) was chartered and in the spring of 1868, it was opened to students. According to the 1870 census, students came from Illinois towns—neither major urban centers nor small hamlets—that averaged populations of about 3,400. Almost all students came from cities located along important transportation corridors—principal state rail lines or towns located along the Ohio River. The Illinois Central Railroad, a

Table 1   Father's Professional or Industrial Class Distinctions,
1850–1880 Census

	1850	1860	1870	1880
Industrial class	55 (71%)	61 (80%)	60 (78%)	42 (55%)
Professional class[17]	9 (12%)	9 (12%)	9 (12%)	7 (9%)
Father deceased	0	1 (1%)	3 (4%)	18 (23%)
No data available	13 (17%)	6 (8%)	5 (7%)	10 (13%)

key participant in the history of the university, played an important role in facilitating access to the campus and was frequently mentioned in student correspondence.

Fathers were of a Protestant religious persuasion with the majority being Baptist. Most held to Lincoln's political beliefs: a four-to-one difference of Republicans to Democrats. Eleven fathers served in the Civil War, with ranks ranging from colonels to privates; all fought for the Union.

Using strict occupational definitions, it was the sons of the industrial class that arrived, in spring 1868. While many students came from fathers of farms, shops, and mercantile pursuits, students from professional backgrounds were consistently represented as well. The university fulfilled its responsibilities to many of the occupational groups within the industrial class.

Although percentages favored industrial class origins, state industrial education leaders were dissatisfied with the student body makeup of their new university. If the ratio of the industrial to the professional class was to be twenty to one, as Turner argued, professional class students were attending in numbers that were inconsistent with their vision. Mathias Dunlap, the university trustee and agriculturalist, led the charge. In several essays that were critical of the university and its leadership, Dunlap warned his readership:

> But, strange to say, the great industrial class for which this grant was designed have sat supinely by and allowed the professions to use the funds for their own advancement.[18]

By 1870, John Milton Gregory, the university's first regent (president), warned Mason Brayman, a university trustee, ". . . A crisis is upon us." Turner, along with other populist leaders, planned to reconsider the "original intention, present condition, and future prospects of the industrial university" in a statewide convention.[19] It appears as though the *Lord's redeemed and anointed* were questioning their salvation.

Table 2   Fathers' Occupational Categories, 1850–1880 Census

	1850	1860	1870	1880
Agriculture	32 (42%)	37 (48%)	35 (45%)	24 (31%)
Professional services	9 (12%)	10 (13%)	8 (10%)	7 (9%)
Manufacturing & mechanical	15 (19%)	11 (14%)	6 (8%)	4 (5%)
Trades	4 (5%)	8 (10%)	13 (17%)	7 (9%)
Public service	2 (3%)	2 (3%)	1 (1%)	1 (1%)
Domestic/personal services	2 (3%)	1 (1%)	2 (3%)	1 (1%)
Transportation	0 (0%)	0 (0%)	3 (4%)	2 (3%)
Clerical occupations	0 (0%)	1 (1%)	1 (1%)	2 (3%)
No data available	13 (17%)	6 (8%)	5 (6%)	11 (14%)
Father deceased	0 (0%)	1 (1%)	3 (4%)	18 (24%)

Notwithstanding these critiques, the Illinois Industrial University appeared to serve the progeny of workers who were employed in various industrial class occupations. The sons of farmers and shopkeepers were enrolling in the university in much higher numbers than were those of the professional class. According to the 1870 census, nearly 80 percent of the new students were from agricultural, mechanical, or mercantile families. This is certainly evidence of service to the industrial classes, albeit not in the ratios envisioned by Jonathan Baldwin Turner.

The economic status of the early attendees offers a different perspective, and suggests another source of the populist discontent with land-grant colleges. The 1870 census shows that many students were coming not from small family farms, but from larger farm enterprises (Table Three).

Approximately 92 percent of the students were from homes in the upper half of the economic spectrum. Census comparisons between Illinois student families and luminaries of the land-grant movement are illustrative. In 1860, the estimated value of a 160-acre Illinois farm was $3,253; for an 80-acre farm, $1,747; and for a 40-acre farm, $1,103.[20] Where data were available, 1860 combined real estate and personal property averages for the university faculty were $9,776; Abraham Lincoln ($17,000); Justin Smith Morrill ($22,000); Jonathan Baldwin Turner ($13,000); and the University trustees at $30,533. The 1860 average for the families of the university students was $10,998.

The 1870 census data tell a similar story. John Milton Gregory, the university's first regent, reported wealth at $14,745. The university

Table 3   Fathers' Economic Class and Occupational Sector, 1870 Census
(Averages, Combined Real Estate, and Personal Property)

Economic Class	Agriculture	Manufacturing & Mechanical	Trades	Transportation	Professional Services	Personal Services	Clerical Occupations	Public Services	Average
I	$59,243 4		$78,824 3		$89,000 1			$76,600 1	$75,917 9
II	$15,226 18	$8,000 1	$25,500 4	$6,200 1	$10,233 3				$13,032 28
III	$5,700 11	$5,280 5	$8,343 6	$3,400 1	$3,800 4	$4,200 1	$3,200 1		$4,846 29
IV	$2,450 2			$3,500 1					$2,975 3
V									
VI									
1									3
2									5

Note: 1–Father DECEASED; 2–No Data Available.

faculty showed averages of $8,318. In contrast, averages for student families were $19,965. Claims that the land-grant movement democratized higher education by providing access to the sons of the toil, if defined as the underprivileged, are inaccurate in the case of Illinois. These students arrived from families of considerable financial means and social standing.

Student age has been used as an indicator of wealth related to college access.[21] The assumption is that more prosperous students would attend college at an earlier age due to economic advantage. In the case of Illinois, no relationship exists between economic class and age of entry. University circulars from 1868 stated that the minimum age for enrollment was fifteen and that the age of eighteen was preferable, assuming greater maturity and responsibility. The actual age range was fourteen to twenty-seven years with an average of eighteen. In the fall 1868 term, and reflecting on student attrition from the previous spring, student James N. Matthews wrote to his father, "I am sorry to say that there are at present but 80 scholars here and most of those are old students that were here last term."[22] Such an observation might suggest that early attendees at Illinois were significantly older, and, therefore, from homes of less economic means; however, Matthew's observation should be framed against his young age of fifteen.

The Land-Grant College Experience: Access, Student Life, Academics, and Persistence

The cost of attending college, without considering the opportunity cost of foregone labor on the farm or shop, posed another challenge to a mission of expanding access to working people. In an attempt to counter this problem, students were encouraged with statements that university expenses should not be considered an impediment to attendance. Circulars addressed the question, "How can I pay my way?" noting that the university had been receiving correspondence from "earnest young men, eager for an education, but without means." The university then issued a manly challenge:

> You will find numbers of fellow students, who are taking care of themselves, and who will, with true brotherly feeling advise and assist you. Come on without fear. What man has done, man can do.[23]

Students could anticipate university expenses between $163 and $195 annually for room, board, tuition, and incidentals.[24] These costs could be reduced to $100 a year by working at the university shops and farms. Work vouchers for the 1868 students suggest that students took advantage of this early version of work-study. The payment was $1.50 per day for shop and farm work—a fair rate, considering that farm laborers in Illinois averaged $16.94/month in 1870.[25] Within the first month of opening, records indicate that the university paid out $126.95 on student labor.[26] The university warned students that textbooks were not in the estimated costs. Student Matthews complained to his father that his botany text cost $3.50 but, ". . . it is nice and I think valuable book containing 832 pages."[27] For an Illinois farm laborer, such a text amounted to more than two days' wages.

Student labor was not enough to address the major challenge to recruiting and maintaining students of the industrial classes: the expense of college relative to average income levels. The cost of an Illinois education consumed more of a family's annual income than could be tolerated for those in a lower economic position. The average daily wage in 1868 for skilled, industrial class occupations was $2.58. The daily wage rates for common labor were as follows: farm laborers ($1.00), blacksmiths ($2.73), machinists ($2.66), and carpenters ($2.67). The annual incomes for nonfarm employees in 1868 averaged $499.[28] The university janitor and handy man were paid $40/month. When compared with Illinois' estimated costs of $163 for annual expenses, the cost of attending the university could consume nearly a third of a families' annual income, not counting the labor lost to the farm or shop.

Board costs could be reduced by living at home, which may explain the high percentage of Champaign County students in the spring of 1868. Forty-nine percent of the seventy-seven students were from Champaign Urbana, and 58 percent were from Champaign County. University critic and trustee M. L. Dunlap, a Champaign County resident, argued that the March 1868 start date restricted statewide enrollments by precluding farmers' sons from spring planting.[29] To Dunlap, inaugurating the university during spring planting was a major slight to working farmers.

Within the first four months of operation, six students requested tuition remission.[30] Five students came from middle-income families. One student who requested tuition remission was from a prominent Illinois family with a 363-acre farm at the time of the request. All were granted their petitions. The only student from the lowest economic strata was awarded the honorary county scholarship.

To reduce college expenses, students prepared their own meals and subsisted on starchy, low-cost foods.[31] The practice of packing students into a room as a cost-saving method was met by a faculty vote to limit occupancy to two students.[32] College costs also spawned entrepreneurship by students. Breads and pies were sold to make extra income.

Student Life at the University

Students arriving at the new university entered an institution that was still defining its scope and purpose. Faculty records for the spring 1868 term reveal a preoccupation with the challenges of an inaugural year. The creation of new policies and procedures dominated faculty meetings. The faculty faced the task of complying with curricular aspects of the Morrill legislation amid the dissent of the agricultural leadership of the state, limited human resources, and without a previous model to guide implementation. The first years of Illinois were marked by acrimony, as the university leadership became the target of suspicion by state industrial and agricultural advocates.

For the spring 1868 students, the typical enrollee attended the university for 1.6 years, averaging four college terms. Information regarding who resided on campus and who boarded off campus is fugitive. Students participated in literary societies, a common nineteenth-century diversion.[33] Pranks and whist parties abounded.

Student descriptions of the university depict meager accommodations and facilities in a barren landscape, jokingly referred to as "no man's land" and "Oklahoma." Sixty-five rooms were available and advertised as 14 x 10 feet designed to house two students. Students were required to furnish their own rooms, including coal stoves that served to heat the room and cook the meals.

Commenting on food expenses, one student recalled, "A carefully kept account of food expenses shows an average monthly cost of $4.10 during one college year. The food was prepared in the dormitory rooms by our own hands . . ."[34] Institutional publications estimated that students were providing meals in their rooms at a cost of $1 to $1.50 a week.

Rooms were described as being similar to a storage locker than a functioning domicile, as students stowed "coal, kindling, dishes, kettles, pails, basins, pitchers, tubs, oil cans, lamps, food, clothing, books, etc. in the cramped quarters . . ."[35] Items were stowed, with the student's trunk, under the bed, hid by a valance.

Admissions, Course of Studies, and Attrition, Spring 1868

One student described the admission process facing the inaugural class of 1868:

> A number of young men who desired to enroll sat in a semi-circle and the good Doctor [Gregory] questioned each as to his qualifications, and after this simple oral investigation of a half hour, all were held as qualified to enter forthwith.[36]

Regent Gregory was known to accommodate a struggling student. When one student failed to pass algebra, Gregory asked what the student wanted to "make of himself." Stating that he wanted to be a lawyer, Gregory, after dutiful admonishment, examined the student's geometry scores and found them to be above average. He pronounced the student accepted.[37] The student eventually became a grain and real-estate dealer.

The university offered a mixed curricula of liberal arts and limited scientific course work in keeping with the Morrill curricular mandate.[38] Preliminary research suggests that the early Illinois curricula was fashioned from Nott's scientific course at Union College (Gregory's *alma mater*), West Point's military and engineering programs, and traditional elements of the liberal arts college. Students took an average of eleven courses, completing nine of them. Students' academic preferences were divided between the liberal (professional) and practical arts (industrial.) Trustee M. L. Dunlap monitored student courses as being an indicator of the university's direction and reported the findings in his articles in the state agricultural newspapers. By 1869, he reported,

> The school opened with 77 students, and 77 of these were put to the study of Latin, to fit them for the plow and the workshop. In May 1869, there were 83 students. These pursued three studies each, as follows, being nine recitations daily: Chemistry, 29; botany, 22; agriculture, 12; geometry and surveying, 43; algebra 31; rhetoric, 27; French, 13; Latin, 24; book-keeping, 27. This was at the opening of the third year. About one half of the students are intending to pursue farming and mechanical trades; and the other half the professions.[39]

Student ledgers (transcripts) for the spring 1868 term support aspects of Dunlap's complaint. Of the seventy-seven attendees, twenty-eight had no recorded courses; fifteen indicated a class in bookkeeping; twenty-four in algebra; eighteen in Latin; eight in German; seven in chemistry; five in natural philosophy; five in English; eleven in French; one in geometry; three in agriculture; eight in trigonometry; five in surveying; four in botany; and two in US history.[40] French, surveying, and trigonometry were standard courses at West Point, and these were consistent with civil engineering and military curricula. German was a useful language due to the immigrant population of Illinois at this time, and faced no complaints; whereas the study of Latin raised the ire of men like Dunlap as an unnecessary vestige of the traditional college. Although not all of the students were taking Latin as Dunlap claimed, a counterpoint could be made with regard to its usefulness to botany, chemistry, and so on. Dunlap also made no mention of bookkeeping, which was immediately useful to a farm or a shop.

Dunlap identified student course preferences and professors as being demonstrative of the imbalance between traditional liberal arts subjects and the industrial arts. He was particularly concerned that students favored, or were compelled to take, Greek and Latin, in lieu of courses he deemed appropriate for the farm or the shop.[41]

Trustee Dunlap's analysis suggested that the state of Illinois was subsidizing a traditional college curriculum. He concluded that most students were not considering industrial but professional pursuits, and new policies were needed that required students to take industrial course work.

Classes	No. of Students	Professor
Greek	11	Gregory
Latin reader	31	"
English composition	17	Baker
Livy	14	"
Latin grammar	11	"
1st Chemistry	18	Stewart
2d Chemistry {sic}	27	"
Agriculture	10	Bliss
French	11	"
Geometry (2 classes)	52	Shattuck
Disc. Geometry	11	"
Botany	14	Burrill
Algebra (2 classes)	38	"
Bookkeeping (2 cls.)	35	Snyder
German (2 classes)	27	"

A comparison between the father's occupational category in 1870 and student choices regarding the course of study reveals that all agricultural students were from farming families, except one. Table Four offers a summary of student choices to the offerings that were available.

Students from professional backgrounds avoided agriculture as an emphasis. The only professional class student indicating a course in agriculture eventually followed his father and became a physician. Students in agriculture and mechanical arts generally had higher completion rates.

The attrition of the spring 1868 group was high. Attempts to explain attrition were that students left the university due to poor academic preparation, financial shortfalls, and health issues.[42] The *Third Annual Circular* (1869–1870) indicates that twenty-six of the original seventy-seven were still enrolled during the 1869–1870 term. Thirteen (16.8 percent) of the original students persisted to graduation. Although some have attributed departure to a lack of academic ability or poor secondary preparation, student examination averages suggest that academic performance was not sub-standard. Students did well in examinations taken at the university. The average examination score on student ledgers was 80.5 percent. Scores indicate that students had the ability to pass examinations and further their program of study, particularly when the faculty set passing at 60 percent.[43] Exam averages were higher for wealthier students (Affluent, 83.4 percent; Moderate, 80 percent; Reduced, 77.6 percent). Admission to the university was predicated on passing examinations in the common branches, and faculty records were free of the usual complaints of under-prepared students.

The central contributor to attrition was the large number of students who failed to attend classes or take examinations. Records illustrate that

Table 4   Student Indicated Course of Study, Spring 1868

Course of Study	Number of Students	Percentage
Agriculture	12	15.6%
Engineering/Mechanical	6	7.8%
Elective	26	33.8%
Commercial/Mercantile	2	2.6%
Military	1	1.3%
No course indicated	28	36.4%
No data available	2	2.6%

students were not making satisfactory progress toward course completion. Twenty-two of the listed enrollees in 1868 did not complete courses or exams (28.6 percent). This can be contrasted with those students who listed courses, and had an 85 percent completion rate.

Early in the spring 1868 term, the faculty established the students' daily regimen so that they would have "a greater amount of uninterrupted time for study . . ."[44] Their schedule was prescribed as follows:

6:45–7:15	Breakfast
7:15–8:15	Recitations
8:15–8:30	Chapel[45]
8:30–9:30	Lectures & Drill alternately
9:30–12:30	Recitations
12:30–1:00	Dinner
1:00–3:00	Labor
3:00–6:00	Access to Library
6:00	Supper
7:00–10:00	Study hours

The faculty may have hoped that such a rigid structure would curb students' lax academic attitudes, but it did not produce the desired results. By November 1868, absenteeism and disciplinary problems reached a new level. Faculty minutes record parents being notified with the hope of prompting changes in behavior. At the meeting conducted on November 23, the faculty expelled their first student, deeming his connection with the institution to be undesirable. The problems with student behavior reached such an ebb that the faculty requested that ". . . the mayors of the cities of Champaign & Urbana be notified that a few of our students have been known to patronize billiard and drinking saloons, and that they be requested that the law is enforced which forbids keepers of saloons to receive the patronage of minors."[46] Furthermore, the faculty attempted to extend their parental oversight by recommending that "boarding-house keepers . . . see that students who board with them are in their rooms during study times, and report to the Regent those who habitually absent themselves at that time."[47]

By the spring of 1869, the faculty went further to address students who neglected their studies and failed to take examinations. Expulsions and notifications to parents became more frequent. One student was cautioned that his enrollment was in jeopardy unless he "keeps from all saloons, remains in his room evenings, and attends to his present studies diligently."[48] Another student found himself before the faculty while explaining his connection to a "public woman." As the faculty crackdown occurred, students sought to withdraw from their courses to escape impending consequences. Regent Gregory's philosophy of student self-governance in lieu of an in *loco parentis* model may have contributed to the discipline issues, as student autonomy may have inadvertently created some of the problems faced by the university.[49]

Another possible contributor to the high student attrition rate was financial challenges. At one point, student James Matthews warned his father,

> Bear in mind that you have sent me just seven dollars this term. Five of that was stolen from me before twenty four hours: knowing your financial embarrassments, I have worried through on the remaining two dollars. I must have money now from some source, or stop school immediately . . .[50]

However, according to the *Faculty Record*, ample support was available for the students who faced economic hardships. On September 28, 1868, faculty remitted tuition on account of a student "being an old student."[51] At the age of twenty-seven, he was the oldest in the original cohort and was from a family of lesser means (Economic Class Level IV.) It was not until February 22, 1869, that another student requested tuition remission which was granted by the faculty. Faculty tuition remission was not a common occurrence. On April 11, 1870, the faculty voted to remit tuition for a student who was identified in the faculty minutes as being "indigent." Curiously, the 1870 census data recorded family wealth at $13,460—hardly indigent by the standards of the day.

Issues of persistence and attrition were high among the first seventy-seven students at Illinois. Less than one-fifth completed their course of study. Like colleges today, some benefited from the experience and moved on; others left Illinois to begin their careers; and still others likely left school due to a lack of interest in the academic enterprise. Occasionally, health issues forced withdrawal.

Plows or Professions: What Did the Sons of Toil Do after College?

University critics were concerned that many of the early attendees were gravitating to careers outside the industrial class. M. L. Dunlap warned readers that students were not utilizing their experience at Illinois as scientific training for the farm or the shop, but were rather pursuing traditional studies as a preparation for the professions.

When occupational categories are considered, there was a migration from agriculture to the professions of medicine, law, ministry, teaching, and academia. Where data are available, thirteen (16.9 percent) of the former land-grant students indicated occupations related to agriculture in the 1880 census; ten (13.0 percent) in 1900 and 1910; and only three (3.9 percent) were still in agriculture by 1920. In contrast, the professions were well represented among the former students. Fourteen (18.8 percent) indicated professional careers in 1880; ten (13.0 percent) in the 1900 and 1910 censuses; and down to seven (9.1 percent) by 1920. Mercantile trades also attracted students away from farming, as they became dealers of dry goods, medicines, grain, and other commodities. Seventeen (22 percent) of the former attendees declared trade-related occupations in 1880; twelve (15.6 percent) in 1900; eight (10.4 percent) in 1910; and seven (9.1 percent) in 1920.

The students may have come from the industrial classes, but they demonstrated a shift away from industrial occupations in favor of the professions or mercantile trades in the new middle class.

Conclusions

The Illinois land-grant students of the class of 1868 became presidents of banks, legislators, professors, inventors, physicians, lawyers, engineers, businessmen, political and agricultural leaders, and a few returned to work on the farm or in the machine shop. Many made a lasting impression and contribution; whereas others quietly vanished into history.

The next fall term brought a new crop of students. Two of them, in particular, are noteworthy. John Alexander, son of the famous Illinois cattle king, arrived at the university as a member of the class of 1869. While his father was a rancher, and he toiled on his father's vast farm holdings, his father's indicated wealth according to the 1870 census, near the time of his arrival, was $1.6 million in real estate, and $30,000 in personal property—a staggering amount for the time.[52] Another student enrolled at Illinois with an intended course of study in military and commercial. He stayed one year before moving on. His name was Charles William Post. Today, his name sits on the breakfast tables of homes worldwide as the founder of Post Cereals.

The Morrill Act opened higher education to the industrial classes with a promise of relevant course work "in the several pursuits and professions in life." The sons of toil, progeny of fathers in industrial class occupations, arrived at the new university. However, the economic status of the early attendees challenges traditional assertions regarding opportunity and access for the underprivileged. If the Morrill Act targeted those from the lower economic strata, they were certainly not present at Illinois in the spring of 1868.

Questions about whether the Morrill Act succeeded in attracting and retaining the industrial classes aside, the land-grant universities were a unique educational experiment. The occasion of the sesquicentennial of the Morrill Act provides an opportunity for reflecting on the accomplishments of the land-grant universities. On the grave of John Milton Gregory, who is interred on the grounds of the University of Illinois, reads the epitaph, "If You Seek His Monument Look About You." In a twist of history, M. L. Dunlap, Gregory's most vocal critic, is interred in a neighboring cemetery in the shadow of, and surrounded by, the university that he judged an abysmal failure. It is doubtful that Gregory, or his detractors, could have imagined what the University of Illinois would become or the land-grant universities would contribute to science and research. Reflecting fifty years later, President Edmund James wrote to the university alumni:

> No one could have anticipated in 1868 that such an institution as this has become would be the result of less than fifty years' growth. Not even Doctor Gregory, the first president, that man of wondrous vision and power, who saw by faith the ultimate outcome, would have dared to expect such an achievement so soon.
>
> The grain of mustard seed planted by the Bone Yard stream in 1867 has indeed become a great tree. When the ground first parted and the bud of promise appeared on that famous eleventh of March, 1868, when the University was opened, two professors and a head farmer, and two non-resident lecturers made up the faculty, and fifty-seven pupils the student body. The former has grown to over 600, (in the present year, -1916,) the latter to 6,500.
>
> It is truly the Lord's doing and marvelous in our eyes.[53]

Notes

1. Adam Gerlach to Willard C. Flagg, November 12, 1868, *Willard C. Flagg Papers, 1863–1878*, Record Series 1/20/7, Box 1, University of Illinois Archives.

2. "Adam J. Gerlach," in *Encyclopedia of Genealogy and Biography of Lake County, Indiana*, ed. T. H. Ball (Chicago, IL: Lewis Publishing, 1904), 283–84.

3. Dr. Newton Bateman, "The Address of Dr. Newton Bateman at the Inauguration of the University," in *Some Founding Papers of the University of Illinois*, ed. Richard A. Hatch (Urbana: University of Illinois Press, 1967), 30–31.

4. Jonathan Baldwin Turner, *A Plan for an Industrial University for the State of Illinois*, Submitted to the Farmers' Convention at Granville, November 18, 1851 (Under the Supervision of the Committee of Publication, 1851), n.p.

5. Mathias L. Dunlap, "Agricultural Education," *Mathias L. Dunlap Papers, 1839–1858, 1867–1877*. Record Series 1-20-2, Box 3, University of Illinois Archives.

6.   Eldon L. Johnson, "Misconceptions about the Early Land-Grant Colleges," *Journal of Higher Education* 52, no. 4 (July–August 1981): 333–51.

7.   J. Gregory Behle and William E. Maxwell, "The Social Origins of Students at the Illinois Industrial University, 1868-1894," *History of Higher Education Annual* 18 (1998): 93–109.

8.   For a context of the land-grant movement, consider Roger L. Williams, *The Origins of Federal Support for Higher Education: George W. Atherton and the Land-Grant College Movement* (University Park: Pennsylvania State University Press, 1991); Roger L. Geiger, ed., *The American College in the Nineteenth Century* (Nashville: Vanderbilt University Press, 2000). The University of Illinois has an exemplary institutional history. Winton U. Solberg, *The University of Illinois, 1867–1894: An Intellectual and Cultural History* (Urbana: University of Illinois Press, 1968).

9.   Frederick Rudolph, "Neglect of College Students as a Historical Tradition," in *The College and the Student*, ed. Lawrence E. Dennis and Joseph F. Kauffman (Washington, DC: American Council on Education, 1966), 47.

10.   Allan Nevins, *State Universities and Democracy* (Urbana: University of Illinois Press, 1962), 16–17.

11.   Ibid., 17–18.

12.   Earle Dudley Ross, *Democracy's College: The Land-Grant Movement in the Formative Stage* (Ames: Iowa State College Press, 1942), 133.

13.   Edward Danforth Eddy, *Colleges for Our Land and Time: The Land-Grant Idea in American Education* (New York: Harper, 1957), 37. Earle Dudley Ross, "On Writing the History of Land-Grant Colleges and Universities," *Journal of Higher Education* 24, no. 8 (November 1953): 412.

14.   Frederick B. Mumford, *The Land-Grant College Movement* (Columbia: University of Missouri, July 1940), 71.

15.   "Address of Mr. Powers from Vermont," *Memorial Addresses on the Life and Character of Justin S. Morrill (Late a Senator from Vermont), Delivered in the Senate and House of Representatives*, 55th Cong., 3d sess. (Washington, DC: Govt. Print. Office, 1899), 104.

16.   Readers interested in student populations might consider Colin B. Burke, *American Collegiate Populations: A Test of the Traditional View* (New York: New York University Press, 1982); Jana Nidiffer and Jeffery Bouman, "'The University of the Poor': The University of Michigan's Transition from Admitting Impoverished Students to Studying Poverty, 1870–1910," *American Educational Research Journal* 41, no. 1 (Spring 2004): 35–67; "The Chasm between Rhetoric and Reality: The Fate of the 'Democratic Ideal' When a Public University Becomes Elite," *Educational Policy* 15, no. 3 (July 2001): 432–51; and Jana Nidiffer, "Poor Historiography: The 'Poorest' in American Higher Education," *History of Education Quarterly* 39, no. 3 (Autumn 1999): 321–36.

17.   "Professional class," as used here, is strictly limited to the occupations of law, medicine, and clergy and is more narrowly defined. Professional services, used in occupational sectors, offers a broader definition to include occupations with predominately intellectual skill sets, such as college professors and presidents, artists, and teachers, which is consistent with Turner's understanding.

18.   "Agricultural Education," *Chicago Weekly Tribune*, February 2, 1870, *John Milton Gregory Press Scrapbook, 1868-1881*, Record Series 2/1/8, University of Illinois Archives; also Dunlap, "Agricultural Education."

19. John Milton Gregory to Mason Brayman, February 25, 1870. *John M. Gregory Papers, 1838–1898*. Record Series 2/1/1, Box 2, University of Illinois Archives. To appreciate this conflict, consider "In the Midst of a Great Conflict," in *The University of Illinois, 1867–1894: An Intellectual and Cultural History*, ed. Winton U. Solberg (Urbana: University of Illinois Press, 1968), 84–117.

20. Jeremy Atack and Fred Bateman, *To Their Own Soil: Agriculture in the Antebellum North* (Ames: Iowa State University Press, 1987), 135. A statewide farm size averaged 146 acres for Illinois in the 1860 census; however, acreage included both arable and unimproved lands. There were 143,310 farms in Illinois according to the 1860 census. Joseph C. G. Kennedy, *Agriculture of the United States in 1860; Compiles from the Original Returns of the Eighth Census* (Washington, DC: Government Printing Office), 222.

21. David F. Allmendinger, *Paupers and Scholars: The Transformation of Student Life in Nineteenth-Century New England* (New York: St. Martin's Press, 1975); Richard Angelo, "The Students at the University of Pennsylvania and the Temple College of Philadelphia, 1873–1906: Some Notes on Schooling, Class, and Social Mobility in the Late Nineteenth Century," *History of Education Quarterly* 19, no. 2 (Summer 1979): 179–205.

22. James N. Matthews to William Matthews, September 15, 1868, *James N. Matthews Papers, 1868–1872, 1966–1968*, Record Series 41/20/26, Box 1, University of Illinois Archives.

23. Illinois Industrial University, *Second Annual Report of the Board of Trustees of the Illinois Industrial University* (Springfield, IL: State Journal Printing Office, 1869), 17.

24. Expenses were estimated as follows: tuition, room rent, and incidentals ($34.50–$39.50); board in hall ($108–$126); fuel and lights ($10.50–$15.50); and washing (75 cents per dozen) ($10–$15). Students were also required to pay a one-time Matriculation Fee of $10 (Ibid., 18). Furniture for the room ($15), Uniform ($27) (Ibid., 17).

25. J. A. Ockerson (1873) recalled, "The University itself furnished employment in digging ditches, laying drain tile, planting trees and various other work paying therefore at the rate of 15 cents per hour. Even at that rate we were *in some cases overpaid* [emphasis added]." "Gregory Recollections – Ockerson, J.A.," *University of Illinois Early History, 1853–1962*, Record Series 35/3/125, Box 1, University of Illinois Archives.

26. *Comptroller Accounting Vouchers, 1867–1904*, Record Series 6/2/3, Box 1, University of Illinois Archives.

27. James N. Matthews to William Matthews, September 15, 1868.

28. *Historical Statistics of the United States: Colonial Times to 1970* (Washington, DC: U.S. Department of Commerce, Bureau of Census, 1975), 165.

29. M. L. Dunlap argues a possible reason for the high percentage from Champaign County when he states, ". . . it began the first of March, at a time when the farmer could ill afford to spare his son to attend. The result was an attendance from the State at large of thirty-two, and from Champaign county of forty-five." Mathias Lane Dunlap, "The State University," *Mathias L. Dunlap Papers, 1839–1858, 1867–1877*.

30. *Faculty Record, 1868–1901*, Record Series 4/1/1, University of Illinois Archives. Tuition was listed as $15 per annum for Illinois residents, $20 for nonresidents.

31. Allene Gregory, *John Milton Gregory: A Biography* (Chicago, IL: Covici-McGee, 1923), 176; "Ancient Manners and Customs of University of Illinois' Students"; "Gregory and Early Recollections – Brown, Ralph L. 1918–20," *University of*

Illinois Early History, 1853–1962, Record Series 35/3/125, Box 1, University of Illinois Archives.

32. September 22, 1868, *Faculty Record, 1868–1890*, Record Series 4/1/1, University of Illinois Archives. Early literature contained the admonishment ". . . for health's sake that each student have a separate bed." "First Annual Report of the Board of Trustees of the Illinois Industrial University (1868)," *Trustee's Reports, 1867*, Record Series 1/1/802, University of Illinois Archives.

33. Thomas Spencer Harding, *College Literary Societies: Their Contribution to Higher Education in the United States, 1815–1876* (New York: Pageant Press International, 1971).

34. "Gregory Recollections – Ockerson, J.A."

35. "Gregory and Early Recollections – Brown, Ralph L., 1918–20." *University of Illinois Early History, 1853–1962*.

36. "Francis Plym," *Alumni and Faculty Biographical (Alumni News Morgue) File, 1882–1995*, Record Series 26/4/1, University of Illinois Archives.

37. "Isaac Chase Sargent to Edmund James, 5 October 1917," *Allene Gregory Research File, 1898–1920*, Record Series 2/1/3, Box 1, University of Illinois Archives.

38. These included the following: Departments of "Science, Literature, and the Arts," "Agriculture," "Mechanical Science and Arts," "Military Tactics and Engineering," "Mining and Metallurgy," "Civil Engineering," "Analytical and Applied Chemistry," "Nat. History, Practical Geology, etc.," and "Commercial Science and Art." All these were to be implemented by limited faculty, including a traveling regent.

39. "Agricultural Education," *Mathias L. Dunlap Papers, 1839–1858, 1867–1877*.

40. *Digitalized Student Ledger Books, 1868–1903*. Record Series 25/3/45, University of Illinois Archives. Ledger books functioned as transcripts recording course title and a course score if available. Ledgers are ambiguous with regard to year and term. For this example, first-year, first-term data were used.

41. "What is Taught in the Industrial University," *Mathias L. Dunlap Papers, 1839–1858, 1867–1877*.

42. At the January 4, 1869 meeting, faculty discussed the admission of young men who were "poorly prepared" on a trial basis. This may have been an attempt to appease the criticism of the institution as neglecting those from smaller farms and increasing institutional enrollments for appropriations. *Faculty Record, 1868–1890*.

43. February 8, 1869, *Faculty Record, 1868–1890*.

44. March 28, 1868, *Faculty Record, 1868–1890*.

45. J. Gregory Behle, "Educating the Lord's Redeemed and Anointed: The University of Illinois Chapel Experience, 1868–1894," *The Master's Seminary Journal* 11, no. 1 (Spring 2000): 53–73.

46. November 23, 1868, *Faculty Record, 1868–1890*.

47. January 4, 1869, *Faculty Record, 1868–1890*.

48. February 10, 1869, *Faculty Record, 1868–1890*.

49. Winton U. Solberg, "The University of Illinois and the Reform of Discipline in the Modern University, 1868–1891," *AAUP Bulletin* 52 (Autumn 1966): 305–14.

50. James N. Matthews to Dr. William Matthews, March 4, 1870, *James N. Matthews Papers, 1868–1872*, Record Series 41/20/26, University of Illinois Archives.

51. Two other students also requested aid with award that was conditional on ". . . the two latter presenting satisfactory testimonials of good character and need for such assistance." September 28, 1869, *Faculty Record, 1868–1890*. Tuition charges in

the 1868–1869 circular were listed as $15 per annum. It is unclear whether the faculty were also remitting room rent charges and fees.

52. C. P. McClelland, "Jacob Strawn and John T. Alexander; Central Illinois Stockman," *Journal of the Illinois State Historical Society* 34 (1941): 177–208; Paul Wallace Gates, "Cattle Kings in the Prairie," in *Landlords and Tenants on the Prairie Frontier* (Ithaca, NY: Cornell University Press, 1973), 196–237.

53. Vergil Vivian Phelps, ed., *University of Illinois Directory, Listing the 35,000 Persons Who Have Ever Been Connected with the Urbana-Champaign Departments, Including Officers of Instruction and Administration and 1397 Deceased* (Urbana-Champaign: University of Illinois, 1916).

Part II

The Politics of Launching Land-Grant Colleges, 1862–1890

Introduction

Nathan M. Sorber

The Morrill Act of 1862 introduced the "leading objects" for land-grant colleges, but offered few specifics on implementation. One clause narrowed curricula by calling for studies "related to agricultural and mechanical arts," whereas the next broadened the scope by stating that scientific and classical subjects as well as military tactics were not to be excluded. Instead of directing colleges toward professional preparation, vocational training, or liberal study, the act, implausibly, suggested that land-grant colleges could do them all. Justin Morrill's speeches on the House and Senate floors provided little clarification; he presented no sample curriculum, no admission requirements, and no guidance on student labor or coeducation. The duty of defining and executing the Morrill Act fell to state legislatures. The result was an eclectic institutional landscape, as the political, economic, and social dynamics of different regions nursed unique land-grant experiments.[1]

States had two years (later extended to five) to accept the terms of the Morrill Act and designate a land-grant college. Some acted immediately; others dragged their feet, but all ultimately accepted the terms. Legislators were eager to sell the public lands (20,000 acres per congressman and senator) that were awarded from the Morrill Act, as concerns mounted over the stability of land values following the Homestead Act of 1862 and the distribution of ten million acres of land to union veterans. Deflation was imminent. States without public lands within their borders were awarded scrip by the General Land Office, and were saddled with surveying, securing parcels, and finding buyers. A few states sent

Perspectives on the History of Higher Education 30 (2013): 97–104
© 2013. ISBN: 978-1-4128-5147-3

college representatives, but most of them either entrusted these complex transactions to third-party agents or simply sold shares to brokers. Peter Moran and Roger Williams argue in "Saving the Land Grant for the Agricultural College of Pennsylvania" that the colleges selling first avoided the glutted market and received the highest returns, as did those that waited (e.g., Cornell and Michigan) until land prices recovered. In Pennsylvania, political wrangling delayed the land-grant sale, and state legislators with a poor understanding of the intricacies of land brokering found buyers for only 22,000 of 780,000 acres by 1867. In order to attract interest in the remaining land, prices were lowered to a paltry average of fifty-five cents per acre, with land broker Gleason F. Lewis purchasing more than half the lot. Lewis' purchase came just weeks after he had bought all of Kentucky's scrip for fifty cents per acre. The south fared better, as the prices of scrip distributed by the General Office rebounded by the time the confederacy was reincorporated into the union. In "An Elephant in the Hands of the State," Susan R. Richardson identifies one such result in Texas, another state that turned in 1871 to Gleason Lewis, who by this time was paying seventy-five cents an acre.[2]

The aim of the federal grants was to provide a perpetual endowment, and only ten percent of proceeds could be used for construction. Legislatures had to determine the degree of state support they were willing to contribute in order to build and sustain these enterprises. This became a central question driving land-grant politics. Fiscally cautious and war-weary legislators looked for ways to fulfill the act at little or no expense, which often meant searching for established institutions to lessen the burden on state coffers. Agricultural society leaders and rural legislators complained that many of these established institutions made poor land-grant candidates, as they followed classical curricula and served the professional class. However, private college officials promised that as land-grant colleges, they would be self-sustaining and not a burden to the state.[3]

Endowed private institutions (Brown University, Yale's Sheffield Scientific School, and Cornell University, and the Massachusetts Institute of Technology) or private scientific branches (Rutgers and Dartmouth) became land-grant designees in the northeast. There were other cases in the north where private aspirants to land-grant status were unsuccessful, as they were overcome by agricultural society opponents. For example, Bowdoin College was considered in Maine until the state agricultural society and journal *The Maine Farmer* rallied supporters for a new state university, as was Princeton in New Jersey, Harvard in Massachusetts, and a smattering of small colleges in Pennsylvania and New York. In Ohio, the private Farmers' College (f. 1852) had a promising claim on the land grant, but financial difficulties and sinking enrollments derailed its case. Several legislatures chose preexisting state universities as land-grant institutions, including Delaware, Georgia, Missouri, North Carolina, South Carolina, Tennessee, Wisconsin, and Vermont. Arkansas, California, Maine, Nebraska, and West Virginia founded new state universities as land-grant colleges; Alabama, Ohio, and Illinois did the same but settled on titles that suggested a narrower, utilitarian scope (the Agricultural and Mechanical College of Alabama, Illinois Industrial College, and Ohio Agricultural and Mechanical College). In New York, Cornell University charted an independent course toward a modern research university. With financial security stemming from the generosity of benefactor Ezra Cornell's philanthropy and subsequent robust returns from land-grant sales, Cornell University did not have to subject itself to the public scrutiny of appropriations hearings and the meddling of legislators. Other variations were the new land-grant colleges founded in Virginia and Louisiana that resembled military academies; Indiana named its new agricultural and mechanical college after its generous benefactor John Purdue; and Texas founded an agricultural and mechanical college which was attached to a nonexistent state university. In Iowa, Maryland, Massachusetts, Michigan, and Pennsylvania, the land-grant college descended from previously established or chartered agricultural schools, and in Colorado and Kansas, new agricultural colleges of varied quality were founded and declared land-grant colleges. However, as Moran and Williams explain, an agricultural foundation did not mean an uncontested path lay ahead.[4]

In 1863, the Pennsylvania Agricultural College was named the state land-grant recipient with little opposition, but the legislature had second thoughts during the next year. Several undistinguished Pennsylvania colleges—many church related with precarious finances—pursued the federal funds to stave off insolvency. These were primarily classical colleges with few resources, hardly contenders for fulfilling the broad scope of the Morrill Act. Yet each college had a local congressman to argue its case in the state legislature, and many were willing to split the fund for a small portion of the prize. Effective college leadership and agricultural society support proved vital in defeating efforts to divide the land grant. Agricultural chemist Evan Pugh received his Ph.D. in Germany, studied under famed scientist Justus Von Liebig, and returned home as president of the agricultural college of Pennsylvania with firm ideas on industrial education. He promoted a broad scientific plan of industrial and agricultural education, dismissed the claims of literary colleges to fulfill the Morrill Act's terms as "absurd and ludicrous," and labored until his untimely death to defend the college's claim. In concert with Pugh's tireless work, Frederick Watts, president of the state agricultural society, rallied his network of members to support the agricultural college and defeated efforts to redistribute land-grant funds to other colleges in the commonwealth.[5]

The first decade of land-grant politics in Pennsylvania were typical in that they were dominated by local concern and economic interest, and only through the interventions of academics such as Evan Pugh did considerations of educational purpose receive fair hearings. Richardson's article presents a second example of how state land-grant politics were driven not by educational concerns, but by the exigencies of intrastate, political and ideological rivalries. It further exemplifies how legacies of war, failed Reconstruction policy, and slavery influenced state politics, and, in turn, the evolution of land-grant education in the south.

In 1858, the Texas legislature approved a charter for the University of Texas, which was presumably to be located in Austin. Fifty leagues of land and $100,000 were appropriated to the project as a permanent endowment. Regional divisions appeared at the outset. Richardson highlights how representatives from east Texas unanimously opposed the bill, displeased that the project would be of little benefit to their constituents. The University of Texas was stillborn, as higher education was subsumed under the all-encompassing shadow of war. Texas seceded from the union, joined the rebellion, and invested the funds promised to higher education in frontier defense and confederate war bonds.[6]

After the surrender of General Robert E. Lee at the Appomattox Courthouse, confederate bonds became worthless, and hopes for the University of Texas floundered. Under the protection of military rule, a Republican legislature was assembled in the capital. Legislative actions included the acceptance of the Morrill Act and the passage of a bill to establish the Texas Agricultural and Mechanical College in 1871. The new land-grant college would be a branch of the yet-to-be-created University of Texas. The exit of northern soldiers and the return of voting privileges to former confederates ushered in a Democratic legislature in 1873, which investigated the Republican-appointed land-grant commission that was tasked with securing a location for the Texas Agricultural and Mechanical College. The commission had gained a notorious reputation, besmirched by lavish spending and financial irregularities. The resurgent Democrats seemed poised to derail the land-grant movement by linking the commission with unpopular Republicans. The Democrats chose not to displease their farming base by sinking the entire project. By 1876, the legislature approved more than $100,000 to finish construction and launch the land-grant college in Bryan, Texas.[7]

The Texas Agricultural and Mechanical College opened its doors to students in October 1876, but soon faced criticism for high tuition costs, a phantom agricultural program with no model farm, and a classical curriculum. As was the national trend, the $250 a year land-grant college was ridiculed as an "aristocratic establishment for the culture of the sons of the wealthy," as farmers demanded access and utility for students who were destined to work for a living. Although unlike the Yankees, the Texans did not build their land-grant mission around agricultural science, but as Richardson explains, they chose a uniquely southern course. Similar to neighboring land-grant colleges in Louisiana and Virginia, Texas Agricultural and Mechanical College attracted its White male student body by emphasizing the military tactic component of the Morrill Act. Student cadets wore uniforms, organized into corps, drilled regularly, and constructed new criteria for Southern honor and White manhood on the ashes of a failed confederacy.[8]

Richardson explains how the new Texas constitution of 1876 established a separate land-grant branch for African-Americans in Prairie View. This "agricultural and mechanical college for the benefit of colored people" was to receive a portion of federal and state funds that had been appropriated to Texas Agricultural and Mechanical College. After the failure of Reconstruction and the loss of Republican allies, the Prairie View School was subjected to decreasing shares of an already pittance in land-grant proceeds from successive Democratic legislatures and administrations. Governor Oran Roberts, the chief promoter of founding the University of Texas, considered closing the segregated institution and redirecting its state support to his state university project in Austin. Prairie View was only saved at the last hour by Barnas Sears and the Peabody fund, promising private financing to refashion the institution as a normal school. Similar events transpired in Mississippi and Arkansas, where the Alcorn Agricultural and Mechanical College and the Arkansas Industrial University were founded during Reconstruction by Republican legislatures. In Mississippi, Alcorn had been founded before the White land-grant college (Mississippi State) in 1871, becoming the oldest historically Black land-grant college in the nation. Hiram R. Revels, the first African-American senator, was a major influence in the college's founding and resigned his post in Washington to become Alcorn's first president. In all these cases, the end of Reconstruction and Republican rule signaled the precipitous decline of state support and the enshrinement of a firmly separate and unequal system of African-American land-grant education. It would not be until the second Morrill Act of 1890 that the federal government would intervene by making some state support of "black land-grant colleges" a condition of receiving annual federal appropriations.[9]

The president of Vermont's land-grant university once equated the Morrill Act to the interstate commerce clause, for its "expansive comprehensiveness [in] those few potent words."[10] The ambiguity of the law allowed each state to tailor the land-grant college or colleges to suit its peculiar needs, politics, and interests. Thus, the first decade of land-grant politics produced numerous forms and guises. Agricultural professor William Brewster of the Sheffield Scientific School disparaged the lack of consensus: The ambiguity allowed "schemes . . . proposed by educators, enthusiasts, cranks, associations, legislators, etc. . . ."[11] Daniel Coit Gilman echoed this sentiment when he criticized the "abrupt passage of the Morrill Act," which precluded "thorough discussion in the periodicals of the day [on what was] possible and desirable in the national education."[12] A flurry of state legislative actions and educational experimentation produced a diverse land-grant scene: schools of science; agricultural colleges; industrial colleges; segregated normal, agricultural, and industrial colleges; military institutes; federally supported classical colleges; science departments in former colonial colleges; agricultural and mechanical colleges; state universities; and a proto-research university in Ithaca, New York.

The political theater launching the land-grant colleges occurred in two acts. The first came before mass farmer organization, with legislative debates dominated by considerations of location, land scrip sales, trustee membership, and state funding. Little time was spent discussing educational criteria or mission. The exceptional cases were found in Pennsylvania and Maine, where agricultural society leaders offered clear articulations of the purposes of agricultural education to counter attempts to divide the land-grant fund and award portions to literary colleges. As the land-grant colleges became established and populist organizations formed after the financial crash of 1873, state capitols became sites for debating the meaning and purpose of the Morrill Act. The outcomes of this second act (see Part III of this volume) influenced the trajectory of land-grant education to the end of the century, attuning many institutions more closely to the needs of agriculture and resulting in several new land-grant institutions in the 1880s and 1890s.

Roger Williams has argued that an idea of a single "land-grant college" is not rooted in historical facts, as it is more similar to a construct invented by historians to give meaning to diverse institutions born from a single law. This is certainly true during the origins and first two decades of the land-grant movement as demonstrated in the articles by Peter Moran, Roger Williams, and Susan Richardson. These articles follow trends in nineteenth-century higher education historiography that a proper conception of the early land-grant movement requires an understanding of regional varieties, state political culture, and local context. It would not be until the dawn of the twentieth century that standardizing forces would bring a more homogenous form to land-grant colleges. The influence of national associations became decisive to this process: In 1895, the Association of Agricultural Colleges and Experiment Station declared that to maintain membership, agricultural and industrial colleges of dubious quality had to elevate curricula and admission standards. The land-grant colleges would avoid populist attacks by maintaining specialized programs in agriculture and engineering as well as extension services, but after the turn of the century, most foresaw futures as "state colleges." The land-grant politics of future generations would focus on expanding access to the "Old State" for a growing middle class of high school graduates.

Notes

1. Earle D. Ross, *Democracy's College* (New York: Arno Press, 1969), 68–85. See "Speech of Honorable Justin S. Morrill of Vermont, In the House of Representatives, June 6, 1862," University of Vermont Archives, No.19: Congressional speeches.
2. Peter Moran and Roger Williams, "Saving the Land Grant for the Agricultural College of Pennsylvania"; Susan R. Richardson, "An Elephant in the Hands of the State"; the text of the Act can be assessed at *An Act donating Public Lands to the Several States and Territories which may Provide Colleges for the Benefit of Agriculture and the Mechanic Arts*, July 2, 1862. In "A Century of Lawmaking for a New Nation: U.S. Congressional Documents and Debates, 1774–1875," 37th Cong., 2d sess., http://memory.loc.gov (accessed February 11, 2011).
3. Nathan M. Sorber, *Farmers, Scientists, and Officers of Industry: The Formation and Reformation of Land-Grant Colleges in the Northeastern United States, 1862–1905* (Diss., The Pennsylvania State University, 2011).
4. For succinct overviews of state developments, see Roger L. Williams, *George W. Atherton and The Origins of Federal Support for Higher Education* (University Park, PA: The Pennsylvania State University Press, 1991), 40–53; Ross, *Democracy's College*, 68–85. For successful and aborted efforts by privately endowed institutions to secure the land grant, see Sorber, *Farmers, Scientists*, chap. 3. More details are available in these representative, institutional histories: David C. Smith,

The First Century: A History of the University of Maine, 1865–1965 (Orono, ME: University of Maine Press, 1979), 1–22; Julianna Chaszar, "Leading and Losing in the Agricultural Education Movement: Freeman G. Cary and Farmers' College, 1846–1884," *History of Higher Educational Annual* 18 (1998): 25–46; Harold Whiting Cary, *The University of Massachusetts: A History of One Hundred Years* (Amherst, MA: University of Massachusetts Press, 1962), 23–37; Robert Manley, *Centennial History of the University of Nebraska, vol. 1* (Lincoln: University of Nebraska Press, 1969); William T. Doherty, Jr., and Festus P. Summers, *West Virginia University: Symbol of Unity in a Sectionalized State* (Morgantown: West Virginia University Press, 1982), 3–37; William Carey Jones, *Illustrated History of the University of California* (San Francisco, CA: Frank H. Dukesmith, 1895); Keith R. Widder, *The Evolution of a Land-Grant Philosophy, 1855–1925* (Lansing: Michigan State University, 2005), 1–90; and George H. Calcott, *The University of Maryland at College Park* (New York: Noble House, 2005).

5.   Moran and Williams, "Saving the Land Grant for the Agricultural College of Pennsylvania."

6.   Richardson, "An Elephant in the Hands of the State."

7.   Ibid.

8.   Quote is cited in ibid., p. 143. For insights on post–Civil War southern politics and southern populism, see the still classic C. Vann Woodward, *Origins of the New South, 1877–1913* (Baton Rouge: Louisiana State University Press, 1971), 1–222. Duncan Lyle Kinnear, *The First 100 Years: A History of Virginia Polytechnic Institute and State University* (Blacksburg, VA: Virginia Polytechnic Institute Educational Foundation, 1972); Thomas F. Ruffin, Jo Jackson, and Mary Herbert, *Under Stately Oaks: A Pictorial History of LSU* (Baton Rouge, LA: Louisiana State University Press, 2006).

9.   George Ruble Woolfolk, *The First Seventy-five Years, 1876–1951: Prairie View Agricultural and Mechanical College* (College Station: Texas A&M University Press, n.d.); George Ruble Woolfolk, *Prairie View* (New York: Pageant, 1962); George Ruble Woolfolk, "Prairie View A&M University,"*Handbook of Texas Online,* http://www.tshaonline.org/handbook/online/articles/kcp06 (accessed May 11, 2011). Published by the Texas State Historical Association. For background on segregated land-grant colleges, see Frederick S. Humphries, "1890 Land-Grant Institutions: Their Struggle for Survival and Equality," *Agricultural History* 65, no. 2, *The 1890 Land-Grant Colleges: A Centennial View* (Spring 1991): 3–11; Robert L. Jenkins, "The Black Land-Grant Colleges in Their Formative Years, 1890–1920," *Agricultural History*, 63–72; C. Fred Williams, "Frustration Amidst Hope: The Land-Grant Mission of Arkansas AM&N College, 1873–1972," *Agricultural History*, 115–30.

10.   *Morrill Centenary Exercises Celebrated by the State of Vermont at Montpelier, April 14, 1910, in honor of the birth of Justin Smith Morrill*, Fulton, NY, 1910, 21.

11.   Cited in Alfred Charles True, *A History of Agricultural Education in the United States, 1785–1925* (New York, NY: Arno Press, 1969), 106.

12.   Daniel Coit Gilman, "Our National Schools of Science," *North American Review* (October 1867): 106.

Saving the Land Grant for the Agricultural College of Pennsylvania

Peter L. Moran and Roger L. Williams

Introduction

Etched into the portico of the Old Main building at Penn State University[1] are the words, "to promote liberal arts and practical education in the several pursuits and professions of life,"[2] followed by the line, "and the faith of the state is hereby pledged to carry the same into effect."[3] The first sentence is from the Morrill Land Grant Act of 1862, which apportioned federal lands to the states for the establishment of colleges that concentrated on agriculture and the mechanic arts. The second line comes from Pennsylvania's acceptance of the act that Governor Andrew Curtin signed into law on April 1, 1863. The placement of these words connotes a seamless process between the congressional grant and Penn State's receipt of the proceeds from the sale of the lands. The reality of that process, however, was an altogether different matter. Penn State's status as the sole beneficiary of the land grant resulted from a contested battle in the legislature that lasted years beyond the state's acceptance in 1863.

The purpose of this article is to develop a better understanding of the college land-grant experience in the Commonwealth of Pennsylvania. In particular, this article discusses the case of Penn State and the process by which this institution became the sole recipient of Pennsylvania's land grant. The study primarily considers the legislative records of sessions between 1864 and 1867, when the General Assembly most seriously

Perspectives on the History of Higher Education 30 (2013): 105–129
© 2013. ISBN: 978-1-4128-5147-3

considered dividing the land grant among other institutions besides Penn State, and archival materials from Penn State, the Commonwealth of Pennsylvania, and other institutions of higher education in an attempt to clarify how Penn State survived challenges to its status as sole beneficiary. Lastly, the article analyzes Pennsylvania's disposition of the land scrip in comparison to other states.

This article shows that Penn State was able to retain the grant by mounting a more effective defense in the legislature, articulating a clearer vision of industrial education, and appealing to a broader base of legislators than its counterparts. Legally, the institution also benefited from receiving the initial grant, as repealing the grant would have required more than a simple majority of votes. Despite having emerged victorious from the protracted battle over land-grant designation, Penn State would not receive a windfall from sales of the scrip. The delay in resolving the beneficiary issue appears to have been both a cause and an effect of the Commonwealth's failure to promptly sell the scrip and realize a favorable return. This delay prevented the legislature from providing the necessary resources to market and sell the scrip. Simultaneously, opponents of Penn State seized on the delay and general confusion surrounding land scrip to accuse the institution of malfeasance in the scrip's disposition. An analysis of the land scrip sales process sheds further light on the political intricacies of the college land-grant experience in Pennsylvania.

Early Support of Higher Education in Pennsylvania

Before the passage of the Morrill Act, Pennsylvania had demonstrated a commitment to higher education and, in particular, to the Farmers' High School. The legislature established an early precedent of support for the Commonwealth's fledgling denominational colleges, which struggled to find sufficient funds for their operations. Generally, the assembly would grant incorporating colleges a parcel of land and/or a small sum of money. Although the legislature provided land and money to multiple institutions during the eighteenth and early nineteenth centuries, consistent legislative support did not materialize until the very end of the nineteenth century. Up until the 1830s, the General Assembly had made one-time appropriations to institutions on inception and periodically as needed. In 1838, the Commonwealth established a policy of sustained support of institutions of higher education[4] and committed annual payments of $1,000 for a duration of ten years "to each University or College, now incorporated, or which may be incorporated by the legislature, and maintaining at least four professors and instructing constantly 100 students."[5] However, before the anticipated date of expiration, the legislature reduced the payments and ultimately opted not to renew them in 1848.

After the 1840s, the General Assembly adopted an even less supportive stance: granting appropriations to institutions only under limited circumstances.[6] The Farmers' High School of Pennsylvania was one of the few institutions of higher education that received significant financial support during the second half of the nineteenth century. Chartered in 1855, the Farmers' High School was founded as "an institution for the education of youth in the various branches of science, learning and practical agriculture."[7] The establishment of an agricultural school had been the principal objective of the Pennsylvania State Agricultural Society, founded on January 21, 1851, and its first president, Frederick O. Watts. Watts, an attorney, judge, and farmer, who maintained a lifelong interest in agriculture and performed soil and crop experiments on his farm, was an indispensable ally to the Farmers' High School. He participated in the founding of the institution and the selection of its location, and also appeared numerous times before the legislature on the school's behalf. The agricultural society was also instrumental in chartering the Farmers' High School. A committee of the society, chartered by Watts, drafted a plan of the general structure and objectives of the school. The committee stated that the school would not only primarily instruct students in areas related to agriculture, but would also provide instruction in classical subjects. The committee also suggested that students perform manual labor in combination with their academic studies and even recommended the title of the Farmers' High School to distinguish the institution from more traditional colleges. From the onset, the society and dedicated proponents such as Watts provided vital financial resources and wise counsel during the institution's difficult early years. Furthermore, representatives from the county and state agricultural societies leveraged their political influence to secure state funding for the college.[8]

In 1857, the state appropriated $25,000 to the institution and provided for an additional payment of up to $25,000 to match the total amount of funds secured from other sources within three years.[9] Between 1857 and 1861, the college received nearly $100,000 in state aid for the construction of buildings.[10] Before it entered into the contest over the land grant, the Farmers' High School had already curried favor with representatives in the state government.

The Farmers' High School

Despite the early support of state government officials and the agricultural societies, the Farmers' High School was plagued by financial problems right from its inception. The construction firm that was hired to build the college's main building for $55,000 went bankrupt before its completion. In addition, due to a financial panic and the failure of crops across the state, the Farmers' High School's trustees did not raise the full $25,000 to receive the conditional state appropriation in 1857. However, through donations and the canvassing efforts of the institution's board members, roughly one-third of the main building was completed before the arrival of the first class in 1859.

The Farmers' High School and its four faculty members—Wm. G. Waring, general superintendent and professor of Horticulture; S. Baird, professor of Mathematics; R. C. Allison, professor of English Literature; and J. S. Whitman, professor of Natural Science—welcomed the sixty-nine students of its first class on February 16, 1859. The students, who hailed from all over the Commonwealth, paid $100 for tuition, room, and board, which represented a fraction of the fee charged by most other institutions in Pennsylvania. Conditions at the school were sparse and dilapidated. The main building, used to board and instruct students, was only partially finished, and the dining hall and kitchen were simple board shanties.[11] The farm was crude and littered with lumber and other construction materials for the main building. The school lacked proper laboratories and recitation rooms for instruction.[12] Adding to the morass, critics throughout the state decried the school's inconvenient location and financial difficulties, and some even advised the school to abandon its grand experiment. The Farmers' High School faced the prospect of failure and needed a unique leader—a leader with the ability to develop an academic program for agricultural education and the political finesse to secure adequate funding that would implement the plan.

The Farmers' High School found this leader in Evan Pugh, whom they hired as the school's first president in February 1859. Pugh possessed the requisite credentials to promote agricultural education at Farmers' High School. His educational philosophy was born from an insatiable thirst for practical scientific investigation, which he first developed while working on everyday problems in his grandfather's blacksmith shop in Chester County, Pennsylvania.[13] Desiring a deeper understanding of agricultural science, Pugh left the blacksmith profession and commenced his graduate studies in Germany, which was a center of research and education during the 1850s.

Pugh studied at the universities of Leipsic, Göttingen, and Heidelberg, and primarily focused on agricultural chemistry, which he believed to be the foundation of a thorough education in scientific agriculture. In particular, Pugh's interests lay with plant nutrition and the effect of gases, oxygen, and other atmospheric components on the life of plants. He earned his doctorate by analyzing meteoric ores from Mexico. This experience further cemented his belief in the application of scientific research to practical problems in agriculture and the mechanic arts, and he aspired to develop an educational system of a similar quality in the United States. While in Europe, Pugh also carried out studies in France and England, where he presented a paper on nitrogen fixation before the Royal Society of London and was elected a Fellow of the Chemical Society of London. His work in England was so well respected that by the time he left to assume the head of the Farmers' High School of Pennsylvania, Pugh had earned a reputation as one of the preeminent researchers in Europe.[14] Thus, Pugh entered his post with a clear understanding of the proper organization of a college focused on agriculture and the mechanic arts, and he would prove to be an effective advocate for the institution before the state legislature.

On the eve of the passage of the Morrill Land Grant College Act, the future of the newly renamed Agricultural College of Pennsylvania remained uncertain. The main building still had not been completed, and the college limped through its first few years with meager resources and low attendance. However, the institution had a passionate leader with a clear vision of agricultural education in the United States. In 1862, Pugh stated that the object of the institution was to "associate a high degree of intelligence with the practice of Agriculture and the industrial arts, and to seek to make use of this intelligence in developing the agricultural and industrial resources of the country, and protecting its interests."[15] To achieve this goal, the Agricultural College of Pennsylvania combined a course of instruction that covered the range of natural sciences with scientific agricultural experiments.

The course options indicate that the Agricultural College of Pennsylvania was a unique institution, one which would simultaneously allow students to pursue an advanced scientific education, while also affording farmers' sons the opportunity to become acquainted with practical agriculture and science. Students had a choice among three types of courses: the full course, the partial scientific and practical course, and the practical course. The full course lasted four years[16] and offered a more expansive range of instruction in mathematics and the natural sciences than "any Agricultural College of Europe."[17] The hybrid and purely practical courses offered less ambitious students the opportunity to learn practical farming techniques.

By its third session, even in the midst of the turmoil of the Civil War, the college graduated eleven students with a Bachelor of Scientific Agriculture degree at the school's first graduation ceremonies in 1861.[18] During its early years, the school and its proponents remained steadfastly committed to the promotion of agricultural education at the college. In September 1862, Pugh foresaw the institution's fortunes changing for the better with the Morrill Act, proclaiming that "with this success amidst the difficulties of the past, there can be no doubt of its ultimate success in the future, now that its college buildings are completed and the Agricultural Bill has passed Congress."[19]

The Morrill Act of 1862

The first Morrill Land Grant College Act, which President Abraham Lincoln signed into law on July 2, 1862,[20] was a landmark piece legislation that established a permanent bond between the federal government and higher education. The act was the product of a movement that emerged in the early nineteenth century. The Land-Grant College Movement was a response to the changing patterns in American life, to the perceived ineptitude of antebellum colleges, to the maturation of democratic ideals, to a desire to apply science to the problems facing the developing national economy, to a disgruntled and vocal agrarian class, and to the growing perception among educators and politicians that literary colleges could not support the quickening changes in American society.[21]

The measure aimed at extending higher education to previously excluded groups and also at applying the principles of science to the fields of agriculture and the mechanic arts. The largest of these excluded groups were the industrial classes. At the close of the Civil War, 80 percent of the American population qualified as members of the industrial classes, a group that consisted of farmers, mechanics, artisans, laborers and small businessmen.[22] This class underpinned the industrial revolution that enveloped the country during the nineteenth century. The Morrill Act of 1862 anticipated the changing landscape of American society and ushered in a new concept of American higher education. George Atherton, the seventh president of Penn State (1882–1906), credited Morrill with introducing a new "theory of education," which endeavored to complement rather than replace the classical education of literary institutions with practical training in agricultural science and the mechanic arts. Atherton quotes Morrill by remarking that

> The act of 1862 proposed a system of broad education by Colleges, not limited to a superficial and dwarfed training such as might be had at an industrial school, nor a mere manual training such as might be supplied by a foreman of a workshop . . . or of an experimental farm.[23]

The Morrill Act of 1862 granted 30,000 acres of land via each member of Congress to the states.[24] At this time, Pennsylvania had twenty-six representatives in the Congress; so, the Commonwealth was eligible for 780,000 acres of land.[25] The Act distributed the grant to the states as either land or land scrip. If the state had enough public land available within its borders, then it could take direct possession of the land. The states that did not have enough available public land, that is, Pennsylvania, were issued land scrip. The scrip granted individual purchasers the right to locate the land in any of the unencumbered federal lands available at the price of one dollar and twenty-five cents, or less, per acre.

In order to receive the land grant, states were required to pass legislation while explicitly accepting the terms of the act. In addition, the act mandated that states establish eligible colleges within five years of acceptance and prohibited land location before January 1, 1863.[26] All thirty-four existing states benefited from the Morrill Act, and the acceptance of land grants followed a number of different patterns.

The Pennsylvania Land-Grant Act

On April 1, 1863, the legislation[27] accepting the grant from Congress, titled "An act to accept the grant of public lands by the United States to the several States for the endowment of agricultural colleges," was signed into law by Governor Curtin.[28] The law accepted the Morrill Act "with all its provisions and conditions, and the faith of the state is hereby pledged to carry the same into effect."[29] The Pennsylvania Land-Grant Act appointed a board of commissioners, including the governor, auditor general, and surveyor general, to oversee the sale of the scrip and investment of the proceeds. The investment of the proceeds was restricted to state and federal stocks, and the act promulgated "that the annual interest from any investment of the funds acquired under the said act of congress, is hereby appropriated, and the said commissioners are directed to pay the same to the Agricultural College of Pennsylvania."[30]

Legislative Challenges to Pennsylvania Land-Grant Act

Introduced into the legislature in January 1863, House Bill No. 119—the proposed bill that became the Pennsylvania Land-Grant Act—did not receive much resistance from legislators. First, the major concern for representatives was deciphering the legal process by which they could legitimately accept the land grant, because the Morrill Act required states to proactively and explicitly accept its terms. Second, the Agricultural College of Pennsylvania and its representatives were largely involved in the preparation of House Bill No. 119. There was also a feeling in the General Assembly that the Farmers' High School was the only institution in the state that qualified as an agricultural college.

However, the 1864 legislative session proved to be much more hostile toward the Agricultural College of Pennsylvania and the Pennsylvania Land-Grant Act. At the beginning of 1864, multiple entities flooded the General Assembly with requests for the land grant.[31] In addition, legislators introduced a number of measures to repeal the Pennsylvania Land-Grant Act. Although the majority of the proposed bills were never called up from committee, legislators in both houses considered Senate Bill No. 617, a partial repeal that would have postponed sale of the scrip.[32]

The bill was motivated by a desire to distribute the fund to multiple institutions. Senator Hiester Clymer claimed that the amendment was prudent, because "this fund can profitability distributed between three institutions,"[33] and the Agricultural College of Pennsylvania had already received its fair share of support from the legislature. Another senator felt the grant was sufficient to fund approximately nine institutions.[34] Senator Morrow B. Lowry of Erie County offered another justification in support of the bill, alleging that the board of commissioners had prepared to sell the scrip for thirty cents per acre despite receiving offers of eighty cents per acre. Some legislators blamed the Agricultural College of Pennsylvania for encouraging a rapid disposition of the scrip at an unfavorable price.[35]

Supporters of the Agricultural College of Pennsylvania warned that a repeal of any portion of the Pennsylvania Land Grant Act could legally nullify the state's acceptance of the land grant, as the terms of the Morrill Act of 1862 required states to explicitly accept the act's provisions. According to these senators, the repeal could permanently exclude the Commonwealth from a share of the grant. In addition, the college's supporters strongly rebuked critics who claimed that the institution had encouraged the sale of scrip at an unfavorable price. Senator Henry

Johnson besmirched the perpetrator who spread this lie as "an enemy" trying to stir "up a feeling against this college, in order to enable outside institutions to get this appropriation from them."[36] Despite the outcry of support from advocates of the institution, the repeal garnered enough support in the Senate to pass by a vote of twenty-three to nine.

However, the House of Representatives did not pass Senate Bill No. 617. Ultimately, the bill was doomed to failure because of procedural rules. Since the House considered the bill so late in the session, the Speaker claimed that the bill needed a two-thirds vote in both houses over the course of days to become law.[37] Although the bill had broad support in the Senate where it originated, the fear that Senate Bill No. 617 would inadvertently revoke the Commonwealth's acceptance of the Morrill Act overrode concerns that the board of commissioners was squandering the scrip away. Due to the insurmountable odds posed by the procedural rule, representatives no longer wanted to consider a dead bill, and the issue was shelved indefinitely. One fatigued representative succinctly captured the situation: "It is obvious, therefore, that every moment which we are spending upon consideration of this subject is a mere waste of time which ought to be devoted to the passage of other bills."[38] The original designation would then appear to have been vital to the Agricultural College of Pennsylvania's success at maintaining the land-grant designation, as the two-thirds rule would have effectively killed any repeal that did not have a groundswell of support in both houses.

During the 1864 session, individual colleges and universities, including the Western University of Pennsylvania (University of Pittsburgh), Allegheny College, and the University of Pennsylvania, also petitioned for a portion of the funds. In addition, the legislature received requests to distribute the funds among several colleges and universities.[39] The widespread demand for the land grant may be evidenced by Senator James L. Graham of Allegheny County, who remarked that "we have had applicants from all parts of the State and from almost every educational institution in the State, asking for a portion of this land."[40]

The petitions and memorials from individual colleges and universities listed the reasons why they deserved a portion of the land-grant fund. These institutions attempted to demonstrate that they were worthy recipients of a fund intended for colleges who focused on agriculture and the mechanic arts. On April 11, 1864, Allegheny College, chartered in 1817, submitted a list of ten "facts" in support of its petition for a one-third portion of the lands donated to the Commonwealth by the

Congress.[41] George Loomis, president of the Faculty, noted its "healthful location in an agricultural district"[42] with nearby railroads and oil wells, boasted of its six competent faculty members, and claimed that its library had a chemical apparatus and "a large geological, mineralogical and conchological cabinet."[43] Loomis also pointed out that more than half of the students who matriculated between 1850 and 1860 hailed from Pennsylvania. Based on these reasons, Allegheny College applied for a one-third share and in return, pledged "to make the leading object of the college the application of science to the industrial pursuits, and grant tuition free."[44]

If Allegheny's petition is emblematic of the pleas from literary colleges, these institutions did not offer a persuasive argument as to why they were deserving of the land grant.[45] The petition did not include any evidence of a current capacity, in terms of faculty members, courses, or infrastructure, to pursue the industrial sciences. Allegheny cited the mere facts that the school was chartered and the governor served as an ex-officio board of trustees' member, a common occurrence at the time, as two of the leading justifications for its petition. The petition also implied that the college was a worthy recipient, because it was located in an agricultural area near railroads and oil wells. Allegheny College had asked the legislature to assume that, by virtue of its location, the school would somehow adopt agriculture and the mechanic arts as leading objects, irrespective of the college's ability to realize this objective.

In response to the bills to repeal its designation and numerous petitions from literary colleges, the Agricultural College of Pennsylvania worked feverishly throughout 1864 to convince legislators that the land grant should remain with the institution. The college engaged with the General Assembly more than any other institution throughout the land-grant designation process. On February 26, 1864, the president of the Board of Trustees sent a letter inviting legislators for a visit at the campus, and representatives from both houses toured the institution on March 19.[46] After institutions had submitted petitions to the General Assembly for a piece of the land grant, President Evan Pugh offered a statement in defense of the legislature's decision to apportion the entire grant to the Agricultural College of Pennsylvania[47] and also drafted a plan for the organization of industrial colleges.[48] In his statement on March 3, 1864, before the Judiciary Committee of the General Assembly, Pugh targeted the literary institutions appealing for a portion of the land grant, claiming that any proposition to combine literary and industrial education was "ludicrous and absurd."[49] Pugh argued that literary colleges trained students for the less rigorous professions, such as medicine and the law, whereas the Agricultural College of Pennsylvania was the only institution in the state that focused primarily on training students in the industrial sciences.

On January 6, 1864, Pugh presented his plan for the organization of colleges of agriculture and mechanic arts to the board of trustees of the Agricultural College of Pennsylvania. Pugh declared that an industrial education institution should be scientifically based and comprehensive, because "the industrial operations of life embrace the *entire range* of human industry, and almost the entire range of human thought."[50] In Pugh's estimation, a broad industrial education required twenty-nine professors and assistants, auxiliaries of study,[51] laboratory spaces, and six distinct courses of study. He also felt that industrial colleges' endowments should be funded at the same level as prominent literary institutions, an amount which was equal to at least $600,000.

Pugh's statement before the General Assembly and his plan for the organization of industrial colleges were a testimony to his ability to describe industrial education and communicate the need for industrial colleges, while simultaneously lobbying on behalf of the Agricultural College of Pennsylvania. First, Pugh acutely articulated the novel character of industrial education. Second, the statement and plan demonstrated how literary colleges had failed to address the industrial exigencies of the nation. Third, Pugh jointly discussed the costs of industrial education and the financial needs of the Agricultural College of Pennsylvania, and, thus, laid the foundation for his argument that the provision of industrial education hinged on the economic stability of the college. Pugh also bolstered the claim that industrial colleges were more deserving of the land-grant than were literary institutions. Painstaking efforts such as these led Pugh to exclaim in a letter to Samuel W. Johnson, professor of agricultural chemistry at Yale University,

> I spent four weeks after the opening of this session in our state legislature, trying to get a bill through donating us the land for agl. colleges. We have such a virtuous legislature that it made it a very very tiresome troublesome disagreeable job. But we secured the entire proceeds of the public lands to our college and we are now taking measures to put the land scrip into the market. Several other parties come forward to get some of this fund but we foiled them and got it all.[52]

Undoubtedly, the Agricultural College of Pennsylvania's early success securing the land grant was due in large part to the efforts of Evan Pugh, the school's first president. A renowned researcher and European-educated scholar, Evan Pugh embodied an unassailable credibility in matters of agricultural education. As evidenced by his tireless efforts politicking with the state legislature, Pugh had the ability to articulate a clear vision of agricultural education that placed the Commonwealth's literary colleges at a severe disadvantage. When Pugh outlined the contours of an industrial education before legislators, he spoke from the perspective of an experienced scholar with concrete ideas about the format of this new type of education, as opposed to representatives from literary institutions, whose mere speculations signaled a deeper interest in the fruits of the land grant than a genuine concern for the industrial classes or industrial education. Unfortunately, Pugh died unexpectedly in April 1864 at the age of thirty-six.

The 1865 legislative session had a similar start to the 1864 one with the appearance of numerous bills proposing to repeal the Pennsylvania Land-Grant Act. Due to the sheer volume of legislation and the remaining uncertainty of whether a partial repeal would result in complete revocation, the House of Representatives adopted a resolution to print 500 copies of the Pennsylvania Land-Grant Act, so that members could acquaint themselves with the text.[53] The legislative record specifically mentions two bills, one of which aimed at redistributing the land among six institutions: the University of Lewisburg (Bucknell), Allegheny College, Pennsylvania College (Gettysburg), Western University (Pittsburgh), Polytechnic of the State of Pennsylvania, and the Agricultural College of Pennsylvania. However, the General Assembly only seriously debated the second bill, Senate Bill No. 120. The Act would have repealed Sections 4 and 5 of the Pennsylvania Land-Grant Act and replaced them with the following section:

> The board of commissioners constituted by the third section of said act are hereby authorized to dispose of the land scrip now on deposit in the office of the Secretary of the Commonwealth, at a price not less than eighty cents per acre, the proceeds to be invested as directed in said third section, and the securities thus obtained to remain in the treasury of the Commonwealth until otherwise ordered.[54]

The debate over Senate Bill No. 120 found the legislature ensnared in personal attacks. Supporters of the Agricultural College of Pennsylvania cited the undue influence of the literary colleges and their religious denominations on multiple legislators. Senator Louis W. Hall's critique centered on the sectarian institutions appealing for a portion of the grant:

> The college in the Meadville district, for instance, a Methodist institution, bringing its influence to bear upon the Senator from Erie, (Mr. Lowry,) the Washington and

Canonsburg college, a Presbyterian institution, calling not in vain on the Senator from Washington, (Mr. Hopkins,) the one in Gettysburg holding its former protégé and pupil, the Senator from Bedford, (Mr. Householder,) under its wings, those in western Pennsylvania, having an eye single to their Senators, all these institutions under the care of religious denominations can, I am fully aware, bring a very powerful influence to bear upon the legislature, because members are not likely to look far outside what seems to be the peculiar interests of their constituents.[55]

Meanwhile, advocates of the repeal labeled the Agricultural College of Pennsylvania as "spoiled" and "wasteful." The tension between the two sides reveals differing conceptions of an appropriate industrial education. The representatives from the Agricultural College of Pennsylvania felt that the land grant should be allocated to an institution that primarily focused on agriculture and the mechanic arts. In a memorial to the General Assembly on behalf of the college, Frederick Watts, president of the Board of Trustees, attached a statement from Ohio Governor John Brough, describing the type of education envisioned by the Morrill Land-Grant Act of 1862. Brough claimed that the Act implemented "a new and distinct species of education"[56] whose purpose was to promote the agricultural and mechanical interests of the nation. This new model of education required a new type of institution, a college whose paramount objective is teaching the industrial sciences. Brough felt that traditional literary institutions were incapable of providing this education, because they had to completely change the nature of their institutions and subordinate all other types of education to the cultivation of industrial sciences.

On the other hand, the advocates of the repeal believed that the land grant should be used "not to propagate a new system of education,"[57] but to disperse practical agricultural and mechanical knowledge to as many people as possible. The two sides also differed on the value of manual labor. The ideology of the Agricultural College of Pennsylvania deemed manual labor necessary to elevate the legitimacy of industrial sciences and to nurture students' fondness for industrial work.[58] School representatives feared that students would abandon industrial occupations in favor of the professions if they did not maintain continuous contact with industrial pursuits throughout college.[59] Proponents of the repeal did not share this virtuous opinion of manual labor. In contrast to a curriculum that featured rigorous academics and arduous labor, the proponents preferred a healthy balance between the two that culminated in an overall student experience which was "pleasant and agreeable."[60]

Senator Clymer broke the stalemate between the two sides with an amendment to assign one-third of the land grant to the Agricultural

College in perpetuity and to place the remaining fund in the state treasury.[61] Clymer proposed this amendment with the intention of appeasing the minds of the friends of the Agricultural College of Pennsylvania, which would have an indivisible share, and the supporters of the literary institutions, which could potentially apply for a portion of the remaining fund. The bill sufficiently satisfied the Senate and was passed on May 8, 1865. The next year, the one-third restriction was codified into law.[62]

Although various measures to redistribute the land grant appeared before the legislature over the next twenty years, Senate Bill No. 120 marked the last time that the Agricultural College of Pennsylvania's status as the sole beneficiary of the land grant was in serious jeopardy. After having prepared and submitted lengthy defenses of the Pennsylvania Land-Grant Act between 1863 and 1865, the Agricultural College of Pennsylvania presented a memorial to the General Assembly on March 2, 1866, requesting the expeditious sale of the scrip, so that the fund could be applied to the college's zealous efforts to proffer industrial education.[63] This memorial represented a change in tone from previous petitions. Instead of focusing on the merits of industrial education or the impropriety of allocating the funds to literary colleges, the Agricultural College discussed its financial difficulties and warned of the dangers of further postponing the sale of the scrip. Although unbeknownst to the actors in this drama, at this time, the question of whether or not the Agricultural College of Pennsylvania would be the beneficiary of the sale of the scrip was more or less settled.

Penn State's Governance and Sponsorship

Penn State's governance structure and board membership also contributed to its success in preserving its land-grant status. The Pennsylvania State Agricultural Society was responsible for founding the institution, providing financial support, and developing the school's early organization and objectives. The state society believed that the institution ushered in a new system of education and would benefit the economic interests of the state, claiming that the school would "invigorate the efforts of those who hold that Science, in combination with Agriculture, will cause two blades to grow where one grew under a less enlightened system."[64]

Unsurprisingly then, the society was greatly involved in the governance of the Farmers' High School. The school's second charter demonstrates the inclusive nature of the institution's governance. The Board of Trustees included the governor, Secretary of the Commonwealth, President of the Pennsylvania State Agricultural Society, Principal, and members of the county agricultural societies in Philadelphia, Center, Allegheny, Erie, Lancaster, Dauphin, Susquehanna, and Cumberland counties.[65] At the meeting held on September 2, 1862, the Board of Trustees established a committee to secure the land grant for the Agricultural College of Pennsylvania. All the members of this committee were members of the Pennsylvania Agricultural Society, including Frederick Watts, who served as both president of the Board of Trustees and president of the agricultural society.

The Board of Trustees also included high-powered figures in the government among its membership. Daniel Kaine, a former lawyer from Fayette County and one of the biggest supporters of the Agricultural College of Pennsylvania in the Pennsylvania House of Representatives, was elected to the Board of Trustees on September 2, 1863. James T. Hale, a member of the US House of Representatives from Center County and a former lawyer and judge in nearby Bellefonte, also served on the Board of Trustees, and was appointed on December 30, 1862 to a committee "to procure state legislation on the subject of the appropriation by the general government of the public lands to the states for agricultural purposes."

An 1862 report on the Agricultural College of Pennsylvania credits Hale with facilitating the passage of legislation on April 18, 1861, which apportioned $50,000 in construction funds to the institution.[66] The report's discussion of the appropriation on April 18, 1861 describes how friends of the college in the General Assembly and the agricultural societies secured favorable legislation. A member from each house took the lead in representing the school's interests. In the Senate, Colonel Andrew Gregg, a member of a prominent Center County family and whose brother-in-law had donated the 200 acres that the Agricultural College was built on, assumed the role. Gregg promised the trustees that he could usher the bill through the Senate if it made it past the House, and only days after the House voted in favor of the bill, he delivered on that promise. In the House, William C. Duncan, a representative from Center County, proved to be a worthy proponent. In Pugh's words, Duncan's "intelligent appreciation of the necessities of agricultural practice, and the financial difficulties of the institution, made him an able advocate in its favor."[67] Duncan initially read the bill before the House, which referred the measure to the Committee of Ways and Means. School officials appeared before the committee describing the purposes and financial difficulties of the institution. The committee reported back to the House favorably on the bill. Duncan passionately defended the bill before the house:

> His honesty and uprightness of character, and personal acquaintance with all the leading friends of the school, and his knowledge of its necessity were sufficient guarantees to his fellow members that the money asked for was needed for the purpose stated, and not for aggrandizement of local interests.[68]

The 1862 report also recognized the work of agricultural societies in guaranteeing the passage of the act on April 18. Representatives from the county agricultural societies and agricultural reformers throughout the Commonwealth visited Harrisburg or sent letters to members, urging them to vote for the appropriation. In addition, the report claimed that "the political press, without regard to party with singular unamity, united with agricultural press in urging the claims of the bill upon the Representatives of the people of our great Agricultural State."[69]

Penn State's origins and governance structure benefited the institution's efforts to secure the land grant. As the product of an agricultural society, the school was linked not only to a statewide economic concern, but also to the national objective of the Morrill Act of 1862. Representatives of the industrial classes throughout the entire Commonwealth participated in the operation of the college, and the expansive range of members on the Board included several prominent government officials. These factors allowed the institution to craft a broad message, which appealed to the agricultural and industrial concerns of all citizens, as opposed to the more locally centered messages of literary institutions. In addition, the widespread membership of the Board helped the college guarantee the passage of favorable legislation in the General Assembly. Due to its governance structure, the Agricultural College of Pennsylvania was perfectly poised to lobby for the entire share of the land grant.

Sale of the Land Scrip

The Agricultural College of Pennsylvania's problems with the land grant were not limited to the legislature. The institution also experienced difficulty in facilitating a swift return on sales of the scrip. The college's opponents seized on this delay in an attempt to erode its support in the General Assembly. Although the Commonwealth accepted the terms of the Morrill Act of 1862 in April 1863, the last of the scrip was not sold until the summer of 1867. Pennsylvania realized a total of $439,186.80, or about 56¢ per acre, on the sale of the scrip.[70] Only six or seven states received lower prices per acre on their scrip. The poor showing by the Commonwealth resulted in unsubstantiated allegations of corruption and mismanagement on the part of the board of commissioners. The delay in sale, however, seems to be the most significant factor explaining Pennsylvania's failure to capitalize on the land scrip.

In accordance with the Census of 1860, Pennsylvania had twenty-six members in Congress, which made the Commonwealth eligible for 780,000 acres of land scrip under the terms of the Morrill Act.[71] Only eleven states had enough public land available for entry within their borders. These states selected 1,770,440 acres of their own land. Land scrip was issued to the states without sufficient public land subject to a private entry at $1.25 per acre. Purchasers of the scrip had the right to locate their property within states with available public lands. Under this method of distribution, twenty-seven states received roughly eight million acres of land scrip. Pennsylvania accepted the land grant on April 1, 1863, but the states could not use the scrip before July 2, 1863, and the backlogged General Land Office did not issue the scrip until sometime after that date.[72]

In 1864, although only a few states swiftly sold their scrip, they attracted notably better offers than those that followed. Vermont sold 150,000 acres for an average of 81.8¢ between March and April 1864. In May 1864, Connecticut received a price of 75¢ per acre for 180,000 acres of scrip. Before 1866, Massachusetts had disposed of 140,000 acres of land scrip at around 81¢ per acre.[73] Around the beginning of 1865, the market for the scrip turned southward, as the anticipation of more lands reduced the offers from prospective buyers.

A couple factors explain the changes in market conditions. First, at this time, public land was freely available. The federal government sold land directly to purchasers at the price of $1.25 per acre. Congress also passed the Homestead Act of 1862, which granted titles to those who entered on land and made improvements. The market was also flooded by roughly ten million acres of soldiers' land warrants and millions of acres of unused lands apportioned to the transcontinental railroads. Second, the Civil War had locked up the attention and resources of many would-be buyers.

Against this backdrop, the Board of Commissioners, charged with disposing of the land scrip, held its first meeting on July 14, 1864.

Recognizing the importance of selling the land in a timely manner, the commissioners declared "that it is expedient immediately to dispose of the land scrip donated by Congress, that the proceeds thereof may be funded for the purpose provided by law."[74] However, the board of commissioners had no resources to market the sale of the scrip. The Morrill Act of 1862 forbade the use of any portion of the land grant to fund expenses related to the marketing and sale of the scrip. Furthermore, until April 1866, the General Assembly refused to vote funds in order to assist with the commissioners' endeavors.[75]

The sale was also impeded by general confusion surrounding the federal government's grant. When Pennsylvania accepted the grant, no state had yet disposed of any land; so, state representatives had no example to follow. In addition, many people were unfamiliar with paper land currency and tended to overestimate its value. The debates in the legislature support this conclusion. During consideration of the Pennsylvania Land Grant Act, legislators incongruously quoted potential minimum prices for the scrip ranging from 75¢ to $1.05 without any regard for actual market value. Land scrip generally sold at a discounted price because of the attendant costs of locating the land. Purchasers not only had to locate the land, often at a far distance, but they also needed to register and clear the land's title with the appropriate authorities. By the time states began to sell their scrip, speculators, who had developed expertise in handling the land warrants of soldiers between 1847 and 1862, had a stranglehold on the market.

Nevertheless, the Board of Commissioners pressed ahead with the sale of Pennsylvania's scrip. In December 1864, the Commissioners decided that 85¢ was a suitable minimum price and accepted twelve bids for about 12,500 acres at that figure. However, the minimum price failed to attract many bids, so the Commissioners lowered the floor price to 75¢ on May 5, 1865. This reduction generated the sale of 3,000 additional acres at prices between 75¢ and $1.00 per acre.

The disposition of land throughout 1865 and early 1866 proceeded at a slow pace. Large land speculators refused to pay high prices on the scrip, and the Board of Commissioners did not have adequate resources to advertise the land. Due to these two factors, the board focused on selling land to small purchasers in Pennsylvania who were willing to pay higher prices than more experienced speculators and whose proximity negated the burden of costly national advertising. By February 8, 1866, the board had sold only 22,400 acres for a total of $18,258, or 81.5¢ per acre. On April 11, 1866, the General Assembly finally passed legislation that authorized funds to cover expenses related to the marketing and sale of the Agricultural College of Pennsylvania's guaranteed one-third share of the scrip.[76] Reinvigorated by the legislature's action, the board embarked on a vigorous campaign to dispose of the rest of the scrip. In May 1866, a representative from the Board traveled to New York and Philadelphia to solicit larger bids.

On February 19, 1867, the General Assembly heeded the calls of the Agricultural College of Pennsylvania and passed House Bill No. 215, which appropriated the income and interest from sales of the rest of the scrip to the institution.[77] During a debate in the House and the Senate, opponents of the college employed familiar methods to stall passage of the bill. Adversarial senators proposed measures to suspend further consideration of the bill, recommit the legislation to another committee, establish a minimum price per acre for the scrip, and apportion a one-third share of realized gains on the land to Allegheny College. The Senate readily rejected these attempts at obstruction, voting twenty-three to seven against the amendment to set a minimum price and twenty-five to five against the amendment to apportion funds to Allegheny College.[78] Similar measures in the House met the same fate.[79] The unsuccessful efforts of the college's opponents amounted to what would be a last ditch effort to deny the Agricultural College the entire benefit of the scrip. Noting that other colleges had not taken the appropriate steps to comply with the Morrill Act and thus avail themselves of the advantages of the grant, Senator George Connell of Philadelphia acknowledged the fact that the Agricultural College had firmly established itself as the sole beneficiary of the land grant by remarking that "the feeling of the public has been gravitating toward this institution."[80] The House echoed these sentiments by passing House Bill No. 215 by a vote of fifty-eight to sixteen on February 14, and the Senate soon followed suit on February 19.

The Board quickly responded by drafting another advertisement on February 27 to sell the remaining 520,000 acres of land. On April 27, the Board received 275 bids on lots between 160 and 520,000 acres. The prices offered ranged from 10¢ to $1.00 an acre, with the majority of bids falling around 55¢. Historian Asa Martin analyzed the seventy-six accepted bids during the entire sale of the scrip. Pennsylvanians figured prominently among the early purchasers of the scrip, whereas a large land speculator, Gleason F. Lewis of Cleveland, Ohio, ended up purchasing more than half of the Commonwealth's 780,000 acres. Lewis eventually acquired a monopoly over college land scrip and between 1866 and April 1873, he purchased about five million acres or 67.7 percent of available scrip in the United States. In July 1866, only weeks before his Pennsylvania purchase, Lewis had bought Kentucky's entire supply of 330,000 acres of scrip for 50¢ per acre.

Based on the low price per acre that the state received for the scrip, we can reasonably conclude that Pennsylvania did not fare well on sales of its share. However, the poor showing was also the result of reasons outside the state's control. Besides the obvious effects of the Civil War, the states were thrown into a competitive market and could not demand high prices on the unfamiliar paper currency. Pennsylvania could not feel very secure about the novel grant of public lands for the support of higher education. The federal government exacerbated the issue by refusing to open up more land for private entry after the Civil War, which restricted the class of land available to the states under the Morrill Act of 1862. The Pennsylvania General Assembly also contributed to the state's unsatisfactory performance. Failure to adequately fund the marketing and sale of the scrip resulted in a scarcity of bids at higher prices. Legislators were also ill-equipped to manage paper currency, and the prolonged debates over the use of the funds, whether intentional or genuine, prevented the sale of the scrip at a more favorable time. Obviously, the Commonwealth would have benefited from a more organized and earlier disposition of the scrip.

Conclusion

In the years after the passage of the Morrill Land Grant of 1862, and despite numerous challenges, Penn State was able to retain its status as the sole beneficiary of the land grant in Pennsylvania. In contrast to literary colleges, Penn State had a broader base of support in the General Assembly due to the lobbying efforts of the college's supporters and its appeal to multiple constituents in the state. Extended legislative debates over the land grant appear to have contributed to Pennsylvania's lackluster effort in disposing of the scrip. Further research into other states' legislative battles may clarify the patterns of land-grant designation and the relationship between actions of state legislators and proceeds derived from the land grant.

Institutions and Amount Received from Land Grant[81]

Name and Location	Amount Derived from Sale	Acres	Avg. Price per Acre
Sheffield Scientific School of Yale College New Haven, CT	$135,000	180,000	$.75
Delaware College Newark, DE	$83,000	90,000	$.92
Illinois Industrial University Urbana, IL	$319,494	480,000	$.67
Purdue University LaFayette, IN	$212,238	390,000	$.54
Agricultural and Mechanical College of Kentucky Lexington, KY	$165,000	330,000	$.50
Maine State College of Agriculture and the Mechanic Arts Orono, ME	$116,359	210,000	$.55
Maryland Agricultural College College Station, MD	$112,500	210,000	$.54
Massachusetts Agricultural College Amherst, MA	$157,538		
Massachusetts Institute of Technology Boston, MA	$78,769	360,000	$.66
Michigan State Agricultural College Lansing, MI	$275,104	240,000	$1.15
New Hampshire College of Agriculture and the Mechanic Arts Hanover, NH	$80,000	150,000	$.53
Rutgers Scientific School of Rutgers College New Brunswick, NJ	116,000	210,000	$.55
Ohio State University Columbus, OH	$507,913	630,000	$.81

(*Continued on next page*)

Institutions and Amount Received from Land Grant[81] (*continued*)

Name and Location	Amount Derived from Sale	Acres	Avg. Price per Acre
Pennsylvania State College, State College, PA	$439,186	780,000	$.56
Brown University Providence, RI	$50,000	120,000	$.42
University of Vermont Burlington, VT	$122,626	150,000	$.82
University of Wisconsin Madison, WI	$244,805	240,000	$1.02

Notes

1. This refers to the different names that Penn State has had throughout the years:
   1855–1862, Farmers' High School
   1862–1874, Agricultural College of Pennsylvania
   1874–1953, Pennsylvania State College (Penn State)
   1953–, The Pennsylvania State University (Penn State)
2. Morrill Act of 1862, ch. 130, 12 Stat. 503 (1862).
3. 1862 Pa. Laws 213.
4. "To encourage the Arts and Sciences, promote the teaching of useful knowledge, and support the Colleges…"
5. 1838 Pa. Laws 332, 333.
6. Asa E. Martin, "Pennsylvania's Land Grant Under the Morrill Act of 1862," *Pennsylvania History* 9, no. 2 (April 1942): 87.
7. 1855 Pa. Laws 46.
8. Michael Bezilla, *Penn State: An Illustrated History* (University Park, PA: The Pennsylvania State University Press, 1985), 3–8.
9. 1857 Pa. Laws 617.
10. Martin, *Pennsylvania's Land Grant*, 3.
11. Amos H. Mylin, ed., *State Prisons, Hospitals, Soldiers' Homes and Orphan Schools Controlled by the Commonwealth of Pennsylvania Embracing Their History, Finances and the Laws, Vol. I* (Harrisburg: Clarence M. Bush, State Printer of Pennsylvania, 1897), 54.
12. Board of Trustees, *The Agricultural College of Pennsylvania; Embracing A Succinct History of Agricultural Education in Europe with the circumstances of the Origin, Rise and Progress of the Agricultural College of Pennsylvania; as also a Statement of the Present Condition, Aims and Prospects of this Institution, its Course of Instruction, Facilities for Study, Terms of Admission, &c., &c.* (Philadelphia, PA: William S. Young, Printer, 1862),37.
13. Jacqueline M. Bloom. *Evan Pugh: The Education of a Scientist, 1828-1859* (Master's Thesis, Penn State University, 1960), 6.
14. Ibid., 68.
15. Board of Trustees, *Agricultural College*, 45.
16. First Year: Arithmetic, Elementary Algebra, Horticulture, Elementary Anatomy and Physiology, Physical Geography and Elementary Astronomy, English Grammar

and Composition, Elocution, History, Practical Agriculture and the details of management on the College Farm.

Second Year: Advanced Algebra and Geometry, General Chemistry, Vegetable Anatomy and Physiology, Zoology and Veterinary, Geology, Paleontology, Practical Agriculture and Horticulture, Logic, and Rhetoric.

Third Year: Surveying, Navigation, Leveling, Drafting with the use of Instruments, Analytical Geometry, Trigonometry, Elementary Calculus, Natural Philosophy, Chemical Analysis, Veterinary Surgery, Entomology, Agricultural Botany, Practical Agriculture and Pomology, Political and Social Economy.

Fourth Year: Analytical Geometry, Differential and Integral Calculus, Engineering, Drafting, Mechanical Drawing, Quantitative Chemical Analysis, Veterinary Pharmacy, Gardening, Agricultural accounts and Farm Management, Moral and Intellectual Philosophy.

17. Pugh, *Agricultural College*, 44.
18. Bezilla, *Penn State*, 45.
19. Board of Trustees, *Agricultural College of Pennsylvania*, 44.
20. Morrill Act of 1862, ch. 130, 12 Stat. 503 (1862).
21. Roger L. Williams, *The Origins of Federal Support For Higher Education: George W. Atherton and the Land-Grant College Movement* (University Park: Penn State University Press, 1991), 11.
22. Alfred C. True, *A History of Agricultural Education in the United States, 1785-1925* (Washington, DC: U.S. Department of Agriculture, 1929), 101.
23. *Atherton*, 20.
24. Ibid., at §1, 503.
25. Martin, *Pennsylvania's Land Grant*, 18.
26. Ibid., at §6, 505.
27. Hereinafter referred to as *The Pennsylvania Land Grant Act*.
28. 1862 Pa. Laws 213.
29. Ibid., at 214.
30. Ibid.
31. On February 4, 1864, Representative Brown noted that the Committee of the Judiciary was already considering a couple bills to redistribute the funds as well as "a number of memorials asking for a portion of this fund arising from the sale of this land," *Legislative Record of 1864*, 153.
32. *Legislative Record of 1864*, 864.
33. Ibid., at 744.
34. Ibid., at 776.
35. Ibid., at 744–45.
36. Ibid., at 746.
37. Ibid., at 1045.
38. Ibid.
39. Ibid., at 278, 311, 356.
40. Ibid., at 776.
41. Ibid., at 606.
42. Ibid.
43. Ibid.
44. Ibid.
45. Numerous other colleges would petition for funds, including Westminster College, Washington and Jefferson College, the Polytechnic Institute of Philadelphia, University of Lewisburg (Bucknell), Gettysburg College, Franklin and Marshall College, and Western University of Pennsylvania, *Legislative Record of 1867 Appendix*, CXXXV.

46. *Legislative Record of 1864,*261, 262, 266–67, 359.
47. Evan Pugh. *A Statement by Dr. E. Pugh of the Agricultural College of Pennsylvania, at a Special Meeting of the Judiciary Committee at Harrisburg, Convened March 3d, 1864, in Reference to the Proposition to Deprive This College of Its Endowment* (Penn State University Archives. 1864).
48. Evan Pugh. *A Report Upon A Plan for the Organization of Colleges for Agriculture and the Mechanic Arts, with Especial Reference to the Organization of the Agricultural College of Pennsylvania, In View of the Endowment of the Institution by the Land Scrip Fund Donated by Congress to the State of Pennsylvania: Addressed to the Board of Trustees of the Agricultural College of Pennsylvania, Convened at Harrisburg, January 6, 1864* (Harrisburg: Singerly & Myers, 1864).
49. *Pugh statement,* 2.
50. Pugh, *Plan for Organization,* 12.
51. For agricultural chemistry, professors "should have collections of different soils, plats, ashes, manures and all other materials that are important in agricultural practice" (19). Similarly, he recommended that professors of civil engineers have access to the materials from which structures are built.
52. *Letter to S.W. Johnson,* April 14, 1863. Evan Pugh Papers. Penn State University Archives.
53. *Legislative Record of 1865,* 132–233.
54. Ibid., at 406.
55. Ibid., at 435.
56. Ibid., at 345.
57. Ibid., at 438.
58. Watts clearly expressed the sentiment in a description of the college's mission, "Our object has been to establish a college, where the minds of youth may be educated to the Science of Agriculture, whilst their habits may be trained to its practical operations; that when a boy returns to the circle of his family, his knowledge, his feelings and disposition will be congenial with those around him, and his inclinations and pleasure will be to improve the methods, while he pursues the occupation of his father," *Report of Board of Trustees to Legislature 1864,*8.
59. Ibid., at 344.
60. Ibid., at 439.
61. Ibid., at 442.
62. 1866 Pa. Laws 100.
63. *Legislative Record of 1866,*382–84.
64. Ibid., at 3.
65. 1855 Pa. Laws §3, 46.
66. 1861 Pa. Laws 392.
67. Board of Trustees, *Agricultural College of Pennsylvania,* 40.
68. Ibid.
69. Ibid., at 40–41.
70. Frank W. Blackmar, *The History of Federal and State Aid to Higher Education.* Contributions to American Educational History, No. 9, ed. Herbert B. Adams. Bureau of Education Circular of Information No. 1, 1890 (Washington, DC: Government Printing Office, 1890), 339–40
71. Martin, *Pennsylvania's Land Grant,* 18.
72. Thomas LeDuc, "State Disposal of the Agricultural College Land Scrip," *Agricultural History* 28, no. 3, (July 1954):100.
73. New York State Senate, *Documents of the Senate of the State of New York,* 97th sess., 1874 (Albany, NY: The Argus Company, 1874), 400–401.
74. *Minute Book of Agricultural Land,* July 14, 1864. Pennsylvania State Archives.

75. 1866 Pa. Laws 100.
76. Ibid.
77. 1867 Pa. Laws 29.
78. The motions to recommit the bill to another committee and suspend further consideration of the bill were withdrawn.
79. *Legislative Record 1867*, 278–79.
80. Ibid., 318.
81. Ibid., at 340.

"An Elephant In The Hands of the State"*: Creating the Texas Land-Grant College

Susan R. Richardson

On October 4, 1876, a few hundred attendees joined the governor, president, and faculty of the Agricultural and Mechanical College of Texas for inaugural festivities. The president was Thomas Gathright, most recently a Mississippi schoolmaster whose major qualification was a recommendation from Jefferson Davis, the Board of Directors' first choice, and an ardent opponent of the 1859 version of the Morrill Act.[1] Gathright possessed little knowledge of agriculture or engineering. He even declared to the crowd that he and the faculty "may not be the proper men to work out success, and may be called to give place to others."[2]

Gathright's faculty totaled five and more or less resembled the average classical college of the time, with the exception of instruction in military tactics and agriculture: Alexander Hogg (pure mathematics), John T. Hand (ancient languages and literature), William A. Banks (modern languages and English literature), Robert Morris (Corps Commandant), and Carlisle P. B. Martin (practical agriculture). The lone agricultural instructor was a minister and part-time farmer. Pinky Downs, Class of 1879, described Martin as "merely a teacher" with "little experience in home farming" who "put out a peach orchard on poor, light land that never did any good. Yet he was the only one . . . to look after the agricultural feature."[3]

The curriculum that Downs and his fellow students took was largely classical and preparatory. A cursory analysis of the backgrounds of

Perspectives on the History of Higher Education 30 (2013): 131–154
© 2013. ISBN: 978-1-4128-5147-3

early students reveals that most came from towns within 100 miles of the college and were the sons of bankers, lawyers, merchants, and educators.[4] Agricultural and Mechanical (A&M) College would be Texas' first public college, but it was not the "university of the first class"[5] that education proponents had envisioned over the previous forty years. Naysayers argued that it was an expensive mistake.

The Texas Legislature passed the act that established the A&M College on April 17, 1871. The former Confederate state was five years removed from the Civil War. Illiteracy was roughly 25 percent—slightly better than in most Southern states and profoundly worse than in midwestern and northeastern states. Texas established its first public college after more than three decades of debate regarding the state's role in providing higher education. Advocates for state higher education envisioned a flagship university, not a farmer's college. The farmer's college, however, would come first and foster unregulated growth and financial competition for years to come. Between the passage of this bill and the fall of 1876, lawmakers and those appointed as Commissioners of the land-grant college selected a location, generally determined how to finance construction, and engaged in partisan squabbles. They crafted policies that would define the tenor of conflicts between Texas A&M, state government, and the University of Texas over the next century.

Antebellum Debates

In 1836, Texas won its independence from Mexico, and it functioned as a republic until gaining admission into the Union as a slave state in 1845. Sam Houston, war hero and Texas icon, served as the republic's first president and later, as US senator and governor. Although not explicitly articulated in his published correspondence and speeches, scholars widely accept the fact that Houston believed higher education was a private matter and opposed legislative efforts to designate land or funds for colleges. Houston allegedly stated that public higher education met the exclusive desires of the rich, and snubbed, even burdened, the poor.[6]

In 1838, Mirabeau Lamar, cofounder of the Texas Philosophical Society, succeeded Houston as president and argued passionately, albeit naively, for a system of public education. Lamar implored the Third Texas Congress to make haste while land was still plentiful and cheap. The new nation could establish an endowment that would support a system in perpetuity. If Texas waited to establish its common schools and universities, land would be scarce; construction, expensive; taxes, necessary; and "sectional jealousies," inevitable. The Texas Congress responded with an 1839 act that provided three leagues (13,284 acres) in each county for common schools, plus fifty leagues (221,400 acres) to establish two universities.[7]

Houston returned as president (1841–1844) and did little to advance public education at any level, although he was instrumental in gaining the Republic annexation as a state.[8] In 1845, when Texas rewrote its constitution on joining the Union, the constitutional convention reaffirmed the commitment to public education in Article X. Under the 1845 constitution, the Legislature would place at least 10 percent of annual state tax revenues into a common school fund. No constitutional provisions were made for higher education. Texas failed to establish a public university, whereas the state issued charters for twenty-nine private colleges, seminaries, and academies between 1837 and 1848.[9]

Anson Jones succeeded Houston as president and then handed over power to the state's first governor George T. Wood (1846–1847), who served briefly before J. Pinckney Henderson (1847–1849). Higher education was not a policy priority during these years until Governor Peter Hansbourough Bell (1849–1853) reintroduced the topic. In his first message to the Fourth Texas Legislature on November 10, 1851, Bell addressed calls to establish the two public universities mentioned in the 1839 Act. He was not willing to make a decision for the Legislature, but referred to "respected sources" which had concluded that the time was not yet ripe for these universities. Money should instead be spent on common schools and scholarships to private Texas colleges. Two years later, Bell changed his mind and kicked off the Fifth Legislature with a call to establish the two universities that Lamar had envisioned in 1839.[10]

The Legislature spent the next few years debating the merits of establishing one, two, or no state university. Governor Elisha Pease (1853–1857) replaced Bell, who left to fill a vacant seat in the US Senate in 1853, and cautioned against creating two universities. Pease wanted to withdraw $250,000 in US bonds from the state treasury to create a single excellent university as opposed to two mediocre ones. In 1855, he increased his recommendation to $300,000.[11]

The most comprehensive debates occurred in December 1855, July–August 1856, and November 1857–January 1858. During the first round in December 1855, one camp stood with Governor Pease's single university plan, and a second argued to two universities. The Senate voted sixteen to ten in favor of founding two.[12]

The senators continued their debate even after they voted for the two-college plan. Edward Palmer of Houston rebutted his colleagues with a few financial figures which he claimed to draw from the Commonwealth of Virginia and concluded, "Our means are not sufficient to support two universities." More compelling was Palmer's reason for opening even one college—the need to protect Texas youth from "doctrines antagonistic to our social institutions, and subversive of the dearest rights of the South." Guy Bryan, a future Congressman who voted against the federal land-grant bill in 1858, enthusiastically agreed. Quick to support the plantation-rich northeastern corner of the state, Jonathan Russell and James W. Flanagan of Rusk and Wood Counties, respectively, echoed Palmer's concern about subversive Yankee influences. In addition, Russell and Flanagan argued that two institutions would allow more students to attend—particularly those from the eastern corridor of the state where transportation to Austin was more difficult.[13]

The Senate returned to the debate between July and August 1856. The body voted fifteen to fourteen to allocate $400,000 to establish a single state university. Next, the assembly reopened the debates of December 1855. With the exception of location, little new information came to light. Earlier, senators refrained from suggesting locations for the second university. There appeared to be an unspoken assumption that one would be located in Austin and the second would be built somewhere in the eastern half of the state. On August 23, 1856, James Flanagan moved to replace the phrase "suitable place" with "Tyhuacana Springs."[14]

After this point, senators would sporadically offer up town names, but took none seriously. Legislation stalled until November 1857 when Governor Pease greeted the Seventh Legislature with a call to act, "No country was better situated to commence such an undertaking."[15] The House responded by charging its education committee with the task of researching the university issue. This committee concluded that the legislature should establish a single well-funded university. Speaking for the Senate Committee on State Affairs on January 16, 1858, Louis Wigfall affirmed the House plan to generously fund one institution. Interestingly, Wigfall wanted to add agriculture to the long list of subjects that the state university might offer.[16]

In what could be interpreted as interest in establishing a land-grant college, a few legislators eschewed professional courses of study such as law and medicine and called for a curriculum that would "be for the universal scientific education of the masses." As some argued in favor of agricultural education, plantation owners such as Representative

Matthew Locke of Upshur County in the northeast responded that the farmers were neither in need of nor desired a college education. Farmers paid the overwhelming share of state taxes and would just as soon not pay for the proposed college.[17]

The university bill finally passed the House and Senate on February 11, 1858. The Senate did not publish the roll call, but the House listed thirteen nays. All the nays came from East Texas representatives who wanted a second school that was close to home.[18] The final bill provided $100,000 of US bonds for the state to finance a single university. In addition, the bill assigned the fifty leagues of land that the Legislature first proposed for education in 1839. The university would be tuition free and would provide instruction in a long list of subjects, including the "principles of agriculture." The 1858 law did not provide a deadline for opening the university. Despite the lack of a timeline, the legislature had finally appropriated money, not just a swath of land that was as available as dust in the Lone Star State.[19]

Hardin Runnels was governor at the time the university bill became law, but he did little to support or discourage the project. The university fund quickly dissolved once Sam Houston became governor in late 1859. On January 13, 1860, Houston asked the legislature to repeal the 1858 university law and proposed liquidating the university fund that was valued at $106,972.26 to beef up frontier protection. Houston argued that private schools were already meeting the educational needs of the state. Texas could build a grand state university someday: "We need money for the protection of our frontier, and to save us from taxation, more than for a fund which promises no immediate benefit." The legislature complied by passing a law that permitted the state treasury to borrow the university fund to pay for military and frontier expenses. In 1861, Texas entered the Confederacy and replaced the US bonds with Confederate bonds. By the close of the Civil War, the university fund was worth fifty-seven cents.[20]

Texas and the Morrill Act

Although the need for an agricultural college may have been discussed, available evidence is thin. The Texas Agricultural Society, established in 1853, listed a state agricultural college and model farm among its proposed initiatives.[21] Despite any interest that Texans may have had in agricultural colleges, US Congressmen Guy Bryan and John Reagan voted against the House version of the land-grant act that narrowly passed 105 to 100 on April 22, 1858. Southerners delivered numerous impassioned speeches against the land-grant act, but none came from Texans.[22]

Reagan said, "Mr. Speaker, I have listened to the reading of the amendment, and I presume there must be some mistake about it. It proposes, as I understand, that double the quantity of land shall be given where the land is selected from the alternate sections of railroad grants. This surely is not what is meant."[23] Reagan may have been worried that the federal government would scoop up large areas of Texas to benefit other states.

Future Confederate President Jefferson Davis provided dramatic oratory against this opinion:

> I have seen the growth of this proposition to do something for the agricultural interest, and I believe it was always delusive, not to say fraudulent. It needs no aid. The agricultural interest takes care of itself. . . . This Government was instituted for no such purpose, and when it invades that prerogative of the States, it commits violence on the sovereign of those by whom it was created.[24]

Regardless of what any Texan thought of Morrill's bill, virtually all conversation halted once South Carolina seceded from the Union. Texas turned its attention to its future in the Union and hosted contentious debates about the merits of secession. Central and western portions of the state fought to remain in the Union, but east Texas planters took control of the conversation and quickly pulled the state into secession.

Accepting the Terms of the Morrill Act

On April 9, 1865, the Confederacy officially surrendered at the Appomattox Courthouse, but it would be five more years before the US Congress seated Texas representatives. Between February and April 1866, Texans assembled in Austin to create a new state constitution.[25] One year later, Congress deemed the Texas constitution unacceptable. In the meantime, in August 1866, the Legislature opened its Eleventh Session. Provisional Governor James Throckmorton, a Unionist turned Confederate turned moderate, called on the Legislature to approve the terms of the 1862 land-grant act if Congress extended the deadline. On July 23, Congress had, in fact, extended the deadline and would make land scrip available to each state once they were "restored to their proper constitutional relation to the Union."[26]

On November 1, 1866, the Legislature approved the terms of the Morrill Act. The House and Senate journals contain only a passing mention of it, and there are no recorded debates as to whether Texas should accept the terms.[27] It is not noted in the legislative journals again until the spring of 1871. The most logical reason for a lapse in its mention is that Texas would not receive access to its land scrip until the fall of 1870 when Congress permitted the state to seat representatives.

The state press mentioned little. In 1869, one exception appeared in *The Plow Boy*, a short-lived agricultural paper out of Austin. A brief article described what several states were doing with their land-grant college benefits. The piece concluded with a hope that Texas would soon claim its land scrip.[28]

Between 1866 and 1869, Texas remained under military control, went through two governors, and revised its constitution again. Approved in 1869, Republicans authored the new constitution. It did not include a provision for higher education.[29]

This constitution endured only till 1876, but it met the approval of the federal government and allowed Texas to hold elections in September 1869 and form a provisional government. Radical Republican Edmund Davis narrowly defeated moderate Republican A. J. Hamilton by just ninety-one votes. A controversial figure, Davis was typical of most radical Republicans in the state. He had been a committed Texas Democrat before the war and even helped write the 1855 party platform that embraced slavery and upheld the Southern flavor of states' rights. Davis never resided in the plantation region of the state. He first settled in Galveston and later served as a customs agent along the Mexican border in Laredo and Brownsville. There were limits to his loyalty to Texas, and Davis eventually opposed secession. He left his family in great danger at home to serve as a general in the Union army and returned to Texas after the war to rebuild his home and community.[30]

Early January 1870, just days into his term, Davis began culling through letters. He found correspondence from Ezra Cornell, dated December 15, 1869. Cornell wanted to make sure that the Texas governor was aware of the impending benefit and the need to sell the scrip quickly at a good price. Given that several Southern states would be moving to sell at the same pace, Cornell was worried that the large supply of land would depress the market. He knew a skilled agent named Gleason F. Lewis who could obtain a good profit for Texas.[31]

On March 30, 1870, Texas was readmitted to the Union and within a few weeks, the US military turned over executive power to Governor Davis. The scrip, consisting of 180,000 acres, became available during the fall of 1870. Davis delegated the scrip disposal task to the Secretary of State James Newcomb. After a few bumps, Newcomb came around to Cornell's advice and relied on the services of Lewis to complete the sale. The scrip was valued $156,600, and bonds were then purchased for $174,000.[32]

On January 10, 1871, Davis informed the Legislature that he had applied for the scrip and was waiting for notification that it was ready. He cautioned that the deadline to establish the land-grant college was fast approaching. Given time constraints, "I think we cannot safely attempt at present the establishment of more than one of these colleges, and suggest that this be incorporated with the state university. I recommend the early passage of an act applicable to this case."[33]

On April 17, 1871, both the House and the Senate honored Davis' request and easily approved "An Act to Establish the Agricultural and Mechanical College of the State of Texas" as a branch of the nonexistent University of Texas. The act provided $75,000 for construction and called for a commission of three who would travel and select a suitable location for the college. After many decades of dithering, Texas finally had a state college along with a deadline for completion. This land-grant college was not the state university that so many had envisioned, but it was an opportunity which no one openly opposed. Congress required each state to establish, or rather, charter, its land-grant college by July 23, 1871. Texas officials interpreted this to mean that they had time until July 23 to locate and build the college. Even if they were required to build a college by July 23, such a task would have been impossible.[34]

The Commissioners

Immediately after the Legislature approved the act to establish A&M, Davis appointed a three-man commission of Republicans from different parts of the state to select a location. Over the next few years, Democrats held this body up as a symbol of Republican corruption. Davis' critics accused him of picking cronies or ingratiating himself to these men by placing them on the Commission. This claim has oft been raised and never substantiated. Although Davis may have handpicked the group, there appears to be no record that these men were friends with Davis or that he had much to gain from appointing them.[35] As Carl Moneyhon has observed, Democrats and Republicans devoted substantial energy during Reconstruction, discrediting policies and legislation introduced by the opposite side. Republicans did not champion public higher education, whereas Democrats eschewed it. Both sides largely agreed on priorities but wanted to deny the other side any voice in decisions.[36]

Records regarding the Commissioners' selection process are scant. John J. Lane stated that the commission traveled to San Antonio, Austin,

Waco, San Marcos, and Tehuacana Hills before arriving in Bryan, the town that would win the prize.[37] Bryan had been incorporated a few months before it was selected to house the agricultural college. What it lacked in age it made up for in motivation. Enthusiastic citizens led by Harvey Mitchell, a Democrat, obtained a state charter for the Central Texas Agricultural and Mechanical Association of Bryan and another for the Bryan Male and Female Seminary mere weeks before they secured the agricultural college.[38]

The selection of a location proved the simplest task. The Commissioners would spend the next several months defending themselves against claims from Davis and the Legislature that they had swindled funds. Fed up with what he believed was gross financial mismanagement, Davis confronted the Commissioners in Bryan on May 16, 1872. After having visited the build site with Austin architect Jacob Larmour, the Commissioners agreed with Davis. Little construction had occurred, and a lot of money had been squandered. Over the next several months, Davis removed and appointed, then appointed and removed several more Commissioners.[39]

Although Davis may have had allies in the Twelfth Legislature, his work with the Thirteenth was contentious. The 1872 elections brought the Democrats back as the majority. In his address to the Thirteenth Legislature in January 1873, Davis declared that he had halted campus construction. He admitted that the Commission had made progress, but not relative to the money they had spent. The college would require an additional appropriation. Davis also acknowledged objections to Bryan as the college's location, but concluded that a move would be impractical at this late stage.[40]

The Democrat-led Legislature believed that it was time to investigate the activities at the college. Andrew Broaddus, a Burleson County (adjacent to Brazos) Democrat and a former secessionist, offered a resolution to refer "that portion of the Governor's message relating to the Agricultural and Mechanical College" to a special committee. The House approved the creation of Broaddus' special committee on January 20.[41]

On February 12, 1873, Broaddus' committee reported its findings. The Commission had selected a good location, whereas they had chosen a poor architect in De Grote. The Commission had wasted money on his services and now required $80,000 to complete a main building that would be "of sufficient size and beauty" for the college. To build their case for this large appropriation, the Broaddus committee included a list of states that had completed their land-grant buildings. Iowa had allotted $227,000, Illinois—$265,544, and Virginia had overcome its reconstruction struggles and given $1,044,364. Many were criticizing the Davis' administration of malfeasance, whereas Broaddus chose to chalk mismanagement in Bryan to incompetence, not corruption.[42]

In December 1873, as his Commissioners seemed to be making progress, Edmund Davis lost the governor's race to Richard Coke, 85,549 to 42,633.[43] Davis refused to accept the results and even appealed to President Grant for federal protection. Grant refused and after several weeks of conflict between Davis and the Democrats, as well as his own party, Davis stepped down. The Democrats now possessed complete control of the state government.[44]

In his first address to the Legislature, Richard Coke proclaimed, "To-day, for the first time since she emerged from the ruin and disaster of the great civil war" Texas had a "government chosen by the free and untrammeled suffrage of her people."[45] Coke made no immediate statements regarding A&M, but the House special committee that was appointed in 1873 did.

George Goodwin, a Brazos resident and supporter of the Grange, replaced Broaddus as committee chairman. According to Goodwin's committee, the Commission withdrew $12,000 from the college account for "pretended purchase" of the Bryan land. Although Goodwin's committee refrained from using the word "embezzle," they concluded that these and others funds totaling $35,458.35 had been "spent, wasted, and chicken-pied away, and nothing whatever accomplished." Fortunately, the present Commissioners had made great progress and restored efficiency and integrity to the project. The college would require an additional appropriation to finish construction. Despite allegations of previous corruption, the Democrat-dominated Legislature appropriated $40,000 to complete the main building on April 2, 1874.[46]

In January 1875, Governor Coke provided the Legislature with a far more detailed list of directives than he had in 1874. The Commissioners had requested $58,000 to complete remaining portions of the main building plus student and faculty residences and to create fences, walkways, and a barn. Coke implored the Legislature to approve the full request so that the college could finally open its doors in the fall of 1876. The majority of the House education committee, chaired by J. H. McLeary, recommended a $32,000 appropriation that the Legislature approved on February 8, 1875.[47]

Constitutional Complications

On March 9, 1875, the Legislature made a governance decision that would create tension for the next several decades. Although established as a branch of the unformed University of Texas, the Legislature approved an independent governing board for A&M. The commission would cease operation, and a board of directors would take over management of the college. Nowhere did the law mention the University of Texas, and A&M board members seemed to possess full authority to act as trustees for the college as if the University of Texas would never exist.[48]

Once the legislative session ended, delegates gathered in Austin to rewrite the state constitution for the third time in ten years. The Democrats wanted to eliminate any systems that they deemed to be too centralized such as the common school system. In contrast to the 1868–1869 delegation, 83 percent were Democrats.[49] The 1876 Constitution included two sections that would shape the agricultural college for decades. As with previous legislation, Article VII declared A&M a branch of the University of Texas, an arrangement that would create bitter conflict between the two schools until a divorce settlement clarified allocations from the Permanent University Fund in 1932. It was B. H. Davis, delegate from Brazos, who introduced the clause that would make A&M the "agricultural and mechanical department."[50] However, the agricultural department would never be just a unit or a branch. It would grow unregulated in competition with the University of Texas once the latter opened in 1883.

The second clause instructed the Legislature to establish a separate college or branch for African Americans. The location would be decided through a public vote. The constitution did not specify whether the segregated school would be a part of A&M, but that detail would become reality on August 14, 1876. This decision solidified segregation as an admissions policy for A&M and the University of Texas until the Sweatt v. Painter decision in 1950. A&M would not admit African Americans until the fall of 1963.[51]

The constitutional convention finished its work on November 24, 1875, and citizens ratified the document in February 1876 at the same time that they re-elected Coke by a landslide. In his message to the Legislature on April 19, 1876, Governor Richard Coke summarized proceedings from A&M Directors' meeting that was held in July 1875. They voted to recommend an additional $40,000 that the Legislature approved. Curiously, the Directors asked Jefferson Davis to serve as president. This was a strange choice given Davis' considerable opposition to the Morrill Act. Not surprisingly, Davis declined the invitation.[52]

After many years of almost exclusive focus on construction, the Directors turned their attention to admissions. Citing the 1876 Constitution, the Directors declared that it was illegal for blacks and whites to attend the same public schools or colleges. Since A&M could not break the law, the Directors would need to wait until the Legislature created a separate land-grant branch to admit African Americans.[53]

Governor Coke called on the Legislature to do whatever possible to ensure that the College opened in October. The Senate and the House responded by forming a joint committee to visit the campus. On their return, the joint committee provided a glowing evaluation of the site, peppering their report with words such as "desirable . . . picturesque and lovely . . . worthy." They advised their colleagues to approve the full appropriation. The legislators recommended that A&M admit men and women, as "The endowment was intended for all." Women would not gain admission until 1963, but it is intriguing to see that some lawmakers championed their presence, even briefly, in the 1870s.[54]

The endowment, "intended for all," meant white citizens. As its closing statement, the joint committee suggested "an available fund at a sufficient amount be appropriated to provide for the colored youth of the country."[55] This school became Prairie View A&M University and would struggle to achieve adequate financial or academic support.

Shaky Start

In October 1876, the Agricultural and Mechanical College opened its doors to students. It was neither the product of a grassroots movement to educate the sons and daughters of farmers nor was it the flagship state university that legislators had proposed in the 1850s. By 1883, there were cries, most notably from the Galveston *Daily News*, to convert the buildings into a "grand central lunatic asylum."[56]

The college struggled to introduce agricultural and engineering courses, but it had little trouble in getting its military program off the ground. The Morrill Act's vague mandate that was intended to provide military training for the land-grant colleges gave them great latitude in meeting this requirement. Most land-grant institutions outside of the south merely expected male students to participate in a few drills each week. The southern land-grant colleges embraced the military requirement enthusiastically and turned to the Citadel and the Virginia Military

Institute (VMI) for models. Able male students who attended southern land-grant colleges wore uniforms, lived in barracks, and participated in a demerit system. A few land-grant colleges took military training as seriously as did Texas A&M. Those hoping for a farmer's college were dismayed by the strong military focus. The *Brenham Weekly Banner* reported that the college had accepted delivery of four, six-pound brass howitzers: "Good gracious! Are we to have war? Has brass howitzers anything to do with agriculture or mechanics?"[57]

Over the next several years, Texas A&M would weather bitter criticism from the Legislature, the state press, the Grange, and the University of Texas boosters. The critique began immediately. On October 4, 1876, the *Galveston Daily News* included several excerpts from other Texas papers. Most of the excerpts attacked the school's $250 annual tuition[58] and focused on classical studies:

> The Victoria *Advocate*: "It was to have given the means to a free education to a number of different regions of the State. The college has been opened in a grand parade, exhibiting a lengthy corps of professors, beginning with Thomas Gathright as President, and ending with Ham P. Bee as Steward. Its catalogue enumerates a long list of studies, many more than is necessary."

> Waxahachie *Enterprise*: "We do not exactly see the justice of building upon an institution of this character at public expense when but a small per cent of people are able to patronize it. . . . To make a success of the institution, men should be educated there who propose to make farmers and mechanics of themselves and who will put the knowledge this obtained into practical operation."

> Goliad *Guard*: "And so this aristocratic establishment for the culture of the sons of the wealthy. Why has this great folly been committed by a Democratic administration? Why are children of the honest yeomanry—the mass of the taxpayers—thus compelled to remain in ignorance. . . . And yet every poor man's and poor widow's cow and calf is taxed to support this college and to pay high salaries to the professors."[59]

Ten days later, the Galveston *Daily News* reprinted an article from the *Brenham Banner* that included the "impractical and . . . ridiculous" curriculum which students would pursue. Only one faculty member was assigned to teach agriculture, and he possessed a degree in divinity.[60] The critics were correct about the cost and noted that the Board had hired Thomas Gathright of Mississippi to serve as its first president. Gathright had no training in agriculture, engineering, or even the pure sciences. Some critics were also concerned about his support of the military requirement, as he had avoided serving in the Confederate army.[61]

The press criticized the curriculum, whereas the Board of Directors had endeavored to design a program that prepared agricultural scientists and engineers. In July 1876, the Board approved seven departments: (1) Commercial; (2) Modern Languages and English; (3) Agricultural and Scientific; (4) Ancient Languages; (5) Applied Mathematics; (6) Pure Mathematics; and (7) Mental and Moral Philosophy. Students were to take different courses in each department over three to four years. They had to attend three classes each day and could choose to study engineering, agriculture, language and literature, or military. After three years, a student would earn a proficiency certificate. If he or she made it to a fourth year, then the student would earn the degree of Scientific Agriculture (S.A.), Civil and Mining Engineering (C.E.), or Bachelor of Arts (A.B.).[62]

Although the Board's plan seemed sound, the faculty quickly discovered that the boys needed a preparatory year followed by a three-year program. Gathright noted that most of the students were not ready for advanced courses, and, therefore, only basic scientific apparatus was required for instruction. We can assume that admission to the college was not difficult. In his effort to obtain a scholarship (available until early 1877), William Trenckman claimed that he was simply asked to recite multiplication tables and name the chief cities in Texas and the capital of New York.[63]

Students were unprepared, yet they were eager to attend college. Enrollment increased from 48 to 106 between the winter of 1876 and the spring of 1877. By the fall of 1877, enrollment ballooned to 200 and 253 by December. Quarters became tight, and there were not even enough bathtubs. The Board reported that it lacked the funds to build machine shops and a model farm that were vital to instruction. In order to meet its expenses (which included paying themselves), the Board decreased an allocation for an orchard from $1,000 to $250, returned mules and a wagon that the college had purchased, and halted all farming projects. Gathright, who reportedly despised farm work, was unwilling to cut any portion of classical curriculum that was in place to free up funds for agricultural and mechanical programs.[64]

In keeping with a national pattern, the Texas State Grange expressed its initial concern for the college's curriculum when, in gathering in Bryan in January 1878, Grange members were appalled by the absence of agriculture. The Grange issued a petition to the Legislature to finance a model farm, but nothing came of it.[65]

The next year, the Board of Directors asked the Legislature to form a committee to evaluate the college. In this request, the Directors quoted directly from the Morrill Act that they were working hard to conform to the call to teach agriculture and the mechanic arts "without excluding other scientific and classical studies." Unfortunately, none of the students were interested in pursuing the new curriculum, because there were no shops, labs, livestock, or farms. Agricultural and mechanical studies were expensive, and the college required more money to "carry out fully the main objects of the grant."[66]

The Legislature assembled for its first session since the College opened in January 1879 and responded to the Board's request by forming a joint committee. Their findings, issued in March, were generally favorable. The faculty were making progress in teaching the young men military tactics. They required an appropriation of $15,000 to furnish laboratories and the library and also to construct a hospital. The legislative committee also recommended that the college form literary and debating societies. Unfortunately, the appropriation bill did not pass, because the House failed to approve it before it adjourned in April.[67]

Although the legislative committee was somewhat positive, Governor Oran Roberts (1879–1883) deemed "the agricultural and mechanical college, so styled" a burden for the State.[68] "So styled" was Roberts' term for the prominence of classical studies at Texas A&M. In his message to the Legislature on February 5, 1879, Roberts even went so far as to take issue with the broad goal of the Morrill Act. In Robert's mind, agricultural and mechanical colleges should exist "to educate skilled laborers" and to secure "the dignity of labor." Roberts was passionately committed to establishing the "university of the first class" in Austin that lawmakers had envisioned in the 1850s, and Texas A&M posed a threat to this dream. As a branch of the University of Texas, A&M's mission would be limited to industrial education.[69]

Governor Roberts was particularly troubled by financial guidelines for A&M. The 1862 Morrill Act barred states from using the proceeds or interest garnered from federal land scrip for the "purchase, erection, preservation, or repair of any building or buildings."[70] A&M would have to rely on state appropriations or proceeds from university lands to expand and maintain the campus. Roberts did not want A&M feeding off the money which he believed that his forbearers had ordained for the University of Texas. Roberts instructed the Sixteenth Legislature during both its regular and subsequent called session to enact a state law that would enable A&M to essentially defy the guidelines set forth in the federal law. Although Roberts acknowledged that the college required funds, he proclaimed that the state had to find the cheapest way to support it, "and then it can more vigorously devote its attention to the promotion of other objects of useful improvements."[71]

It is curious that Roberts, a noted attorney, would pursue a law which would violate the principle of federal preemption. Reason prevailed, and Education Committee Chairman James Henderson declared that the bill could not go forward, "for reasons too obvious to require mention." In spite of the governor's wishes, A&M received $15,000 from the University Fund to pay for library and agricultural equipment at the close of the special session in July.[72]

The remainder of 1879 would prove to be difficult for the college. President Gathright attempted to mediate a conflict between a faculty member and a student who was passed over for a promotion in the Corps of Cadets. The conflict exploded into a student revolt and became statewide news in November. In the end, the Board of Directors dismissed Gathright and all but one faculty member. This crisis exacerbated anger that A&M was not educating farmers. The Houston *Telegram* even declared that the college was a "humbug" and failed to graduate a single farmer.[73]

The Board of Directors responded by hiring John G. James, a military man with strong ideas about industrial education, to replace Gathright. James, a graduate of Virginia Military Institute and a respected Confederate officer, had served as president of Texas Military Institute since 1869. James' faculty initially resembled the old one in disciplinary composition: Charles Estill (Ancient Languages), James Cole (English Literature), Dr. D. Porte Smythe (Anatomy), and Benjamin Allen (Mathematics). Allen did not approve of the state of affairs on campus and quickly departed. Louis McInnis, the lone remaining professor from the Gathright administration, soon replaced Allen. Curiously, the Board did not initially replace agriculture professor Carlisle Martin.[74]

James settled in and drafted his first report to Governor Roberts in late spring. He contended that Gathright's administration had created an environment that was hostile to agricultural and mechanical studies. The elective curriculum was prime evidence of this opposition. He suggested two rigid tracks: one in agriculture and one in mechanics. In addition, James announced that students would participate in compulsory field or shop labor. Anyone seeking a liberal arts degree would need to pursue studies at another college.[75]

The 1880–1881 curriculum featured a great deal more structure than the one devised in 1876:

1880 Curriculum

Common Curriculum	Agriculture	Mechanics
•First Year: arithmetic, geometry, algebra, U.S. history, English grammar, composition and declamation. •Second Year: geometry, trigonometry, physics, surveying, chemistry, history and rhetoric. •Third Year: astronomy, geology, English literature, Texas and U.S. constitution	•First Year: Breeds of horses, cattle, sheep and swine; soils; structural botany and history of agriculture. •Second Year: Practical agriculture, farm irrigation, field crops, fertilizers, tillage, drainage, dairying and zoology •Third Year: Farm engineering, farm management, nursery business, meteorology, veterinary science, entomology, rural law and forestry.	•Freehand and mechanical drawing as well as shop work taught throughout course; engineering occurs in third year and includes civil engineering, millwork, iron work and steam engines

Source: *Industrial Education in the United States: A Special Report Prepared By the U.S. Bureau of Education* (Washington, DC: Government Printing Office, 1883), 231.

Just because the College had an A&M curriculum did not mean that students were interested in it or prepared to complete it. In 1881, one agriculture instructor noted that first-year students were still not prepared to take on the agricultural courses. Of the eight older students whom he was able to teach, three had dropped out during the session.[76]

Although students were not yet ready for the coursework, A&M finally had a few qualified faculty members to teach the technical courses. James hired Charles Gorgeson to introduce veterinary science. Gorgeson, a graduate of Michigan State, organized the first cattle herd at the college, but students showed little interest in his courses. Engineering professor Franklin Van Winkle was more successful. Many students left after Gathright's departure, and this exodus freed up space that had been used as makeshift housing when enrollments skyrocketed between 1877 and 1879. He was able to build a machine shop out of the former barracks. The Legislature appropriated $7,500 for 1880–1881 to outfit the shop, and Van Winkle purchased equipment, including a steam engine, lathes, and anvils. Students found shop work more engaging than milking cows. Of the ninety students who had enrolled in the spring of 1881, eighty-six opted for the mechanical track.[77]

In spite of some progress in developing the agricultural and mechanical curriculum, a legislative committee visited campus in early 1881 and reported that the college had still to elevate these subjects to

Sampling of Student Backgrounds and Careers

Student	Hometown/ Proximity to College	Father's Occupation	Career After Graduation
William Sleeper	Waco/92 miles	Attorney	Attorney
William Trenckman	Millheim/ 70 miles	Educator, 1st president of agricultural society Cat Springs Landwirtschafflicher Verein	Newspaper publisher
Pinckney "Pinky Downs"	Waco/92 miles	Head of Waco Female College, died and then raised by uncle	Banker and supporter of experiment stations
Edward Fitzhugh	Waco/92 miles	Farmer	Insurance
Edward Cushing	Houston/ 100 miles	Newspaper publisher	Military and railroad
G.W. Hardy	Millican/16 miles	Unknown, father convicted of murder	Military
Pinkus Levy	Navasota/ 25 miles	Merchant	Real Estate
Foster Fort	Waco/92 miles	Banker	Merchant
Louis Kopke	Austin/110 miles	Died in Civil War	Civil Engineer
John Stewart	Houston/ 100 miles	Attorney	Attorney
Charles Rogan	Waco/92 miles	Unknown, but Rogan attended private schools	Attorney and state land commissioner at the time of Spindletop

Source: US Census, 1870, 1880, 1900, and 1920.

an acceptable level. James and the Board of Directors responded by eliminating Estill, professor of ancient languages.[78] In March 1881, the legislative committee concluded that wealthy students were attending the college in large numbers and enrolling in classical courses. Judging from available background data, it was difficult to find students who came from the "industrial classes."

If the college admitted three needy students from each of the thirty-one state senatorial districts, enrollment in the agricultural program would increase. To that end, the committee recommended an $800 (later increased to $7,500) appropriation to provide scholarships. Knowing that students might not opt to study agriculture, the Legislature added a provision that required half of the scholarship students to enroll in the agricultural course and the other half in the mechanical course.[79]

The law temporarily helped bolster enrollments. In the fall of 1881, 93 scholarship students matriculated. The agriculture department grew from four students to fifty-nine, and mechanics increased from 81 to 199. The next fall, however, enrollment in agriculture decreased to forty-five.

As of 1883, the college had not received the scholarship funds approved by the Legislature in 1881. Not only did A&M lack the state funds to educate the scholarship students, but also it did not receive an appropriation to purchase equipment for the agricultural and mechanical departments.[80] In addition, students complained that they were required to work in the fields. James eliminated the labor requirement, but agriculture still failed to attract as much interest as did engineering.

Charles Gorgeson described the challenge of teaching students about stockbreeding without much livestock, "I did the next best thing and illustrated the lectures with crayon drawings," but it was hard to hold student interest without experiential opportunities. Franklin Van Winkle added that boys chose mechanics in lieu of agriculture, but "The majority of students do not come here for a technical training in agriculture or mechanics. They come for a general education, and these will always choose the course they imagine to be the most pleasant."[81]

Gorgeson and Van Winkle were not alone in their frustrations. After three years of financial, curricular, and enrollment challenges, James resigned in March 1883. He could not adequately build the agricultural and engineering departments without funds and also could not attract enough students without expanding the classical curriculum that Governor Roberts and others wanted to reserve for the University of Texas.

The Elephant and State

Texas spent the years between independence and the Civil War debating the role that the state would play in providing higher education. It did not plan on an agricultural college, but rather a state university that might include agriculture as a part of the curriculum. After the Civil War, it joined the other former Confederate states in accepting the terms of the Morrill Act. Although Texas might have tried to refuse federal land scrip before 1861, the cash-strapped and rebellious state had little choice after 1865. The Texas Legislature had envisioned a state university that it could support with a land endowment. By the 1870s, the University Fund was small and did not yield enough to support even one, much less two universities. Almost immediately, A&M's critics deemed it an elephant—too large to move and too voracious to nourish.

In the next few years, A&M would take hits from the agricultural community, the Legislature and governor, the University of Texas, and the public. Agricultural leaders and the Grange would fault A&M for spending far too much time in training young men to be soldiers. Indeed, the Corps of Cadets distinguished the college far more than any degree program well into the twentieth century. The Legislature and governor found fault with A&M's constant (biennial) requests for funding and routinely cut requests for needed farms and labs. Many lawmakers failed to grasp that the Morrill Act did not permit A&M to use the proceeds from its land scrip for permanent improvements. The University of Texas rebuked A&M for duplicating its engineering programs and for requesting its share of the Permanent University Fund. Despite its struggle with the Legislature and UT, A&M increased its enrollment to 316 by 1890, 382 by 1900, and 782 by 1910.[82] The 1887 Hatch Act provided the college with the funds it needed to build a strong agricultural experiment station system. Texas A&M would eventually become a competitive and comprehensive research university that conformed to Morrill's vision.

Notes

*   *Galveston Daily News*, January 5, 1879, quoting the *Houston Age*.
1.   The Morrill Act was introduced in 1857, revised and debated in 1858, and vetoed by President Buchanan in February 1859.
2.   Henry C. Dethloff, *A Centennial History of Texas A&M University, 1876–1976*, II vols. (College Station, TX: Texas A&M University Press, 1975), 37.
3.   Ibid., 31; David Brooks Cofer, *First Five Administrators of Texas AM College, 1876–1890* (College Station, TX: The Association of Former Students, 1952), 13.
4.   Exploratory research using 1870 and 1880 Census and voting records. See table titled "Sampling of Student Backgrounds and Careers" for more details.
5.   The phrase that legislators and University of Texas regents, faculty, and alumni used and continue to use to identify its goals.
6.   John J. Lane, *History of the University of Texas Based on Facts and Records* (Austin: Henry Hutchins State Printer, 1891), 4–5; Roger A. Griffin, "To Establish a University of the First Class," *Southwestern Historical Quarterly* 86, no. 2 (1982): 136–37.
7.   *Journal of the House of Representatives of the Republic of Texas*, Regular Session of the Third Congress hereafter referred to as *Texas House Journal* (Houston, 1839), 168–70, H. P. N. Gammel, comp., *The Laws of Texas, 1822–1897* hereafter listed as *Gammel's Laws*, vol. 2 (Austin, 1898), 134–36. Lamar's naïveté is best summarized in the opening sentence of his remarks to the Third Texas Congress (*Texas House Journal*, 168), "Education is a subject which every citizen and especially

every parent feels a deep and lively concern. It is one in which no jarring interests are involved, and no acrimonious political feelings excited; for its benefits are so universal that all parties can cordially unite in advancing it."

8. Lane, *History of the University of Texas Based on Facts and Records*, 4–5; Griffin, "To Establish a University of the First Class," 136–37.
9. Constitution of the State of Texas (1845), Article X, Eby, 94.
10. *Texas House Journal*, Fourth Legislature, 49–50; Fifth Legislature, 27–28.
11. *Texas House Journal*, Sixth Legislature, 21; *Texas Senate Journal*, Sixth Legislature, 17.
12. H. Y. Benedict, *A Source Book Relating to the History of the University of Texas* (Austin: University of Texas, 1917), 23–46.
13. Ibid., 28–30; Palmer quotes on 28.
14. *Texas Senate Journal*, Sixth Legislature, 88–90; Flanagan reference on 330. Tyhuacana Springs was south of Dallas.
15. *Texas Senate Journal*, Seventh Legislature, 20.
16. *Texas House Journal*, Seventh Legislature, 80–82, *Texas Senate Journal*, 345–49. Described as one of the most vocal of the fire-eaters, Wigfall was an arch enemy of pro-Union Sam Houston and was passionate about expanding slavery.
17. H. Y. Benedict, *A Source Book Relating to the History of the University of Texas*, 159–62, quote on 162.
18. *Texas House Journal*, Seventh Legislature, 809.
19. *Gammel's Laws*, vol. 4, 148–51.
20. *Texas Senate Journal*, Eighth Legislature, quote 272, Griffin, "To Establish a University of the First Class," 139.
21. *Transactions of the Texas State Agricultural Society: Embracing the Proceedings Connected With Its Organization, the Constitution and an Address by the President* (Austin: Printed for the Society, by J. W. Hampton, 1853).
22. Sarah T. Phillips, "Antebellum, Republican Ideology, and Sectional Tension," *Agricultural History* 74, no. 4 (Autumn 2000): 799–822. Phillips takes a critical look at the long-held view that Southern opposition to federal control trammeled Morrill's Act. Once the eleven states seceded, Congress easily passed the land-grant bill. Phillip's counters that the southern states took full advantage of federal support when it suited constituent needs. Southerners even advocated establishing land-grant colleges. As previously mentioned, the Legislature added agriculture to the list of subjects that the University of Texas offered. American farmers were almost uniformly interested in advancing the science of their work, but the south wanted to preserve slavery alongside modern techniques. They did not want northern and western critics to remold their system. There were Republican agricultural reformers whose primary goal was to rid the south of its slave system. Many of these same reformers wanted to establish land-grant colleges and a federal agricultural department.
23. *Congressional Globe*, April 22, 1858, 1740 and 1742, quote on 1740.
24. *Congressional Globe*, February 1, 1859, 722.
25. *Journals of the Constitutional Convention 1866*, 119, Constitution of the State of Texas (1866). The convention consisted of extreme secessionists, unionists, and, to a lesser degree, moderate Democratic and Republicans. Delegates took an oath of loyalty to the United States, but much of the constitution resembled antebellum law. While slavery ceased to exist, the 1866 constitution did not extend suffrage to Blacks. The following from Oran Roberts, future governor and University of Texas law professor, provides a glimpse of the racial attitudes present at the convention, "the permanent preservation of the white race being the paramount object of the people of Texas, the Legislature shall have power to pass all such laws, relating

specially to the African race within her limits." As a part of this racial preservation plan, the constitution authorized the Legislature to levy a tax on Black citizens to provide for their own schools.

26. *Texas House Journal*, Eleventh Reg. Sess., 198; *Journal of the Senate of the United States of America* 58: 707; *Fortieth Congress*. Sess. I Res. 25, 1867, 26.
27. *Texas House Journal*, Eleventh Reg. Sess., 367–68, 664–65; *Gammel's Laws*, vol. 5, (Austin, 1898), 1103–5. After considerable opposition to the land-grant bill in 1858, it is striking that all the Southern states accepted the terms of the Morrill Act after the war without significant debate. The war had left the southern states both financially and physically in shambles, and it is fair to assume that all were compelled to take the much needed proceeds which would come from the land scrip.
28. *The Plow Boy* (Austin, TX), vol. 1, no. 5, ed. 1, Saturday, May 1, 1869, 1.
29. David Minor, "Throckmorton, James Webb," *Handbook of Texas Online*, http://www.tshaonline.org/handbook/online/articles/fth36 (accessed April 6, 2011). Published by the Texas State Historical Association; Randolph B. Campbell, *Gone to Texas: A History of the Lone Star State* (New York: Oxford, 2003), 276–77.
30. Campbell, *Gone to Texas*, 280, Carl H. Moneyhon, "'Texas Out-Radicals My Radicalism': Roots of Radical Republicanism in Reconstruction Texas," in *The Texas Left: Radical Roots of Lone Star Liberation*, ed. David O'Donald Cullen and Kyle G. Wilkison (College Station, TX: Texas A&M University Press, 2010), 13–35.
31. Ezra Cornell to Dear Sir, 12/15/1869, Edmund J. Davis Papers, hereafter referred to as Davis Papers, Box 301-60, Folder 6, Texas State Library Archives Commission (TSLAC).
32. William T. Hooper Jr., "Edmund J. Davis, Ezra Cornell, and the A&M College of Texas," *Southwestern Historical Quarterly* 78, no. 3 (1975): 308–10, Walter Smith to Edmund Davis, 4/1/1871, Davis Papers, Box 301-72, Folder 180; Lane, *History of the University of Texas*, 6.
33. *Texas House Journal*, Twelfth Legislature, Regular sess., 54; *Gammel's Laws of Texas*, vol. 6, 938–40.
34. *Texas House Journal*, Twelfth Legislature, 1023; Dethloff, *Centennial History of Texas A&M University*, 12–14.
35. William Saylor to Edmund Davis, May 1, 1871, Davis Papers, Box 301-72, Folder 185; Dethloff, *Centennial History of Texas A&M University*, 15–26.
36. Carl H. Moneyhon, "Public Education and Texas Reconstruction Politics, 1871–1874," *Southwestern Historical Quarterly* 92, no. 3 (1989): 395–416.
37. Lane, *History of Education in Texas*, 267; Clarence Ousley, "History of the Agricultural and Mechanical College of Texas," *Bulletin of the Agricultural and Mechanical College of Texas* 6, no. 8 (1935): 39.
38. *Gammel's Laws*, vol. 6, 517, 1186–87.
39. Dethloff, *Centennial History of Texas A&M University*, 23.
40. *Texas House Journal*, Thirteenth Legislature, Regular sess., 37.
41. Ibid., 61.
42. Ibid., 195–99, quote on 197.
43. *Texas Senate Journal*, 14th Legislature, Regular sess., 16.
44. The state press pledged overwhelming support for Coke. The *Waco Daily Examiner*, for example, published this bit of rhyme on January 6, 1874, "We have had the election. And Coke's away 'head, And the whole Radical lay-out Was killed very dead." The *Galveston Daily News* had routinely demonized Davis. *Waco Daily Examiner* 2, no. 57, ed. 1, January 6, 1874.
45. *Texas Senate Journal*, 14th Legislature, Regular sess., 17. Although African Americans could vote in 1874, it is important to note that the state instituted a poll tax before the election.

46. *Texas House Journal*, 14th Legislature, Regular sess., 310–13, first quote on 311, second quote on 312; *Gammel's Laws*, vol. 8, 50–51.

47. *Texas Senate House Journal*, 14th Legislature, Second sess., 89–91, 126–27; *Gammel's Laws*, vol. 8, 387.

48. *Gammel's Laws*, vol. 8, 444–45.

49. Campbell, *Gone to Texas*, 285.

50. *Journal of the Texas Constitutional Convention of the State of Texas Begun and Held in the City of Austin September 6, 1875* (Galveston, 1875), 134.

51. Constitution of the State of Texas (1876), *Gammel's Laws*, vol. 8, 972–73. Surprisingly, the 15th Legislature chose a similar method to organize what would become Prairie View University. They directed the governor to appoint a commission of three to travel the state and select the most suitable location. After so much talk about corruption within the A&M Commission, it is interesting that they proposed this path again.

52. *Texas House Journal*, Fifteenth Legislature Regular sess., 50–51, full text of Davis' letter printed in *Galveston Daily News*, July 23, 1875.

53. *Texas House Journal*, Fifteenth Legislature Regular sess., 51.

54. *Senate Journal*, 15th Legislature, Regular sess., 149, first quote on 308, second quote on 309.

55. Ibid.

56. Dethloff, *Centennial History of Texas A&M University*, 88.

57. Rod Andrew Jr., *Long Gray Lines: The Southern Military Tradition, 1839-1915* (Chapel Hill: University of North Carolina Press, 2001), 5, 40–41, 52; *Brenham Banner Weekly*, January 31, 1879.

58. The Board decreased tuition to $200 after it abolished need-based scholarships in 1877.

59. *Galveston Daily News*, October 4, 1876.

60. *Galveston Daily News*, October 14, 1876, Clarence Ousley, "History of the Agricultural and Mechanical College of Texas," *Bulletin of the Agricultural and Mechanical College of Texas* 6, no. 8 (1935): 45.

61. Dethloff also notes that Gathright sympathized with the Conservative Republicans during Reconstruction, 33–34.

62. Dethloff, *Centennial History of Texas A&M University*, 31, 40.

63. Ibid., 40; David Brooks Cofer, *Early History of Texas A and M Through Letters and Papers* (College Station, TX: The Association of Former Students, 1952), 10, 130.

64. Dethloff, *Centennial History of Texas A&M University*, 38–39, 42–43, 45.

65. Ibid., 47; Frederick Eby, *Education in Texas: Source Materials* (Austin: University of Texas, 1918), 501.

66. *Senate Journal*, Sixteenth Legislature, Regular Sess., 205–7 first quote on 205, second quote on 207.

67. *House Journal*, Sixteenth Legislature, Regular Sess., 675–677.

68. Ibid., 111.

69. *Senate Journal*, Sixteenth Legislature, Regular Sess., 202–5.

70. 37th Cong., 2d sess., chap. 30, 504 (see also U.S.C.A. 301).

71. *Senate Journal*, Sixteenth Legislature, Regular Sess., 204; Special Sess., 8, 18–19, quote on 19.

72. *House Journal*, Sixteenth Legislature, Special sess., 217; *Gammel's Laws*, vol. 9, 44–46.

73. Dethloff provides a detailed account of what is known as the "Crisp Affair," 50–69. Louis McInnis, adjunct professor of mathematics, was spared his job. Houston *Telegram* quote cited in *Brenham Banner Weekly*, December 5, 1879.

74. Dethloff, *Centennial History of Texas A&M University*, 70–71.
75. Ibid., 72–74.
76. *Industrial Education in the United States: A Special Report Prepared By the U.S. Bureau of Education* (Washington, DC: Government Printing Office, 1883), 231.
77. Dethloff, *Centennial History of Texas A&M University*, 75.
78. Ibid.
79. *Texas Senate Journal*, Sixteenth Legislature, Regular sess., 153; *Gammel's Laws*, vol. 9, 183.
80. Dethloff, *Centennial History of Texas A&M University*, 78, 84.
81. *Galveston Daily News*, June 25, 1883.
82. Annual Catalogue of Texas A&M, 1890; *Report of the Commissioner of Education for the Year 1900–1901* (Washington, DC: Government Printing Office, 1902); *Report of the Commissioner of Education for the Year Ended June 30, 1910* (Government Printing Office, 1911).

Part III

Agriculture and Engineering, 1880–1900

Introduction

Roger L. Geiger

In 1880, land-grant colleges and universities were operating in thirty-seven states. Most of these were young institutions, still finding their bearings pedagogically and often politically. Just five antedated the Morrill Act; the rest began operating about equally in the 1860s and 1870s. In 1880, the academic revolution that shaped the American university was still inchoate, and only a handful of land grants, led by Cornell, embraced the university ideal. Among state universities, those in California, Minnesota, Wisconsin, Illinois, Ohio, and Nebraska were more or less committed to a university model, despite recurrent frustrations. Other universities, especially in the south, regarded their land-grant units more as appendages, having little or no integration with their colleges. The University of Mississippi gladly shed its land-grant unit to a new A&M college in Starkville (1880), and both North and South Carolina would soon, less happily, repeat that pattern. In the north, Yale segregated its land-grant units in the Sheffield Scientific School, and similar arrangements existed at Rutgers, Brown, Dartmouth, and Vermont. In all the would-be universities, disagreements arose over whether the land-grant revenues were meant to support the university or just agriculture. Eight of the land-grant institutions enshrined a dedication to agriculture and the mechanic arts in their titles (A&M), and a similar number were simply named "agricultural colleges." Since the 1870s, farmers' groups had claimed ownership of the agricultural colleges, against the protests of advocates for more inclusive national schools of science. By 1880, two-thirds of the land grants had agriculture in their title, but

Perspectives on the History of Higher Education 30 (2013): 157–164
© 2013. ISBN: 978-1-4128-5147-3

the battle over the content and control of these institutions had only begun.[1]

Agriculture, in general, had fallen on hard times. The financial crash of 1873 ushered in more than two decades of falling prices and worsening conditions for American farmers. Agrarian discontent was soon organized into political movements—the National Grange in the 1870s, Farmers Alliances in the 1880s, and the Populist Party in the early 1890s. Farmers' grievances were directed against railroads, banks, and the gold standard—all associated with the political domination of capitalists. An extensive network of regional and national publications allowed these interests to weigh in on numerous issues, including the agricultural colleges.[2] There was cause for discontent in these colleges as well. The agricultural departments of the land-grant institutions had failed to find ways to offer education for farming or to improve agriculture. The model farms that were created were dismal failures, as was the practice of requiring all students to perform manual labor. Knowledge that could be usefully applied to farming was limited, and individuals who could teach what was known were scarce. After a disastrous start, Cornell developed an effective program after 1875; Michigan Agricultural College was perhaps most focused on teaching primarily agriculture. Other institutions, for the most part, had produced neither graduates nor agricultural knowledge. Consequently, universities faced intermittent crusades to remove agriculture and the land-grant endowment to separate institutions; in other states, A&M institutions were assailed for failing to live up to their mission.[3]

Scott Gelber's paper on "The Populist Vision for Land Grant Universities" examines these developments in Nebraska, Kansas, and North Carolina, where populists gained the upper hand for a time over land-grant institutions.[4] Their complaints and designs convey the basic themes that animated agrarian hostility toward these institutions throughout this period, as well as the egalitarian values of the land-grant movement. In general, populists were most concerned about the social composition of the colleges and an agricultural curriculum, but these matters were closely linked in their minds.

At a time when public high schools were largely limited to urban areas, it was difficult for farm youth to obtain the proper qualifications for college entry. In 1880, most colleges in the country maintained preparatory departments, including the land grants in Illinois, Indiana, Ohio, Iowa, and Pennsylvania. Most students were admitted by examination. Populists often sought lenient admission standards which were consistent with the common school education that rural youth could obtain. They also demanded remedial offerings. The University of Minnesota resolved this dilemma by creating separate admissions and curricula for an agricultural school, actually a technical high school. Admission requirements constituted a significant difference between land-grant universities and agricultural or A&M institutions. By 1906, most universities in the Midwest and West required a full high school course (fourteen or fifteen units) for admissions, whereas only four A&Ms did.[5]

Populists instinctively objected to manifestations of privilege in keeping with the Morrill Act spirit of melding the professional and industrial classes. Fraternities provided a flash point on this issue, as they segregated the well-to-do from the humble. Gelber notes Nebraska's failed attempt to outlaw fraternities, but this could have been a dangerous step. When the president of Purdue outlawed fraternities, he first lost a challenge in court and then lost his job when the legislature retaliated by withholding Purdue's appropriation. In 1881, the head of Illinois also was forced from office, in part for his ban against fraternities.

Land-grant institutions faced enormous difficulties in connecting agricultural knowledge with agricultural practitioners. Few agricultural students graduated, and few of those few went back to the farm. From early days, agricultural professors had sought to reach farmers through traveling lectures or institutes, with little success. The University of Wisconsin found a more effective strategy when it made professors offer short courses for farmers during winters, a practice that was soon widely imitated. Progress was made in the 1880s, and experimental farms soon displaced ineffective model farms. These examples, and vigorous lobbying by land-grant presidents, led to the passage of the Hatch Act in 1887, which provided annual federal support for agricultural experiment stations.[6] With agriculture at the peak of its political influence, the Second Morrill Act followed in 1890, granting a federal appropriation to all land-grant institutions. The Hatch Act, at last, provided for organized and coordinated agricultural research, and the 1890 Act provided a significant infusion of funds at the moment the academic revolution and the expansion of secondary education made growth imperative. Before long, a new relationship emerged among farmers and departments of agriculture, one that made agriculture a special enclave in land-grant universities, sustained by a dedicated stream of federal funds.[7]

In the short run, these acts incensed agrarian opponents, who felt that the land-grant colleges had failed to serve their interests and did not deserve public support. Emboldened, they renewed campaigns to remove the land grant from comprehensive universities. In 1887, North Carolina populists wrested the land grant from Chapel Hill, founding the North Carolina College of Agriculture and the Mechanic Arts (later, N. C. State University). "Pitchfork" Ben Tillman, governor of South Carolina, did the same to found Clemson University (1890). Similar measures followed in New England, where Yale and Brown relinquished their land-grant designations to new state agricultural colleges.[8]

Gelber's study captures the high tide of agrarian populism through its impact on the land-grant colleges. Although these colleges evoked the land-grant mission to cultivate the practical arts and bring higher education to the industrial classes, it was hard to accommodate these social goals with the "other scientific and classical studies." However, precisely the preference for low admissions and academic standards, and for practical subjects to the neglect of scientific and literary disciplines, made the populist vision increasingly anachronistic in the waning years of the nineteenth century. The identification of land-grant institutions with agriculture consequently impeded the difficult evolution into modern universities. This was not the case for the two institutions that were dedicated to engineering—Purdue and the Massachusetts Institute of Technology. These institutions as well as the comprehensive land-grant universities would exemplify the Morrill legacy in the development of engineering.

Although agriculture and the mechanic arts received equal billing in the Morrill Act, their disposition was quite different in the land-grant colleges. The "mechanic arts" in contemporary parlance referred to the activities of the numerous, relatively small machine shops, most dense in the Northeast, that manufactured tools and machinery. Justin Morrill used his blacksmith father as an example of the mechanics that he wished to aid.[9] Such workers were not engineers. The term referred to civil engineers, the most prominent of whom were college graduates. The United States Military Academy had been the first to graduate civil engineers, but by 1860, these engineers were being educated at Yale's Sheffield School, Union College, and Rensselaer Polytechnic Institute.[10] The Massachusetts Institute of Technology was the only land-grant institution that was specifically devoted to nonagricultural studies. The fruit of a concerted campaign by William Barton Rogers to establish a "School of Industrial Science," his project only became feasible when he secured one-third of the state's land grant.

Unlike agriculture, industrial science had competitors outside of land-grant institutions. In the decade after the Civil War, scientific schools were founded at Lafayette, Dartmouth, Penn, and Princeton, among others; and independent schools of technology were founded in Pennsylvania (Lehigh), Worcester, and Hoboken (Stevens Institute of Technology). MIT, nevertheless, emerged as the most effective and fully developed institution of this kind. It pioneered a four-year course, in which students received basic grounding in math, science, English, and modern languages during the first two years. They could then specialize in mechanical engineering, civil engineering, chemistry, geology, the nation's first course in architecture, or general studies. Above all, MIT was dedicated to bringing modern science to bear on these practical arts, particularly through the use of instructional laboratories.[11] However, the most problematic area was mechanical engineering. What still passed for mechanic arts was dominated by a shop culture, which held that skills needed to make tools and machinery could only be learned through hands-on immersion in the workplace. Worcester Polytechnic and other schools established workshops in which students learned by manufacturing commercial products. Thus, until the mid-1880s, the mechanic arts remained a viable approach to this field with limited academic content.

Gregory Zieren's study reveals the crucial role of Robert H. Thurston in remolding this field into mechanical engineering. Thurston combined a B.S. degree from Brown University with experience in the shop culture, but his most formative experience was working in steam engineering at the Naval Academy. Steam engines were powering America's industrial revolution, and their development needed science-based engineering. Thurston's expertise was recognized by the founders of Stevens Institute of Technology, who hired him specifically to develop mechanical engineering. They sponsored his travels to investigate engineering education throughout Europe and the United States, but the distinctive four-year curriculum that he devised for mechanical engineering was essentially grounded in his American experience. He stressed a laboratory approach to engineering education that gradually advanced students from the physical properties of materials through to machine applications.

Thurston's curriculum not only prepared competent mechanical engineers, but also created laboratories that could be utilized for testing and design—engineering research. His reputation quickly grew, and he became an advocate for the new approach to mechanical engineering education. He was instrumental in founding the American Society of Mechanical Engineers and served as its first president (1880–1883). He soon obtained a larger field of operation when President Andrew

D. White appointed him Dean of the Sibley College of Engineering at Cornell. At the college, Thurston had the resources to pursue research and graduate education, as well as a more prominent platform from which to proselytize for mechanical engineering. Zieren notes that Thurston quickly built the largest and most respected program in the country, one that was soon admired internationally.

After 1885, all forms of engineering education took off. Civil engineering remained a vital field, which was relevant to the expanding railroad network as well as the infrastructure needs of America's burgeoning cities. Mining engineering was launched in 1864 by the Columbia School of Mines, emphasizing chemistry and metallurgy, and this institution dominated the field. Electricity, which had long been studied in physics departments, was transformed into electrical engineering in the 1880s, complementing the appearance of telephones, electric lights, and power generation. Applied chemistry, which was a major subject in all scientific schools, developed more gradually into programs for chemical engineering. The integration of science with practical arts that had been advanced at MIT and by Thurston transformed engineering into a college-educated profession. By the twentieth century, metallurgy and electrical engineering demanded college degrees, and this was increasingly true for many applications of chemistry. Thurston made mechanical engineering attractive for industry by combining science with the hands-on traditions of shop culture. After 1900, a college education came to be valued more highly than experience in a shop.

With the rise of engineering, many land-grant colleges were transformed into engineering schools. By the mid-1890s, engineering students constituted the majority of undergraduates at Cornell and Illinois, two-thirds at Pennsylvania State College, and four-fifths at Purdue. In 1900, engineering was the largest college as well at Kentucky, Maine, LSU, and Ohio State. Zieren notes that agricultural interests feared being displaced by the growth of engineering in Ohio, Iowa, and Kansas. Engineering experiment stations were created at Illinois (1903) and Iowa State (1904), although agricultural interests were wary of this development. By the end of the 1920s, land-grant colleges in thirty-one states had such stations, but most were poorly funded and repeated attempts to elicit federal support failed.[12]

In contrast, agriculture enrollments remained weak at most land grants through the end of the nineteenth century. In 1894, the land-grant colleges produced 229 graduates in agriculture, half of them in Kansas, Massachusetts, Wisconsin, and Michigan.[13] However, the colleges were reaching a far larger audience through short courses, institutes, and correspondence courses. Minnesota, for example, enrolled more than 500 students in its sub-college School of Agriculture, but only 27 in its College of Agriculture (1900). The fortunes of agriculture departments changed markedly in the first decade of the new century. Regular (i.e., collegiate) agriculture students rose from less than 100 before 1900 to more than 500 in 1910 at both Cornell and Illinois, and other land grants experienced the same explosive growth at roughly the same time. Several factors converged. The great depression in agriculture had dissipated by 1900, and opportunities arose for agriculturalists in the government and industry. As the experiment stations created by the Hatch Act matured, they brought research, sometimes for the first time, into agricultural colleges. The Adams Act in 1906 accelerated this development by doubling the appropriations for agricultural experimentation. Research spawned greater expertise, which translated after 1900 into specialization in the agricultural curriculum, as separate courses were established for agronomy, horticulture, animal husbandry, dairy, and others. Finally, even as regular students grew, the colleges multiplied their interaction with farmers through flexible courses and the development of extension programs. The latter were consecrated with federal support by the Smith–Lever Act of 1914. By this date, the agricultural colleges truly lived up to their name.[14]

Engineering schools or agricultural colleges? The land-grant colleges and universities became both, though on rather different terms. American industry became the patron of academic engineering, first through the philanthropy of industrialists such as Hiram Sibley, later through direct relationships with industrial firms. MIT, foremost in electrical engineering, forged working arrangements with AT&T and General Electric; Purdue became renowned for railroad engineering, obtaining its own locomotive for research and instruction; and everywhere, industrial patrons contributed equipment or dollars to assist favored departments. Agriculture overcame a generation of ineptitude to perform increasingly valuable services for its farming constituency. However, the government was the indispensible handmaiden of this success. The federal government established a compelling superstructure—accepted by every state—through the two Morrill Acts, funding for the experiment stations, and finally support for agricultural extension. However, states had to supply the bulk of support to realize the goals of these federal programs. The land-grant institutions, thus, became highly segmented organizations, with their parts dependent on various resources from different parties. By the twentieth century, they also faced the challenge of forming the whole into a modern American university (Part IV).

Notes

1. *Report of the Commissioner of Education for 1880* (Washington, DC: GPO, 1881), 677–83; Daniel Coit Gilman, "Report on the National Schools of Science," in *Report of the Commissioner of Education for 1871* (Washington, DC: GPO, 1872), 427–44.

2. Alan I. Marcus, *Agricultural Science and the Quest for Legitimacy: Farmers, Agricultural Colleges, and the Experiment Stations, 1870–1890* (Ames, IA: Iowa State University Press, 1985).

3. Alan I. Marcus, "The Ivory Silo: Farmer-Agricultural College Tensions in the 1870s and 1880s," *Agricultural History* 60, no. 2 (Spring 1986): 22–36.

4. See also, Scott M. Gelber, *The University and the People: Envisioning American Higher Education in an Era of Populist Protest* (Madison: University of Wisconsin Press, 2011).

5. New Hampshire, Iowa, Purdue, and Washington, *Bulletin of the Carnegie Foundation for the Advancement of Teaching*, I (1907): 22, 34.

6. Roger L. Williams, *The Origins of Federal Support for Higher Education: George W. Atherton and the Land-Grant College Movement* (University Park: Pennsylvania State University Press, 1991), 87–173.; Marcus, *Agricultural Science*, 188–221.

7. Alfred Charles True, *A History of Agricultural Education in the United States, 1785–1925* (Washington, DC: GPO, 1929).

8. Nathan M. Sorber, *Farmers, Scientists, and Officers of Industry: The Formation and Reformation of Land-Grant Colleges in the Northeastern United States, 1862–1906* (Ph.D. diss., Pennsylvania State University, 2011).

9. William Belmont Parker, *The Life and Public Services of Justin Smith Morrill* (Boston, MA: Houghton Mifflin, 1924), 262; Monte A. Calvert, *The Mechanical Engineer in America, 1880–1910: Professional Cultures in Conflict* (Baltimore, MD: Johns Hopkins University Press, 1967), 29–40.

10. Robert V. Bruce, *The Launching of Modern American Science, 1846–1876* (Ithaca, NY: Cornell University Press, 1987).

11. Julius A. Stratton and Loretta H. Mannix, *Mind and Hand: The Birth of MIT* (Cambridge: MIT Press, 2005); A. J. Angulo, *William Barton Rogers and the Idea of MIT* (Baltimore, MD: Johns Hopkins University Press, 2009). By 1884, MIT offered ten courses that students entered as freshmen.

12. David L. Harmon, "Collegiate Conflict: Internal Dissension at Land-Grant Colleges and the Failure to Establish Engineering Experiment Stations," in *Engineering in a Land-Grant Context*, ed. Alan I. Marcus (West Lafayette: Purdue University Press, 2005), 7–26.

13. True, *History of Agricultural Education*, 213. Before 1900, the graduation rate for engineering was estimated to be 25 percent, but agriculture was much lower. Ironically, the abysmal graduation rates were the best evidence that land-grant institutions were reaching the target population of the Morrill Act—the industrial classes who tended to be poorly prepared educationally and financially.

14. True, *History of Agricultural Education*, 220–72; Michael Bezilla, *The College of Agriculture at Penn State* (University Park: Pennsylvania State University Press, 1987), 58–111.

The Populist Vision for Land-Grant Universities, 1880–1900

Scott Gelber

The ambiguities of the Morrill Act created conflicts over the mission of land-grant universities from the beginning. Roughly speaking, the rival visions for these institutions can be characterized as elitist and populist. Historians, in general, have had better access to sources documenting the elitist perspective. This article uses the original capital "P" Populists of the late nineteenth century as a proxy in order to better understand the small "p" populist vision. Fueled by rural dissatisfaction, the Populist movement of the late nineteenth century promised to defend small producers against exploitation by bankers, wholesalers, and railroad executives.[1] A subset of the movement believed that higher education could also advance the cause of Populist egalitarianism. Somewhat unexpectedly, Populist legislators often advocated for generous, occasionally record-setting, appropriations to land-grant colleges. These Populists, who were participants in what was arguably the United States' last mass democratic campaign, promoted a variant of the land-grant vision that warrants careful consideration.[2] A reexamination of this original Populist vision illuminates classic and celebrated elements of the land-grant mission. Just as importantly, this history reveals the vestigial aspects of early debates that, for better or worse, have disappeared from discussions about the Morrill Act.

This article focuses on Populist efforts to shape land-grant programs in North Carolina, Kansas, and Nebraska, locations that provide

Perspectives on the History of Higher Education 30 (2013): 165–194
© 2013. ISBN: 978-1-4128-5147-3

particularly dramatic examples of Populist pressure (Populists also gained varying degrees of formal influence over land-grant institutions in states such as Missouri, Colorado, the Dakotas, and Washington). Leaders of the agrarian revolt in North Carolina were instrumental to the founding of the North Carolina College of Agriculture and Mechanic Arts (NC-CAMA—currently North Carolina State University). During the 1890s, Populists intermittently governed Kansas State Agricultural College (KSAC—currently Kansas State University). They also controlled appropriations for the University of Nebraska (NU) for most of that decade and elected a majority of the school's board of regents between 1900 and 1904.

The first part of this article briefly reviews aspects of the Populist vision that remain familiar to twenty-first advocates of land-grant universities. To varying extents, land-grant universities continue to emphasize the Populist themes of accessibility and practicality. Next, the article discusses forgotten aspects of the Populists' demands, especially their expectation that these schools could serve as an antidote for invidious professional distinctions between manual and mental labor and a cure for the estrangement of working-class college graduates from their home communities. In these ways, land-grant colleges were supposed to level inequalities between elites and "the people." Ultimately, the article explains the failure of this leveling agenda, while indicating the manner in which the land-grant mission, nevertheless, exhibits a combination of Populist and elitist elements.

The Familiar: Accessibility and Utilitarianism

Aspects of the Populist vision of land-grant universities are neither unprecedented nor unfamiliar. A substantial portion of the movement's lobbying efforts promoted a somewhat more shrill version of the two most common expectations for public higher education: accessibility and utilitarianism.[3]

Populists believed that land-grant colleges should enroll a critical mass of low-income students. Contrary to Populist insinuations, nearly every public university leader (and even most elite private university presidents) shared this goal.[4] Some state constitutions, such as Indiana, mandated free tuition, whereas other states passed legislation to this effect. When Justin Morrill conceived of the federal land-grant program, he also assumed that A&M colleges would be free.[5] Some land-grant universities also felt compelled to be free of charge in order to attract enough students to justify their existence.[6] Most land-grant institutions that charged tuition still managed to subsidize the enrollment of between one-third and one-half of their campuses, typically by providing scholarships to a number of students from each legislative district.[7] Nevertheless, familial obligations and even modest costs of living prevented the children of many poor farmers and laborers from attending and graduating from land-grant universities. For example, during the 1880s and early 1890s, NCCAMA professors frequently informed their students that they would have to leave if they did not pay their debts for tuition, fees, room, or board.[8] Of course, other factors contributed to low attendance and high attrition in this period. During the late nineteenth century, a diploma was far from essential for ambitious youth, and it was not uncommon for students to leave college in favor of more attractive opportunities.[9] Nevertheless, student bodies tended to be disproportionately wealthy even at land-grant campuses, as demonstrated by J. Gregory Behle's chapter.

Populists were especially concerned about the underrepresentation of poor students. Movement leaders accused students at the University of Georgia of being "dandies and dudes," who spent their time "dancing and rioting and drinking liquor."[10] Nebraska Populists asserted that Cornell University exemplified the manner in which land-grant institutions sometimes betrayed their original dedication to accessibility by charging tuition and building expensive laboratories. "What good old uncle Ezra founded for the benefit of the poor," stated the *Nebraska Independent*, "has been stolen by the rich."[11] Populists were particularly vigilant critics of college fraternities, which appeared to promote extravagance and institutionalize class distinctions within the student body. In 1897, a Nebraska Populist legislator attempted to outlaw fraternities and sororities at NU in order to keep all students "on a level footing."[12] Populists were troubled by the discomfort that poor students experienced when surrounded by classmates who spent freely on clothes, fees, and parties. The *Nebraska Independent* worried that students from modest rural backgrounds were "already ill at ease" on campus and would be easily discouraged by social exclusion.[13] Alvin Johnson, an NU student from a Populist family, recalled that his peers "adored" Chancellor James Canfield, because he was "a true democrat, who used all his influence to abate the snobbishness of the students from families that composed the rising middle class."[14] For Populist leaders, increased attendance of poor rural students was insufficient; they argued that colleges should enroll a large percentage of these students in order to form a supportive campus culture.[15]

To this end, Populists defended the principle of free or inexpensive higher education against critics who raised concerns about the potential moral hazards of tuition subsidies. The very notion of scholarships could provoke controversy during the nineteenth century; even some leaders of state universities questioned the wisdom of enrolling students free of charge. Chancellor Henry Tucker of the University of Georgia worried that free higher education might attract "indolent" or "undeserving" students. Chancellor of the University of Nebraska, E. Benjamin Andrews wondered whether free tuition might make students ungrateful for their educational opportunities.[16] In contrast, Arkansas politicians aligned with the Farmers' Alliance and forbade the state land-grant university from charging tuition to students taking vocational courses.[17] In North Carolina, Populist leader Leonidas L. Polk argued that NCCAMA should be free or inexpensive in order to serve those "unable to send their children to high graded and expensive schools and colleges."[18] During Missouri's brief era of Populist–Democrat governance, the land-grant university first started a scholarship program and then eliminated tuition altogether.[19] In Nebraska, the organ of the state Farmers' Alliance applauded the public university, which had always been legally barred from charging tuition. "The son of a rich man can go to Harvard, Yale, Columbia, or Princeton, and pay the $150 to $200 per year demanded by these institutions for tuition," the *Farmers' Alliance* stated, "but the boy from the poor man's home cannot do this . . . the free state university is his only hope."[20]

In addition to supporting free tuition and scholarships, Populists opposed additional laboratory, library, diploma, and incidental fees. In 1894, Kansas Populists objected to a proposal to introduce a five-dollar library fee at KU, which had a longstanding tradition of tuition-free education. When eighty students refused to pay the fee, a movement newspaper supported their protest and then celebrated when the Populist attorney general and Populist-controlled state supreme court agreed that the fee violated a state law forbidding tuition charges.[21] The next year, a proposal to legalize fees inspired Populist predictions that KU would eventually exclude "every poor boy or girl in the state." Under the headline "Education Must Be Free," *The Jeffersonian* called another proposed ten-dollar fee "an exhibition of asinine stupidity."[22] Similar to their counterparts in Kansas, Nebraska Populists also protested against fees at the state university. Although NU was legally prohibited from charging tuition, other expenses, including fees, room, and board, ran as high as $175 per semester during the 1890s.[23] In 1901, after the Republican Governor Charles Henry Dietrich vetoed a $90,000 appropriation bill, NU regents raised funds by instituting a three-dollar fee per semester. The *Nebraska Independent* labeled the new fee the "Dietrich Tax" and complained that the governor's veto made "poor students have to foot the bill" for their education.[24] These sorts of concerns continue to exert some degree of countervailing pressure against proposals to compensate for inadequate state funding by increasing tuition or fees at land-grant universities.

Populists also promoted the still familiar, though even more controversial, notion that land-grant colleges should be relatively accessible in terms of admissions standards. Often only requiring an eighth- or ninth-grade level of preparation, many state agricultural colleges maintained an intermediate status between secondary and higher education during the late nineteenth century.[25] Presidents of land-grant institutions risked inciting protests if they attempted to make their schools more "selective" by increasing minimum requirements beyond the level of the average student. Well before the peak of Populist political power, public outrage prompted the trustees of Ohio State University to veto an increase in the rigor of its entrance examinations. Southern land-grant institutions felt particular pressure to shed the perception that they were training grounds for heirs of the antebellum plantation elite. A professor at the University of California claimed that "popular clamor" also compelled western institutions to maintain low standards. Even in New England, not typically regarded as fertile ground for populistic agitation, New Hampshire legislators attempted to compel the state agricultural college to admit all common school graduates.[26]

In states where they came to power, Populists advanced to the vanguard of this longstanding campaign for low entrance requirements. When Leonidas L. Polk campaigned to divert North Carolina's land-grant proceeds from the University of North Carolina (UNC) to a separate state agricultural college, he argued that the new school would recognize "the disadvantages under which the farmer's boy labors in the struggle for education." Polk envisioned that North Carolina's land-grant institution would be within the reach of "any farmer's boy who has obtained the rudiments of a common school education."[27] Led by Polk, farmers lobbied for the establishment of NCCAMA, which originally admitted any white male over fourteen years of age who could demonstrate moral character as well as comprehension of "ordinary English," "simple arithmetic," and "a fair knowledge of geography and state history."[28] Along with most colleges in the nation, NCCAMA also issued conditional acceptances to applicants who failed one or two entrance examinations and required professors to provide remedial tutoring.

In the event of "some unusual circumstance or promise in the applicant," NCCAMA trustees also authorized the enrollment of students who had failed three or more exams.[29] However, North Carolina Populists never obtained full control over the institution, which began to drift toward conventional academic norms. The college added an algebra requirement and closed its remedial department in 1899, even though large portions of North Carolina remained without access to free high schools. Afterward, NCCAMA denied admission to significant numbers of applicants.[30]

During their administration of KSAC, Kansas Populists' permissive attitude toward admission standards also clashed with the outlook of traditional academic leaders. Similar to their counterparts in North Carolina, Kansas Populists tolerated high requirements at the flagship state university while defending relatively low standards at the state land-grant institution. KSAC's Populist regents refused to increase the college's relatively low standards, rejecting a personal request from Harvard University President Charles Eliot.[31] In contrast, the Republican *Manhattan Nationalist* protested that any student who completed the seventh grade could enter KSAC. The paper urged, "Elevate the standard regardless of the numbers attending." The *Nationalist* also argued that the college's modest requirements had been enforced more strictly before the start of the Populist reign. The paper claimed that forty to sixty applicants had failed each examination during the several years preceding 1897, whereas virtually all students had passed the test in 1897.[32]

In Nebraska, Populists were pleased with the lax approach to admissions promoted during the administration of Chancellor Canfield (1891–1895). Unlike North Carolina and Kansas, which established independent A&M schools, Nebraska created an "Industrial College" within the flagship state university. Although NU had initially maintained lower standards at this land-grant program, in 1885, the university raised the Industrial College's entrance requirements to the equivalent of its liberal arts division.[33] These standards were similar to NU's peer institutions—applicants either presented diplomas from accredited high schools or passed examinations in common school branches, plus algebra, geometry, history, and foreign languages.[34] Nebraska Populists did not demand that NU reverse this decision, but they expected the university to administer its admission policy with a measure of sympathy for rural youth. Canfield agreed that NU's gates should not be guarded "with locks that respond only to golden keys." In his letter accepting his post at the university, Canfield announced his intention to "minister to the needs of the greatest number" instead of attempting to reach an academic ideal that was far removed from the level of the typical country school system.[35] Canfield instructed entrance examiners to conduct oral interviews of applicants who ran out of time, and to be conscious of the "rust" that students accumulated over the course of the summer, or during the years between leaving school and applying to university. He urged examiners to "let our entrance gates turn rather easily."[36]

In the late 1890s, after Canfield had left NU to become president of Ohio State University, the *Nebraska Independent* worried about his successor's attitude toward entrance requirements. The newspaper was concerned that Chancellor George MacLean (1895–1899), a former professor of English at the University of Minnesota, sought to raise admission standards beyond the level of the average rural school system. "City blood is no better than country blood," the *Independent* argued, warning that high requirements would be viewed as tantamount to discrimination against rural students. Asserting that any student who was capable of doing college work should be enrolled even if other students were far more advanced, the *Independent* also opposed any movement toward selective admissions.[37]

In addition to lobbying for low entrance standards, Populists fervently supported remedial programs that were designed to prepare students who could not even meet these modest requirements. In contrast, most professors reluctantly tolerated these "preparatory" courses and regretted the manner in which preparatory departments impeded the growth of high schools and distracted universities from their primary mission.[38] President Edward Orton of Ohio State University complained that remedial courses designed "to bring up the work of backwoods districts" created mongrel institutions that clashed with the "sacred" purpose of higher education.[39] University of Missouri President Richard H. Jesse questioned whether it was even possible for land-grant institutions to maintain these programs without violating the terms of the Morrill Act.[40] Encouraged by the growth of public secondary schools, most professors supported the termination of remedial programs during the 1880s and 1890s.[41]

Drawing attention to the contentiousness of this issue, Populists expressed greater concern about the extent to which the elimination of preparatory departments would limit the educational opportunities of rural youth. As late as 1895, 17 percent of full-fledged college students had finished their preparation in these programs rather than proceeding directly from public or private high schools.[42] Other schools cut remedial programs, whereas KSAC's Populist administrators applauded a

65 percent increase in attendance at the college's preparatory courses between 1897 and 1899. Furthermore, in the fall of 1898, KSAC's regents hired the college's first fulltime instructor for preparatory courses.[43] The Populists who monitored developments at NU also believed that widespread remediation was consistent with the institution's land-grant designation. In 1890, when NU faculty voted to close the university's remedial "Latin School", the board of regents overruled this decision after protests from the State Farmers' Alliance.[44] Chancellor Canfield pleased his Populist supporters by arguing that public colleges without preparatory departments were unable to enroll large numbers of rural students.[45] Canfield recognized that Populist legislators might cut the university's funding if the school cancelled remedial courses.[46] George MacLean, his successor, rejected the Populist perspective on remediation and announced plans to close the Latin School.[47] Unconvinced, the *Nebraska Independent* charged that ending the preparatory courses was "a scheme to shut the 'hayseeds' out of the university and reserve its privileges for the benefit of Nebraska's aristocracy."[48] During a decade in which public high school enrollment rose dramatically, Populists epitomized this sort of argument for the preparatory function of state colleges and universities.

Populism tended to conceive of these academic and financial struggles in terms of college access for rural men, whereas the movement also occasionally advocated for the now-familiar principle of equal access for women applicants to land-grant institutions. Populist rhetoric often stressed the fact that both rural husbands and wives labored to sustain the economic viability of the farm, and the movement's organizations welcomed women as members, organizers, lecturers, and editors.[49] Populists supported the expansion of college access for women by promoting coeducation in the West and single-sex colleges in the south, approaches that were consistent with regional tendencies.[50] Populists believed that college training could reduce the drudgery of fieldwork and prepare women to work as teachers, telegraph operators, or clerks in case of economic depression or widowhood. The North Carolina Farmers' Alliance resolved in favor of college access for women at its annual meeting in 1890, explaining that higher education "alike for males and females" would benefit all of "the industrial classes." The next year, a state legislature that was dominated by members who were loyal to the Alliance established the North Carolina Normal and Industrial College (NCNIS) for white women.[51] In Kansas and Nebraska, Populists advocated for coeducation and, sometimes, women's access to faculty appointments and governing board seats. Populist editor Frank Eager attacked NU for having replaced two female teachers with men and for only hiring women to fill low-level administrative positions. Eager accused Chancellor MacLean of snobbishly favoring east-coast elites while alienating the "earnest young women" who attended the university.[52] When Populist regents had the chance to act on these concerns in Kansas, they filled the KSAC chair of mathematics with Mary Winston, the first woman with a Ph.D. to ever teach at the college.[53] Fusionist Governor John Leedy also appointed Susan St. John (a prohibition activist and wife of a former governor) to the KSAC board of regents.[54] In Nebraska, the Populist Party nominated Elia Peattie to run for a seat on the NU board of trustees.[55]

Efforts to forge a movement that encompassed men and women were moderately successful, whereas Populism's potential as a basis for interracial solidarity fell tragically short. Notwithstanding some efforts to build biracial coalitions during election years, most white Populists remained reluctant to share political power or patronage with potential African-American allies.[56] The Southern Farmers' Alliance excluded African Americans altogether. In North Carolina, Leonidas L. Polk personified the racism of many white Populists. An opponent of proposals to found a state industrial college for African Americans, Polk speculated that black people would be incapable of learning scientific agricultural methods.[57] Most white Populists in the Great Plains also rejected the concept of social equality with their black counterparts, and expressed little concern for racial inequalities in higher education. In Kansas, where some older Populists had participated in abolitionist campaigns, the movement's advocacy for college access only indirectly affected African-American students.[58] Uninterested in race-based advocacy, white Kansas Populists apparently ignored the Western University, the one institution in the state that was dedicated to the higher education of African Americans.[59]

This indifference toward racial disparities in higher education is consistent with the broader history of white Populism. Less predictably, there is little evidence that black Populists in the southern Colored Farmers Alliance or state Populist Parties campaigned against discrimination in public higher education. Risking their lives by advocating for fundamental human rights and equal funding for common schools, black Populists may have viewed access to higher education as an issue of marginal importance.[60] Black Populists may have also believed that the historically black land-grant colleges which were supported by the Second Morrill

Act of 1890 were already fully committed to accessibility.[61] Alternatively, it is plausible that black Populists may have had low expectations for state colleges which were governed by white legislators and trustees. Black colleges with a land-grant designation faced an external mandate to focus on vocational education and often answered administrators who hailed from outside of local communities.[62] Regardless of race, the black wing of the Populist movement did not persuade white Populists to campaign vigorously for the expansion of access to land-grant colleges. Instead, despite occasional rousing calls for unity, the white majority of the movement organized its higher education platform around the perceived interests of white farmers and mechanics.

Concern for the status of these producers shaped the Populist stance toward college curriculum in both familiar and foreign ways. To some extent, Populists epitomized the narrow interpretation of the Morrill Act, which saw the legislation as mandate for a predominant focus on practical subjects such as agriculture, home economics, and engineering.[63] Populists joined an ongoing campaign for applied higher education that included supporters inside and outside of land-grant institutions. These reforms signified revolutionary changes to academic definitions of scientific inquiry. The spread of utilitarian pursuits within higher education also resonated with strong currents of modern America, especially industrialization and professionalization.[64] Although they sometimes repeated traditional agrarian skepticism about college training, Populist leaders ultimately joined this movement for applied higher education.[65] To be sure, Populists tended to frustrate scientists by expecting them to demonstrate profitable methods and to respond to personal queries from farmers. Despite this shortsighted opposition to basic scientific research, the movement did not object to agricultural science altogether. Indeed, Populists complained that land-grant colleges were not committed enough to the endeavor. The national umbrella organizations of the Grange and the Farmers' Alliance supported the Hatch Act of 1887 and the Second Morrill Act of 1890. Populists remained hopeful that these fledging institutions would improve crop yields and spearhead economic development in rural America.[66]

North Carolina Populists typified this response when they attacked UNC and campaigned for the establishment of a separate state college of agriculture. "Shoot in the direction of Chapel Hill," exhorted Daniel McKay, a farmer from Harnett County. McKay told Leonidas Lafayette Polk that "our people have had enough of junk in that stereotyped lecture defining the *relations* the university has to the farming interests of N.C . . . we want something more tangible."[67] Starting with the very first issue of his newspaper, the *Progressive Farmer*, Polk attacked UNC's use of land-grant funding for courses in zoology and geology.[68] These concerns explain why NCCAMA initially required all students to study agriculture, horticulture, shop-work, and mechanical drawing. The college's daily schedule consisted of three hours of classroom recitation followed by three hours of manual training.[69] Although the movement never assumed full control of the college, Populists used the opportunity provided by NCCAMA's brief period of Populist–Republican rule (1897–1899) to support Professor Wilbur Fisk Massey and experiment station head W. A. Withers, both of whom prioritized utilitarian advice.[70]

Western Populists advocated for vocational higher education with equal fervor. In Kansas, Populists complained that KSAC President George T. Fairchild increased offerings in the humanities and core sciences rather than adding agricultural courses.[71] The *Jeffersonian* accused "a class of pig headed professors" of disrespecting farmers and laborers.[72] Frustration with the college's lack of commitment to agricultural education motivated the Populist reorganization of KSAC during the 1890s, a period when a new administration established more specialized curricular tracks, instituted a three-fold increase in the number of agricultural courses, and directed the experiment station to focus on the "cash value" of experiments.[73] Kansas Populists also supported the construction of a building that was dedicated to the college's program in domestic science.[74] Similarly, Nebraska Populists pressurized administrators to increase investment in utilitarian education at NU. Similar to most land-grant institutions, NU's Industrial College struggled during its early years and attracted criticism from farmers.[75] Chancellor Canfield agreed that the university was not using its land-grant proceeds to maximize vocational offerings and added a forge room, a carpentry shop, and an electrical program.[76] Nevertheless, Populist legislators still claimed that the school provided insufficient attention to agricultural students. Populist criticism intensified during the administration of Chancellor MacLean. The *Nebraska Independent* wryly predicted that land-grant proceeds might someday be redirected to the College of Fine Arts.[77] Between 1900 and 1904, when an alliance of Nebraska Populists, Democrats, and Silver Republicans controlled the board of regents, NU doubled its agricultural teaching force.[78]

Although these attacks on the curriculum of land-grant colleges may have been demagogic to some degree, they also expressed a common belief that agricultural and mechanical higher education would attract larger numbers of poor students. For example, the Populist superintendent of Kansas' public schools asserted that "popularizing" education required making it more "practical." The superintendent concluded that colleges taught "too much lawyer, teacher and doctor and too little merchant, mechanic, and farmer; too much preparation to live in the parlor and too little for the kitchen and the workshop."[79] Leonidas L. Polk agreed that farmers' sons would not or could not attend university in order to master "the dead languages, mathematics, polite literature and all the ologies."[80]

The Foreign: Class Leveling

This Populist emphasis on applied subjects is both familiar and predictable, whereas other aspects of the movement's curricular vision are more radical and almost completely absent from twenty-first century discussions of the land-grant mission. In particular, Populists argued that land-grant colleges could not just boost the fortunes of farmers and mechanics, but also soften the edges of class distinctions.

A part of the Populist pursuit of this objective entailed somewhat unexpected advocacy for moderate amounts of the humanities and social sciences. Although vocational training was central to the Populist vision of the land-grant college, the movement did not entirely reject the liberal arts. Some Populists, especially those who had themselves attended college, embraced classic tributes to the antimaterialism and democratic idealism of liberal education (particularly the study of Ancient Greece). A letter to the editor of the *Wealth Makers of the World* asserted that colleges could provide students with "higher conceptions of success" instead of ambition for mere wealth and self-promotion. Written by a "Populist educator," the letter argued that NU could help inoculate students against enslavement to material temptation and counteract the influence of "these sordid, mammon-worship times."[81] Disappointed by his own experience as a Harvard undergraduate, Populist Regent Carl Vrooman also believed that KSAC's liberal arts courses could dissuade students from becoming "materialistic and cynical."[82] Indeed, after the Populist reorganization of the college, KSAC students could still opt for a general course featuring English, history, science, and mathematics.

Populists were not opposed to traditional academic courses as long as these subjects could be harnessed to discourage plutocracy or shrink the cultural distance dividing humble country-dwellers from influential elites. Some of the more intellectually inclined Populists believed that literary courses were necessary to the education of the next generation of movement leaders. Populists expected land-grant colleges to transform the children of farmers and mechanics into representatives, not just of their occupations, but also of their social class and communities of origin. They believed that higher education could promote a more egalitarian society by endowing these young people with the social and political status that was earlier associated with educated cosmopolitans. For example, a Kansas Populist urged the state's land-grant college to provide young people from humble backgrounds with similar sort of knowledge "as can be learned in the schools and universities of the foremost army-ridden countries of Europe."[83]

Populists also increased offerings in the social sciences at land-grant institutions under their control, because they believed that these courses would empower the children of farmers and mechanics to protect their parents from exploitation. Many Populists recognized that a narrow emphasis on utilitarian and manual training courses could become a double-edged sword. Vocational education promised to elevate the status of America's producers, but did not necessarily encourage students to negotiate for better financial terms or to participate confidently in a democratic society. Indeed, a utilitarian curriculum could have an altogether different emphasis. For instance, a committee of state legislators hoped that the new Georgia Institute of Technology would "stop drift the drift towards communism, and insure subordination to law and order in all classes."[84] Years before John Dewey and Jane Addams translated similar ideas into more refined language, leaders of State Farmers' Alliances and Populist Parties advocated for an expansive vision of vocational education that included substantial and critically inclined offerings in political economy. Conventional wisdom held that increasing agricultural productivity would improve the condition of farmers, whereas Populists believed that cutting-edge social science proved that lawyers and bankers drained profits away from the rural masses. The *Nebraska Independent* exalted that training the children of farmers and mechanics "in the higher powers of analysis, science and organization" would doom any efforts to monopolize higher learning for the benefit of the "privileged classes."[85] The *Weekly Commoner* of Washington State argued that limiting the education of farmers to vocational subjects would doom rural youth to remain "mere hewers of wood and drawers of water."[86] At KSAC, Populist President Thomas Elmer Will declared that those who opposed teaching political economy to farmers were akin to masters who opposed the education of slaves. Will accused capitalists of supporting narrow vocational training in order to educate "blind Samsons, left to grind through life in the prison house of the modern Philistines of wealth." KSAC's Populist board of regents and the Populist press of Kansas agreed with this assessment.[87]

Populists hoped that rural youth who received a broader form of vocational higher education would continue to identify with the producing classes and return home to advance the political interests of their communities. The *Progressive Farmer*, for example, editorialized that farmers' lack of higher education handicapped them in a political sphere that was dominated by lawyers and doctors. "Any class that is not educated," stated the paper, was "at the mercy of all educated classes."[88] Hamlin Garland, who lectured on behalf of the Farmers' Alliance and People's Party, illustrated this vision of higher education in his novel *A Spoil of Office*. Garland told the story of Bradley Talcott, a farm laborer who became a Populist politician. After realizing that "a feller ought o' know how to speak at a school meetin' when he's called on," Bradley saved up in order to attend a small-town seminary. Ultimately, Bradley flourished in the seminary's rhetoric class and debating club, attended law school, and ran successfully for public office. Garland's fictional account of Bradley mirrored the experience of Populist leaders such as William Jennings Bryan, who honed their oratorical skills during college courses and extracurricular activities.[89]

Nevertheless, vocational courses remained at the heart of the Populist vision for land-grant colleges—but not just because they were supposed to attract the masses and provide practical training. Populists hoped that utilitarian courses could prevent privileged as well as humble students from becoming corrupted by their time in college. With regard to children of the professional classes, Populists hoped that vocational courses could blur the distinctions which encouraged them to exploit the labor of farmers and mechanics. Populists predicted that college students from elite backgrounds would be less likely to feel superior or heartless if they were required to take some practical courses, especially those involving manual labor. In this spirit, NCCAMA pledged to increase labor's "respectability."[90] At NU, Chancellor Canfield supported a college-wide vocational course requirement, because he agreed that agricultural students would be stigmatized if no other students worked with their hands. Unless all students worked in the university's shops or fields, Canfield feared that agricultural students would feel that they were told to "go over there in the corner and stay there."[91] The *Nebraska Independent* went so far as to forecast that NU's vocational courses could destroy "the old division of mankind into wealth producers and wealth consumers."[92] During its Populist period, KSAC broadcast similar messages. A graduate of the college boasted that KSAC taught students to be "imbued with a deeper and more wholesome respect for the average walks of life." After the end of the Populist era, the KSAC catalog continued to state that physical work "awakens and deepens sympathy with industry and toil" and "impresses the student with the essential dignity of labor."[93]

Vocational curricula also attracted Populist support, because these courses could theoretically preserve the moral virtue and class identity of the college-educated children of the producing classes. Many Populists believed that emphasizing A&M subjects was the only way to prevent higher education from alienating rural students from their wholesome roots. Populists feared that a curriculum which exclusively comprised the liberal arts would estrange young people from manual labor and transform them into members of parasitical professions, such as law and banking. These concerns echoed a time-honored tradition—many advocates for vocational education expressed a romanticized vision of manual labor and claimed that classical colleges directed students away from the ranks of noble producers.[94] Senator Justin Morrill, for example, believed that colleges were graduating too many lawyers and bankers rather than workers who "do not produce, vend, or consume luxuries."[95] Populists joined this chorus. A Populist editor in Mississippi complained that the state's A&M college neglected vocational training and "educated our boys out of the ranks of the producers into those of consumers."[96] An ally of the North Carolina Farmers' Alliance agreed that agricultural higher education would bolster "the manhood of the yeoman," whereas traditional higher education taught "the smith to despise his anvil and the clodhopper to look with contempt upon the plow."[97]

Those Populists who were most interested in higher education supported vocational courses, in part, because they were supposed to encourage land-grant college graduates to remain associated with agrarian or industrial labor.[98] Leonidas L. Polk explained that vocational courses would help land-grant college students to "keep sympathy with the interests they are being educated to benefit."[99] At NCCAMA's opening, therefore, President Alexader Holladay assured Polk's allies that the school would teach students to pursue an "honest living" instead of careers "secured by doubtful methods and modern tricks of the trade."[100] When discussing the higher education of women, Populists also recommended applied training in domestic science in order to reinforce an attachment to labor, rather than courses where young women merely learned how to "smile, sing, recline, and languish."[101] Populists believed that land-grant colleges, if conducted in this spirit, could minimize the gulf that separated workers and elites. They hoped that the graduates of these institutions would identify to some extent with the struggles of the so-called "producing classes" rather than focusing primarily on obtaining (or preserving) their own status as professionals.

However, this vision of land-grant education conflicted with the aspirations of most students and with the credentialing function of the college degree. A few students attended college in order to maintain close-contact agricultural or industrial labor.[102] Instead, most students hoped to achieve or reinforce middle-class status by entering a commercial or professional field.[103] Regardless of the extent to which the college curriculum might honor manual labor, the diploma elevated graduates into holding privileged occupations.[104] Similar to most boosters of A&M education, Populists were slow to realize that white-collar occupations had become the fastest growing sector of the labor market.[105] Populists also failed to realize that many students preferred liberal arts education in order to increase their career options by delaying vocational specialization.[106]

Regardless of whether they were in regions with strong Populist organizations, land-grant colleges struggled to attract students to courses in agriculture—the subject dearest to the movement. Farming provided deep satisfaction; rural life also entailed long hours, hard labor, and financial volatility.[107] Many students attended college precisely in order to escape the strain and insecurity of farming. The president of the Colorado State Agricultural College argued that Populist rhetoric about the superiority of farming rang hollow, because all people wanted to work less, earn more, and abandon the "slave life of labor."[108] A member of the first class of NCCAMA decided to enter school, because he was tired of hollering at an uncooperative mule.[109] A student at the University of Nebraska reported that the agricultural college was viewed with "contempt" and that "nobody went back to the farm."[110]

Enrollment and occupational trends confirm these observations. During the Populist administration of KSAC, just 10–15 percent of students opted for the agricultural track. In each of NCCAMA's graduating classes from 1898 through 1901, only two students took a full agricultural course of study.[111] Land-grant institutions produced growing numbers of engineers and teachers nationwide; whereas by 1900, less than 2 percent of their graduates engaged in farming or other agricultural pursuits. Between 1889 and 1922, the most common occupation for graduates of

A&M colleges consisted of some form of commercial activity, followed by teaching, and then engineering.[112] Even within the pool of students who decided to take agriculture courses, roughly half ultimately worked in other fields.[113]

Among the small number of students who worked in agriculture after having attended land-grant colleges, the ambiguity of that vocation frustrated Populist hopes that land-grant colleges could muddy the distinction between laborers and professionals. Despite Populists' monolithic use of the term, the manner in which "farmer" encompassed field hands as well as managers obscured the extent to which graduates of agricultural colleges constituted a privileged class.[114] Unimpressed by romantic Populist rhetoric about the wholesomeness of the rural work ethic, most students pursuing agricultural courses were preparing to supervise the labor of others. Land-grant courses that were tailored to women students also tended to assume that graduates would hire assistants to perform the most menial tasks.[115] In general, agricultural colleges promoted large-scale commercial production managed by experts rather than the small-scale owner-operated farms idealized by Populists.[116] The NCCAMA catalog, for example, announced that the college's agricultural courses taught students to supervise "the great army of uneducated muscle which constitutes our farm hands."[117] The North Carolina A&M College for the Colored Race also advertised that its graduates could manage farms and handle unskilled laborers.[118] The KSAC *Industrialist* reprinted an article arguing that native-born white farm youth should train to become effective employers of immigrant laborers from Italy and China.[119] At least as many graduates of land-grant agricultural programs in North Carolina and Kansas became salaried managers or experts rather than working farmers.[120] Perhaps because of their inability to afford fertile land of their own, 60 percent of students taking agriculture courses in land grant colleges between 1889 and 1922 proceeded to postgraduate study—more than double the percentage of arts and science students who continued their formal education.[121]

Anecdotal evidence suggests that Populist students contributed to the exodus of educated country youth from the ranks of agricultural labor. Even though children of Populist parents often attended rallies, marched in parades, sang campaign songs, delivered speeches, and sold newspaper subscriptions, they did not pledge their lives to farming, especially after having attended college.[122] A Populist sympathizer and son of a Wisconsin Granger, Hamlin Garland recalled that the local institution of higher education "gave farmers' boys like myself the opportunity of meeting those who were older, finer, more learned than they, and every day was to me like turning a fresh and delightful page in a story book, not merely because it brought new friends, new experiences, but because it symbolized freedom from the hayfork and the hoe." Garland and his brother spent only a year attending the seminary, but it was enough to place "the rigorous, filthy drudgery of the farm-yard in sharp contrast with the care-free companionable existence led by my friends in the village."[123] Frank O'Connell, who grew up in a family of Nebraska Populist farmers, wanted to attend college in order to become an engineering expert. Frank told his brother of his intention to pursue a college degree in order to "be a perfessor. Teach the lunks around here how." Full of ambition, Frank eventually moved to New York City, took a self-help course from Dale Carnegie, and pledged "to become a leader or to hold any worth-while position."[124] Mamie Boyd, a KSAC student with a Populist background, eventually became a journalist. During the heyday of Populism at KSAC, even a self-proclaimed radical student graduated and promptly started working for a bank.[125]

Many rural parents, Populists, and conservatives alike encouraged their children to pursue courses that could train them for nonfarm careers. According to the president of Arkansas Industrial University, most parents wanted their sons to "take the course of study that will best open the way for distinction. Hence preference is given to the classics, to literature, oratory, etc."[126] Indeed, even Daniel McKay, a proud farmer engaged in North Carolina agrarian politics, told Leonidas L. Polk that he hoped his children would learn "*anything* else but farming." McKay told Polk that if he had sons, he would "*break their legs* if they had any inclination that way."[127] Hamlin Garland's mother supported his desire to raise himself "above the commonplace level of neighborhood life."[128] Frank O'Connell's Populist mother was also determined that her children attend college so that they might "amount to something." She did not let her anger at "nasty bankers" prevent her from hoping that a college education could transform her son into "a doctor—or an engineer, lawyer, or the like" or even take him "right to the top in some big corporation or the like of that."[129]

Since the goal of dignifying work seemed irrelevant to many students, most land-grant colleges encountered resistance to their manual labor requirements—a core element of the Populist prescription for these institutions. At the Michigan State Agricultural College, the labor program evolved into a meaningless routine of brute farm work and campus maintenance. Resentment toward Professor Samuel Johnson's supervision of this three-hour-a-day requirement boiled over in 1885. After a student had been expelled for repeatedly calling Johnson "Sammy," the ex-student led his classmates to Johnson's house, where he threw the professor to the ground before Mrs. Johnson dispersed the crowd with a horsewhip.[130] At land-grant colleges across the nation, many professors of agriculture opposed manual labor sessions, because they drained students' intellectual energies and reduced the resources available for scientific experimentation. By 1898, the Association of American Agricultural Colleges and Experiment Stations resolved that land-grant schools should no longer require physical work.[131]

Even schools in Populist regions eventually abolished these requirements. At NCCAMA, a policy mandating that all freshman work on the college farm was discontinued in 1895. Attempts to inspire enthusiasm by awarding a medal to the most hard-working student could not prevent students from shirking their responsibilities or flinging produce and clods of dirt at each other. Within ten years of its founding, NCCAMA evolved into a traditional academic and preprofessional school.[132] According to Chancellor Canfield, manual training was also a "bugaboo" among NU faculty, who believed that it would lower the "tone" of the institution and displace other courses. A faculty committee expressed concern that requiring manual training might discourage prospective students and decrease support for the university among "some of the best people of the state." Ultimately, manual labor became optional for liberal arts students after the end of Canfield's tenure in office.[133] Despite its Populist administration, KSAC converted manual labor in its agriculture course into an elective after the first year. According to school newspapers, many KSAC students exhibited a prejudice against labor.[134]

The demise of manual training requirements was merely the most visible symptom of the failure of Populist advocacy for a synthesis of labor and professionalism. Despite Populist hopes that vocational education could meld elite and mass forms of higher learning, schools continued to reinforce these distinctions. Although land-grant universities established a new class of professional agriculturalists and engineers, the increased status of these occupations did not fundamentally alter the elitism that was inherent in higher education. Indeed, the Carnegie Foundation for the Advancement of Teaching would instruct land-grant colleges to differentiate between "agriculture as a profession and farming as a trade."[135]

Conclusion

Populists endorsed the classic goals of accessibility and practicality, albeit with more radical (perhaps demagogic) objectives and overtones than most land-grant administrators.[136] The history of the movement highlights how Populist interpretations of these land-grant functions competed against other visions of the Morrill Act. Populists promoted minimal admission requirements and widespread remediation, and stood opposed to requiring four years of high school. Populists demanded free tuition or generous scholarships, whereas some commentators complained that these policies were inappropriate uses of public funds. Populists lobbied for increasing the study of applied subjects, whereas many land-grant presidents promoted pure science and training for prestigious professions.

The mission of the land-grant university, as we understand it today, evolved from a fractious but productive relationship between these Populist and elitist perspectives on access and curriculum. Land-grant institutions continued to seek increased college access among disadvantaged students, though they emphasized expanding opportunity rather than the Populists' zero-sum rhetoric of class tension. Populists insisted on wide access to regular undergraduate seats, whereas land-grant institutions have increasingly advertised the public contributions of their research expertise and extension programs rather than attendance in the university proper.[137] Land-grant colleges have always modified or co-opted Populist demands for access and practicality, and the movement has communicated a fundamental hopefulness about higher learning that remains integral to these most celebrated contours of the land-grant mission.

In contrast, the movement's desire to use land-grant colleges as tools of class "leveling" has virtually disappeared. The movement believed that colleges could mobilize students on behalf of the collective interests of farmers and mechanics. This aspect of their vision was ambitious and perhaps misguided; Populists hoped that trade training at the college level could erode status inequalities between professional and physical occupations. Land-grant institutions have expanded the number of professional occupations and widened the pipeline to these jobs, but rarely have they encouraged students to reject upward mobility or question the line separating professionals from workers. Students would either attend relatively prestigious institutions (with land-grant status or not) where they were inclined to migrate into (or remain within) the professional class, or they would earn second-class vocational credentials at other schools. Increases in overall college access could assuage some Populist anxieties, whereas persistent concerns over this inherent elitism fueled questions about the legitimacy of social and political status predicated on higher education. To be sure, the goal of training leaders for marginalized communities has lingered to a certain degree—undoubtedly, land-grant institutions are gratified when graduates from humble roots become hometown leaders. However, compared with the regional, national, and international scope of the land-grant university, even this aspect of the Populist vision can seem quaint.[138] However, it was this sort of belief in the potential of public colleges to mitigate inequalities of status and power that encouraged Populists to promote other, more enduring, egalitarian aspects of the early land-grant mission.

Notes

1. The ideological and organizational diversity of Populism has generated substantial debate over which regions, leaders, policies, and/or political strategies have represented the purest form of the movement. However, it was the Populists' fundamental antielitism that formed the core of their vision of land-grant colleges. It is appropriate, therefore, for this article to employ a fairly broad definition of the movement, including members and fellow travelers of the Grange, Farmers' Alliance, Populist Party, and "fusion" coalitions. Due to length limitations, this article does not discuss the Grange, an organization whose influence peaked before the heyday of the Alliance and the Populist Party. For definitions of Populism, see Charles Postel, *The Populist Vision* (New York: Oxford University Press, 2007); Michael Kazin, *The Populist Persuasion: An American History* (Ithaca, NY: Cornell University Press, 1998).

2. This subject is analyzed with greater detail in Scott Gelber, *The University and the People: Envisioning American Higher Education in an Era of Populist Protest* (Madison: University of Wisconsin Press, 2011).

3. For a classic treatment, see Merle Curti and Vernon Carstensen, *University of Wisconsin: A History, 1848-1925* (Madison: University of Wisconsin Press, 1949). For a discussion of "grassroots" visions of state universities, also see Laurence R. Veysey, *The Emergence of the American University* (Chicago, IL: University of Chicago Press, 1965), 70–72.

4. John R. Thelin, *A History of American Higher Education* (Baltimore, MD: Johns Hopkins University Press, 2004), 171. Also see Daniel A. Clark, *Creating the College Man: American Mass Magazines and Middle-Class Manhood, 1890–1915* (Madison: University of Wisconsin Press, 2010), 122.

5. Frederick Jackson Turner, "Pioneer Ideals and the State University," *The Frontier in American History* (Huntington, NY: Krieger, 1976), 282; Jana Nidiffer and Jeffrey P. Bouman, "The Chasm Between Rhetoric and Reality: The Fate of the 'Democratic Ideal' When a Public University Becomes Elite," *Educational Policy* 15 (July 2001): 437. G. F. Mellen, *Popular Errors Concerning Higher Education in the United States and the Remedy* (Leipsic, OH: Gressner & Schramm, 1890), 46–47; Curti and Carstensen, *University of Wisconsin*, 492.

6. Hal Bridges, "D.H. Hill and Higher Education in the New South," *Arkansas Historical Quarterly* 15 (Summer 1956): 117–18; John Thelin, "Higher Education's Student Financial Aid Enterprise in Historical Perspective," in *Footing the Tuition Bill: The New Student Loan Sector*, ed. Frederick M. Hess (Washington, DC: American Enterprise Institute, 2007), 21; Eldon L. Johnson, "Misconceptions about the Early Land grant Colleges," *Journal of Higher Education* 52 (July–August 1981): 338.

7. Thomas J. Giddens, "Origins of State Scholarship Programs: 1647–1913," *College and University* 46 (Fall 1970): 37–45.

8. Applicants for admission who arrived in Raleigh without sufficient money were preemptively rejected. NCCAMA faculty meeting minutes of December 2, 1889 and January 12, 1892, Chancellors Office, North Carolina State University Archives and Special Collections (hereafter NC Fac Mins).

9. See, for example, *Catalogue of the Kansas State Agricultural College, 1893–94*, 66 (hereafter KSAC Catalog).

10. *Atlanta Constitution*, November 17, 1894, 7.

11. *Nebraska Independent*, March 13, 1902, 4.

12. *Nebraskan*, February 26, 1897, 1–2.

13. *Nebraska Independent*, March 13, 1902, 4, October 14, 1897, 4, and October 21, 1897, 4.

14. Alvin Johnson, *Pioneer's Progress* (New York: Viking, 1952), 81–87. Also see "Canfield to All Students," October 2, 1894, James H. Canfield General Correspondence, 1891–1895, James Hulme Canfield Papers, Archives, and Special Collections, University of Nebraska-Lincoln Libraries.

15. *Wealth Makers of the World*, May 10, 1894, 3.

16. Thomas Dyer, *The University of Georgia: A Bicentennial History, 1785–1985* (Athens: The University of Georgia Press, 1985), 124–25; Elisha Benjamin Andrews, "Eastern Universities and Western," *The Independent* 57 (July–December 1904): 676. Also see Nidiffer and Bouman, "The Chasm between Rhetoric and Reality," 439.

17. Harrison Hale, *University of Arkansas, 1871–1948* (Fayetteville: University of Arkansas Press, 1948), 57–60.

18. Although the state legislature of 1887 rejected two proposals for free tuition at NCCAMA, it limited tuition to $20, required the college to grant 120 scholarships, and authorized the college president to accept promissory notes in lieu of tuition. Including living expenses, annual student costs ranged from $100 to $130, which was half the cost of attending UNC. *Progressive Farmer*, February 10, 1886, 4–5 and March 3, 1887, 4; untitled document dated March 2, 1887, "Legislation" box, UA50.1.14, North Carolina State University Archives; NCCAMA Trustee Meeting Minutes of May 22, 1889 and December 5, 1889, North Carolina State University Archives and Special Collections (hereafter NC Trustees Mins); Catalog of the North Carolina College of Agriculture and Mechanic Arts, *1890*, 38, 41–42 (hereafter NCCAMA Catalog). *North Carolina General Assembly, Public Laws, Regular Session, March 7, 1887*, 469; *Biennial Report of the Superintendent of Public Instruction of North Carolina, 1887–88*, 116.

19. *Biennial Report of the Board of Curators of the University of the State of Missouri, 1895–1896*, 16; *Biennial Report of the Board of Curators of the University of the State of Missouri, 1897–1898*, 10, 22.

20. *Farmers' Alliance*, March 7, 1891, 4. *Compiled Statutes of the State of Nebraska, 1922* (Columbia, MO: E.W. Stephens, 1922), sec. 6727.

21. F. S. Snow to C. S. Gleed, September 30, 1893, Chancellor's Office, Francis H. Snow, Correspondence—Regents et al., Spencer Research Library, University of Kansas; *Student's Journal*, May 4, 1894, 2; F. H. Snow to C. F. Scott, November 3, 1894,

box 16, Chancellor's Office, Francis Huntington Snow, General Correspondence, Spencer Research Library, University of Kansas; *Jeffersonian*, November 8, 1894, 4 and November 29, 1894, 2.

22. Untitled Typescript, 189(5), William Henry Sears Papers, Kansas State Historical Society, box 1, Letterbook, 239–42; *Jeffersonian*, January 28, 1897, 2.

23. Robert Manley, *Centennial History of the University of Nebraska*, vol. 1 (Lincoln: University of Nebraska Press, 1969), 114.

24. Record of the Proceedings of the Board of Regents of the University of Nebraska, vol. 4, April 9, 1901, NU archives; *Biennial Report of the University of Nebraska Board of Regents, 1900–02*, 9 (hereafter NU Report); *Nebraska Independent*, September 12, 1901, 4, October 3, 1901, 1, October 24, 1901, 1, and October 31, 1901, 1.

25. *Proceedings of the Annual Convention of American Agricultural Colleges and Experiment Stations, 1896*, 19 (hereafter AACES Proceedings).

26. James E. Pollard, *History of the Ohio State University: The Story of its First Seventy-Five Years, 1873–1948* (Columbus: The Ohio State University Press, 1952), 37–39; Michael Dennis, *Lessons in Progress: State Universities and Progressivism in the New South, 1880–1920* (Urbana: University of Illinois Press, 2001), 4, 92–93; AACES Proceedings, 1897, 61; University of New Hampshire, *History of the University of New Hampshire, 1866–1941* (Durham, NH: University of New Hampshire Press, 1941), 117–20.

27. *Progressive Farmer*, November 24, 1886, 3.

28. NCCAMA Catalog, 1890, 39–40.

29. NC Fac Mins, December 30, 1889, January 27, 1890, February 10, 1890, and October 27, 1891; *Annual Report of the North Carolina College of Agriculture and Mechanic Arts, 1890*, 4 (NCCAMA Report); NC Trustees Mins, June 17, 1891 and December 3, 1891. These requirements situated NCCAMA within the lowest tier of land-grant colleges in terms of admission standards. AACES Proceedings, 1896, 19.

30. NCCAMA Catalog, 1901, 14; NC Trustee Mins, August 2, 1899; NC Fac Mins, March 5, 1900. NCCAMA Report, 1899–1900, 6; *Progressive Farmer*, September 12, 1899, 2. Until 1907, North Carolina did not have a statewide network of high schools. Louis R. Wilson, *The University of North Carolina, 1900–1930: The Making of a Modern University* (Chapel Hill: University of North Carolina Press, 1957), 22.

31. Eliot was representing the "Committee of Ten," a prestigious panel on admissions standards that was sponsored by the National Education Association. *Industrialist*, June 23, 1894, 163 and October 1898, 558–62; *Manhattan Republic*, September 10, 1897, 75–76.

32. *Nationalist*, October 7, 1897, 2, October 21, 1898, 2, and November 18, 1898, 2.

33. *The University of Nebraska Industrial College: A Brief Historical Sketch* (Lincoln: The University of Nebraska, 1892), 12–13. The Industrial College required the same number of high school credits, though it required fewer English and foreign language credits and more science credits. Minutes of April 11, 1900, Record of the Proceedings of the Board of Regents of the University of Nebraska, vol. 4, Archives and Special Collections, University of Nebraska-Lincoln Libraries (hereafter NU Regents Mins).

34. NU Report, 1887–1888, 10–11.

35. LaVon M. Gappa, "Chancellor James Hulme Canfield: His Impact on the University of Nebraska, 1891–1895" (Ph. D. diss., University of Nebraska, Lincoln, 1985), 43, 45; *Nebraska State Journal*, July 12, 1891; Manley, *Centennial History of the University of Nebraska*, 114–16.

36. Canfield to Examiners, September 8, 1892, James H. Canfield General Correspondence, 1891–1895, James Hulme Canfield Papers, Office of the Chancellor, Archives and Special Collections, University of Nebraska-Lincoln Libraries.

37. *Nebraska Independent*, May 20, 1897, 4, June 10, 1897, 4, June 17, 1897, 3, September 2, 1897, 4, September 23, 1897, 4, September 30, 1897, 4; December 29, 1898, 4, and January 26, 1899, 3.

38. *Journal of Proceedings and Addresses of the National Educational Association, 1886*, 290 (hereafter NEA Proceedings); Joseph L. Henderson, *Admission to College by Certificate* (New York: Teachers College, 1912), 73, 83; NEA Proceedings, 1877, 71.

39. Pollard, *History of the Ohio State University*, 43. Also see James Gray, *The University of Minnesota, 1851–1951* (Minneapolis: University of Minnesota Press, 1951), 49; Dennis, *Lessons in Progress*, 76, 92, 112–13.

40. AACES Proceedings, 1897, 59.

41. However, universities typically continued to offer similar remedial courses in some form or another for years after the official closure of preparatory departments. Henderson, *Admission to College by Certificate*, 82; Harold Wechsler, *The Qualified Student: A History of Selective College Admissions in America* (New York: Wiley, 1977), 6, 11, 21.

42. Frederick Rudolph, *The American College and University* (New York: Knopf, 1962), 284.

43. Attendance in the KSAC preparatory department increased from 67 in 1896–1897 to 110 in 1898–1899. *Biennial Report of the Kansas State Agricultural College, 1899–1900*, 47 (hereafter KSAC Report); Minutes of the KSAC Board of Regents, Kansas State University Archives, vol. B, March 25, 1898; *Industrialist*, October 1898, 580.

44. NU Regents Mins, vol. 3, June 11, 1890 and June 12, 1890; *Nebraska State Journal*, February 27, 1891, 4; *Farmers Alliance*, March 7, 1891, 4; Report of the Committee Appointed by the General Faculty on Extensions of Courses of Study, June 6, 1893, box 11, folder 86, Papers of the Board of Regents, University of Nebraska, 1869–1910, Archives and Special Collections, University of Nebraska-Lincoln Libraries (hereafter NU Regents Papers); Manley, *Centennial History of The University of Nebraska*, 126.

45. *Hesperian*, February 15, 1894, 2–4; NEA Proceedings, 1889, 384; Gappa, "Chancellor James Hulme Canfield," 182.

46. Untitled clipping, February 10, 189(5), University of Nebraska Newspaper Clippings Scrapbook, 1895–1897, Archives and Special Collections, University of Nebraska-Lincoln Libraries.

47. Johnson, *Pioneer's Progress*, 82; *Nebraskan*, September 27, 1895, 1; Manley, *Centennial History of the University of Nebraska*, 127; George E. MacLean, "Inaugural Address," February 14, 1896, George E. MacLean Papers, Office of the Chancellor, box 1, folder "Speeches," Archives and Special Collections, University of Nebraska-Lincoln Libraries.

48. *Nebraska Independent*, May 13, 1897, 4, May 20, 1897, 4, June 10, 1897, 4, June 17, 1897, 3, September 2, 1897, 4, September 23, 1897, 4, and September 30, 1897, 4.

49. In the West, Populist women also won election to minor political offices, such as school superintendent and register of deeds. Pressure from the southern wing of the movement also dissuaded national Populist organizations from endorsing full legal or political rights for women. Michael L. Goldberg, *An Army of Women: Gender and Politics in Gilded Age Kansas* (Baltimore, MD: Johns Hopkins University Press, 1997); Postel, *The Populist Vision*, 69–101; Maryjo Wagner, "Farms, Families,

and Reform: Women in the Farmers' Alliance and Populist Party" (Ph.D. diss., University of Oregon, 1986), 35–44.

50. Roughly half as many women attended college as men during the heyday of Populism. Barbara Solomon, *In the Company of Educated Women: A History of Women and Higher Education in America* (New Haven, CT: Yale University Press, 1985), 53; Thomas D. Snyder, ed., *120 Years of American Education: A Statistical Portrait* (Washington, DC: National Center for Education Statistics, 1993), 75–76. Also see Andrea G. Radke-Moss, *Bright Epoch: Women and Coeducation in the American West* (Lincoln: University of Nebraska Press, 2008); Lynn D. Gordon, *Gender and Higher Education in the Progressive Era* (New Haven, CT: Yale University Press, 1990). For Populist support of coeducation, see *Industrialist*, April 1899, 212; *Jeffersonian*, October 28, 1897, 2; James E. Hansen II, *Democracy's College in the Centennial State: A History of Colorado State University* (Fort Collins: Colorado State University Press, 1977), 111.

51. *Proceedings of the North Carolina Farmers' State Alliance, 1890*, 35; *Prospectus of the Normal and Industrial School of North Carolina, 1892–93*, 6. Also see Postel, *Populist Vision*, 91.

52. *Nebraska Independent*, February 10, 1898, 4 and March 10, 1898, 4.

53. Judy Green and Jeane Laduke, "Contributors to American Mathematics," in *Women of Science: Righting the Record*, ed. G. Kass-Simon and Patricia Farnes (Bloomington: Indiana University Press, 1990), 127–29.

54. George Thompson Fairchild, "Populism in a State Educational Institution," *American Journal of Sociology* 3 (November 1897): 399.

55. *Peoples Poniard*, October 25, 1895, 1; *Lincoln Independent*, October 4, 1895, 4 and October 11, 1895, 4.

56. Gerald Gaither, *Blacks and the Populist Revolt: Ballots and Bigotry in the "New South."* (Tuscaloosa: University of Alabama Press, [1977], 2005), 36, 76, 112–13, 123–27; Omar Hamid Ali, "Black Populism in the New South, 1886–1898" (Ph.D. diss., Columbia University, 2003).

57. Stuart Noblin, *Leonidas Lafayette Polk: Agrarian Crusader* (Chapel Hill: University of North Carolina Press, 1949), 92; Lawrence Goodwyn, *Democratic Promise: The Populist Moment in America* (New York: Oxford University Press, 1976), 658 n26. After the Second Morrill Act of 1890 required North Carolina to offer some form of A&M education to African Americans, white Populists supported the establishment of the North Carolina Colored Agricultural and Mechanical College (now North Carolina Agricultural and Technical State University) rather than the integration of NCCAMA. Frenise Logan, "The Movement in North Carolina to Establish a State Supported College for Negroes," *North Carolina Historical Review 35* (April 1958): 167–70; Warmouth T. Gibbs, *History of the North Carolina Agricultural and Technical College, Greensboro, North Carolina* (Dubuque, IA: Wm. C. Brown, 1966).

58. KSAC was officially colorblind, but did not graduate a black student until 1899. KSAC Report, 1885–86, 166; James Carey, *Kansas State University: The Quest for Identity* (Lawrence: The Regents Press of Kansas, 1977), 61–62.

59. Thaddeus T. Smith, "Western University: A Ghost College in Kansas" (M.S. thesis, Kansas State College of Pittsburg, 1966), 2–10, 13–23, 27–37, 41–42.

60. Louis R. Harlan, *Separate and Unequal: Public School Campaigns and Racism in The Southern Seaboard States, 1901–1915* (New York: Athenaeum, 1958, 1968); Postel, *Populist Vision*, 61.

61. South Carolina's black land-grant college charged no tuition for children whose parents earned less than $1,000 a year. North Carolina's college admitted all literate students. John F. Potts, *A History of South Carolina State College, 1896–1978*

(Orangeburg: South Carolina State College, 1978), 31; Gibbs, *History of the North Carolina Agricultural and Technical College*, 12.

62. The President of Mississippi's Alcorn State College, for example, reported that nearly half of the school's trustees actually questioned the higher education of African Americans. In contrast, private black colleges, especially those founded by black churches such as the African Methodist Episcopal denomination, could be expected to be more responsive to the wishes of their students and their families. Fred Humphries, "Land-Grant Institutions: Their Struggle for Survival," in *A Century of Service: Land Grant Colleges and Universities, 1890–1990*, ed. Ralph Christy and Lionel Williamson (New Brunswick, NJ: Transaction, 1992); Fred Williams, "The Second Morrill Act and Jim Crow Politics: Land-Grant Education at Arkansas AM&N College, 1890–1927," *History of Higher Education Annual* 18 (1998): 81–92; Leedell W. Neyland, *Historically Black Land-Grant Institutions and the Development of Agriculture and Home Economics, 1890–1990* (Tallahassee: Florida A&M University Foundation, 1990), 19; Henry Drewry and Humphrey Doermann, *Stand and Prosper: Private Black Colleges and Their Students* (Princeton, NJ: Princeton University Press, 2001).

63. Roger L. Williams, *The Origins of Federal Support for Higher Education: George Atherton and the Land grant Movement* (University Park: Pennsylvania State University Press, 1991); Coy F. Cross II, *Justin Smith Morrill: Father of the Land grant Colleges* (East Lansing: Michigan State University Press, 1999).

64. Julie A. Reuben, *The Making of the Modern University: Intellectual Transformation and the Marginalization of Morality* (Chicago, IL: University of Chicago Press, 1996), 62; Veysey, *The Emergence of the American University*, 90; A. J. Angulo, *William Barton Rogers and the Idea of MIT* (Baltimore, MD: The Johns Hopkins University Press, 2009); Roy V. Scott, *The Reluctant Farmer: The Rise of Agricultural Extension to 1914* (Urbana: University of Illinois Press, 1970), 29.

65. Accustomed to managing their fields according to intuition and experience, farmers had often expressed ambivalence toward the science of agriculture, which threatened farmers' prized ethic of self-sufficiency. Advocates of scientific agriculture also tended to promote capital-intensive techniques that could be implemented only by the wealthiest landholders. Agricultural experiment stations directed by A&M colleges also struggled to win farmers' appreciation. Station scientists disappointed farmers whenever they focused on basic research rather than the dissemination of best practices, evaluation of soil samples, and inspection of commercial fertilizers. Alan Marcus, *Agricultural Science and the Quest for Legitimacy: Farmers, Agricultural Colleges, and Experiment Stations, 1870–1890* (Ames: Iowa State University Press, 1985); Margaret Rossiter, *The Emergence of Agricultural Science: Justus Liebig and the Americans, 1840–1880* (New Haven, CT: Yale University Press, 1975).

66. Elizabeth Sanders, *Roots of Reform: Farmers, Workers, and the American State, 1877–1917* (Chicago, IL: University of Chicago Press, 1999), 314–16; Postel, *Populist Vision*, 32, 48, 53–56. Also see Theodore Mitchell, *Political Education in the Southern Farmers' Alliance, 1887–1900* (Madison: University of Wisconsin Press, 1987), 134.

67. D. McKay to LL. Polk, June 12, 1880, Leonidas L. Polk Papers, Southern Historical Collection, Wilson Library, University of North Carolina, box 4, folder 45 (hereafter Polk papers).

68. *Progressive Farmer*, February 10, 1886, 4–5, May 19, 1886, 4, and January 19, 1887, 3.

69. NCCAMA Report, 1890, 10; *North Carolina General Assembly, Public Laws, Regular Session, March 7, 1887*, chap. 410, sec. 9, 718–22; NCCAMA Catalog, 1890, 2–3.

70. "Wilbur Fisk Massey: North Carolina Botanist, Horticulturalist, and Agriculturalist," *Journal of the Elisha Mitchell Scientific Society* 116 (2000): 101–12; Ira O. Schaub, *North Carolina Agricultural Experiment Station: The First 60 Years, 1877–1937* (Raleigh: Agricultural Experimental Station Bulletin, January 1955), 55; "Administration of Dr. W.A. Withers, Acting Director 1897–99" (undated) and "Report and Recommendations of the Director of the Experiment Station and Professor of Chemistry," April 21, 1899, William J. Peele Papers, NCSU Archives.

71. KSAC Report, 1891–1892, 40; KSAC Catalog, 1881–1882, 13–14; *College Symposium of the Kansas Agricultural College* (Topeka: Hall and O'Donald, 1891), 32; *Industrialist*, January 4, 1897, 69.

72. *Jeffersonian*, June 24, 1897, 2. Also see *Manhattan Republic*, April 30, 1897, 4; Ralph Sparks, "To Serve the People: The Populist Era at Kansas State," unpublished manuscript, Kansas State University Special Collections.

73. *Industrialist*, July 15, 1897, 161, August 16, 1897, 171, January 1898, 56–61, and May 1899, 301–18; KSAC Report, 1897–1898, 1, 4, 37–38, 43; KSAC Report, 1899–1900, 26–27.

74. *Industrialist*, February 1899, 123.

75. Robert P. Crawford, *These Fifty Years: A History of the College of Agriculture of the University of Nebraska* (Lincoln: University of Nebraska Press, 1925), 56–57; Thomas R. Walsh, "Charles E. Bessey and the Transformation of the Industrial College," *Nebraska History* 52 (1971): 395–96, 404–5; *The University of Nebraska Industrial College*, 16.

76. Entries dated September 8, 1891, December 9, 1891, and December 10, 1891, James Canfield's Chancellor's Journal, James Hulme Canfield Papers, Office of the Chancellor, Archives and Special Collections, University of Nebraska-Lincoln Libraries (hereafter Canfield journal); Gappa, "Chancellor James Hulme Canfield," 126–27, 186.

77. *Nebraska State Journal*, April 1, 1893, 3; *Nebraska Independent*, October 14, 1897, 4, October 21, 1897, 4, and September 8, 1898, 4, 6; Manley, *Centennial History of the University of Nebraska*, 117–19.

78. "Preliminary Report of the Committee on Agricultural Education in the University," April 11, 1900, NU Regents Papers, box 14, folder 115; NU Report, 1901–1902, 8, 13–14.

79. *Industrialist*, April 1899, 213; *Manhattan Republic*, February 19, 1897, 4. Populists were not unanimous on this point. See *Manhattan Republic*, September 10, 1897, 1.

80. *Progressive Farmer*, February 10, 1886, 4–5, February 17, 1886, 4, April 21, 1886, 4, July 28, 1886, 4, July 7, 1886, 3, and October 13, 1886, 4.

81. *Wealth Makers of the World*, November 8, 1894, 8. Also see Caroline Winterer, *The Culture of Classicism: Ancient Greece and Rome in American Intellectual Life, 1780–1910* (Baltimore, MD: Johns Hopkins University Press, 2002).

82. Helen M. Cavanaugh, *Carl Schurz Vrooman: A Self-Styled "Constructive Conservative"* (Chicago, IL: Lakeside, 1977), 19.

83. *Topeka Advocate*, February 3, 1897, 2. Also see *Nebraska Independent*, December 29, 1898, 4, and January 26, 1899, 3.

84. Herbert Kliebard, *Schooled to Work: Vocationalism and the American Curriculum, 1876–1946* (New York: Teachers College Press, 1999); Robert C. McMath, Jr. et al., *Engineering the New South: Georgia Tech, 1885–1985* (Athens: University of Georgia Press, 1985), 18.

85. Mitchell, *Political Education in the Southern Farmers' Alliance*, 135–38; *Nebraska Independent*, June 15, 1899, 4.

86. *Weekly Commoner*, March 26, 1897, 4 and May 12, 1899, 4; George A. Frykman, *Creating the People's University: Washington State University, 1890–1990* (Pullman: Washington State University Press, 1990), 32.

87. *Industrialist*, May 1899, 301–18; KSAC Report, 1893–1894, 10; *Manhattan Republic*, April 8, 1898, 4; *Kansas Commoner*, October 21, 1897, 4. Also see T. E. Will to J. Walters, April 10, 1909, Thomas Elmer Will Papers, Kansas State University Archives, Folder 5 (hereafter Will papers); KSAC Catalog, 1896–1897, 31.

88. *Progressive Farmer*, September 17, 1895, 2.

89. Hamlin Garland, *A Spoil of Office* (Boston, MA: Arena, 1892), 30. Regarding Garland's political sympathies, see Postel, *Populist Vision*, 231. On Bryan, see George R. Poage, "College Career of William Jennings Bryan," *The Mississippi Valley Historical Review* 15 (September 1928): 177–80.

90. NCCAMA Catalog, 1890, 10.

91. *Canfield Journal*, May 4, 1893.

92. *Nebraska Independent*, June 15, 1899, 4.

93. "Farewell: Address on behalf of the Alumni Association of the KSAC," Will papers, folder 9; *Industrialist*, October 1898, 558–62; KSAC Catalog, 1900–1901, 24.

94. Both radicals and conservatives endorsed the idea that physical labor provided the backbone of morality. Daniel T, Rodgers, *The Work Ethic in Industrial America, 1820–1920* (Chicago, IL: The University of Chicago Press, 1978), xi, 211–13; Kliebard, *Schooled to Work*, 1–25.

95. Joseph F. Kett, *The Pursuit of Knowledge Under Difficulties: From Self-Improvement to Adult Education in America, 1750–1990* (Stanford, CA: Stanford University Press, 1994), 230–31.

96. *Chickasaw Messenger*, June 28, 1888, 1.

97. *Caucasian*, December 18, 1890, 2.

98. *Progressive Farmer*, February 10, 1886, 4–5 and July 26, 1898, 1.

99. *Progressive Farmer*, July 21, 1887, 4.

100. *Progressive Farmer*, October 15, 1889, 1.

101. *Country Life*, December 1890, 4.

102. *The Weekly Toiler*, February 5, 1890, 1; *Canfield Journal*, October 3, 1891.

103. Burton J. Bledstein, *The Culture of Professionalism: The Middle Class and the Development of Higher Education in America* (New York: Norton, 1976); David K. Brown, *Degrees of Control: A Sociology of Educational Expansion and Occupational Credentialism* (New York: Teachers College Press, 1995), 138–39; David F. Labaree, *The Making of an American High School: The Credentials Market and the Central High School of Philadelphia, 1838–1939* (New Haven, CT: Yale University Press, 1988).

104. Kett, *Pursuit of Knowledge under Difficulties*, 230–31, 511 n22.

105. Especially after 1890, the growth in higher education occurred primarily in the fields of teacher training, law, and medicine. Colin B. Burke, *American Collegiate Populations: A Test of the Traditional View* (New York: New York University Press, 1982), 221–22.

106. See, for example, *Student Herald* (KSAC), January 29, 1896, 4.

107. Pamela Riney-Kehrberg, *Childhood on the Farm: Work, Play, and Coming of Age in the Midwest* (Lawrence: University Press of Kansas, 2005), 79–81, 203–6; Liahna Babener, "Bitter Nostalgia: Recollections of Childhood on the Midwestern Frontier," in *Small Worlds: Children and Adolescents in America: 1850–1950*, ed. Elliott West and Paula Petrik (Lawrence: University Press of Kansas, 1992).

108. Michael McGiffert, *The Higher Learning in Colorado: A Historical Study, 1860–1940* (Denver: Sage Books, 1964), 101–2.

109. Alice Reagan, *North Carolina State University: A Narrative History* (Ann Arbor, MI: Edwards Brothers, 1987), 1.
110. *The University of Nebraska Semi-Centennial Anniversary Book* (Lincoln: University of Nebraska Press, 1919), 47.
111. O. P. Hood to G. T. Fairchild, February 20, 1898 and J. T. Willard to G. T. Fairchild, May 4, 1899, Kansas State College History in Letters, 1897–1899, Collected and Arranged by J. T. Willard, Kansas State University Archives; William L. Carpenter, *Knowledge is Power: A History of the School of Agriculture and Life Sciences at North Carolina State University, 1877–1984* (Raleigh: North Carolina State University, 1987), 67, 99; Christopher Allen, "The Land Grant Act of 1862 and the Founding of NCCAMA" (M.A. thesis, North Carolina State University, 1984), 87–97; Johnson, "Misconceptions about the Early Land grant Colleges," 339–40.
112. Although graduates contrasted themselves with laborers, early engineering programs, and blurred vocational/professional lines by moving the profession away from its elite roots and closer to a middle-class occupation. Bruce Sinclair, "Episodes in the History of the American Engineering Profession," in *The Professions in History*, ed. Nathan O. Hatch (Notre Dame: University of Notre Dame Press, 1988), 138. Arguably, teacher education, the largest vocational field within many universities, could also be considered a successful example of egalitarian higher education because of the ambiguous class status of teachers. Paul H. Mattingly, *The Classless Profession: American Schoolmen in the Nineteenth Century* (New York: New York University Press, 1975).
113. Burke, *American Collegiate Populations*, 220; Arthur J. Klein, "Survey of Land Grant Colleges and Universities," *United States Office of Education Bulletin*, no. 9 (Washington: Government Printing Office, 1930), 369, 382.
114. Dwight B. Billings Jr., *Planters and the Making of a "New South": Class, Politics, and Development in North Carolina, 1865–1900* (Chapel Hill: University of North Carolina Press, 1979), 72–73.
115. Radke-Moss, *Bright Epoch*, 152–59.
116. Mary Neth, *Preserving the Family Farm: Women, Community, and the Foundations of Agribusiness in the Midwest, 1900–1940* (Baltimore, MD: Johns Hopkins University Press, 1995), 100–106; Rudolph, *American College and University*, 251, 264–65.
117. NCCAMA Catalog, 1890, 14. Also see G. T. Winston to W. H. Page, December 15, 1902, Houghton Library, Harvard University, Walter Hines Page Papers, Letters from Various Correspondents, American Period, bMS Am 1090 (45).
118. *Annual Catalog of the North Carolina Agricultural and Mechanical College for the Colored Race, 1901–02*, 7.
119. *Industrialist*, September 23, 1893, 9.
120. *The Agricultural and Mechanical College Record, 1902*, 109–10; KSAC Report, 1895–1896, 5.
121. Klein, "Survey of Land Grant Colleges and Universities," 357.
122. MaryJo Wagner, "'Helping Papa and Mamma Sing the People's Songs': Children in the Populist Party," in *Women and Farming: Changing Roles, Changing Structures*, ed. Wava G. Haney and Jane B. Knowles (Boulder, CO: Westview Press, 1988), 322–23.
123. Hamlin Garland, *A Son of the Middle Border* (New York: Macmillan, 1941), 197, 205.
124. Frank O'Connell, *Farewell to the Farm* (Caldwell, ID: Caxton Printers, 1962), 117, 135, 190, 195.
125. F. J. Smith to J. T. Willard, March 30, 1937, KSU archives, vertical file, presidents, Thomas Elmer Will, 1897–1899; Mamie Alexander Boyd, *Rode a Heifer Calf through College* (Brooklyn: Pageant-Poseidon, 1972), 94.

126. Hal Bridges, "D.H. Hill and Higher Education in the New South," *Arkansas Historical Quarterly* 15 (Summer 1956), 114.
127. D. McKay to L. L. Polk, July 14, 1880, Polk papers, box 4, folder 46.
128. Garland, *A Son of the Middle Border*, 210.
129. O'Connell, *Farewell to the Farm*, 44, 94, 102, 147, 166.
130. Ray Stannard Baker, *Native American: The Book of My Youth* (New York: Scribner's, 1941), 201; Richard H. Harms, "Farmers vs. Scientists," *Michigan History* 67 (1983), 26–31. Also see Morris Bishop, *A History of Cornell* (Ithaca, NY: Cornell University Press, 1962), 127–28.
131. Marcus, *Agricultural Science and the Quest for Legitimacy*, 33; AACES Proceedings, 1898, 74.
132. Reagan, *North Carolina State University*, 23, 36.
133. *Canfield Journal*, May 4, 1893, May 13, 1893, November 4, 1893, and November 6, 1893; "Report of the Committee Appointed by the General Faculty on Extensions of Courses of Study," June 6, 1893, NU Regents Papers, box 11, folder 86; NU Regents Mins, vol. 3, April 17, 1896.
134. Students still had to perform a few hours of labor as freshmen, when all of them took the same set of basic courses. *Industrialist*, February 2, 1895, 87; *Student Herald*, March 24, 1897, 2 and May 26, 1897, 2; Julius T. Willard Diary, KSU Archives, June 20, 1897; Kansas State Agricultural College Faculty Records, KSU archives, vol. D, November 30, 1897, 31.
135. *Carnegie Foundation for Advancement of Teaching, Fourth Annual Report, 1909*, 103–5.
136. The Populist emphases on accessibility and practicality remain familiar to land-grant university leaders in the twenty-first century. For example, the mission statement of Pennsylvania State University states that the institution provides "unparalled access" and coordinates activities to "generate, disseminate, integrate, and apply knowledge that is valuable to society." It is debatable whether Populists would approve of the actual student bodies and curricula of most land-grant institutions these days. http://www.psu.edu/ur/about/mission.html (accessed September 20, 2011).
137. Even in Kansas, the annual reports of KSAC stopped emphasizing the enrollment of ordinary rural youth. Instead, KSAC added a lengthy section on the "Public Work of the KSAC," which described applied research, open lectures, and bulletins. See KSAC's annual reports between 1900 and 1912. Also see Dennis, *Lessons in Progress*, 28–32. Making matters worse (from the Populist perspective), the research and extension programs of land-grant colleges tended to conform to the interests of large commercial farmers and resisted input from dissident agricultural organizations. Neth, *Preserving the Family Farm*, 100–106.
138. See Lou Anna K. Simon, *Embracing the World Grant Ideal: Affirming the Morrill Act for a Twenty-first-century Global Society* (Lansing: Michigan State University, 2009).

Robert H. Thurston, Modern Engineering Education, and Its Diffusion through Land-Grant Universities

Gregory Zieren

In October 1939, as the world started coming to terms with the opening salvoes of World War II, American engineering educators took time out to celebrate the one-hundredth anniversary of the birth of one of their leaders and forebears. Cornell University and the American Association of Mechanical Engineers jointly sponsored the event and honored Robert H. Thurston, who had died in 1903 at the age of sixty-four. All four universities in which Thurston had studied or taught sent representatives, including Admiral Wilson Brown, superintendent of the US Naval Academy, to memorialize the man who, as one speaker noted, "establish(ed) educational standards and programs that set the pattern for modern engineering education." Representatives from British and Canadian universities also paid tribute to Thurston's powerful influence in fashioning the late nineteenth century curriculum even outside the United States. Stanford University emeritus professor William F. Durand, friend and biographer of Thurston, delivered the keynote address and extolled Thurston's pioneering efforts at Stevens Institute of Technology in the 1870s and at Cornell University after 1885. In a fitting tribute to the spirit of Thurston, guests at the commemoration took part in guided tours of Cornell University's College of Engineering laboratories.[1]

Perspectives on the History of Higher Education 30 (2013): 195–214
© 2013. ISBN: 978-1-4128-5147-3

Robert H. Thurston and Laboratory Instruction

Robert H. Thurston was the father of instructional laboratories for engineering students, first as chair of mechanical engineering at the Stevens Institute of Technology in Hoboken, NJ, and dean of the Engineering College at Cornell University. Born in 1839 in Providence, RI, to a well-to-do family, Thurston grew up spending time in his father's machine works. The firm constructed steam engines and textile machinery, and his time spent there exposed him to what Monte Calvert called "the shop culture" of skilled workmen and hands-on education in making tools and machinery. However, as the scion of a prosperous family who was expected to take over the family business, Thurston also studied mathematics, natural sciences, and languages at Brown University, graduating with a B.S. in the class of 1859. He worked as a salesman for the firm for a year, then quarreled with his father, and promptly left for a two-year apprenticeship at the firm of William Sellers in Philadelphia, a second important center of American machine tool production.[2]

In 1861, Thurston enlisted in the US Navy and met Benjamin F. Isherwood, chief of the Navy's Bureau of Steam Engineering, and the two began a lifelong friendship. Isherwood was one of the Navy's foremost scientific minds, and he conducted exhaustive testing of steam engines for marine purposes in the 1850s. Among a myriad of other Civil War duties, Isherwood recruited engineers to serve in the Navy as it expanded during the Civil War from several dozen steam-powered vessels to its maximum of 600 ships overall by the end of the war.[3]

At the war's end, Isherwood and Vice Admiral David D. Porter, the postwar Superintendent at the US Naval Academy, selected the most talented young engineers from the ranks of young officers and installed them as instructors in a new program to train engineers at Annapolis. A year earlier, the Navy had secured from the Congress an appropriation of $20,000 to build a new facility with classrooms, steam engines, and laboratories for instructional purposes. Earlier, it was decided that all naval cadets take part in engineering training, but the delay in moving the Academy back to Annapolis from its wartime home in Newport, Rhode Island, changed the plans and provided an opportunity for experimenting with the curriculum. The triumph of steam in navies around the world was becoming an accomplished fact, and the nation's foremost institution that was devoted to training naval officers clearly required a curriculum which adapted to the new demands. In a tribute to Isherwood's role in creating the new program, the Navy named its first engineering building

Isherwood Hall, but it is clear that Porter, Thurston, and other instructors also contributed to shaping the two-year program.[4]

In 1866 and 1867, two atypical groups were recruited as subjects to endure the rigors of engineering training. One small group of young mechanics with little or no secondary school academic preparation followed the typical curriculum of mathematics, physics, chemistry, and technical drawing. A larger group of fifteen recent college graduates went through the same program. Only one of the mechanics completed his education and was commissioned as an officer, and all but two of the college graduates succeeded. The lesson to be drawn from the experiment clearly favored the academically trained student compared with the "shop culture" journeyman. Thurston later described his experience: "the practice of basing all engineering work on applied and exact science (would) continue to be the method of the engineer."[5]

Unfortunately for Thurston's career at the Naval Academy and the short-term prospects for effective engineering education there, Isherwood and Porter feuded over the future of the program and the relative status of line versus staff officers. By 1869, both experiments in educating young mechanics and recent college graduates ended. Isherwood lost his battle with Porter and was forced to accept a posting at the Mare Island naval base near San Francisco. Thurston lasted less than two more years without his mentor at Annapolis. The Navy began the reconversion to a mixed sail and steam fleet, and for staff engineers such as Thurston, as Lance Buhl noted, "uncertainty about career status became intense." In 1871, after Porter's departure from Annapolis, engineering education slowly returned to the curriculum as a three-year course in 1873 and a four-year course in 1874. Brendan Foley's study of engineering education at the US Naval Academy has shown that it would become one of the cradles of modern engineering education by the end of the decade, but by then, Thurston had moved on to the decidedly greener pastures of the Stevens Institute of Technology.[6]

The Stevens Institute of Technology was founded in 1871 with a $600,000 bequest from Edwin A. Stevens of steam engine and steam packet fame. The bequest reflected the founder's intention to create a college that was devoted to engineering education, specifically mechanical engineering. President Henry Morton offered Thurston the first chair of mechanical engineering at the new college and gave him virtual carte blanche in designing a curriculum. The first small class began its studies in 1871 and graduated in 1875. Newly recruited faculty such as Thurston and former University of Michigan engineering professor DeVolson Wood dipped into their own resources initially to pay for the basic machinery that was used in instruction. This included a complete set of carpenter's tools, several lathes, a forge, planning and milling machines, and a steam engine. Thurston regarded the collection as basic for his methods. The Stevens endowment helped finance his more ambitious goals, including Thurston's extensive tour of American engineering schools and technical universities in France and Germany. In 1872 and 1873, Thurston spent time between semesters traveling in search of best practice in engineering education. An additional source of revenue to pay travel expenses was the commission to write the four-volume report on the Vienna World's Fair of 1873 for the Federal government. By 1874, he was ready to submit his proposed curriculum to the Stevens Board of Trustees and petition for funds to finance his extensive machinery purchases to stock mechanical engineering laboratories.[7]

Engineering education in post–Civil War America came primarily from the shop culture of machine shops, from mechanics institutes that taught part-time or evening classes, and from a handful of institutions such as Rensselaer Polytechnic Institute and the US Military Academy at West Point that offered postsecondary degrees. However, the emphasis at RPI and USMA was on civil engineering. The Columbia School of Mines, the University of Michigan's engineering program, Yale's Sheffield, and Harvard's Lawrence Science Schools offered instruction in the natural sciences and mathematics, and their graduates often called themselves engineers to describe their skill sets. Mechanical engineering, as distinct from civil engineering, had promising beginnings in the 1870s at several institutions, but there was little consensus on curriculum, length of study, or mode of instruction. Stillman Robinson, by training a civil engineer who had taught at Michigan, began teaching a mechanical course in 1870 at the University of Illinois, but he left for a post at Ohio State University in 1879. About the same time, practical engineer John Edson Sweet inaugurated a mechanical course with laboratory-based instruction at Cornell University. On a much smaller scale, Worcester Polytechnic Institute used workshops to teach students, and then sold the work produced on a contract basis to help pay college costs. By the end of the decade, Allen D. Conover at the University of Wisconsin started a course in mechanical engineering, and in the 1870s, William Barton Rogers and John Runkle at the Massachusetts Institute of Technology planned a curriculum for mechanical engineering that also emphasized the role of laboratories. Still, there seems to have been relatively little influence from one program to another, no consensus on curriculum, and no notion of best practice, therefore no template for future programs in mechanical engineering.[8]

Among the students of engineering education, there is widespread agreement that the *École Polytechnique* in Paris provided the basic model for all types of nineteenth-century engineering schools in the United States, the German States, Austria–Hungary, and Switzerland. Founded in 1794 by French Revolutionaries who were dedicated to providing engineers for both civilian and military applications, the *École* also provided the model for the curriculum of the USMA at West Point and for the Rensselear Polytechnic Institute in 1851, which was the first engineering college in the United States. Students at the *École* spent two years in learning theoretical mathematics and natural science, and then spent another year or two at applied engineering institutions—the *Écoles des Mines*, *École des Ponts et Chaussees*, or *École Centrale des Arts et des Manufactures*. Some of the most brilliant minds in French science, mathematics, and engineering studied or taught at the *École Polytechnique*, and for most nations in search of a training institution for the education of engineers, the Paris school provided the model.[9]

The German States provided a second source of inspiration for Thurston and other early pioneers of engineering education in the United States. Building on the French model, the Duke of Baden founded the first *Technische Hochschule*, or technical university, in Karlsruhe in 1838; schools in Prussia (Berlin and Aachen), Bavaria (Munich), and another in Saxony (Dresden) followed. These institutions differed from the Paris model in significant ways. For example, students typically studied at these institutions for three or four years but they earned certificates, because the *Technische Hochschulen* did not possess degree-granting powers and were not reckoned as equals with traditional universities until 1899. As observed in Kees Gispen's study, the struggle for equal status with the universities drove many of the initiatives of the technical schools. Furthermore, they occupied a place at the highest rank of what Germans called "the dual system," namely the division of common school graduates into academic or vocational tracks in secondary schools. Among their occupational training tasks, the technical universities also filled the need for qualified graduates to teach those vocational students. Despite the limitations of their status within the framework of German higher education, the best of the *Technische Hochschulen* by 1880 were highly respected institutions of higher learning.[10]

Continental examples could inspire and inform Thurston's curriculum, but copying from them was out of the question. By the 1870s, Germany especially had adopted relatively uniform systems of secondary education—systems that were certified by the state to ensure a *Gymnasium* graduate, for instance, had learned Greek, Latin, and perhaps a modern language, had undertaken at least a year of chemistry and physics, and had studied mathematics up to the level of calculus. Though American common or elementary schools in New England, the Middle Atlantic, and Middle Western States had begun to achieve uniform standards of literacy, numeracy, and civics instruction, the status of secondary or grammar schools was still fluid, and only a minority of any age cohort attended, much less graduated from high school. The so-called "Michigan Idea" of accepting high school graduation and preparation of academic subjects as prerequisite for admission to a university was just beginning in the decade. In 1893, Professor George F. Swain of MIT estimated that a student entering his institution was approximately two years behind his German counterpart. The very diversity of American secondary education, split between rural and urban school districts, public and private schools, academy, grammar, or high school, with standards differing from state to state, created a host of problems for Thurston. The solution that Stevens and other engineering schools adopted was to set a list of prerequisites in science and math for admission and further to test candidates in order to determine their skill levels. Later, Stevens, Cornell, and other universities set up special preparatory courses to provide instruction for one or two years to students who failed to pass the entrance exam or whose secondary school training did not satisfy the list of prerequisites.[11]

The primary influence on Thurston in devising the curriculum came from his experience at Annapolis and from practicing engineers. He sent copies of his proposed curriculum to prominent engineers for commentary and revision. Little of the correspondence from this period in his career at the US Naval Academy or the earliest years of his career at Stevens has survived in his manuscript collection at Cornell. His Navy mentor Benjamin F. Isherwood would likely have contributed his ideas and so might have prominent Navy-trained engineer Erasmus D. Leavitt, who later sent his son to Stevens. Thurston's correspondence during the 1880s and 1890s includes exchanges with some of the most notable engineers in the United States, Great Britain, France, Belgium, Germany, and Austria. His network of friends and acquaintances in the science and engineering world was extensive. He was a prominent member and officer of the American Association for the Advancement of Science, and he chaired sessions at their annual meetings in the 1870s on teaching science and mathematics. Moreover, he believed in the educational value of inviting successful engineers to speak to students, and his correspondence is filled with invitations to potential speakers, including Thomas Edison, George Westinghouse, Nicola Tesla, Andrew Carnegie, and many others. In other words, though Thurston recognized the shortcomings of "shop culture" for educating engineers, he was acutely aware of the benefits of hands-on training and learning-by-doing. He sought guidance from practical engineers in fashioning a curriculum of what students needed to learn in order to be successful in their careers.[12]

Thurston devised a four-year curriculum for mechanical engineers that emphasized physical materials in the first year, including concepts such as strength, measures of elasticity, friction, and lubrication; the second year was devoted to tools and tool making, machinery, millwork, power, loads, and power transmission; in the third year, students focused on prime movers, from waterwheels to steam engines, compressed air, and electrical motors; and in the fourth year, students applied this learning to railroads, ships, factories, and foundries and took a course in general business as it applied to practicing engineers. Physics, chemistry, and higher mathematics were integral to the curriculum in the sense that they were taught independently in the first two years and later, in conjunction with engineering applications. Seniors also took part in extensive tours of foundries, factories, shipyards, steel mills, and other industrial facilities to see for themselves the might of industrial America and where they might spend professional careers.[13]

In 1874, when the trustees of Stevens Institute approved Thurston's request to set up a mechanical laboratory and purchase tools, equipment, testing devices, and a steam engine, Thurston's master plan for a distinctive education in mechanical engineering evolved past the efforts of other pioneering educators at Annapolis, Illinois, Cornell, and elsewhere. His conception of using machine tools for instruction offered three clear advantages: First, it fostered a working knowledge of machinery for his students; second, it created opportunities for professors and students to conduct real research and contribute to the progress of engineering; and finally, it provided business and government with a venue to test, design, and develop products and machines. He promoted the first and second objectives by requiring students to complete a senior thesis before their graduation.

With regard to product development, he returned from Europe with an early Otto and Langen piston-driven atmospheric engine. He tested it along with internal combustion engines, compressed air machines, and every variety of steam engine imaginable. In 1875, his dedication to laboratory testing was rewarded when he was selected to serve as secretary on the US Testing Board, a special agency of government that was created to carry out strength tests on iron and steel and metal alloys for use in Navy vessels and Army ordnance. Most of the iron and steel testing was carried out at the Watertown Arsenal in Massachusetts, whereas the nonferrous metal and alloy testing took place at Stevens' laboratories under Thurston's supervision between 1875 and 1877. His inventive skills showed up in his twenties when he patented a magnesium light for use by the Navy. In the 1870s, he invented metal stress testing equipment that was used in laboratories to determine strength and elasticity, created tools to determine coefficients of friction and lubrication testing, to measure power transmission, and to compare engines of all sorts. In other words, in addition to simply familiarizing students with tools and machinery, Thurston's vision of engineering education included scientific testing, primary research, and opportunities for publishing the results. Such characteristics would soon serve as a function of graduate education in engineering, but circumstances at Stevens limited what Thurston could accomplish there.[14]

The Philadelphia Centennial and the Diffusion of Mechanical Engineering Education

Thurston's first opportunity to show off his laboratory and popularize his educational ideas among engineering educators came in 1876 at the Philadelphia Centennial. Alexander Lyman Holley, one of the nation's most distinguished engineers, pioneer of the Bessemer process in the United States, and partner in Andrew Carnegie's Edgar Thomson Steel Works, used his presidential address with regard to the American Institute of Mining Engineers in February 1876 to call for more practical instruction of engineering students as apprentices or interns in private industry. Holley's suggestions were taken up by a combined meeting of the associations of both the AIME and American Society of Civil Engineers in June 1876 and later secured a place on the program of the International Conference on Education in Philadelphia. Holley and Thurston were friends who had together served on the US Testing Board and corresponded on the subject of engineering education. The Stevens laboratory display on the grounds of the Centennial attracted favorable notice from both national and international educators. Thurston also publicized his ideas on the use of laboratories in engineering education in articles in *Scientific American* in 1874 and 1876 and another in *The Journal of the Franklin Institute* in 1875.[15]

A more enduring impetus came in 1879 when a small group of men, including Thurston, Holley, and John Edson Sweet, met in the offices of Jedson Bailey, editor of *The American Machinist*, in New York to promote the creation of a new professional organization of mechanical engineers that was patterned after the associations for civil and mining engineers. In his 1915 history of the American Society of Mechanical Engineers, long-term secretary Frederick Remsen Hutton recognized three factors that fostered the creation of such an organization at precisely that time: first, the growing industrial prowess of the United States in comparison with Great Britain and other nations; second, the brilliant display at the Philadelphia Centennial of the Corliss steam engine and many other technological innovations; and third, the need to direct and promote engineering education at the new land-grant universities which had inaugurated its study but were still experimenting with the curriculum and instruction for mechanical engineering students. Both the preliminary meeting in April and the first convention in October 1880 took place on the grounds of the Stevens Institute. Thurston was elected the ASME's first president and served two terms. The proceedings of the ASME's yearly conference featured papers on education, curriculum, and a variety of topics related to student preparation for mechanical engineers.[16]

In 1879, the federal government provided a second, unexpected boost to the fortunes of laboratory-based engineering instruction when the Congress passed a law permitting the secretary of the Navy to transfer naval officers to academies, colleges, and universities for a four-year term to promote instruction in steam, mechanical, and naval engineering. In 1871, the re-introduction of the engineering curriculum at Annapolis was providing more trained officers than the still stagnant US Navy could employ. The drafters of the 1879 law hoped to enhance the career prospects of participants, foster a curriculum that the Navy might find useful in the future, and promote the Navy's image to the public at large.[17]

During the decade of the 1880s, more than fifty naval officers taught in engineering schools around the country. Many eventually resigned their commissions and became fulltime engineering professors. Colleges and universities that benefited from their services typically used the opportunity to start new courses in mechanical engineering. Laboratory-based instruction as practiced by Annapolis-trained engineers and Thurston at

Stevens received a major boost from the program. Among the universities that took part in the program were Harvard, University of Pennsylvania, Purdue University, the University of Wisconsin, Michigan Agricultural College (now Michigan State University), Pennsylvania State College, Ohio State University, and the University of Michigan. Among the young instructors who achieved the greatest renown were Dugald Jackson, the long-serving dean of the College of Engineering at MIT, and Mortimer E. Cooley, his counterpart at Michigan.[18]

By the middle of the 1880s, laboratory-based mechanical engineering programs were springing up all over the nation. The model featured a four-year curriculum with instruction using tools, machinery, steam engines, and an intensive science and mathematics concentration. The experience of Michigan Agricultural College was typical. The first class of thirty-five students enrolled in 1885, and the first graduates finished the course in 1889. At the fiftieth reunion of that first class in 1939, one alumnus fondly recalled the three professors who taught the students and the laboratory instruction using machinery and tools. However, he noted that some technical high schools in the 1930s had more machinery than MAC did in its first years. The criticism was a reflection of the problems that mechanical engineering instruction encountered in its earliest decades. Machinery was expensive, and trustees were often reluctant to authorize the expenditures at Land Grant and other public universities. Even a laboratory with basic equipment might cost between $2,000 and $3,000. In states such as Ohio, where the state legislature voted only very modest appropriations to operate the Ohio State University, $2,000 might represent 20–50 percent of an entire yearly budget for the cost of instruction. In addition, state legislators, responding to their farmer constituents, expressed fears that engineering instruction would direct resources and institutional priorities away from agricultural education. Such fears limited the growth of engineering programs at Ohio State, Kansas State, and Iowa State universities, among others.[19]

In the south, the enthusiasm for engineering education lagged a few years behind the rest of the nation until boosters such as Georgia's Henry Grady began promoting industrialization as a means of catching up with the rest of the United States. His efforts met success in 1888 when the Georgia School of Technology opened its doors in Atlanta. The chair of mechanical engineering went to John Saylor Coon, a Cornell graduate and protégé of John Sweet. Unfortunately, the Georgia state legislature insisted on the Worcester model of instruction, which included setting up woodworking and metal shops and the sale of student-made products to finance the school. Georgia Tech tried and failed to procure an Annapolis graduate to jumpstart its program but modernized its curriculum to follow the Thurston model in the 1890s. The engineering branch at Vanderbilt University was luckier, both because it was able to recruit a Naval Academy-trained mechanical engineer as a professor and because Cornelius Vanderbilt's grandson, Cornelius II, donated the funds to build Mechanical Engineering Hall in 1888, the first building anywhere in the state which was dedicated to that purpose. The Agricultural and Mechanical College of Alabama, now Auburn University, opened its mechanical division in 1885 and added instructors from Purdue and Cornell in 1888. Institutions such as the Agricultural and Mechanical College of the State of Mississippi were quick to add civil engineering and set up woodworking shops, but lack of funding typically delayed the mechanical engineering branch until later.[20]

Scarce resources were a key concern for Thurston at Stevens, and he addressed them candidly at his graduation speech to the class of 1885, the tenth full class to complete his four-year curriculum since the Institute's opening in 1871. The bulk of the Stevens bequest had already been expended on classroom space, laboratories, and salaries. The Institute had reached a size limit of no more than 200 students, and throughout much of its brief history, it enrolled no more than 150 students. Late in his tenure at Stevens, Thurston introduced a program in electrical engineering and marine engineering, each with dedicated staff and laboratory facilities, but he had reached the limits of the institution's resources. Unless it removed the preparatory school or found a new financial benefactor, Stevens would have to limit the freshman class to a maximum of fifty students.[21]

Thurston's graduation speech addressed the financial limitations and the future of engineering education. He likened it to the training of doctors and lawyers, who were expected to complete a four-year curriculum first before beginning their professional education. Thurston believed that the engineers of the twentieth century would earn the appropriate salary levels and public recognition they deserved when they earned graduate degrees in their subject matter. Proper graduate instruction was out of the question in the constrained circumstances of Stevens Institute. Thurston's speech turned into his valedictory at Stevens as he drew the obvious conclusion from his own logic. In order to complete his vision of engineering education for elite professionals, he would have to move to another university with more ample resources. He wrote to Andrew Dickson White at Cornell in 1885 and explained his vision of turning engineering education into graduate education on the model of Johns Hopkins University, the nation's first foremost graduate university.[22]

Thurston's Career at Cornell University

In 1884, Andrew Dickson White began his final year as president and was looking for a leader to take charge of the floundering Mechanical Arts division of the Sibley School of Engineering. He called Thurston the new dean of the college, and as had Morton at Stevens, gave him almost unlimited authority to shape the curriculum. White was already one of the best known and most successful university presidents, and Cornell University served as a model for other land-grant universities. Promoters of the Ohio State University looked to Cornell; for instance, skeptics in Ohio questioned whether there was room for another land-grant university in the nation with the wealth, talent, and quality of Cornell. However, the same praise did not necessarily apply to the Mechanical Arts division. Despite a promising start under John Edson Sweet in the 1870s, since his departure for the industry in 1879, the division had become disorganized and demoralized. Thurston inherited a program with just seven faculty and sixty students, which was significantly smaller than that of Stevens.[23]

Unlike Stevens, Cornell had a donor who could be approached for additional financial support, namely Hiram Sibley. Sibley was a long-time friend and business associate of Ezra Cornell, who had made a fortune at Western Union and later at American Telephone and Telegraph. Until his death in 1888, and thereafter by his descendants, the Sibley family contributed nearly $200,000 to Cornell. Thurston worked closely with the donor and his heirs to secure the necessary funds to re-create and improve on the facilities he had once fashioned at Stevens, especially the laboratory and testing equipment. Cornell also enjoyed the benefits of the largest of the land grants and the wisdom of retaining the land until prices rose. Thurston used the funding to create programs in electrical, marine, and railroad engineering. He also set up the first chair in experimental engineering, which was filled by Rolla C. Carpenter from Michigan State University. Eventually, an entire department at the Sibley School was devoted to experimental engineering. The value of machinery, tools, and equipment in the early 1890s was more than $200,000.[24]

Thurston spent the final eighteen years of his career at Cornell. As he had done earlier at Stevens, he promoted his curriculum, laboratory-based instruction, and engineering research in a dozen more articles in *Scientific American* and other journals. He also undertook to promote his curricular reforms through personal visits to budding engineering schools. In 1931, the MIT Department of Engineering Chair Dugald C. Jackson recalled Thurston's visit to the University of Wisconsin School of Engineering in 1894, when Jackson was a young faculty member there. Thurston praised the attempts of the School to install laboratory-based instruction and encouraged them to expand its extent. He recommended the proper balance between lecture and laboratory to be no more than 60–65 percent of a student's time to the former method of instruction and 35–40 percent to the latter. Laboratory instruction, of course, was costlier in terms of machinery, apparatus, testing equipment, class size, and instructor workload. However, it was the only means of delivering the hands-on experience that young engineers needed and employers valued, as well as the research that would advance the field. Thurston also spread the message by personally attending groundbreaking ceremonies for new machinery halls at the University of Illinois and Iowa State University. Certainly, by the early 1890s, Cornell's engineering education was considered the best in the United States, and among the best in the world. Only MIT's program constituted serious competition. By the time of his death in 1903, Thurston had expanded the engineering program to 46 faculty and nearly 1,000 students.[25]

International Recognition of American Engineering Education

The Centennial provided the occasion for foreign observers to take note of Thurston's methods. Hermann Grothe's *American Industry* (1877) was the work of a civil engineer who became an expert in textile machinery, patents, and technical journalism. Most of the book lauded the development of American industry from the perspective of a German industry spokesman who wanted to copy America's protective tariff legislation. However, Grothe also noted Thurston's work in metallurgy at Stevens and the general progress of scientific and engineering education at the land-grant institutions and the Columbia School of Mines.[26]

More closely focused on the question of laboratory-based instruction was another Centennial visitor, Hermann Wedding, who was a professor at the School of Mines in Berlin. In a lecture in 1877, later an article for the Association for the Promotion of Economic Efficiency, titled "Notes on Technical Education in North America," Wedding sketched the outlines of the work of Thurston and others in the field. Wedding was often a judge and reporter at late nineteenth-century world's fairs, especially in the fields of mining and the iron and steel industry. He reviewed the short history of American technical education but reserved the majority of his analysis to extended discussions of Stevens Institute and the Columbia School of Mines. He declared that the New York City school was probably the best equipped mining school in the world, though it was clearly Stevens Institute that captured his imagination. He devoted half of his article to Stevens' curriculum, its facilities and professors, and the innovation of the mechanical testing laboratory. Wedding especially liked the fact that students had the "the opportunity to participate in the experiments on steam engines, boilers, and other operations that occur in practical life." Nowhere in Germany was there such emphasis on laboratories, a significant lapse because they were "the connecting link between science and industrial practice" that had been missing until then.[27]

Anyone interested in the history of science and technology education might find it ironic that a German professor was complaining about the absence of laboratories when Germany considered itself the birthplace of the university laboratory. Furthermore, German technical universities, especially the earliest one in Karlsruhe, inspired practices at MIT, Cornell, and Stevens. The chemical laboratory of Justus von Liebig at the University of Giessen dated its founding to the 1820s; indeed Eben N. Horsford, one of Liebig's American students, is usually credited with introducing laboratories to American universities when he became professor of chemistry at Harvard University in 1847. Furthermore, the distinction of hosting the first laboratory at a technical university belongs to the one in Munich, where in 1871, Professor Johann Bauschinger created a materials testing laboratory at the insistence of the government of Bavaria. However, Bauschinger's laboratory was not yet a part of the curriculum in the 1870s.[28]

The technical universities in Germany faced a struggle for standing in the academic world with traditional universities just as the land-grant institutions strove for equality with traditional universities in this country. In their quest for legitimacy, the technical universities accepted only those students with the traditional *Gymnasium* education in the sciences and languages or from the newer comprehensive schools, known as *Real-gymnasien*. Furthermore, professors at technical universities before 1890 sought to turn engineering into pure applied science, which was more or less based on the French model. They believed that practical application was reserved for vocational schooling, not universities. The consequence was that German technical universities were graduating mechanical engineers with high-level skills in mathematics, physics, and chemistry but no work experience and no knowledge of the day-to-day routine of the mills and factories where they would be employed. The opportunity to change the status of German technical universities came in 1893 and with the visit of Germany's most distinguished engineering professional, Alois Riedler, to the World's Columbian Exposition.[29]

The year 1893 marked the triumph of Thurston's vision for engineering education. At the World's Columbian Exposition in Chicago, American and Canadian professional engineering societies invited guests to the inaugural World's Engineering Congress. Promoters of the Congress in 1891 initially set up a program which was based on functional specialties, that is, sessions devoted to mechanical, maritime, civil engineering, and so on. Thurston proposed to include a session that was devoted to engineering education, and his prestige persuaded the promoters to include the subject. The result was the first international gathering devoted to the subject, and from that impetus came the formation of the American Society for the Promotion of Engineering Education, which is now the American Society for Engineering Education (ASEE). In effect, the ASEE institutionalized Thurston's curriculum as best practice for American higher education in the field.[30]

The second acknowledgment of his curricular design came from a study of American engineering education that was commissioned by the Prussian Ministry of Education. Professor Alois Riedler of the Royal Technical University of Berlin carried out this work by visiting major engineering schools throughout the United States during the summer and fall of 1893. He published his findings during the next year, with recommendations to adopt American-style laboratory instruction in German engineering universities. Riedler celebrated the accomplishments of engineers and, by extension, their training. He exclaimed, "America owes its greatness, achieved in such an unparalleled short time span, to the civilizing influence of the engineer. The engineer is not only the pioneer of civilization in the wilderness . . . but nowhere else in the world is the work of the engineer of greater importance." Riedler insisted that so powerful was the force of rapid American development in the world that Germany had no choice but to study it carefully and see what lessons it might yield for the Old World. Riedler was no stranger to the New World, having visited the Philadelphia Centennial of 1876 and composed reports on American technology for the Austria–Hungarian Commission in 1876 and the Paris World's Fair of 1878. In 1893, Riedler's praise was not reserved for accomplishments of individual inventors such as Thomas Edison or George Corliss. He focused his attention instead on the achievements of a corps of professional engineers and on the qualities of an educational system that had fostered such excellence.[31]

In this context, he praised Cornell's laboratories as being the best equipped in the world. He was also deeply impressed by the extent of private philanthropy in the United States as a source of university funding, a practice that was uncommon in Germany. In addition, despite the unevenness of their educational preparation before they attended universities, American students also impressed him with their receptiveness to hands-on, practical training. He maintained, "Students born in America and raised in the spirit of the land simply refuse to acknowledge that there is a contradiction between practical work and science," and he insisted further that if their secondary school preparation had been better, American engineering students would be superior to German ones.[32]

Conclusion

In conclusion, the results of Riedler's efforts at the turn of the twentieth century to reform German engineering education demonstrated the high quality of American methods in preparing young men and a few young women for careers in engineering, quality that was held in high esteem by knowledgeable European observers. However, this example also shows the convergence of methods in the two most advanced industrial nations of the time. The success of German industrial products in winning awards at the Columbian Exhibition of 1893 gave a boost to the manual training movement in the United States to improve the education of secondary schools students along the lines of the German model of technical training. The education of engineers, technicians, and mechanics in both countries profited from the cross-fertilization of practices and ideals.[33]

Both Thurston and Riedler were also keenly aware that more than pedagogy was at stake in the training of engineers. In 1893, Thurston noted, "the Atlantic Ocean has ceased to be a defense against foreign competition" and quoted the Scottish engineer John Scott Russell, who maintained that "in the energetic rivalry of competing nations," the winners would be those who could "do the work of the world better, more ably, more honestly, more skillfully and less wastefully" than others. "If we are less skilled or less honest than others, we are beaten in the race of life." Riedler's address as Rector of the Royal Technical University in 1899 echoed the Darwinian tone of Thurston and Russell: "Germans need fear in the industrial world neither the English nor the French, only the Americans; and to compete with the American engineer, we must strive constantly to improve and extend our engineering courses."[34]

In October 1903, Thurston died unexpectedly on his sixty-fourth birthday just before he was about to attend a dinner in his honor. He lived long enough to see Annapolis transformed into a modern engineering college, because, as Mortimer Cooley explains, a modern ship is "one mass of machinery, mechanical and electrical." He also lived long enough to see his model of engineering education based on research in laboratories become the standard in both the United States and abroad. In the context of 1939 when engineers celebrated the one-hundredth anniversary of Thurston's birth, such expressions of international rivalries and competitiveness took on far more dangerous connotations than they had had in the 1890s. Human capital in the form of education and training of mechanical, naval, aeronautical, and electrical engineers turned out to be a decisive factor in victory during World War II as Thurston's protégés crafted Sherman tanks, Liberty Ships, and B-17s to crush the threat of European fascism. For the United States, the enduring value today of such training as it was shaped in the land-grant institution in the late nineteenth and twentieth centuries, can be no less compelling than it was in 1939.[35]

Notes

1. *Exercises Commemorating the One-Hundredth Anniversary of Robert Henry Thurston, Held at Cornell University, 25 October, 1939* (Ithaca, NY: Cornell University Press, 1940). See also "The 100th Anniversary of the Birth of Robert H. Thurston," *Science* 90, no. 2329 (1939); for a recent assessment of Thurston's Cornell University model, Jonathan Harwood, "Engineering Education between Science and Practice: Rethinking the Historiography," *History and Technology* 27 (Spring 2006).

2. The standard account is William F. Durand, *Robert Henry Thurston, a Biography* (New York: American Society of Mechanical Engineers, 1929); Monte Calvert, *The Mechanical Engineer in America, 1830–1910* (Baltimore, MD: Johns Hopkins University Press, 1967).

3. On the US Naval Academy after the Civil War, see Brendan Patrick Foley, "Fighting Engineers: The U.S. Navy and Mechanical Engineering, 1840–1905" (unpublished doctoral diss., Massachusetts Institute of Technology, 2003); Edward W. Sloan III and Benjamin Franklin Isherwood, *Naval Engineer: The Years as Engineer in Chief, 1861–69* (Annapolis, MD: United States Naval Institute, 1966).

4. Ibid., 148–54; Robert H. Thurston, "Benjamin Franklin Isherwood," *Cassier's Magazine* 18 (August 1900): 347.

5. Lance C. Buhl, "Marines and Machines: Resistance to Technological Change in the American Navy, 1865–1869," *Journal of American History* 61, no. 3 (December 1974); Foley, "Fighting Engineers," 240–56.

6. Geoffrey W. Clarke, *History of Stevens Institute of Technology* (Jersey City, NJ: Jensen/Daniels, 2000); Durand, *Thurston*, 46. Thurston may have benefited from Stevens Institute's political influence in obtaining his position as editor of the American Commission's report on the 1873 Vienna World's Fair. See Merle Curti, "America at the World Fairs, 1851–1893," *The American Historical Review* 55, no. 4 (July 1950): 833–85.

7. Frederick Rudolph, *The American College and University: A History* (New York: Random House, 1962), 228–31; Edwin D. Eddy, *Colleges for Our Land and Time: The Land-grant Idea in American Education* (New York: Harper & Brothers, 1957); A. J. Angulo, *William Barton Rogers and the Idea of MIT* (Baltimore, MD: Johns Hopkins University Press, 2009).

8. Charles R. Mann, *A Study of Engineering Education* (New York: Carnegie Foundation, 1917); William E. Wickenden, *A Comparative Study of Engineering Education in the United States and in Europe* (Lancaster, PA: Society for the Promotion of Engineering Education, 1929); Winton U. Solberg, *The University of Illinois, 1867–1894, an Intellectual and Cultural History* (Urbana: University of Illinois Press, 1968), 107, 142–45; C. W. Butterfield, *History of the University of Wisconsin from Its First Organization to 1879* (Madison, WI: University Press, 1879), 200–31; Morris Bishop, *A History of Cornell* (Ithaca, NY: Cornell University Press, 1962). A survey of post–Civil War engineering education can be found in Robert V. Bruce, *The Launching of Modern American Science, 1846–1876* (Ithaca, NY: Cornell University Press, 1987), 331–34.

9. Kees Gispen, *New Profession, Old Order: Engineers and German Society, 1815–1914* (New York: Cambridge University Press, 1989); Karl-Heinz Manegold, *Universität, Technische Hochschule und Industrie; ein Beitrag zur Emanzipation der Technik im 19. Jahrhundert unter besonderer Berücksichtigung der Bestrebungen Felix Kleins* (Goettingen: Vandenhoek & Rupprecht, 1970).

10. James C. Albisetti, *Secondary School Reform in Germany* (Princeton, NJ: Princeton University Press, 1983); Rudolph, *American College*, 252; on the uneven levels of high school preparation for higher education, see David F. Larabee, *How to Succeed in School Without Really Learning: The Credentials Race in American Education* (New Haven, CT: Yale University Press, 1999), *Proceedings of the Society for the Promotion of Engineering Education* 1 (1893), 54 (hereafter *Proceedings*) for Swain's observation.

11. Robert Henry Thurston Manuscripts (hereafter Thurston MSS), Box 2, File 2, Correspondence, Cornell University Archives.

12. Durand, *Thurston*, 240–56; Clarke, *History of Stevens Institute*, 54–67; Thurston's textbook, available in many editions, was titled *Materials of Engineering*, 3 vols. (New York: Wiley, 1882).

13. Durand, *Thurston*, 51, 214; Thurston MSS, see especially Correspondence, 1884–1903; Calvert, *Mechanical Engineer*, 216.

14. Clarke, *History*, 54–67; Durand, *Thurston*, 75–80; Robert H. Thurston, "Instruction in Mechanical Engineering," *Scientific American* (Supplement April 19, 1874), 6904; Theodore T. S. Laidley, Lester A. Beardslee, and Robert H. Thurston, *Report of the United States Board to Test Iron, Steel, and Other Metals* (Washington, DC: GPO, 1878).

15. Eddy, *Colleges for Our Land and Time*, 137, 142; See the list of Thurston's publications appended in Durand, *Thurston*, 210–23.

16. *Engineering News* 7, February 21, 1880, 66–67; Frederick Remsen Hutton, *A History of the American Society of Mechanical Engineers from 1880 to 1915*

(New York: The Society, 1915), 3–4. Another interpretation of the founding of the ASME can be found in Edwin Layton, *The Revolt of the Engineers: Social Responsibility and the American Engineering Profession* (Cleveland, OH: Press of Case Western University, 1971), 34–36.

17. Foley, "Fighting Engineers," 223–44; Mortimer E. Cooley, "The Detail of Naval Officers to Colleges," *Transactions and Proceedings of the National Association of State Universities and Land-grant Colleges* 10 (Burlington, VT: Free Press, 1912), 187–202.

18. Mortimer E. Cooley, *Scientific Blacksmith* (New York: Arno Press, repr. 1972).

19. Keith R. Widder, *Michigan Agricultural College: The Evolution of a Land-grant Philosophy, 1855–1925* (East Lansing: Michigan State University Press, 2005), 131–35; Madison Kuhn, *Michigan State: The First Hundred Years* (East Lansing: Michigan State University Press, 1956), 146–51; William A. Kinnison, *Building Sullivan's Pyramid: An Administrative History of the Ohio State University, 1870–1907* (Columbus: Ohio State University Press, 1970), 66; Dorothy Schwieder, ed., *A Sesquicentennial History of Iowa State University's Traditions and Transformation* (Ames: Iowa State University Press, 2007), 19, 28–29.

20. James E. Brittain and Robert C. McMath, Jr., "Engineers and the New South Creed: The Formation and Early Development of Georgia Tech," in *The Engineer in America: A Historical Anthology from Technology and Culture*, ed. Terry S. Reynolds (Chicago, IL: University of Chicago Press, 1991); Paul K. Conkin, *Gone with the Ivy: A Biography of Vanderbilt University* (Knoxville: University of Tennessee Press, 1991); http://www.eng.auburn.edu/about/history/history/index (accessed April 15, 2012); http://www.bagley.msstate.edu/ (accessed April 15, 2012).

21. Robert H. Thurston, "Stevens and Her Faculty," *The Stevens Indicator* 2 (June 6, 1885): 81–84. See also the account of one of Thurston's successors, Franklin de Ronde Furman, *Morton Memorial: A History of the Stevens Institute of Technology* (Hoboken, NJ: Stevens Institute of Technology, 1905), 210–14.

22. Ibid., 83; Robert H. Thurston to Andrew Dickson White, December 20, 1885, Correspondence, Thurston MSS.

23. Morris Bishop, *A History of Cornell* (Ithaca, NY: Cornell University Press, 1962); Kinnison, *Building Sullivan's Pyramid*, 42, 48, 69; *Exercises Commemorating the One-Hundredth Anniversary*, 39.

24. Ibid., 256; Rolla C. Carpenter, *A Textbook of Experimental Engineering; for Engineers and Students in Engineering Laboratories* (New York: J. Wiley and Sons, 1892). I am indebted to John Blake for making me aware of this source.

25. Dugald C. Jackson, "Research Laboratories in Engineering Education," *Science* 74 (August 21, 1931); Karl L. Wildes and Nilo A. Lindgren, *A Century of Electrical Engineering and Computer Science at MIT, 1882–1892* (Cambridge, MA: MIT Press, 1985), 146; Solberg, *University of Illinois*, 367; *Exercises Commemorating the One-Hundredth Anniversary*, 24.

26. Hermann Grothe, *Die Industrie Amerikas: Ihre Geschichte, Entwicklung und Lage* (Berlin: Burmester & Stempel, 1877), 144–45.

27. Hermann Wedding, "Mittheilungen über die technische Erziehung in Nord-Amerika," *Verhandlungen des Vereins zur Beförderung des Gewerbefleiss* 56 (1877): 516–27.

28. Claus Priesner, "Justus von Liebig," *Neue Deutsche Biographie* 14 (Berlin: Duncker & Humblot, 1985), 497–501. Lyman C. Newell, "Eben Norton Horsford," *Dictionary of American Biography* 5: 236–37 (New York: Charles Scribner's Sons, 1933);

Hans Ludger Dienel and Helmut Hilz, *Bayerns Weg in das Technische Zeitalter: 125 Jahre Technische Universitat Munchen, 1868–1993* (Munich: Hugendubel, 1993), 49–51.

29. Gispen, *New Profession*, 245.
30. *Proceedings* 1, 24; Thurston MSS, Lecture, World's Educational Congress, Chicago, July 26, 1893.
31. Karl-Heinz Manegold, "Alois Riedler," in *Berlinische Lebensbilder: Techniker*, ed. Wilhelm Treue and Wolfgang Konig (Berlin: Colloquim Verlag, 1990), 293–307; Georg Grüner, "Johann von Radinger," *Ōsterreichisches Biographische Lexikon* 9: 375–76 (Wien, 1988); Alois Riedler, "Dampfmaschinen," *Bericht über die Weltausstellung in Paris 1878* (Wien: Faesy & Frick, 1879); Paul Rieppel, "Alois Riedler, Nachruf," *Zeitschrift des Vereines Deutsche Ingenieure* 80, no. 51 (November 10, 1936): 1517.
32. Alois Riedler, *Amerikanische technische Lehranstalten* (Berlin: Springer Verlag, 1893).
33. Donald S. Linton, "American Responses to German Continuation Schools during the Progressive Era," in *German Influences on Education in the United States to 1917*, German Historical Commission, ed. Henry Geitz, Jurgen Heideking, and Jurgen Herbst (New York: Cambridge University Press, 1995).
34. Volker Hünecke, "Der "Kamp ums Dasein" und die Reform der technischen Erziehung im Denken Alois Riedlers," in *Wissenschaft und Gesellschaft*, ed. Reinhard Rürup (Berlin, 1979); Gispen, *New Profession*, 139; Thurston MSS, Lecture, World's Educational Congress, Chicago, July 26, 1893. Riedler quoted Wildes and Lindgren, *Century of Electrical Engineering*, 146.
35. Cooley, "The Detail of Naval Officers," 202.

Part IV

Land-Grant Universities, 1900–1940

Introduction

Roger L. Geiger

The American university assumed its modern form in the years bracketing the turn of the century. The academic revolution of the 1890s institutionalized the academic disciplines as the basis for the college course. However, as observed in Part III, this same transition to a science-based curriculum affected first engineering and then agriculture. The distinguishing feature of a university was the pursuit of some or all of these subjects to the highest level—to the discovery and dissemination of new knowledge.[1] During these same years, enrollment growth in higher education accelerated, and universities accounted for the bulk of this growth. Private universities experienced their greatest growth before 1900, but public universities led the expansion in the new century. They did so, above all through the variety of their offerings. The University of California listed nine undergraduate colleges, plus five professional schools; the University of Illinois had fifteen undergraduate divisions besides professional schools. Land-grant subjects accounted for more than half of these units, and the land-grant spirit made the universities open to new applied fields, such as commerce. Thus, they combined both scale in terms of growing enrollments and scope in terms of a wide coverage of subjects. The key to success as an American university involved the combination of scale and scope with a commitment to academic advancement—to graduate education and research.[2] However, these developments widened the gulf between land-grant institutions that adopted a university model with full development of the arts and sciences, and those which were erected as agricultural or A&M colleges.

Perspectives on the History of Higher Education 30 (2013): 217–223
© 2013. ISBN: 978-1-4128-5147-3

Becoming a full-fledged university became a goal of different institutions at different points in time.

Both the articles in this section address the issue of leadership in pursuit of the university ideal. Winton Solberg's study of the presidency of Edmund James at the University of Illinois (1904–1920) represents what could be called the "first generation of land-grant universities." Jane Robbins' examination of Ralph Hetzel at New Hampshire and especially Pennsylvania State College represents a second generation in terms of their ability to join the ranks of universities. Leadership was essential, because rising into the top ranks of research universities—and staying there—imposed multiple challenges.

After 1900, the competition for prestige in American higher education became more overt and more focused on academic quality. During that year, the Association of American Universities was organized as an exclusive club of doctoral-granting institutions.[3] Solberg notes how important it was for Illinois to obtain membership. In 1905, the Carnegie Foundation for the Advancement of Teaching was founded ostensibly to provide pensions for college teachers. However, it quickly embraced the mission of raising academic standards. To this end, it published comparative statistics and clearly identified those institutions that were good enough to be included in the pension system.[4] In 1906, *Science* compiled a list of the 1,000 Leading American Men of Science, which revealed the stark inequality of scientific prowess between Harvard (66), thirteenth-ranked Illinois (6), and 38 other colleges and universities having even fewer.[5] In addition, several schemes were offered that rated the relative attainments of graduates of colleges and universities.[6] The stakes clearly rose for institutional reputation, and presidential leadership was imperative to raise expectations and implement policies that enhance quality.

Presidential leadership was also necessary to obtain the resources needed for enlarging the scale of operations. In part, this meant not only establishing good relations with governors and legislatures, something that was not always possible, but also staying in favor with trustees and a university's multiple constituencies. Regular state appropriations were not yet standard, as Hetzel found in New Hampshire, and special appropriations were still essential for capital expenditures. Discrepancies in resources were huge among the land grants and accounted for much of their relative capabilities (Table 1).

The "first generation" of land-grant universities stand out simply by their scale of operations and the scope of subjects made possible by large faculties. The challenge facing aspiring universities with smaller

Table 1   Instructional Salary Budgets and Instructional Faculty, Selected
Land-Grant Universities, 1908

Institution	Instructional Budget ($000)	Instructional staff (total)	Instructional staff (u.grad colleges)
Cornell	511	507	283
Illinois	492	414	190
Wisconsin	490	297	231
California	408	350	218
MIT	301	n/a	211
Minnesota	263	303	116
Ohio State	244	127	87
Nebraska	240	173	90
Missouri	239	144	101
Iowa State College	140	n/a	108
Kansas State Ag. C.	129	n/a	69
Purdue	129	124	119
Michigan St. Ag. C.	110	n/a	78
Pennsylvania St. C.	97	n/a	81
Clemson Ag. C.	94	n/a	41
Tennessee	78	106	34
Texas A&M	74	n/a	52

budgets and faculties half or less as large—Ohio State, Nebraska, and Missouri—is also evident. Agricultural or A&M colleges generally commanded much less resources. Only Iowa and Indiana supported their flagship and land-grant universities comparably: Iowa State was the leading college of this type in agriculture, and the same could be said of Purdue with regard to engineering. Elsewhere, the A&Ms had a constricted scope, especially in arts and sciences. Leadership undoubtedly interacted with other contextual factors. Pennsylvania, with the largest state economy, provided little funding for public higher education. Trustees dominated Ohio State, leaving presidents with little ability to lead. In 1909, Nebraska, after decades of relative overachievement appointed an uninspiring chancellor who sought continuity rather than distinction.[7]

Academic leadership was crucial internally, above all, in order to articulate and advance the university ideal. Especially in developing institutions, presidents need to take ownership of the university mission, rather than allowing more parochial interests to define purpose. The identification of individuals who are capable of advancing the university may have been most crucial. Andrew D. White's appointment of Thurston, for example, brought transformational change to engineering at Cornell. Edmund James at Illinois and Ralph Hetzel at Penn State understood this dimension of their role.

The University of Illinois expanded its scope and scale dramatically under the presidency of Andrew S. Draper (1894–1904). Undergraduates tripled; five professional schools were added; and the state appropriation, including capital, almost quadrupled. Illinois advanced from being the fourteenth to the seventh largest university, but its academic standing was far lower. In a detailed study of the Draper administration, Winton Solberg has faulted his leadership for the university's relative backwardness.[8] Draper was a schoolman who had attended law school but not college. He was an autocratic micromanager who had little appreciation for academic values. His treatment of faculty was particularly heavy-handed, and he was dismissive toward research. The university advanced along many fronts during his decade in the presidency, but Edmund James inherited an institution of huge unrealized potential.

James deserves greater recognition as one of the foremost builders of American universities. Assuming the presidency of Illinois in the decade that saw the retirement of university pioneers Daniel C. Gilman and Charles W. Eliot, he, nonetheless, articulated university ideals as eloquently as any contemporary, and worked methodically to realize them. Having earned a PhD in political science at the University of Berlin, he combined a Germanic commitment to the scientific nature of university studies with a very American desire to make the university serve the state and civil society. One signal achievement was to rescue the graduate school from its previous neglect. The formal organization of the Graduate School in 1908 coincided with the university's admission to the AAU. In 1903, Illinois had only granted its first PhD, but during James' administration, it vaulted into the company of the nation's premier universities, in science no less than doctoral education. After his retirement in 1920, seven land-grant institutions claimed substantial participation in research and graduate education, two of them being private (Table 2). The fact that Illinois ranked third among the public land grants in the early 1920s is ample testimony to the accomplishments and the legacy of Edmund James.

Table 2   Leading Men of Science (1927) and PhDs Awarded (1920–1924), Land-Grant Universities.[9]

Institution	No. of men of science	Rank	PhDs	Rank
California	40.5	6	184	8
Cornell	34.5	8	258	6
Wisconsin	28	11	272	5
Illinois	26	13	176	9
MIT	20	19	57	20
Minnesota	18.5	21	105	13
Ohio State	13	24	88	15
Iowa State	8.5	27	23	28
Rutgers	*	20	31	
Nebraska	*	17	34	
Missouri	5	43	16	35

Note: *Less than 3.

Pennsylvania State College had the sixteenth largest instructional budget in 1908 (Table 1) and did not award its first PhD until 1926. Under president George W. Atherton (1882–1906), regarded as the "second founder," the institution developed from a struggling multipurpose college to a thriving engineering school with significant agricultural research. Afterward, however, it endured the kind of breakdown in leadership that had assured mediocrity between founding president Evan Pugh (1859–1864) and Atherton. The head of the trustees who became acting president sided with students against the faculty and inflicted a dictatorial vice president on them as well. The next president, Edwin Sparks (1908–1921), had never held a regular faculty position. Similar to Draper at Illinois, he sought to expand the scope of the college but not its quality. He bragged of hiring "as few instructors as we can possibly get along with, for the least possible compensation." He explicitly rejected any wish "to aspire to the much-abused title of university." The college was woefully supported by the state, which refused (then and now) to accept it as the flagship university.[10] Sparks' successor, John Thomas (1921–1925), possessed a university vision and endeavored to transform Penn State into a full university, in both fact and name. However, he confronted a governor in Gifford Pinchot (Yale, '89) who disdained public higher education, in general, and Penn State, in particular. When the state appropriation was slashed, Thomas resigned to accept the challenge of advancing Rutgers as a land-grant university.[11]

Through the interwar years, the A&M land grants felt increasing pressure to move in the direction of conforming to the university model. Most lacked any distinguished scientists or doctoral students, and agricultural constituencies persisted in trying to define the mission, as they did in New Hampshire, despite accounting for a minority of students. As complete public universities expanded enrollments, curricula, research, and graduate education, A&M schools became increasingly aware of their deficiencies. Overcoming them presented a succession of challenges; but perhaps the greatest was obtaining academic leaders who embraced the university ideal; could sell it to faculty, trustees, and legislators; and could implement the necessary changes in university administration. From this perspective, Jane Robbins' homage to Ralph Hetzel elucidates the many facets of this protracted process. In contrast to John Thomas, who may have aimed too high too fast, Hetzel addressed the quotidian issues that produce incremental change. Robbins rightly focuses particular attention on research, where Hetzel immediately elevated the profile and salience by establishing a Council on Research. This body included all the key administrators, focusing their attention on fostering research and resolving obstacles. Hetzel led Penn State through the steps that made it a university, in fact, and thereby laid the foundation for it to take advantage of postwar conditions to expand enrollment, curriculum, and research. In 1953, his successor, Milton Eisenhower, made Penn State a university in name.

Notes

1.   In 1908, the National Association of State Universities defined the "standard American university," which, among other things, required the resources to offer graduate education to the PhD in five departments: Hugh Hawkins, *Banding together: The Rise of National Associations in American Higher Education, 1887–1950* (Baltimore, MD: Johns Hopkins University Press, 1992), 82–84.
2.   Roger L. Geiger, *To Advance Knowledge: The Growth of American Research Universities, 1900–1940* (New Brunswick, NJ: Transaction, 2004 [1986]); Edwin E. Slosson, *Great American Universities* (New York: Macmillan, 1910).
3.   Hawkins, *Banding Together*, 10–15, 37–41.
4.   Daniel S. Webster, *Academic Quality Rankings of American Colleges and Universities* (Springfield, IL: Charles C. Thomas, 1986), 77–84; *Bulletin of the Carnegie Foundation for the Advancement of Teaching*, no. 1 (1907), no. 2 (1908); Bulletin no. 4 (1910) was Abraham Flexner's devastating Report: *Medical Education in the United States and Canada*.
5.   Geiger, *To Advance Knowledge*, 38–39. James McKeen Cattell continually updated this list: In 1927, nine land grants had three or more leading men of science

(Table 2): J. McKeen Cattell and Jacques Cattell, eds., *American Men of Science: A Biographical Dictionary*, 4th ed. (New York: Science Press, 1927), 1127.

6. In 1911, the US Bureau of Education classified most colleges and universities into four strata on the basis of their graduates' readiness for graduate work. A&M institutions were generally ranked low; for example, LSU and Michigan Agricultural College were in Class III (one-year deficient); and Auburn, Kansas State, NC A&M, Virginia Polytechnic, and Oregon State were in Class IV (two-year deficient). Due to criticism, this classification was never published. In 1914, the AAU developed a similar classification to identify which institution's graduates were prepared for graduate study: Webster, *Academic Quality Rankings*, 33–43, 85–91.

7. William A. Kinnison, *Building Sullivant's Pyramid: An Administrative History of the Ohio State University, 1870–1907* (Columbus: Ohio State University Press, 1970); Robert E. Knoll, *Prairie University* (Lincoln: University of Nebraska Press, 1995), 186–206.

8. Winton U. Solberg, *The University of Illinois, 1894–1904: The Shaping of the University* (Urbana: University of Illinois Press, 2000).

9. Cattell and Cattell, eds., *American Men of Science*, 1127; Lori Thurgood et al., *U.S. Doctorates in the 20th Century* (Washington, DC: National Science Foundation, June 2006), 104.

10. Michael Bezilla, *Penn State: An Illustrated History* (University Park: Pennsylvania State University Press, 1985), quotes on 93, 106. Pennsylvania has a remarkable record of never establishing a public institution of higher education: Penn State was founded by agricultural societies, and the other "state-related" universities were founded privately; the institutions that comprise the Pennsylvania State System of Higher Education were privately founded as normal schools. Governor Edward Rendell attempted to disown Penn State as a state university, and his successor, Governor Thomas Corbett, wished to privatize all of Pennsylvania's public universities.

11. Bezilla, *Penn State*. Thomas repeated his Penn State experience in his five years at Rutgers: Renamed "The State University of New Jersey" in 1917, it retained a private Board of Trustees and received little state support. Thomas presented an ambitious plan to create a comprehensive flagship university, but was frustrated by the growing opposition among trustees and state officials. No regular support was forthcoming, and the title, "State University of New Jersey," was withdrawn! In 1930, Thomas resigned and joined an insurance company. The interwar experiences of Penn State and Rutgers reveal the obstacles to gaining university status: Richard P. McCormick, *Rutgers: A Bicentennial History* (New Brunswick, NJ: Rutgers University Press, 1966), 186–207.

President Edmund J. James and the University of Illinois, 1904–1920: Redeeming the Promise of the Morrill Land-Grant Act

Winton U. Solberg

As president of the University of Illinois in the early twentieth century, Edmund J. James redeemed the promise of the Morrill Land-Grant Act. In its first half century, the state of Illinois had been remarkably laggard in advancing public education. The achievement of James is best understood in the context of the situation that he inherited when he arrived in Urbana in 1904.

Higher Education in Illinois: 1818–1904

The birth of the nation kindled the belief that the public has a responsibility to support higher education. By 1860, twenty of the thirty-four American states had founded a university, including all of Illinois' immediate neighbors: Kentucky (1792), Indiana (1816), Missouri (1821), Iowa (1846), and Wisconsin (1848). Fourteen states had failed to establish a publicly supported university before the Civil War. Seven of these were original states in which private colleges of the colonial period remained strong, and seven were new states, including Illinois (1818), Maine (1820), Arkansas (1836), Florida (1845), Texas (1845), Oregon (1859), and Kansas (1861). Illinois was the oldest and most prestigious of the delinquent new states.[1]

Perspectives on the History of Higher Education 30 (2013): 225–246
© 2013. ISBN: 978-1-4128-5147-3

Universities are a part of an educational landscape that presupposes primary and secondary schools. Publicly supported common schools were late bloomers in Illinois. One reason was the pattern of settlement. The migrants who flooded into southern Illinois by way of the Ohio and Mississippi rivers in the early nineteenth century came mainly from Kentucky, Tennessee, Virginia, and the Carolinas. In 1818, when Illinois became a state, 75 percent of its people were southern in origin, and a high degree of illiteracy prevailed among them. The pioneers came from states that lacked a tradition of tax-supported common schools, and they strongly opposed taxation for education.[2] This attitude took deep root and shaped the manner in which the residents of Illinois thought about the state's responsibility to educate its citizens.

Another reason for the delay was legislative perfidy. When Illinois was admitted to the Union, Congress conferred lands and moneys on the state for a permanent fund. This gift included four separate funds, the income of each that was to be spent for public education. This largesse provided the means to develop schools and a college, but the first state constitution was silent on education, and none of the early laws recognized the school as a public function. In 1825, Joseph Duncan, a state senator, secured the passage of a common-school law that provided for a tax-supported common school in each county. This law, however, was undone by legislation in 1827 and 1829. Subscription funds and itinerant preachers got up a few pay schools, but the public schools suffered. Politicians used the state's educational patrimony to pay current expenses.[3]

Although the state defaulted on its obligation to establish a system of public education, the churches assumed the responsibility for doing so. In the 1820s, Presbyterians, Congregationalists, Baptists, and Methodists established colleges in Illinois which perpetuated a model of education that was ill-suited to the needs of a democratic, utilitarian, and westward-moving nation.

A movement that was designed to reconstruct higher education began in 1820, gathered momentum in the 1840s, and culminated in the Morrill Act. In Illinois, the demand for reform was largely identified with Jonathan B. Turner. Meanwhile, a crusade to create a system of free public schools began in New England, New York, and Pennsylvania in the late 1820s. It spread to Illinois, where educational reformers agreed on the need to establish free common schools but disagreed on other issues. Some wanted an industrial college with a regular school, whereas others wanted a regular school with an agricultural department.

Illinois passed a common school law in 1855, and it established Illinois State Normal University in 1857. Illinois State was an excellent school for the training of teachers, but it was not a true university.[4]

The Morrill Act and the University of Illinois to 1904

It took the Morrill Act to prod the people of Illinois into establishing a state university, the culminating point of the educational system of the state. Chartered in 1867, Illinois Industrial University opened for instruction in 1868. The language of the Morrill Act permitted many different interpretations. In its early years, the University was largely an engineering school with a predominantly male student body. In the 1890s, the trustees concluded that the University needed to stimulate the liberal arts and to attract more female students, and in 1894, they chose Andrew S. Draper to lead in the new direction. Draper had attended a proprietary law school in Albany, New York, for one year, but he lacked any college or university experience. He had made a reputation as the commissioner of education in New York and as superintendent of the Cleveland public schools. An autocrat who had held office for ten crucial years in the development of American higher education, Draper failed to understand that the university was then replacing the college as the paradigmatic form of American higher education.[5]

Edmund J. James: The Man and His Early Career

Edmund J. James, who served as president of the University of Illinois from 1904 to 1920, was superbly equipped to transform a land-grant college into a genuine university. He was born in Jacksonville, Illinois, on May 21, 1855. Colin James, his father, was a presiding elder in the Methodist Church and an advocate of higher education. Edmund attended grammar school and high school at Illinois State Normal University. He spent one year at Northwestern and another year at Harvard, but was unhappy with their offerings. In October 1875, James went to the University of Halle, where he studied political economy under Johannes Conrad. Conrad believed that the state played a positive role in socioeconomic affairs. He taught his students how to formulate and administer policy. In 1877, at the age of twenty-two, James graduated with a PhD in political economy and a strong reverence for German culture and institutions.

Returning home, James served for a year as the principal of the Evanston High School and for two years as the principal of the Model High School at Illinois State Normal University. In 1881, he and

Charles DeGarmo became proprietors of the *Illinois School Journal*, in which James urged that the federal government should promote higher education. James contributed articles to a national cyclopedia in which he brought the German school of economic thought to the attention of American readers. He was a pioneer in the revolt against laissez-faire thought in the United States. His articles won James a national reputation and in 1883, led to his appointment to the University of Pennsylvania.

It was here that James laid the foundations on which the Wharton School of Finance and Economy was built. He introduced the first research seminar at the Wharton School at Penn and applied policy-oriented research to the solution of economic, social, and political problems. His studies led to the conclusion that as society grew in complexity, the government had to expand its sphere to protect the public welfare. James also took an active part in the larger academic world. He was one of the founders of the American Economic Association; he helped establish the American Academy of Political and Social Science, which published the *Annals of the American Academy of Political and Social Science*; and he was a pioneer in promoting higher commercial education in the United States. A paper in which he urged the people of Philadelphia to take back their gas system from the venal "Gas Ring" won him a reputation as a reformer, and he played a key role in establishing the Municipal League of Philadelphia. James' addresses and papers on controversial issues made him enemies among those wedded to the status quo. In April 1894, the new acting provost of the University, a wealthy man who was a member of the Board of Trustees and strongly disliked James, indicated that James had no future at the school. On October 1, 1895, James resigned.

James went from Philadelphia to the University of Chicago. He served there as a professor of public administration and the director of the University Extension, an autonomous enterprise that was designed to supply beyond the campus what the academic departments offered on the campus. President William Rainey Harper approved of the program, but it aroused criticism. In 1898, when the College of Teachers was created, James became its dean. Harper admired James. "There is no man whom I have esteemed more," he wrote, "and with whom I have worked more affectionately than yourself."[6]

In January 1902, James was elected president of Northwestern University, a dream fulfilled. Northwestern was a Methodist school, and James was a devoted Methodist. Northwestern was then at a critical juncture in its affairs. For a decade before James arrived, President Henry Wade Rogers had tried to move the college into the modern age, but the financial resources were inadequate and the trustees were recalcitrant. Soon after taking office, James proposed several long-range objectives to advance the school, but his appeals to donors for financial support met polite refusal and the Methodist Church offered only rhetorical encouragement. James feared spending most of his time on administrative details rather than on doing large things at Northwestern, so he accepted with alacrity an offer from the University of Illinois.[7]

James and His Inauguration

In 1904, James arrived in Urbana with a vision of transforming a land-grant college into a genuine university. A skilful promoter, he used his installation as president in October 1905 to advertise both the University and himself. These exercises lasted the greater part of a week. They included a religious service, the dedication of a new building, addresses on the state and education and on the military training of the citizen soldier, and conferences on college and university trustees, religious education in a state university, and commercial education. The ritual of the inaugural perpetuated the tradition of the medieval university. In the morning, nearly two hundred invited delegates from universities in seven countries attended a formal reception; while in the afternoon, a seventeen-gun salute to the governor of Illinois preceded the academic procession to the Armory. Later that day, the University awarded twenty-five honorary degrees.

James' inaugural address, "The Function of the State University," was the high point of the program. He defined a university as an institution that afforded the ultimate institutional training of the youth of the country for all the various callings for which a scientific training, based on liberal preparation, was necessary. In a true university, the training should be scientific in nature. The model for such training was the German university. A university should provide scientific preparation not only for the old professions but also for any department of community life. James would extend the scientific character of the work done inside the institution and discontinue all secondary work, which could just as well be done elsewhere (e.g., in junior colleges). The University would not have a theological faculty, but it should reflect the character of society, and most Americans wanted their children to remain under proper religious influence during their college years.

James praised the generic state university for its influence on the older, endowed private colleges and universities—it forced them into a larger and more liberal view, helped maintain the democracy of education, helped keep education progressive, and made higher education the expression of the people's needs. A state university was the crown of the state system of public education, and it had to rest on a solid foundation of elementary and secondary training.

James went on to suggest some directions in which the state university should develop. First, it should become a great civil service academy. Second, it should become the scientific arm of the state administration. Third, along with the normal schools, the state university should become for many purposes the state department of education. In sum, the state university "should be as universal as the American democracy . . . ready to take up into itself all the educational forces of the state . . . tying together all the multiform strands of educational activity into one great cable whose future strengths no man may measure."[8]

The press reaction to the address was favorable. Much of the reportage observed that James described the endowed colleges and universities as bulwarks of opposition to educational progress while celebrating the progressive nature of the state universities. The press failed to note how much James emphasized the word "scientific" to validate the work of the university. At that time, the notion that scientific methods could be used in the pursuit of knowledge was prevalent in American thought, but James came close to invoking the word "scientific" as a talisman.

In his inaugural address, James envisioned the possibilities inherent in the Morrill Act. He believed that a true university could be built for the people of Illinois in what was then a small town on the Illinois prairie. As James once said, "if great universities could be created at Oxford and Cambridge, so too could a great university be erected in Urbana."

James possessed the professional and personal qualities that were needed in order to implement his vision. Medium in stature but commanding in presence, he worked hard and required his colleagues to work hard as well. He was democratic and agreeable in conversation. Frequently ill, he was once hospitalized for some months with a stomach ulcer. He had the capacity to disagree with others while maintaining cordial relations with them. He was able to admit his own failings. After a tense meeting with the Board of Trustees, he wrote to Trustee Ellen Henrotin and expressed regret for having lost his temper.[9] James had a healthy ego and large ambitions. He sent along with a faculty member who was going to Washington, DC, to take up a federal appointment a note saying, "if you see President Theodore Roosevelt, tell him I am available for a cabinet appointment."

President James and the Board of Trustees

Legal authority over the University was vested in the Board of Trustees. In addition to three ex officio members (the governor, the president of the State Board of Agriculture, and the Superintendent of Public Instruction), it consisted of nine members who were nominated by the Alumni Association to the political parties and elected by the people for six-year terms. During James' tenure, the board included a few able members, some eccentrics and lightweights, and others. Most board members were ill-prepared to know how to create a great university. Their strength lay in the fact that they reflected the will of the people. James assumed responsibility for setting educational policy. He relied on the board for advice and consent.

James was a progressive Republican, as were the trustees from 1904 to 1912. In 1912, however, three Democrats were elected to the board, including John R. Trevett, a Champaign banker, who was known to have a "violent dislike" for James. After an interview with Trevett on May 20, 1913, James wrote in his diary in Greek a phrase that translates, "he is a supreme jackass." Trevett, allying himself with Mary Busey, a trustee from Urbana, sought to gain control of the board's executive committee (which consisted of three people), reduce the power of the president to that of a clerk, and manage the University for his own purposes. The conflict became very nasty. When it became public knowledge, a delegation of twenty-one local pastors presented James with a Memorandum that praised him for resisting "all forms of graft of illegitimate influence local, family, church, or political." Knowing that he was under attack, James invited all faculty members who held an appointment for more than one year to meet to test the validity of the rumors that he had lost the confidence and esteem of his colleagues. He proposed a secret ballot on the question as to whether his presidency had been "liberal and progressive" and had promoted the "substantial development" of the University on "broad and scholarly lines," and whether the faculty had confidence in his administration. James then left the room and a confidential ballot was taken. Out of 194 votes, 188 were yes, two showed qualified support, and four were no. The faculty on one-year appointments balloted on their own initiative, with but one dissenting vote.[10]

President James and the State Appropriation

As president, James envisioned the creation of a German university that was adapted to American conditions. To realize his goal, he proceeded along several lines simultaneously. He appealed to wealthy donors to support various initiatives, whereas he relied on the Illinois legislature for the funds needed to build and operate the University. He was persistent and successful in securing money from the state. From 1869 to 1885, the average annual state appropriation to the University had been $27,603. From 1886 to 1904, the average annual appropriation had been $215,630. From 1904 to 1919, the average annual state appropriation had been $1,812,382.81. In sum, from 1869 to 1903, the state appropriated a total of $4,378,194.32 to the University, and from 1905 to 1919, it had appropriated a total of $28,998,125.00.[11]

The Graduate College and Research

When James assumed office, the University was mainly engaged in undergraduate education. Illinois was behind Michigan, Wisconsin, Minnesota, and others in offering graduate studies, and it was not a member of the elite Association of American Universities. James wanted to develop graduate work so that Illinois would rank with the best universities at home and abroad, and he wanted to supplement the system of higher education that had been built up in Illinois by private effort and the churches. Convinced that legislators did not understand the value of a graduate school as well as they understood the value of agriculture and engineering, James initiated a campaign to lobby for a special grant. He wrote to two thousand superintendents, principals, and school teachers, urging them to convince their legislators that a graduate school was necessary to secure for the University its proper standing among the higher educational institutions of the country, and he appealed to newspaper editors to endorse the proposition.[12] In doing so, he publicly argued that a graduate school was necessary to train school teachers, although in his inaugural address he had declared that the university's prime duty was to promote science and discover new knowledge. The legislature appropriated a sufficient sum for him to proceed, and James began to reorganize the existing Graduate School.

James wanted David Kinley to direct the Graduate School. Kinley, an economist with a Wisconsin PhD, was reluctant to give up his position as dean of the College of Literature and Arts and head of the economics department to head a new organization without separate funds, without a distinct faculty, with no authority over appointments, without a constituency, and with a certain sentiment in the state against it. However, after having defined his terms, Kinley accepted the deanship, and on May 4, 1906, the Graduate School became a separate unit.[13] Kinley sought to enlist the private colleges in Illinois to support an appropriations request for the Graduate School, and James appealed to the presidents of the private colleges to lobby for the appropriation. The University would emphasize graduate and professional studies, James said, leaving to the colleges as far as possible the elementary work of college grade while maintaining a college of literature, arts, and sciences. Most of the presidents were willing to support the Graduate School if the University would agree to concentrate on the advanced work, "leaving," as President Charles A. Blanchard of Wheaton College wrote, "the arts schools to furnish the Christian training which every nation must have or rot down." President J. A. Leavitt of Ewing College wrote that it did not seem "economically wise for all the Christian people of this State to be taxing themselves to build up an institution to rival those of their own."[14]

Kinley had a clear vision of the role of the Graduate School. Its main objectives were to advance knowledge by research and publications and to train a younger generation of scholars and school, college, and university teachers.

In the fall of 1907, University authorities planned the formal opening of the new venture for the fall of 1907, but events dictated otherwise. In September, the Graduate School opened unofficially with an enrollment of 168 students—134 in residence and 34 in absentia. By the end of the year, the enrollment rose to 211. The official opening was rescheduled for February 1908. The University had hoped to have its efforts to create a Graduate School rewarded by admission to the Association of American Universities. However, since its formation in 1900, the AAU had become elitist and was not eager to expand. The University had twice applied for and been denied admission because of the adverse votes of Columbia University and the University of Chicago. Exclusion did not become a serious handicap until 1904, when Dutch and German universities refused to recognize graduate work done at any American university that was not a member of the AAU. President Charles W. Eliot of Harvard prompted the AAU to consider enlarging the association, and on January 9, 1908, Illinois was finally elected to membership. The joyous news arrived on the eve of the formal inauguration of the Graduate School.[15]

This event took place on February 4–5 along with the installation of a new dean of the College of Engineering. On the first day, President G. Stanley Hall of Clark University, Dean Andrew F. West of Princeton, and the presidents of two Illinois colleges spoke on graduate study, while Kinley spoke on the relationship between the land-grant college ideal and the promise of American life. He declared that democracy required devotion not only to technical research, but also to research in the theoretical and abstract sciences and in the humanities. State universities as well as private universities should promote things of the spirit along with knowledge that has utilitarian value. In supporting the Graduate School, Kinley added that the people of Illinois demonstrated their belief that scholarship was necessary to democracy. The weekly magazine *Science* published the text of Kinley's address.[16] In describing the opening of the Graduate School, in *Science* Kinley wrote, "This is the first time in the history of American education that the people in their corporate capacity have put themselves on record as definitely in favor of that kind of work the graduate school is doing."[17]

In his address to the General Assembly on January 18, 1909, Governor Charles S. Deneen declared that the Graduate School promoted original research and investigation of all subjects which were of interest to people of the state, and it had raised the University to the plane occupied by the great universities of this and other countries.[18]

James and Kinley were eager to cultivate good relations with the Illinois private colleges.

Joseph R. Harker, the president of Illinois Woman's College, complimented James on the friendly attitude he had taken toward the independent colleges; it was very different from the former attitude at the University. On January 22, 1909, the University held a conference attended by seventeen college presidents. Those present discussed how to induce students to complete all of their general college work before entering the University for purely technical or advanced work and related matters.[19]

The Graduate School met a pressing need and grew steadily. In 1910, in his book, *Great American Universities*, Edwin E. Slosson wrote that the graduate work was the "the most interesting line of development" at Illinois.[20] Kinley insisted that the University should provide a medium for publishing research results of scholarly and scientific value. In 1908, the Graduate School sponsored the *Journal of English and Germanic Philology*. Two years later, it replaced *University Studies*, for which it had assumed responsibility in 1906, with *University of Illinois Studies in the Social Sciences*, a quarterly. In 1914, both *Studies in Language and Literature* and *Illinois Biological Monographs* began to appear. James was eager to expand into areas that might win the University a reputation as a center of research, and he shifted the costs of these ventures on to the Graduate School. Perhaps the most notable of these came in 1913 when the University became one of the sponsors of the Crocker Land Expedition to the Arctic.

The Graduate College met a need and prospered. In 1917–1918, the total enrollment was 451 students, including 98 women (21.7 percent). The constituency was largely local, but students from forty-one other states and the District of Columbia were registered along with twenty-three students from six foreign countries. China sent twelve, and Japan sent six. Of the students in residence, 79.5 percent were in the arts and sciences, 15 percent were in agriculture, and 5.3 percent were in engineering. The largest enrollments were in chemistry (seventy-four), English (thirty-two), education (twenty-two), animal husbandry (nineteen), Romance languages and agronomy (both twelve), and economics and physics (both eleven). The university did not award its first PhDs until 1903, but it graduated thirty-two in 1919.

James and Professional Education

James was an apostle not only of graduate education but also of professional education. When he assumed office, the University had a library school and a law school, both in Urbana, and a medical center in Chicago. James was dissatisfied with the law school. He wanted the law faculty to reform the law, not merely to teach it, and he wanted the dean to provide the school with more and better direction. The dean, Oliver Harker, a former state appellate court judge in southern Illinois, was politically well connected. James apparently concluded that it was best to let well enough alone. In any case, he was heavily involved with the reform of medical education. At the turn of the twentieth century, the United States had a multitude of medical schools, most of which were proprietary enterprises that were dependent on tuition and fees to meet expenses and yield a profit. Entrance requirements were low, medical faculties were usually practitioners, and instruction was largely didactic. Chicago had a large proportion of all the medical schools in the United States and a greater number than some European countries. Most of the proprietary schools taught some form of sectarian medicine, and their graduates were poorly prepared. The three medical schools that were affiliated with universities taught regular or allopathic medicine. They were Rush Medical College affiliated with the University of Chicago, Chicago Medical College affiliated with Northwestern, and the College of Physicians and Surgeons affiliated with the University of Illinois.[21]

The College of Physicians and Surgeons had been founded in 1881. The University of Illinois leased the college in 1897, believing that with its share of the profits the University would be able to acquire the school in twenty-five years. However, the advent of scientific medicine increased operating costs and made this goal impossible. Such was the situation in 1904.[22]

James was a notable reformer of medical education. He labored to get an appropriation from the state to raise the quality of the education offered by the medical school, but the sectarian medical schools, especially the homeopaths, fought him fiercely. Beginning in 1909, Abraham Flexner investigated the medical schools of the country as the agent of the Carnegie Foundation for the Advancement of Teaching. In his report on *Medical Education in the United States and Canada*, published in 1910, Flexner wrote that the city of Chicago was "in respect to medical education the plague spot of the country."[23] Many doctors and others in the Chicago medical community denounced Flexner for his criticism, but James declared that Flexner had not gone far enough. In 1912, when the medical school could not meet the higher standards required by James, the two institutions cut their ties with each other. A year later, James acquired the school for the University, where he worked with the two leading doctors in the Rush Medical School to create in Chicago a world center of medical research and education by the union of Rush and the University of Illinois. He was close to realizing his goal when circumstances intervened: The nation went to war, and the University of Chicago acquired the resources to erect its own medical college. Nevertheless, by 1920, the University of Illinois College of Medicine was established on the Near West Side, and Chicago was a world center of medical research and education.[24]

The University library, a fledgling enterprise in the early history of the University, took a new direction with the appointment in 1897 of Katharine L. Sharp as head librarian, professor of library science, and director of the Library School. Sharp was an 1892 graduate of Melvil Dewey's New York State Library School. Dewey described her as "the best woman librarian in America," and she was his devoted disciple. Sharp brought with her to Urbana the Library School of the Armour Institute in Chicago and a new level of professional expertise. She systematized the library and trained a number of women librarians who became her devoted disciples. On April 1, 1907, Sharp informed James of her desire to resign her positions during the next September. She confided to friends that she had been at loose ends since James arrived. As librarian, her strength was in techniques and procedures. James wanted a librarian who would build the collection and serve the research needs of scholars.[25]

James floundered for the next two years in dealing with the library. He appointed the former order librarian as acting librarian, brought in a new director of the Library School, and soon asked him to resign. While in Washington, he consulted Herbert Putnam, the Librarian of Congress, about his course of action. Early in 1909, James hired Phineas T. Windsor as the librarian and director of the Library School. Windsor was an 1899 graduate of the New York State Library School. Since 1903, he had been the librarian at the University of Texas. James and Windsor differed in temperament. James was bold and decisive; Windsor was retiring and deferential. James kept close watch on Windsor. He badgered Windsor about details, and on occasion, sharply reprimanded him. However, Windsor was the master of his own domain, which included both the general library and the departmental libraries.[26]

James himself strove to build a splendid library. In 1911, he began enlisting ethnic and religious groups in the United States to contribute materials related to their own history and culture. He persuaded the Board of Trustees to appoint two commissions whose object was to increase the University's collections—one on Jewish–American history and culture and another on German–American history and culture. Then, he announced his intention to appoint commissions on Dutch, French, Hungarian, Irish, Polish, Scandinavian, and Slavic elements in America for the same purpose. James habitually perused the catalogs of foreign booksellers, and in 1912, while in Germany, he bought from the widow of Gustav Gröber of the University of Strasbourg, one of the world's leading scholars of Romance philology, a library of 6,367 volumes and pamphlets for 10,000 marks ($2,500).[27]

While in Berlin in January 1912, James discovered that the library of the University of Berlin and the Royal Library together possessed more than one and a half million books, and they were augmented by special and departmental libraries which were connected with the university as well as special collections of government departments. As a result, within twenty-five miles of the city hall, scholars had access to five million volumes. This experience shaped James's notion as to what should be done to build a great library at Urbana. On June 7, 1912, he laid his views before the Board of Trustees. No part of a university, he began, was of more fundamental necessity than the library. A great library would under favorable conditions become a great university. However, the Illinois library was inadequate for the purposes it ought to serve. Comparative data showed that its holdings were very far inferior to those of universities located near other substantial library collections, and the Illinois library was inferior to that of the leading American universities. The university could not hope to take its place as a great center of learning until it had much larger library facilities. James complained that more prospective faculty members had turned down job offers because of the lack of library facilities than for any other reason. The University should look forward to the accumulation of at least a million books as rapidly as possible.

After having addressed the board, James asked the faculty senate to create a special committee to study the problems involved in library development. The committee reported that the University should make every effort to build up a library of at least a million volumes in the next ten years, and it recommended the construction of a new library building. James, speaking on invitation to an overflow student audience in October 1914 on the present and future of the University, demonstrated his passion about the future greatness of the University. The library had contained 60,000 volumes in 1904, he said, and 300,000 as he spoke. However, the present collection was a mere start. "We must have a library to begin with . . . of at least a million, and when we have a library of two million it will only be a fair beginning, and when it is four or five millions, as it must be if it is going to serve our purposes, it will have become one of the great libraries of the world."[28]

The library continued to grow by gift, exchange, and purchase. James himself gave generously to the library, and was closely involved in the purchase of whole libraries. In 1915, the University bought the Ratterman collection of books on German–American history. In 1846, Heinrich A. Ratterman had immigrated to the United States from Germany and settled in Cincinnati. A self-made man, a self-educated scholar, and a wide reader, Ratterman had a library of seven thousand volumes besides pamphlets, periodicals, manuscripts, and newspapers, and was especially rich in materials on the German element in the United States. A year after the Ratterman purchase, the University bought from a Leipzig bookseller manuscripts dealing with the period from 1570 to 1770 that illustrated the relation of Venice and the Ottoman Empire and of Venice and its Levantine possessions. The seventy-nine volumes of *Venetian Manuscript Documents* occupied more than six feet of shelf space in the Rare Book and Special Collections Library. Also in 1916, James sent Windsor a catalog of books related to Ireland, and a year later, the University bought the library of James Collins, a native of Dublin who had collected about seven thousand volumes on Irish history, topography, biography, and antiquities. The collection was particularly strong in nineteenth-century political and religious history. At the time of the purchase, only one faculty member was identified with Celtic and Irish studies. James built for the future.[29]

American entry into the First World War interrupted the book trade with Europe. In August 1918, shortly before the Armistice, the University purchased the library of Julius Doerner, an eccentric book collector and antiquarian of Chicago who died in 1916. The catalog of his collection, which contained more than fifty thousand books and a great deal of artwork, classified more than thirty subjects, including newspapers, periodicals related to American history, and nearly six hundred rare and valuable books and pamphlets. The material arrived in more than three hundred cases. Uncrating and cataloging it took years.[30]

The most important acquisition after the war was the Cavagna Library. Count Antonio Cavagna Sangiuliani di Gualdana, the last of a family of Cavagna counts, had fought for the unification of Italy, received a degree in law, been in public life from 1873 to his death in 1913, and had been a member of many societies, academies, and institutions. He had built up a library that contained more than forty thousand books and pamphlets and several thousand manuscript documents and maps. The collection included seven incunabula, rare and early printed books, first editions, and many books printed before 1560. Mostly in Italian, the library included French editions of Italian works, Italian editions of French works, Latin works, translations from Italian works, and some German works. In 1914, when James had learned about the Cavagna Collection, he asked Windsor to check it out. The price asked by a German bookseller was $40,000. James told the dealer that he would like the collection but lacked funds for it.

Shortly after the Armistice, James asked the head of the University's Romance languages department, who was then in Rome, to inspect the Cavagna Library, which was located at La Zaleta, near Milan. The agent reported that the collection was strong in Italian history from the Middle Ages to the present, was in excellent condition, and offered unlimited opportunities for study. The owners, the count's daughters, were willing to sell at the same price in lira as in 1914, which at the current exchange rate was about $20,000, half of the earlier price. University faculty members in related subjects said that the library was an extraordinary bargain, would furnish material for theses for graduate students, and would give the University real distinction in the Italian field. James approved of the purchase, which cost $17,989.31. Its acquisition was a landmark in the development of the library.[31]

James envisioned the University library as "one of the great libraries of the world." He set it on a path that enabled it to become the third largest university library in the United States.

President James and the Faculty

The faculty is the heart of a university. A great university president builds up a great faculty. Charles W. Eliot at Harvard, Daniel C. Gilman at Johns Hopkins, and William R. Harper at Chicago are examples. So too is James at Illinois. As the University grew, it needed a larger faculty. James interviewed a large number of candidates who were recommended to him by departments and deans. He did not want to hire anyone as an assistant professor without confidence that the person had the ability to advance to a full professorship. His appointees had to be efficient teachers as well as productive scholars. James was handicapped in recruiting by the location of the University and his inability to pay competitive salaries. Even so, he added a number of distinguished scholars to the faculty, several of whom testified to their pleasure in working with him. An atmosphere of productive scholarship began in the University shortly after James assumed office. He appointed several Jews to the faculty, in the humanities as well as in technical fields. What James did in getting a new faculty into the University of Illinois, Guy Stanton Ford wrote, transformed it within a decade into a relatively great university. Other presidents saved themselves trouble in recruiting by going to Illinois first.[32]

James and the Students

James did not pander to students. He viewed them as responsible adults and left the details of their care to others. Thomas Arkle Clark was the dean of men when James became president. Gifted in dealing with young men and determined to control them, Clark used an outside offer to consolidate his position at Illinois. Later, James and Clark worked well together. James insisted that his dean of women have a PhD, because she would be a member of the Council of Administration. He did not retain one woman who was successful in office because she lacked a PhD, and the women with doctorates whom he appointed were failures as deans. When important issues that affected students arose, James invited student leaders to present their views to the Council of Administration and at mass meetings of the entire student body. Students knew that he respected them, and they, in turn, respected him.

Hazing was an entrenched college custom in which sophomores subjected freshmen to initiation and discipline. It was a product of the class system, in which students were considered members of a single class throughout their college career. Hazing was difficult to control because it took place outside of class hours, frequently at night, and ranged from the practical joke to the cold-blooded offense. Hazing troubled all American colleges in the nineteenth century.

The practice took root at Illinois soon after the school opened. It flourished most vigorously at the opening of the academic year. The hazing of freshmen ranged from forcing them to recite a verse or climb a pole to scalping, paddling, or ducking them in the Boneyard Creek. A large gang made hazing a sport by going into rooming houses, where they asked students to perform various antics, and tossed the resisters into the creek that meandered through the campus. So-called "innocent" hazing always threatened to get out of hand. For example, a freshman waiter in the dining hall was told that according to "sophomore law," his mustache had to come off. He replied that his mustache was his own business; he would shoot anyone who tried to remove it. One evening, the hapless freshman was jumped by several men with scissors when he left the dining hall. The freshman fired his revolver and the assailants scattered. Hazing led some students to carry guns as protective measures.

The authorities informed students that hazing posed a physical danger and endangered public support of the University. They disciplined some offenders, expelled a few, and persuaded the sophomores and freshmen to promise to give up the familiar custom. Resolutions and pledges were unavailing. In the fall of 1903, hazing made the campus a battlefield. Gangs consisting of from twenty to fifty sophomores (and others) roamed the streets, entered rooming houses uninvited, and forced unfortunate freshmen to do their will.

Hazing was becoming increasingly dangerous. It was the sport of rowdies more than an expression of class rivalry. James, who assumed office in 1904, was eager to get rid of it. In October 1905, a sophomore compelled a freshman to push a peanut with his nose through the filth of the highway under penalty of being paddled. The Council of Administration suspended the assailant for the remainder of the year. The offender's father pleaded for reconsideration, which the council denied. A state senator then intervened for the culprit, but James was determined to stamp out "the brutal practice of hazing," and the only way to do so was by dismissing every student who was implicated in any way in these affairs.

Hazing did not suddenly vanish, but students were beginning to realize that under James the penalties for hazing would be enforced. Some learned slowly. In 1908, two sophomore ruffians were expelled for hazing, one having incited an incident "by means of gun shots and eloquent language." James admitted that it was extremely difficult to end hazing, "for the general public, in spite of some indications to the contrary, is at bottom in favour of hazing, at least opposed to any such punishment as is necessary if the custom is to be stopped." In 1911, when a student was dismissed for hazing, his parents used their influence with the state superintendent of public instruction and the governor, both of whom were ex officio members of the Board of Trustees, to get their son reinstated. James informed these officials that the university's position was difficult. The school was criticized if it did too little or too much to abate the "detestable and dastardly custom." In 1913, a sophomore from Peoria was dismissed for hazing. His father asked the council to reconsider its penalty for a "boyish prank," and he prompted the governor, a state representative, and a state senator to intercede with university authorities on his son's behalf. The sophomore offender had forced his way into the room of another student and with the aid of others had subjected the student to personal indignities, all of which James did not regard as a boyish prank. James now believed that public sentiment backed up the universities in their determination to stamp out hazing. He offered to help the student secure admission to some other institution, and he wrote to Princeton on the student's behalf.

By 1913, hazing at Illinois had apparently run its course. Several forces converged to end the practice. First, James demonstrated that educational leadership made a difference He was responsible for the policy that participation in hazing of any kind would lead to dismissal from the university. Second, as the university grew rapidly in size, there was a growing emphasis on university spirit rather than class spirit. Third, the rise of intercollegiate athletics and Greek-letter societies led to change. Youthful energy was increasingly directed to football and fraternities. Hazing disappeared as a campus activity but took on new life in the fraternities.[33]

James and Intercollegiate Athletics

James was conventional in his attitude toward intercollegiate athletic sports. He was not a sports enthusiast, and did not regularly attend the University's football games, though football was then the favorite intercollegiate sport. Similar to other university presidents, James endorsed intercollegiate athletics for various reasons that were accepted at the time: They promoted good relations between the universities, brought the student body together, encouraged students to participate in intramural sports, and made the public aware of the university. Nevertheless, he insisted that athletics be subordinated to the academic work of the university.

James and Academic Freedom

James had good relations with his faculty. Many faculty members testified to their pleasure in working with him, and in a crisis, as previously noted, the faculty endorsed his leadership. However, his handling of the alleged disloyalty of several faculty members during the world war deserves criticism. When Queen Lois Shepherd, a philosophy instructor, adamantly refused to buy war bonds, William H. Kerrick, a Department of Justice investigator, came to Urbana to investigate rumors related to faculty resistance to the Liberty Loan drive. At a public hearing, Kerrick questioned Shepherd sharply. He considered her answers "belligerent and antagonistic." Frustrated, Kerrick exploded, "You're a damned, rotten, vile, socialist, anarchist." A classics professor rushed to the defense of Shepherd. He and other faculty members then came under suspicion at a time when war hysteria was high. Reports of the local affray attracted national attention. James was known to be an admirer of German culture, and he feared that he might come under suspicion. Rather than defend the academic freedom of the accused faculty members, he advised them to write him a letter in which they made a declaration of their loyalty. Five faculty members complied with the request. The trustees appointed a special committee to look into the charges. After a long hearing, the board reported that there was no disloyalty, but faculty members were required to be "above the suspicion of disloyalty." James was satisfied

\e report. No one had been dismissed, but academic freedom had been compromised.[34]

Retrospect

In early September 1918, not long after the disloyalty dispute, James submitted his resignation. The Board of Trustees declined to accept it. The next June, in light of his age and the condition of his health, the board granted James a leave of absence on full pay until the opening of the school year in 1920. James then moved to California. He did not regain full vigor, and on March 3, 1920, he resigned as of September 1, 1920.[35] James died in 1925.

Edmund J. James was one of the outstanding university presidents of his generation.

He took a land-grant college that had not yet found its destiny, adapted the model of the German university to local conditions, and transformed Illinois into a leading American university. In 1910, Edwin Slosson's *Great American Universities* included Illinois among the nine endowed universities and the five state universities described. At the time, Illinois rated in about the middle of the fourteen universities evaluated. In later years, James propelled the University farther forward, and in his letter of resignation, he wrote that Illinois "has become one of the great universities of the world."[36] He looked forward with confidence to an even greater future for the University. However, oddly and inexplicably, no tangible memorial on the campus bears the name of the man who redeemed the promise of the Morrill Act by transforming a public institution into a true university and propelling the University of Illinois into greatness.

Notes

*   The primary sources cited are located in the University of Illinois Archives housed in the University Library in Champaign-Urbana. The reports of the Board of Trustees are cited by giving the number of the report in Arabic numerals, the year of publication in parentheses, and page references: e.g., *23rd Report* (1906), 311–12. Documents are cited by giving the number of the Record Series, the box, and the folder that contains the document, e.g., 2/5/5, B:13, F:Graduate School. The names of the Records Series cited are as follows:

- 2/5/3 James General Correspondence
- 2/5/4 James General Letterbooks
- 2/5/5 James Subject Files
- 2/5/6 James Faculty Correspondence
- 15/1/4 College of Literature and Arts Letterbooks

1. Donald G. Tewksbury, *The Founding of American Colleges and Universities before the Civil War, with Particular Reference to the Religious Influences Bearing upon the College Movement* (New York: Teachers College, Columbia University, 1932; repr. Archon Books, 1976), 154–207.

2. Clarence W. Alvord, "The Illinois Country, 1673-1818," in *The Centennial History of Illinois*, vol. 1 (Chicago, IL: A. C. McClurg, 1922), chap. 19–21; William V. Pooley, "The Settlement of Illinois from 1830 to 1850," *Bulletin of the University of Wisconsin*, no. 220. History Series vol. 1, no. 4 (Madison, 1908), 309–10, 313–29.

3. W. L. Pillsbury, "Sketch of the Permanent Public School Funds of Illinois," *Superintendent of Public Instruction, 14th Report* (1880–1882), cvii–cviii, cxxiv–cxxxi: Samuel Willard, "History of Early Education in Illinois," *Superintendent of Public Instruction, 15th Report* (1882–1884), cix–cx.

4. John B. Freed, *Educating Illinois: Illinois State University, 1857–2007* (Virginia Beach, VA: Donning Publishers, 2009).

5. On the history of the University to 1904, see Winton U. Solberg, *The University of Illinois, 1867–1894: An Intellectual and Cultural History* (Urbana: University of Illinois Press, 1968); Winton U. Solberg, *The University of Illinois, 1894–1904: The Shaping of the University* (Urbana: University of Illinois Press, 2000).

6. Harper to James, 29 February 1904: 2/5/1 (James Personal Correspondance), B:4, F:Correspondance, 1901-04.

7. For a biographical sketch, see Winton U. Solberg, "James, Edmund Janes," in *American National Biography*, ed. John A. Garraty and Mark C. Carnes (New York: Oxford University Press, 1999), 11:813–14.

8. Edmund J. James, "The Function of the State University," *Science* 22 (November 17, 1905): 609–28.

9. Edmund J. James to Ellen Henrotin, May 3, 1915, 2/5/3, B:64, F:Henrotin, Ellen.

10. Winton U. Solberg, "A Struggle for Control and a Moral Scandal: President Edmund J. James and the Powers of the President at the University of Illinois, 1911-14," *History of Education Quarterly* 49 (Spring 2009): 39–67.

11. *Sixteen Years At the University of Illinois: A Statistical Study of the Administration of Edmund J. James* (Urbana: University of Illinois Press, 1920), 15–17.

12. James to J. E. Armstrong, January 4, 26, 1905; James to C. W. Groves, January 19, 1905; James to George W. Hinman, January 23, 1905; James to Alice A. Abbott, January 31, 1905; J. W. Wilson (James's secretary) to J. E. Armstrong, February 9, 1905, 2/5/4, B:1: Ltrbks. 36, 37.

13. Kinley to James, December 12, 13, 1905, 2/5/6, B:2, F:David Kinley; Kinley to James, January 24, 1906, 15/1/4, B:4; *23rd Report* (1906), 311–12, 313.

14. Blanchard to James, October 6, 1906; Leavitt to James, October 20, 1906, both in 2/5/5, B:13: F: Graduate School, 1906–1907.

15. Kinley to James, February 22, 1907, 2/5/5, B:13, F:Graduate School 1906-1907; Evarts B. Greene to James, March 4, 1907, 2/5/6, B:6, F:Evarts B. Greene; Association of American Universities, *Journal of Proceedings and Addresses of the Ninth Annual Conference* (1905): 10–11; (1908): 10–11. The universities of Minnesota and Missouri were elected to membership at the same time as Illinois.

16. David Kinley, "Democracy and Scholarship," *Science*, n.s. 28 (October 16, 1908): 497–509.

17. *Science*, n.s. 27 (March 6, 1908): 394–95.

18. *Journal of the House of Representatives of the 46th General Assembly of the State of Illinois* (1909): 56.

19. Harker to James, April 18, 1908; "Report of Dean David Kinley on the Conference of College Presidents of Illinois," 2/5/5, B:13, F:Graduate College 1908–1909: Conference of College Presidents.
20. Edwin E. Slosson, *Great American Universities* (New York: Macmillan, 1910), 294.
21. Winton U. Solberg, *Reforming Medical Education: The University of Illinois College of Medicine, 1880–1920* (Urbana: University of Illinois Press, 2009), 7–32.
22. Ibid., 33–94.
23. Abraham Flexner, *Medical Education in the United States and Canada*, Bulletin Number Four, Carnegie Foundation for the Advancement of Education (New York, 1910), 216.
24. Solberg, *Reforming Medical Education*, 133–245.
25. Winton U. Solberg, *The University of Illinois, 1894–1904: The Shaping of the University* (Urbana: University of Illinois Press, 2000), 40–41, 189–201 (quotation at 192).
26. Winton U. Solberg, "Edmund Janes James Builds a Library: The University of Illinois Library, 1904–1920," *Libraries and Culture* 39 (Winter 2004): 42–56.
27. Solberg, "Edmund Janes James Builds a Library," 58.
28. Ibid., 60–63.
29. Ibid., 63–64.
30. Ibid., 65–66.
31. Ibid., 66–67.
32. Guy Stanton Ford, *On and Off the Campus* (Minneapolis: University of Minnesota Press, 1938), 301–2.
33. Winton U. Solberg, "Harmless Pranks or Brutal Practices? Hazing at the University of Illinois, 1868–1913," *Journal of the Illinois State Historical Society* 91 (Winter 1998): 233–59. Reprinted in *Schools as Dangerous Places: A Historical Perspective* (Youngstown, NY: Cambria Press, 2007), 309–37.
34. Bruce Tap, "Suppression of Dissent: Academic Freedom at the University of Illinois during the World War I Era," *Illinois Historical Journal* 85 (Spring 1992): 2–22.
35. *30th Report* (1920), 131, 309–10, 416, 709, 715.
36. Ibid., 709.

Transforming the Land Grant:
The University of New Hampshire and
the Pennsylvania State University under
the Leadership of Ralph Dorn Hetzel

Jane Robbins

Clark Kerr once noted that universities are "remarkably understudied institutions."[1] It was a statement about a surprising paradox: At the same time that there are numerous histories of higher education in America in general, and both historical and contemporary accounts of individual colleges and universities and their students in particular, little has been written on universities *as* universities—as institutions. From an institutional theory perspective, universities have been, in macro-organizational terms, largely ignored by educators.[2]

Even when colleges and universities have been studied from an organizational perspective, individuals, and the decisions they make, may be neglected. Presidents are described as "presiding" over change or growth, as if they just happened to be there while it occurred. Changing fortunes or changing interests are often attributed to an abstraction such as the economy, or the "market," or to shifting public priorities. Groups may join this list of outside forces in pushing the university into particular directions or forms: not only policy makers, foundations, and industry in particular, but also alumni, even students. Rarely, particularly in today's highly decentralized institutions, do we hear of the university itself—its leaders—choosing a course of action, and decisively bringing

Perspectives on the History of Higher Education 30 (2013): 247–274
© 2013. ISBN: 978-1-4128-5147-3

about change or growth. With the recognition that leader decision making and behavior is closely tied to performance, understanding successful leadership is of pressing importance to universities that seek to retain a hold on their own futures.[3]

This article explores the leadership and management of Ralph Dorn Hetzel, who spent his entire career in the land-grant system (and was himself a product of the system), beginning in 1908 as professor and later first head of the experiment station at Oregon Agricultural College (now Oregon State College); to his first college presidency at New Hampshire College of Agriculture and the Mechanic Arts (now University of New Hampshire) in 1917, through his presidency of Pennsylvania State College from 1927 until his untimely death in 1947. As context for this exploration, it utilizes documentation of two of his signature initiatives—the transformation of New Hampshire College into a university along with securing a permanent fund for its support, and of Penn State into a well-positioned research institution. It argues that it was Hetzel's individual capacities, skills, and habits of mind and behavior, not his position per se or any structural advantage, that allowed him to build his institutions to new heights, and to do so under the worst possible circumstances. It argues that the growth of Penn State as a research university was a mindful strategic choice that was carefully engineered and managed by Hetzel.[4] Hetzel's unusual combination of a highly analytical, methodical mind with compelling leadership skills drove Penn State's success and positioned it for the academic stature it enjoys today.

In the next few sections, I briefly review Hetzel's time at New Hampshire before providing a more detailed account of his purposeful efforts to build research capacity and reputation at Penn State. In the final section, I evaluate Hetzel as a leader and link both his accomplishments and his strategic choices to his internalization of and commitment to the spirit of the Morrill Act.

Before Penn State: Background on Ralph Dorn Hetzel

Ralph Dorn Hetzel was born on New Year's Eve, 1882, in Merrill, Wisconsin. In 1906, he received his A.B. from the University of Wisconsin. A multisport athlete during high school, Hetzel joined the crew team in his freshman year but soon dropped sports to work on the newspaper, reflecting an early interest—and talent—in communication. He quickly followed his A.B. with an L.L.B., and admission to the Wisconsin bar, in 1908, and was hired as an Instructor in English at Oregon Agricultural College (OAC, now Oregon State University) that same year. In the summer of 1909, Hetzel studied at the University of California and received an L.L.D.; in 1910, he was admitted to the Oregon bar. Hetzel's nine years at OAC illustrate the energetic productivity, broadly inquisitive and analytical mind, and general managerial competence that propelled him toward higher education leadership. He was promoted from instructor to full professor of English within three years; organized a Department of Political Science and became Professor of Political Science and Professor of Public Speaking shortly thereafter; and was named the first Director of Extension when OAC Agricultural Extension was formed in 1913. During his four years as Extension Director, he increased the college's appropriation from $2,500 to $221,000, taking a broad view of extension work as comprising work in the liberal arts, commerce, engineering, forestry, home economics, and other subjects. He was instrumental in increasing attendance to Extension events from 450 to 1,750. When he was hired by the New Hampshire College of Agriculture and the Mechanic Arts to be its seventh president in 1917, the student paper *The New Hampshire* reported that at Oregon Hetzel had played "an active and important part in advertising the institution to the state and securing financial aid for further work." His accomplishments showed that "President Hetzel, therefore, comes to New Hampshire keenly in sympathy with student affairs and practically equipped to manage various problems." He was thirty-four years old.[5]

Hetzel did not disappoint, despite having a "what have I done" moment on stepping off the train to take his post and looking around him at the Durham station to see—nothing. A man of commitment and simplicity, however, he simply set to work; there was no inauguration, not merely for war economizing but also because of Hetzel's low-key personal style. There were 562 students and 56 faculty members when he arrived at his office on August 17, 1917, and 1,784 students and 103 faculty on the day of his departure, January 1, 1927.[6]

The shift from an essentially agricultural college to a more educationally diverse institution occurred neither by accident nor with ease. It was an idea that, like many others, Hetzel sold to both the legislature and the state at large, which was deeply suspicious, even resentful, of suggestions that the college's primary focus should not remain on agriculture, and often raised the possibility of abolishing Arts and Sciences. He frequently reminded those who questioned him that it was written into law (the Morrill Act) that public institutions should not exclude "scientific or classical studies," but should "prepare the industrial classes for all the professions and industries of life." Hetzel was committed to this idea, and quoted the law by heart. But beyond that, he skillfully argued that a liberal education fed right back into the stimulation and success of agriculture and was required for all who would return to the farm as well as those whose work was required to support the industry as marketers, home economists, and others trained in the Arts and Sciences course. He also argued that, without such education, there would be no institution of higher learning in the state to which women could go—meaning the state would be cutting off the source of its teachers. He knew how to connect with the state's interests: "If you want to do harm to Agriculture, and of course that is the one thing we are trying to look at, you could not hurt it any more severely than by cutting out the Arts and Science Division, I believe, because 60% of our boys and girls come from our farms and small villages and it would be saying to the people who go back on to our farms, 'All right, you may go there, but you must remember with your limited income you can only get agriculture.' If there is anything that would prompt them to go to the Middle Western states it would be just that type of thing. What is the justification for curtailing? The matter of economy? All right, look at that." Then he would launch into another persuasive case of why nothing would be saved because agriculture students were still required to take liberal arts courses. He showed what had happened in other states that had tried eliminating liberal requirements. Next, he would compare their relatively modest demands with those of other states, showing through careful calculation that New Hampshire actually delivered more value for money than any other state institution in the country. He always showed where he had already cut, and from what, to get at his requests. He was fond of concluding with, "And there are your facts." However, he would always end with the moral argument: that students not only want and need, but also "ought" to have that education.[7]

The most visible evidence of Hetzel's persuasive power and legacy at New Hampshire was "two great legislative victories" related to his transformation of the rural farming college into a growing state university. The first was a name change to the University of New Hampshire (UNH), an effort that had been previously crushed in the face of opposition from the agricultural interests, who even objected that "mechanic arts" was in the name. The second was the establishment of a permanent fund known as the University of New Hampshire Fund through a millage tax on property at a time when the New Hampshire legislature's principal focus was keeping down taxes, and business lobbyists opposed funding because the state had Dartmouth.[8]

Hetzel's approach to both these accomplishments was similarly methodical, and characterized by high levels of information gathering and analysis; broad, focused communication of well-supported argument targeted to the objections and interests of legislatures and lobbying groups; and inclusionary and persuasive personal involvement. Although the name change came first, in 1923, and the Mill Tax Act in 1925, Hetzel had begun thinking about the mill tax as his strategic focus almost as soon as he arrived, and the campaigns were closely related. Indeed, it might be said that the name change was a necessary first step to achieving permanent funding, or, at the very least, that it proved insufficient to generate enough support for a growing student body and rising costs.

In many ways, the time was right, but it was Hetzel who, first, recognized this and, second, overcame objections by making the reasons clear to the public. "Why The Name of the New Hampshire College of Agriculture and the Mechanic Arts Should be Changed to University of New Hampshire," published and widely circulated by the Alumni Association Committee at Hetzel's behest, updated previous arguments for the present situation.[9] Hetzel was in the habit of consulting widely, and he incorporated the advice of numerous correspondents into the public document. It used speeches by Justin Morrill that justified broad, liberal studies to counter arguments from farm interests that the name change would be in opposition to the Morrill Act intent of agriculture education, and it noted that all but three states had changed the original names of their state colleges. It argued that the name inhibited interaction with all the industries of New Hampshire and concealed its public purpose of accepting students from all secondary schools, in contrast to aristocratic schools such as Dartmouth that "will never encourage the attendance of women." In fact, it demonstrated that the name made it difficult to market to women, who dominated the liberal arts, and drove both women and men out of the state because of confusion over college offerings; it was even suggested that the name was discriminatory to women. Hetzel and his network of supporters worked to convince the farm bureau that the change was good for agriculture. House Bill 385, "Act Relating to the New Hampshire College of Agriculture and the Mechanic Arts and Establishing the University of New Hampshire," was overwhelmingly passed by the legislature and signed by Governor Fred H. Brown on April 23, 1923. When President Hetzel returned from Concord (the capital) with the signed charter, he received a hero's welcome: he was met at the station and carried back to campus in Tom Thumb's coach, "followed by a parade of students."[10]

Hetzel did not rest on his laurels; he knew that institutional finances were his biggest challenge. Hetzel had done his homework in preparation for his next task, securing a source of stable income, by compiling detailed data and preparing briefs on subjects ranging from enrollment distributions, tuition, and budgets across the nation State and federal funds were only 54.7 percent of university income compared with 72.8 percent nationally—less if building funds were taken into consideration. At the same time, tuition was the second highest in the nation. Faculty salaries were low, and buildings were overcrowded. New Hampshire students were going elsewhere: The public universities of Vermont and Maine had attracted the most students, whereas Bates, Boston University, Harvard, MIT, Simmons, Smith, Brown, and Bowdoin had drawn substantial numbers among the privates.

Hetzel was not one to complain, but rather to act—and engage. Within months of the name change, he announced in the August 24, 1923 *Herald* a movement "to rehabilitate New Hampshire by a program for making agriculture and industry more prosperous" and to create "a bigger and richer New Hampshire." Hetzel himself would direct a "searching survey and catalog of the resources of New Hampshire." The goals of the survey included actively enlisting participation of the people of the state, particularly through its organizations and associations, and attracting to the state "people and resources for growth, prosperity, and well-being."[11]

Announcement of the survey produced an enthusiastic response from agricultural and industrial interests, and Hetzel quickly organized and led a conference of representatives from more than thirty citizen, agriculture, and business groups. Subcommittees were created in order to study every conceivable segment of the economy, from agriculture, education, finance, population, and transportation to recreation and resorts, minerals and soil, climate, water, and electric power. The survey made Hetzel a visible, and trusted, figure in the eyes of state interests and also focused those eyes on the university and its potential to assist the state in a wide range of developmental needs.

By the beginning of 1925, Hetzel felt ready to pursue the proposal he had been planning since his arrival: to seek permanent funding from the legislature. By that date, there was a UNH student for every 503 people in the state, almost 75 percent of whom earned some or all of their tuition. Keeping costs down was important for them. Out-of-state tuition, the fifth highest in the nation, was keeping students away. He prepared a special report calling for "a comprehensive plan for the support and development of the University over a period of years," and outlining its necessity, beginning with "The State University is in a critical condition".[12] Brief but well argued and supported, it laid out a plan for expansion and proposed a "mill on a dollar" tax, or 1/10 of a cent of property tax, as sufficient for the maintenance of the university. Since 1917, Hetzel had been researching the funding of state universities around the country and had an extensive file of correspondence that supported a mill tax. His special report was submitted on January 16, 1925, and a committee was organized to develop legislation.

Eleven days later, Rep. James Chamberlin of Durham submitted House Jt. Resolution 54 and House Jt. Resolution 59 for an appropriation and a special survey investigation about the university, and by March 25, 1925 the survey committee unanimously submitted House Bill 403, "An Act Providing for a Fund to Be Known As the 'University of New Hampshire Fund' and Regulating the Enrollment of Students at the University of New Hampshire" with a recommendation that it should be passed. Hetzel had already gained endorsements from numerous groups throughout the state, and he had also gone to work on the legislators. Using a kind of Facebook of the day, he learned about the legislators and their leanings, noting who was on what committee and making other notes in the margins next to the pictures of each representative.[12] He invited them to tour the university, arranging festivities every Friday for months that included coffee and doughnuts at the Faculty Club (an old war building); a tour of the best and worst buildings; dinner; an ice cream cone from the dairy; a carnation from the greenhouse; and a convocation in which legislators would be asked to speak, beginning with a "friend to the institution," and followed by others who, often as not, would fall into line. Photographs were taken early in the day, and by the time the lawmakers left on the afternoon train, Hetzel presented them with prints to take with them."[13]

In less than three months from the decision to submit legislation, House Bill 403 was passed and was signed by the Governor on April 22, 1925. Hetzel had "so thoroughly prepared the minds of the people for such a procedure" that there was little opposition.[14]

New Challenges Ahead: Penn State

It is no wonder, then, that when President John Thomas of Penn State College resigned and took a position at Rutgers, Hetzel was unanimously chosen by the board to be the tenth president of Penn State. The trustees saw in him something that Thomas had lacked—an ability to work with an unsympathetic state government. Political conditions were particularly difficult in Pennsylvania, with a governor who had little interest in higher education and a tendency toward punitive action against those, like Thomas, with whom he came into conflict. Indeed, Thomas had left Penn State in frustration at having been so unsuccessful at gaining the kind of support and recognition for the institution that he ambitiously sought—in part, it seems, because he lacked judgment and perceptiveness about how his plans and communications might be received.[15] In contrast, Hetzel had effectively demonstrated that he possessed precisely these skills of judgment and perception in interpersonal relations that Penn State believed it needed to move forward.

Many veterans of administration might have avoided what looked like a situation doomed to failure, but not Hetzel. Young—at forty-three, one of the youngest college presidents in the country—he seemed to relish the challenge and have confidence in his ability to succeed. The UNH trustees tried desperately to keep him, but he was ready to move on to the next challenge, and students and faculty seemed to understand this. "Literally, the university has been put on the map since the President's arrival here," read an article in *The New Hampshire* on September 30, 1926 about his resignation; Penn State, given its treatment by the legislature, "requires a man who has the power and ability to set forth clearly and to the best advantage the needs of such a state institution." He was feted with a chicken dinner and an hour and a half of toasts, presented a silver service and a bound testimonial, and bid farewell.[16]

Hetzel took up his post at Penn State on January 1, 1927. As at New Hampshire, Hetzel arrived without fanfare and went straight to work. He declined to have a separate inaugural; instead, he combined a simple inaugural ceremony, forgoing the usual invited dignitaries, with commencement later that spring. In his words, he "presumed to depart from custom by the severest simplification of procedure possible and consistent with progress toward the large objectives on which we are intent." Reflecting his humility as well as his external orientation and high level of accountability, he stated "the necessity of conserving our resources of energy and substance as to be without justification for any measure of ceremony not essential to the serious prosecution of our task. So we address ourselves today in a manner which we hope always will be characteristic of this administration, soberly and without pomp, to our important work."[17] As we might say today, it was not about him.

Hetzel began at once to make a difference. Over the course of his presidency, his significant accomplishments included major development of the physical plant—supported by the good timing of a change of governor and his own skill at working with the legislature—and bringing intercollegiate athletics, under fire nationwide for its corruption, particularly in football, under his control.[18] These two examples reflect Hetzel's canny ability to balance growth and effectiveness with clarity about public university purposes and integrity, an ability made possible by keeping the latter always a visible part of the conversation. When pressured to expand into branch campuses, for example, an initiative being promoted as a revenue generator during the Depression, Hetzel was cautious, expressing concern for the larger system of higher education (he saw branch campuses as threatening the new emergence of junior colleges, a movement that he saw as a valuable public benefit and whose purposes he did not believe the university should usurp). He would expand only in places where displaced faculty could be employed, and where no junior college or other institution of higher learning could serve area students.[19]

Hetzel entered the presidency at a time of impending crisis, the Depression, which influenced both what he chose to focus on and how he handled decision making. In the matter of state appropriations he was not as overtly aggressive as he had been at New Hampshire but continued to be remarkably successful in the face of seemingly impossible odds. He simply used a different touch. When former President Thomas's nemesis, Governor Pinchot, was elected for a second term in 1930, the combination of the Depression and the Governor's antipathy toward higher education made the prospect of cuts in state appropriations nearly inevitable. But Pinchot did not cut a dime, and a few years later, at the height of economic hardship and budget-slashing, he recommended only a 10 percent cut, a tribute to Hetzel's influence and approach. Rather than fighting and complaining, Hetzel sized up Pinchot and instead publicly announced that Penn State would absorb its fair share of cutbacks, and that 10 percent seemed reasonable and understandable. The result? The legislature voted to keep Penn State funding intact, and the Governor signed on, providing an appropriation *greater* than for any period since 1929.[20]

Rather than begging for more money, Hetzel chose to focus his strategic mind on building an infrastructure for research. Whereas at New Hampshire he had drawn attention to the university as a place for research beyond extension services and begun to lay the foundation for its growth, at Penn State he found an institution where research activities were farther advanced but neither well-organized nor controlled. Penn State had hired him to do what he had done at New Hampshire: make it a university and bring the legislature into alignment with Penn State interests. But Hetzel did not see these as Penn State's most pressing needs, and he crafted his own view of what ought to be done first. He determined from the start that he would make research his priority, sending a clear signal of his intent during inauguration[21]:

> If we of Pennsylvania are going to continue to be prosperous we have got to look in increasing measure to the ministration of science and scientific methods. Our wealth of natural resources is being rapidly depleted; our forests are mostly cut away; our oil reservoirs resist with heightened stubbornness our drafts upon them; we are immensely rich in minerals, but it is with increasing difficulty that we get them advantageously into the markets of the world; the original fertility of our soils has been largely exhausted. From henceforth our wealth will come more and more as the result of increased skill and decreasing waste; and for these two aids we must look almost entirely to the further perfection of scientific method. We are concerned therefore most vitally in stimulating and developing the agencies of scientific research. And it is important, vastly important, that a measurable control of scientific research shall be vested in a public agency. Pennsylvania will pay the penalty if for long she fails to equip this College, this public servant in the realm of educational ministry, so that it may control and make available for public benefit this vital and potential wealth-producing agency of science. Not only the wealth of the State, but her health, her comfort, her pride, her place in the sun, will be largely affected by what she does for herself in this important concern.[22]

While dealing with immediate issues such as the power struggle over athletics and launching the construction plan, Hetzel quickly set out to develop a coordinated and efficient program of research and increased graduate education, and unified policies and procedures to govern it. Consistent with his strong belief that the university should be of service to the state, but always concerned with the consequences of decisions for the long term, he saw an emerging set of issues associated with both public and private research; these ranged from patenting, already being discussed in a rather unsystematic way at the university when he arrived, to questions of faculty consulting and cooperative relationships with industry.[23] Hetzel also knew how vulnerable the institution was to state appropriations, despite his success at holding the line in that area. As Depression hardships mounted, building not just the capacity but also the reputation and efficient organization for doing research in a way that preserved the land-grant mission became a top priority of his administration.

President Hetzel and the Council on Research

Within months of arriving, on April 1, 1927, Hetzel formed a university-wide Council on Research with the approval of the Board of Trustees to serve as advisory committee to the President on all matters of research. Hetzel himself served as initial chair, presiding over early meetings (later delegated to S. W. Fletcher, Vice Dean of the Graduate School and Professor of Horticulture). Dean Gerald Wendt (Dean, Chemistry and Physics Department) was vice chair and assistant to Hetzel on the Council, and E. K. Hibshman was secretary (see Table). The Council's objective "was to outline the institutional policy on research," particularly as related to a range of questions that were arising in response to growing requests from and interaction with commercial firms, especially the industries of oil, anthracite coals, millings, and baking. These questions included everything from the contractual terms and conditions for commercial work, patent policy, consulting, and publication concerns, to the role of graduate students in research, release time for research, proper use of travel funds, and the effects of research on teaching. The "proper correlation of research" and "institutional responsibility rather than . . . school or departmental responsibility for research" was Hetzel's overarching goal for the Council. Here as elsewhere, Hetzel's belief in the leader's role in coordination and strategic agenda-setting comes through.[24]

A consummate manager, Hetzel was particularly interested in the question of how best to avoid "the uneconomic duplication of research" throughout the college, especially as a means of conserving funds; this, and a later question of an "appraisal" of research, would prove to be an area of some resistance from his committee, but one that Hetzel successfully converted into a means of fostering collaborative, interdisciplinary projects.[25]

He also strongly encouraged the funding of noncommercial research oriented to public purposes and research on pedagogy. Consistent with his commitment to the comprehensive purposes of the land-grant mission, he ensured, in his low-key way, that every area of the university, not just the sciences, was included in the Council's conception of research, and was represented thereon. He appointed several committees, including industry-specific committees, the most important of which were the Committee on Cooperative Research and the Committee on Patents and Copyrights.[26] The Council and its committees made detailed recommendations to Hetzel and, ultimately, the Board of Trustees, that resulted in policies to guide the conduct and disposition of research that persisted well beyond Hetzel's presidency. In the case of the Pennsylvania Research Corporation, they live on today in the form of The Penn State Research Foundation.

The Council's legacy is, perhaps, exceeded only by its productivity. By the end of its first year, it had recommended that research be adopted as the primary function of the institution in all subjects and that policies be created to oversee patents, an area of concern that would take up a good deal of its attention. The Council met two or three times a month over its first two years, and a minimum of once a month for many years thereafter, with special committees meeting and pursuing their own tasks outside these regular meetings. Its schedule of meetings was encouraged and prodded by Hetzel, who expressed concern if meetings lapsed, stating "I am desirous that the Council on Research should continue to do all that it can to carry forward the research program of the Institution."[27] Under Hetzel's executive guidance and according to his requests, it debated and formalized in considerable detail broad, philosophical questions such as what the function of research should be in the college, and the scope of the Council's work and authority.[28] The development of policy and procedure was goal-oriented. To meet Hetzel's desire to avoid duplication of research and promote collaboration, all projects had to be outlined and submitted for approval, and annual reports on research approval, progress, and completion submitted; preference was given to cross-departmental cooperative research, what we would call "interdisciplinarity" today. To foster research generally and aid Hetzel in his legislative requests for money, all departments were required to budget separately for research from instruction, a new way of thinking about budgeting for many departments. Hetzel had considered the pros and cons of having more detailed versus more general budgets when seeking appropriations, and decided that he could achieve more, and have greater accountability from departments as well, through itemization than by blanket request. To curb abuse and emerging concerns, specific policies were laid out regarding consulting and travel, with Hetzel determining that travel budgets should be administered by Deans. To guide research within the College, categorizations according to type of funding were developed, and policies regarding publication, type of work that could or could not be done (routine testing for private interests was, for example, discouraged), and patents were put in place. To further develop the graduate school, the connection between graduate study and research was laid out. And to increase awareness of research activities both within and outside the College, the Council created venues and funds for publication.[29]

Many of these policies, and the structures to support them, involved considerable study and disagreement, and several went through various iterations. Two of the most difficult areas were patents and cooperative research. The Divisions of Engineering and Agriculture at the time refused to conduct private studies that would assign any rights and rejected offers to do cooperative research, while Mining, Chemistry, and Physics thought that such work should be encouraged. At stake in this disagreement was the trade-off between public trust and the availability of research funds. Another contentious area was Hetzel's request during the height of the Depression for a "re-appraisal" of research for the purposes of determining, if financially necessary, where research expenditures could be cut back.[30] In Hetzel's view, this was contingency planning, but the Council generally resisted, requiring Hetzel to ask repeatedly for their consideration. Unsurprisingly, policies and procedures for gearing up and promoting research were put in place rather quickly, such as proposals for research, reports of research in progress, and publication of research activities in the *Faculty Bulletin*.[31] In 1930, a survey of research across the College was completed and published as *Seventy-five Years of Research, 1855–1930: Contributions of the Pennsylvania State College* "to direct attention to the steps that have been taken to strengthen this important function [research] to the College." Consistent with Hetzel's views of service and the notion of what constitutes a university, every school of the College was included; with his prodding, the Council had determined that "research" should include "creative writing," including fiction and poetry; criticism; histories; economic studies; and pedagogical materials. Research in the School of Education included such varied work as development of the Pennsylvania State College Psychological Examination, a test used for admission; a study of the ease of remembering number combinations; a bibliography on learning and teaching; and a simplified technique for computing regression coefficients. As of the report date, 456 projects were in progress across the institution, most having "important application to the welfare of the State," reflecting the College's "duty" to meet the many requests for research "so far as funds may be made available for this purpose by the State."

In 1931, "Recommendations of the Council on Research as approved by the President and as adopted by the Board of Trustees on March 20, 1931" was issued as a Supplement to the *Faculty Bulletin*, fulfilling Hetzel's overall goal of establishing both a coherent approach and common sensibility toward research across the institution. It covered nearly all the topics that the Council had been charged with for examination, except those still under discussion, most notably patents. A few years later, a policy and procedures for handling patents through the

Council were added, and the document name was changed to *Policy and Procedure in Research.*[32]

The addition of a patent policy marked the resolution of years of debate, changed opinions, and pressure emanating from the Board of Trustees to set up a separate body to handle patents in a manner similar to the Wisconsin Alumni Research Foundation. As was common in such debates at the time, the College was well aware of the potential "embarrassment" and tax status risk that could arise from administering patents and of the risks of litigation (three primary reasons for turning to setting up separate corporations for the purpose), and of the negatives associated with the Wisconsin structure. In the end, everyone got a little of what they wanted, a kind of hybrid system in which the College, including the Council, retained control over questions of evaluating patent potential, but a separate corporation would take and administer patents. With a separate patent committee that had been appointed by the Board of Trustees, Hetzel lost some control over the issue, though he did his best to slow it down and communicate concerns that had arisen from the College's experiences with patents to date. However, after coming precariously close to being established as a for-profit corporation—a status that would surely have altered the future of university patenting not only for Penn State but for all of higher education—The Pennsylvania Research Corporation (TPRC) was chartered as a nonprofit corporation on March 16, 1934.[33]

With the establishment of TPRC, the basic structure for growing and governing research at Penn State was in place. In addition to handling the ongoing work of publication of research news, research approvals and disbursements, and patent handling, the Council continued to handle requests from the President's office to consider and make recommendations on matters of policy as they arose: In 1935, a policy for trademarks and trade names for varieties developed at Penn State; in 1936, a proposed contract from Parke, Davis and Company to fund a lab in organic chemistry in exchange for exclusive rights (initiated by Wendt's department, but sent back by Hetzel for reflection). But the influence had shifted from formulating policy under Hetzel's guidance to interpreting and implementing it under faculty control, a change that gradually broadened the Council's activities. Fiscal concerns remained, and in 1937 the Council made a decision to actively canvas foundations, corporations, and private interests for research funds, in part because Hetzel had no funds available for departments that did not have their own resources. In 1938, seeking to mitigate faculty conduct of applied industry work that he thought might have negative consequences for research, Hetzel authorized a Central Fund for Research of $2500 to promote research throughout the institution, intended for fundamental research, which the Council directed to aid in publishing, research assistance, and buying out teaching time. But the focus on fundamental and public research also gradually shifted toward the private and applied, and by the time the Depression had ended, and the country had entered World War II, cooperative research and patent and licensing issues (including litigation and pilot manufacturing efforts to demonstrate patent viability or proof of concept to business) dominated the Council agenda.[34] Penn State had become a modern research university.

Leadership and the Hetzel Legacy

On the morning of October 3, 1947, President Hetzel made a telephone call from home. During the call, at 11:25 a.m., he suffered a stroke and died. He was sixty-four, and had been President of Penn State for more than twenty years, the second longest tenure of any president in its history.

At the time of his death, Penn State had grown into a diversified educational institution with more than 11,000 students and undergone great physical expansion. Between New Hampshire and Penn State, he had overseen their management during two world wars, starting out one presidency with one war, and ending another presidency after another. In both cases, he exhibited his usual can-do attitude of "courage and Herculean effort to surmount the obstacles and shoulder the load," handling as many as 2,500 armed services personnel on the campus of Penn State in 1943. He had received numerous honorary degrees, including the Litt.D.D. from Lafayette College and the LL.D. from the University of Pennsylvania, Dartmouth, the University of Maine, the University of Pittsburgh, and the University of New Hampshire. His service to higher education and the state comprised membership on the executive committee of the American Council on Education, the presidency of the National Association of State Universities and Land-Grant Colleges, and, for sixteen years of his presidency at Penn State, the Board of Directors of the Pennsylvania Chamber of Commerce.[35]

Beyond the external criteria of honors and titles, however, Hetzel's accomplishments and service to the universities and states where he spent his life were assessed by those who experienced his presidencies as permanently and remarkably transformative. For New Hampshire, his decade of administration was "probably the most productive in the history of the university," in which he had put a small college on the road to becoming "one of the State's largest businesses, with important economic implications for southeastern New Hampshire."[36] Speaking at his memorial service at Penn State, Chaplain Emeritus John Henry saw that Hetzel's perspective went well beyond Penn State itself: "What he has accomplished in bringing about a recognition of the land grant college in the eastern states is, in itself, a memorial to his wisdom."[37]

What allowed Ralph Hetzel to do what he did? Not a particularly warm or popular man, in the conventional people-person sense, he had a "rather severe mien." Yet he was widely respected by students, faculty, and trustees at New Hampshire, who had "unlimited faith in him."[38] Such trust and respect is consistently associated with the most effective and evolved leaders. In every case of his presidency, he did not enjoy the luck of location, and infrastructure, that so often is credited with making a difference to university success: He was in the country, a "turnip patch" as former President Johnson of New Hampshire put it, far from a port or major city or any other center of commerce and concentrated population.[39] He did what he did under the worst possible circumstances: wars, the Depression. He did not ride a wave, such as the post–World War II boom in higher education funding or the explosion of scientific, particularly NIH, research funding of recent decades. What was the source of his achievement?

Most likely, it was the man himself. Hetzel possessed the characteristics of leaders—not merely the trappings of someone in a "position of leadership." The history of his leadership of New Hampshire and Penn State bear this out. It is tempting to say that Hetzel was particularly strong in one or another aspect of running a university, but he proved himself a leader by virtue of balance and integration in everything he did. Hetzel saw Penn State as a part of a larger system, not merely of state universities, but of a system of *education* that comprised all institutional types. Seeing Penn State in relation to other colleges and institutions, he was thoughtful about neither encroaching on their proper places, nor shirking the development of Penn State's own. He did not believe in expansion for expansion's sake, filling a need that others could do better, or otherwise making decisions on the basis of what he called "institutional ambition." An expert problem solver, he was highly goal oriented within a long-term vision of the university and its needs, demonstrating intuition and wisdom, as Chaplain Henry noted, gained from depth of experience. In both strategy and execution, particularly in relation to legislative accomplishments, he demonstrated a highly analytical mind and the leader's habit of voraciously seeking not only information, data, and multiple perspectives but also further learning for himself.[40]

Hetzel forged this breadth of understanding into visions that were both long term and firmly rooted in the land-grant mission: service to the state through, first, education, and second, research. A highly strategic but not at all grandiose planner, he crafted well-supported and realistically nuanced visions that suited the schools and the states as he found them. Repeatedly hailed as a change agent, Hetzel was very comfortable with (indeed embraced) change, and always cautious not only about over-reaching, but also about "the limitation of vision which characterizes every generation. . . ."[41]

Hetzel's fairness, honesty, and moral courage in taking a stand independent of popular opinion were repeatedly cited as the basis for his wide respect. He was deeply committed to the university but also detached—not warm—allowing prudence and judgment in decision making. Perhaps nowhere was this more visible than his quest for "strict amateurism" in sports, "eschewing scholarships, scouting, and other 'professional' trappings," and his willingness to see revenues decline. A model of intrinsic motivation and external orientation, his hard work and high levels of preparation were oriented to making decisions that were focused on the greater good of the state and the institution and never on his own personal glory, or even internal glory. For Hetzel, growth occurred through service and learning; growth was not, in and of itself, the mission. He clearly saw his role as a preserver of values, questioning and reminding everyone about how any particular choice fit in with the land-grant mission or what its consequences might be for institutional character in the future. He explicitly labeled himself as "steward." He said the college should have a soul—that it was "concerned with the task of weaving into the structure of our civilization culture and idealism and morality."

In other regards, Hetzel was a man who balanced risk and return—who would not do something for short-term advancement. Although a strong believer in both research and service to the state, Hetzel was aware of the risks to integrity of both science and the institution that it presented, and demonstrated a tendency both to treat all researchers equally and to maintain relatively tight control over outside research activities; as shown, he was prepared to cut back on research if it threatened the college's fundamental priority of providing a quality education to the public. Concerned about over-reliance on industrial cooperation, he saw hypocrisy as well as danger of loss of public trust in the assertion that, as public institutions, they should serve private industrial labs. Each time he looked at a contract or proposal he asked that faculty "anticipate" consequences, and develop "contingency" plans, a hallmark of the ethical leader.[42] He modeled this behavior to the entire institution, holding himself and others accountable for every dollar spent, and every choice made.

Hetzel's extraordinary communication skill, particularly relationship skill, was frequently cited by those who had worked with him as a basis for his achievements. He was an energetic and inspiring advocate for his causes. Particularly skilled at creating the contagious enthusiasm for which leaders are known, he was able to engage large and diverse sets of followers, utilizing a democratic and participatory style instinctively suited to each. He knew when to be eloquent and poetic, when to be firm and matter-of-fact. These interpersonal abilities were the manner in which he achieved buy-in of his vision, often, as in New Hampshire, against long-held resistance.

Communication skills were also important in the way he consistently modeled behavior, particularly the need to consider moral aspects of decision making, to faculty. He was, verbally, the moral compass and conscience for both institutions, always reminding, in his low-key, questioning way, faculty and others to whom he had delegated responsibility what those responsibilities were. He was equally effective as a moral compass with students and in his interactions with other institutions. He consulted with students on matters where others might be more authoritarian and took their wishes into account—for example, repealing mandatory chapel attendance through pragmatic, logical discussion with the trustees, loosening outmoded social restrictions on students, and accommodating students who wanted to participate in political demonstrations. In exchange, students worked hard, and respected Hetzel's tough stand against what he saw as destructive adolescent activities such as hazing. This collaborative, empathetic give-and-take style—he had a reputation for giving people the benefit of the doubt—was another hallmark of his presidency.

Hetzel worked tirelessly to achieve what he believed was needed, often in the face of discouraging odds. He was readily adaptive to whatever came his way, and had a high tolerance, what in the leadership literature is sometimes called "a preference," for uncertainty. From taking on a "cow college," to turning down a comfortable position after World War I to help with international reconstruction in order to stay and build New

Hampshire, to accepting the Penn State offer after the legislature had literally thumbed its nose at it, Hetzel intentionally sought out challenges. Selfless, modest, hardworking, persistent, methodical, curious about all things, and fiscally conservative, he ran the institution according to his beliefs in coherent management and decisions that were in the best interests of the university as a public service institution, and not any individual (including his own), department, or private interest. Supporting his understanding of change as a constant, he had the confidence in his skills to believe that he could make it happen, and push through times of hardship; at the same time, he was totally lacking in hubris: "I formally assume the responsibility of this office today, conscious of the enormity of the task and humble in the knowledge of the inadequacy of my equipment."[43]

In many ways, Hetzel reflects the ideal leader-manager. Both efficiency and effectiveness were important to him, and he saw duplication of effort as a waste, evidenced by his centralization of many functions, including athletics, student government, research, and extension, as well as the consolidation of programs.[44] Interestingly, centralization created a powerful avenue for public awareness and promotion, and ultimately for the fulfillment of vision and adherence to the land-grant ideal, because it worked. Hetzel knew how to recruit and assign good people to work with him rather than independently, and to free up time and resources to focus on achieving needed goals. He did all this with vision, humility, fearlessness, cooperative spirit, and total commitment.

What might Hetzel think of land-grant universities today? He would be proud of the accomplishments of both New Hampshire and Penn State, and of every area in which they and their land-grant counterparts contribute to the well-being of their states. To the extent that they have grown to serve larger numbers of undergraduates, he would be pleased. But he would be appalled by the cost of an education and by the fact that there seemed to be little change in students' struggles to pay for college despite these institutions' achievement of considerable wealth; as he said, high tuition defeats the public purpose. Although he would laud its democratic effects, most likely he would question global expansion by public universities as not directly aiding the state and thereby not being a prudent and fair use of its resources. He would be chagrined by the enormous decentralization of administration, which he would see as grossly inefficient and duplicative, and disappointed in the overspecialization and siloization of the university, which he would see, again, not only as inefficient, but also as limiting interdisciplinary thinking and innovative productivity. He would be shocked at the state of intercollegiate athletics, which he would see as a distortion of everything the land-grant institution was set up to accomplish, and the failure of the efforts of those who, like him, tried to keep it in check. Most of all, he would be concerned about conflict of interest, and the failure, or neglect, of presidents to balance growth in attention to science with maintaining public trust and institutional integrity, and with equal growth in and attention to ensuring the highest-quality pedagogy and learning experience for students. But he would have faith in the possibility of change, and hope for a new and courageous vision of leadership.

I close with some of Hetzel's own words about what it means to be responsible for a public institution—both his reverence for it, and his caveats:

> . . . these public institutions . . . have survived and grown great because they served greatly. By virtue of this service untold wealth has been added to the material resource of the Nation;. . . . But more than this they have contributed greatly to the dignity, the satisfaction and the happiness of all of the people of this Nation. They have been the largest single factor not only in the democratization of education but in the democratization of idealism. They have carried idealism into the realm of everyday things. They have influenced all education; they have forced higher education in America to be ever attentive and sympathetic with the needs and ambitions of all of our people; they have been a great factor in making higher education available to the American youth irrespective of inheritance, of station or of wealth; they have been a great force in preserving public confidence in educated leadership. They have ever been the alert champions of democracy."[45]

> . . .

> "We have in our temporary keeping and under our direction an agency which has been created to give substance to a great ideal—an ideal of social justice by which recognition shall be given to the rights and the privileges of all our people; an agency which must minister to the security of our State by preparing its people to assume in constantly increasing measure the responsibilities of each new day; an agency which is charged with enlarging our prosperity through the increase of wealth by adding knowledge and skill to our processes of production; an agency which is charged with enlarging our vision, strengthening our hopes, enriching our faith. The enormity of this responsibility justifies our pause in the activities of this day in order that we may acknowledge with gratitude the gift of our fathers, and make solemn pledge that we shall during the course of our brief day of responsibility carry on and move forward the great, vital trust which they have placed in our keeping, and by whose ministry we are permitted to profit.[46,47]

Council on Research, Members as of October 31, 1928

G. Wendt, Dean of Graduate School, Professor of Chemistry and Physics

R. H. Smith, Comptroller of the College

R. L. Watts, Dean of Agriculture

R. L. Sackett, Dean of Engineering

C. W. Stoddart, Dean of Liberal Arts

R. G. Kern, Dean of the Graduate School

E. B. Forebers Dir. Institute of Animal Nutrition, Professor of Animal Nutrition

E. Steidle, Dean of Mines and Metallurgy

S. W. Fletcher Vice Dean and Dir. Research, Professor of Horticulture

C. C. Peters, Dir. of Educational Research, Professor of Education

W. J. Sweeney Dir. Division of Industrial Research, School of Chemistry and Physics

F. G. Hechler, Professor of Engineering Research

Notes

1. C. Kerr, *The Uses of the University, with a "Postscript—1972"* (Cambridge, MA: Harvard University Press, 1972).
2. Notable exceptions have tended to come from outside the realm of higher education historians and scholars from the fields of sociology or economics. They include T. Veblen, *The Higher Learning in America: A Memorandum on the Conduct of Universities by Businessmen* (New Brunswick, NJ: Transaction Publishers, 1918); R. Collins, *The Credential Society: An Historical Sociology of Education and Stratification* (New York: Academic Press, 1979). Recent additions to examining the nature of universities as institutions include J. Robbins, "Toward a Theory of the University: Mapping the American Research University in Space and Time." *American Journal of Education* 114 (February): 243–72 plus online supplement; R. Barnett, *Realizing the University in an Age of Supercomplexity* (Buckingham: Society for Research into Higher Education and Open University Press, 2000); J. A. Douglass, "The Entrepreneurial State and Research Universities," *Higher Education Management and Policy* 19, no. 1 (2007): 84–120, and a spate of books aimed primarily at understanding university purposes; these include B. A. Weisbrod, J. P. Ballou, and E. D. Asch, *Mission and Money: Understanding the University* (Cambridge: Cambridge University Press, 2010); M. Bousquet, *How the University Works: Higher Education and the Low-Wage Nation* (New York: NYU Press, 2007); H. Thorp and B. Goldstein, *Engines of Innovation: The Entrepreneurial University in the Twenty-first Century* (Chapel Hill: University of North Carolina Press, 2010); and E. Schrecker, *The Lost Soul of Higher Education Corporatization, the Assault on Academic Freedom, and the End of the American University* (New York: The New Press, 2010).
3. Biographical studies of college leaders, such as P. Gilpin and M. Gasman, *Charles S. Johnson: Leadership behind the Veil in the Age of Jim Crow* (Buffalo, NY: SUNY Press, 2003); A. Padilla, *Portraits in Leadership: Six Extraordinary*

University Presidents (Westport, CT: American Council on Education/Praeger, 2005); M. A. Dzuback, *Robert M. Hutchins: Portrait of an Educator* (Chicago, IL: University of Chicago Press, 1991); D. S. Jordan, *Leland Stanford's Views on Higher Education* (Stanford, CA: Stanford University Press, 1901); D. Kampel, *Learning Leadership: Women Presidents of Colleges and Universities* (Lampert Academic Publishing, 2010); A. Levine, "Succeeding as a Leader: Failing as a President," *Change* (January–February 1998); F. S. Gulley, *The Academic President as Moral Leader: James T. Laney at Emory University* (Macon, GA: Mercer University Press, 2001); C. M. Perry, "Henry Philip Tappan: Philosopher and University President," *Journal of Philosophy* 31, no. 2 (January 18, 1934): 52; and C. Gonzalez, *Clark Kerr's University of California: Leadership, Diversity, and Planning in Higher Education* (New York: Transaction Publishers, 2011) focus on people who shaped their institutions or higher education, and can provide good insight into the evolution of the role and questions of its differentiation across segments of higher education. There are too few of them, and their publication dates evidence the general lack of interest in presidential studies in the postwar period up until recent decades, a period when leadership as an area of study was neglected in general. Since the 1990s and particularly since 2000, there is renewed interest in leadership, both in higher education and in management in general. Volume 28 (2011) of *Perspectives on the History of Higher Education* is devoted to articles on "iconic leaders." For studies of the office of the college presidency and its role, which suffered from the same midcentury neglect but is now enjoying a surge of interest, see G. P. Schmidt, *The Old Time College President* (New York: Columbia University Press, 1930); D. G. Brown, *University Presidents as Moral Leaders* (Westport, CT: ACE/Praeger Series on Higher Education, 2006); M. D. Cohen and J. G. March, *Leadership and Ambiguity: The American College President* (New York: McGraw-Hill, 1974); H. K. Brodie and L. Banner, *The Research University Presidency in the Late 20th Century: A Life Cycle/Case History Approach* (Westport, CT: Praeger, 2005); A. H. Goodall, *Socrates in the Boardroom: Why Research Universities should be Led by Top Scholars* (Princeton, NJ: Princeton University Press, 2009); D. W. Breneman and P. J. Yakaboski, eds., *Smart Leadership for Higher Education in Difficult Times* (Edward Elgar Publishing, 2011). Presidential memoirs and essay collections provide a complementary lens through which to view particular issues related to particular presidents' perspectives and their times. This large genre includes, as a few examples, R. Rosenzweig, *The Political University: Policy, Politics, and Presidential Leadership in the American Research University* (Baltimore, MD: Johns Hopkins University Press, 1999); D. Bok, *Universities in the Marketplace: The Commercialization of Higher Education* (Princeton, NJ: Princeton University Press, 2003); W. G. Bowen and H. T. Shapiro, *Universities and Their Leadership* (Princeton, NJ: Princeton University Press, 1998); M. A. Wachman, *The Education of a University President* (Philadelphia: Temple University Press, 2005); J. J. Duderstadt and F. W. Womack, *The View from the Helm: Leading the American University during an Era of Change* (Ann Arbor: University of Michigan Press, 2007); D. P. Gardner, *Earning My Degree: Memoirs of an American University President* (Berkeley: University of California Press, 2005); C. V. Newsom, *A University President Speaks Out: On Current Education* (New York: Harper, 1961); and A. Draper, "The University President." *The Atlantic Monthly* 97 (1906).

4.   For historical background on the land-grant system related to the time period and developments documented in this article, see, for example, G. E. Howard, "The State University in America," *Atlantic Monthly* 67 (1891): 332–42; I. L. Kandel, *Federal Aid for Vocational Education*, Bulletin of the Carnegie Foundation for the Advancement of Teaching, no. 10 (New York: Carnegie Foundation for the

Advancement of Teaching, 1917); A. C. True, "A History of Agricultural Education in the United States, 1785–1925," *U.S. Agriculture Dept Miscellaneous Publication* 36 (July 1929); E. D. Eddy, Jr., *Colleges for Our Land and Time: The Land Grant Idea in American Education* (New York: Harpers, 1956); A. H. DuPree, *Science in the Federal Government: A History of Policies and Activities to 1940* (Cambridge, MA: Belknap Press, 1957); L. R. Veysey, *The Emergence of the American University* (Chicago, IL: University of Chicago Press, 1965); H. Hawkins, ed., *The Emerging University and Industrial America* (Malabar, FL: Robert E. Krieger Publishing, 1985); A. Brody, *The American State and Higher Education* (Washington, DC: American Council on Education, 1935); F. Rudolph, *The American College and University: A History* (Athens, GA: University of Georgia Press, 1962); A. Nevins, *The State Universities and Democracy* (Urbana: University of Illinois Press, 1962); J. S. Brubacher and R. Willis, *Higher Education in Transition: A History of the American Colleges and Universities, 1636–1976* (New York: Harper & Row, 1958); R. Hofstadter and C. D. Hardy, *The Development and Scope of Higher Education in the United States* (1952); D. O. Levine, 1986. *The American College and the Culture of Aspiration, 1915–1940* (Ithaca, NY: Cornell University Press, 1952); J. Thelin, *A History of American Higher Education* (Baltimore, MD: Johns Hopkins University Press, 2004); and J. A. Douglass, *The Conditions for Admission: Access, Equity, and the Social Contract of Public Universities* (Palo Alto, CA: Stanford University Press, 2007a). Many of these also serve as general histories of higher education. Also of interest are public university presidential addresses from the period, such as L. D. Coffman, *The State University: Its Work and Problems. A Selection from Addresses Delivered between 1921 and 1933* (London and Minneapolis: Oxford University Press and University of Minnesota Press, 1934) (Coffman was President of the University of Minnesota); Edmund J. James, "The Function of the State University," *Science* 22 (November 17, 1905): 609–28; and J. R. Angell, *American Education* (New Haven, CT: Yale University Press, 1937) Angell was President of the University of Michigan.

5. *The New Hampshire*, October 13, 1917. Biographical information from this issue and University of New Hampshire, University Archives, Vertical Files, folder "Hetzel, Ralph D." (primarily a clip file, many articles/obits without sources or dates); William E. Marks, *Biographic Survey of Centre County, PA*,1941(105), online at www.libraries.psu.edu/do/digitalbookshelf/29242719/29242719_part_05.pdf ; Ralph Dorn Hetzel, 1917-27 Papers, Presidents, UA 2/1/4University of New Hampshire, University Archives. During his presidencies, Hetzel received honorary doctorate degrees (in Letters or Law) from Dartmouth, the University of Maine, Bucknell University, Lafayette College, the University of Pennsylvania, and the University of New Hampshire. He served in executive positions on national scholarly and higher education organizations, including but not limited to Phi Beta Kappa, Association of Land-Grant Colleges and Universities, and the National Association of State Universities.

6. Sackett, Everett B. for the Class of 1924, "Ralph D. Hetzel, President of the Earlier College and the University of New Hampshire, 1917–26," no date, in Hetzel, Ralph D., Vertical Files, op. cit. This appears to be a commemorative note; other content suggests perhaps it was for a fiftieth class reunion. Hetzel predicted that by 1975, New Hampshire would have between 2,000 and 2,500 students. It surpassed his estimate within thirteen years: As of 1956, it had exceeded that estimate by nearly 40 percent, and by 1973, with two years left to go on the clock, enrollment was nearly 10,000 (Johnson 1956, 23; E. B. Sackett, *New Hampshire's University: The Story of a New England Land Grant College* (Somersworth, NH: New Hampshire Publishing, 1974), 76, 91. In fact, Hetzel tried to waylay fears among the legislature

that New Hampshire was growing too rapidly when discussing future budgets; for example, in 1921 he attributed some of the growth to a post-war spike, and chose an average growth rate to suggest that it would take ten years for enrollment to hit 1,300 (less than it was when he left in 1926). It is possible that Hetzel's underestimates were deliberate (Untitled transcript, Hetzel Papers, PSU, Subgroup 5, Box 2, Folder 17).

7. (Untitled transcript, Hetzel Papers, PSU, Subgroup 5, Box 2, Folder 17). Probably 1921. This appears to be a transcript of one of Hetzel's favorite relationship strategies: inviting legislators to campus to see for themselves both its assets and, particularly, its needs, sandwiching detailed money talk between eloquent historical discussions of land grants and telling of stories of student hardships or accomplishments, and entertainment, from ball games to ice cream socials. At this time, enrollment was 867, almost all from rural or labor classes (Hetzel was a master of data; he knew, e.g., how many came from single-mother households); the average assistant professor salary was $2200; and the total budget for the institution, including extension, experiment work, and other activities, was $741,656 for the coming year, including a tuition increase. Instate tuition was $100.00 and out-of-state $150.00; most of instate tuition was covered by scholarship, plus fees of $50.00. The cost of educating each student ("maintenance") was estimated to be around $400.00. New Hampshire had the highest tuition of any state, which was one of Hetzel's concerns; forty-seven states had free tuition for instate students and Hetzel believed that all should. "If you get your charge up to a point where it becomes prohibitive for boys and girls, then you are defeating the very purpose of the institution."

8. Sackett, *New Hampshire's University*, 88.

9. University of New Hampshire, University Archives, UA 6/5/3.

10. Sackett, *New Hampshire's University*, 88; F. Engelhardt, *History of the University of New Hampshire, 1866–1941* (Durham and Rochester, NH: University of New Hampshire/The Record Press, 1941). A copy of the Act, together with notes and correspondence related to support for the bill, is in F-32, Box 1 of President Hetzel's papers, UA 2/1/4. The Act, in establishing the university, required the establishment of a College of Technology or Engineering and a College of Arts and Sciences, and teaching and research "as may be necessary and desirable in the education of youth and the advancement and development of the arts, the sciences and the industries."

11. New Hampshire State Survey Committee, New Hampshire State Survey Records, 1923-25, MC131, Box 1, Folder 1 "Correspondence to/from President Hetzel, Aug 1923–Jan1924" and Folder 10 "Undated Material," 30. "A Brief Statement Relative to the University of New Hampshire: Prepared by the President of the University Under Authorization of the Board of Trustees," UA 2/4/2, University of New Hampshire, University Archives.

12. *The Brown Book: Biographical Sketches of the New Hampshire Legislature of 1925* (Concord, NH: Joseph M. Lucier, Publisher). In Folder 23, Box 3 of President Hetzel's papers.

13. Engelhardt, *History of the University of New Hampshire*; Sackett, *New Hampshire's University*, 93.

14. Engelhardt, *History of the University of New Hampshire*, 271. The Act limited out of state enrollment to between 4 and 8 percent, depending on the state of student origin. The percentages were lower for non–New England states. Its support by farm interests was likely smoothed through the introduction and passage of a separate law, the Purnell Act, which increased funds for agricultural research up to $90,000/yr.

15. Ralph D. Hetzel, Vertical Files, University of New Hampshire, University Archives; M. Bezilla, *Penn State: An Illustrated History* (University Park: The Pennsylvania State University, 1985).

16. Ralph D. Hetzel, Vertical Files, Program for Faculty and Staff Dinner and *The New Hampshire*, December 2, 1926.

17. Sackett, *New Hampshire's University*; Inaugural Address, Tuesday, June 14, 1927. University Archives, PSU, Papers of Ralph Dorn Hetzel, Subgroup 5, Box 2, Folder 33. Sackett is a summary of an unfinished, seven-volume typescript by Professor Marston, who died before it was published.

18. Thomas had laid the foundation for the building plans, but had been unable to get legislative support. Hetzel essentially centralized authority over athletics in order to rein in unethical activity. An interesting series of articles titled "Wanted: Honest Football" written by another university president during the 1930s, Henry Apple of Franklin and Marshall, gives a good, and eerily familiar, overview of corruption in athletics during the period.

19. Sackett, *New Hampshire's University*; Bezilla, *Penn State*. Branch campuses at that time were referred to as "undergraduate centers."

20. Bezilla, *Penn State*.

21. When Governor Earle himself made a proposal for a name change to a university, Hetzel remained noncommittal, although he dutifully presented it to the Trustees. Hetzel distanced himself from Earle, who was known to be corrupt, but still maintained friendly relations and good influence over the legislature, for which he was well respected (Bezilla, *Penn State*).

22. Inaugural Address, 22–23. As discussed elsewhere in this article, Hetzel balanced his belief in science with the need for "intellectual and moral controls," citing Frankenstein as a warning, and the need for culture, beauty, skill, humane industry, and philosophy. "If our great mechanical structure—our mechanistic culture—is to continue forward and upward, we must make sure that we have set over it a spiritual control that is adequate to this task" (24). In addition, Hetzel did not believe that science should take precedence over teaching. In fact, his push for "appraisal" of research was related to his commitment to ensuring that there were adequate funds for students as well. Given the choice: "The President has stated that in the event that there is a very serious reduction of funds, curtailment should be more severe, relatively, in the budgets for research and extension than in the budget for resident instruction. Instruction is considered to be the paramount obligation of the College, under the Land-Grant College Act ('for the training of youth')" (Minutes, November 7, 1932).

23. The issue of patenting of university research had arisen during World War I, and became a major topic during the interwar years, in large part due to an aggressive marketing campaign on the part of the National Research Council, working with industry and the patent bar, to convince universities that they should patent their research. The patent system had been under fire from Congress and the courts since the turn of the century, and universities were seen as a potential ally in shoring up the system. See J. Robbins, "Shaping Patent Policy: The National Research Council and the Universities form World War I to the 1960s," *Perspectives on the History of Higher Education* 25 (2006): 89–122.

24. Letter, Hetzel to Council, June 3, 1931, quoted in Minutes, November 2, 1931. AZ/PSUA/01299.

25. Review of Activities, November 21, 1929; Minutes, February 13, 1928, February 6, 1928, January 6, 1930. The Pennsylvania State University, University Archives, AX/PSUA/01778: The Minutes of the Council on Research from 1926. Prior to Hetzel's involvement, there had been a Committee on Research that reported to

the Senate; this committee had done some preliminary thinking about patents in 1926 at the request of the Trustees, which had resolved to formally recognize the potential value of university inventions on January 18, 1926. The faculty committee had recommended that patenting be favorably considered and suggested policy provisions, including that patents be handled by the Board of Trustees. Gerald Wendt, F. G. Hechler, C. W. Hasek, and E. B. Forbes, four of the five members of this early committee, were eventually became members of Hetzel's Council on Research. (Policy and Procedures in Research, 1970 (50), AX/PSUA/06344; Report of the Committee on Research, Adopted by the Senate, March 18, 1926, AX/PSUA/01778).

26. These and a Committee on the Scope of the Council were appointed on October 29, 1928 to focus in greater detail on issues generally discussed by the Council since its inception. (Minutes of the Council on Research from 1926, AX/PSUA/06344.) The talented Hetzel himself held a patent. (Folder, "Organization for Patent Administration, Box AX/PSUA/01299 (29)).

27. Letter, President Hetzel to the Council, October 31, 1929. It was at this point that Hetzel appointed Fletcher chair, and asked him to call a meeting.

28. Some of the questions explored were as follows: "Is it wise for the college to permit unlimited earnings on the part of members of the staff whose abilities have industrial value?"; whether the college should participate in organizing and setting rates for work, or require faculty to "register" the fact that they were doing work outside of their teaching duties; how graduate work fit into patent policy; how to value research; the circumstances under which it would or would not be acceptable to engage in cooperative research with industry; and the "dangers of public embarrassment" from doing exclusive or "closed or semiclosed" work. (AS/PSUA/01778, Minutes of the Council on Research, various dates). Although considerable work of commercial benefit was being done, all departments at the time still "consistently refused to accept such researches as would assign any property rights or publication rights to the donors of the funds" (Minutes, May 27, 1929).

29. Letter, Hetzel to Fletcher, March 3, 1931. Hetzel had very successfully used detailed itemization of costs as a means of justifying expenditures to the legislature in New Hampshire. He viewed being very specific in his budget requests, and devoting substantial attention to explaining them, as a means of overcoming objections; in this, he was consistently right.

30. Minutes, May 27, 1929; Minutes, June 3, 1029; Letter, President R. D. Hetzel to Doctor S.W. Fletcher, Chairman of the Council on Research, September 28, 1932; Minutes, November 7, 1932, AX/PSUA/01778.

31. Some, such as the policy on consulting, were not sent to the President for approval, as the faculty decided they were a "just a statement of practice" (Minutes, March 9, 1931). Both faculty and Trustees would find ways such as this to bypass the President's control over behavior that he believed was inconsistent with public purpose. See Philip Selznick, *TVA and the Grass Roots* (Berkeley: University of California Press, 1949) on "recalcitrant tools" and self-interested elites.

32. *Faculty Bulletin of the Pennsylvania State University College*, vol. 10, no. 32 (May 19, 1931) and vol. 13, no. 20 (July 1934). *Patent Policy and Procedure* was revised/reprinted in 1940, 1958, and 1970; patent details in particular increased and changed over time, but the roots of the Council's early work is evident everywhere, and in some areas of the publication modifications were minimal.

33. Minutes, January 4, 1932; Minutes, February 8, 1932, Minutes, February 22, 1932; "An Analysis of Three Possible Methods of Handling College Patents"; "Report to the Council on Research of the Committee on Patents," May 23, 1932; Memo, Committee on Patents (G. E. Deike, Chair) to Col. J. Franklin Shields, President,

Board of Trustees, November 21, 1932; Letter, Smith to Deike, March 14, 1933; Minutes, April 3, 1933; Letter, Hetzel to Deike, December 29, 1933; Minutes, January 27, 1936, AZ/PSUA/01299. In addition to the Wisconsin format, two other common benchmarks of the time were Purdue (which "does make large profits for the benefit of its stockholders," Letter, Blanchard & Blanchard to Sackett, March 3, 1932) and Research Corporation (F. G. Cottrell, whose patent launched Research Corporation, was consulted in the matter, Cottrell to Forbes, December 11, 1931), both of which were discussed; on Research Corporation, see D. C. Mowery and B. N. Sampat, "Patenting and Licensing University Research Inventions: Lessons from the History of Research Corporation," *Industrial and Corporate Change* 10, no. 2 (2001): 317–55; F. G. Cottrell, "The Research Corporation, an Experiment in Public Administration of Patents," *8th International Congress of Applied Chemistry*, New York, 1912. There was also a group that believed the Trustees themselves should handle patents—although the Trustees, of course, were against this. The Foundation was no sooner set up than, as Hetzel had been worried, the Council was experiencing a form of buyer's remorse.

34. Minutes of the Council on Research, May 14, 1938. The focus on fundamental research gradually weakened; by 1944, the Council was offering a $500 grant to the faculty member "who submits the most acceptable research project with commercial possibilities." Letter, O. Morse to President Hetzel and Secretary Hostetetter, June 22, 1944, AX/PSUA/01278. Numerous cooperative agreements with industry associations, and several patents, were handled by the Council in the late 1930s through 1940s. While beyond the scope of this article, these included the Sinden patents on mushroom spawn; Fuchs patent for a process improvement on coal oxidation (furfural); and the Fenske process patent for manufacturing packing materials related to distillation columns. Total royalties on all patents for the eight years between 1935 and 1943 was $62,046.64, almost entirely from seventeen licenses for mushroom spawn. Most of the money went to operations and litigation, and about $16,000 of it went for further research on the Sinden and Fuchs patents. Report by Mr. Deike, President of the Pennsylvania Research Corporation, January 22, 1944, AXPSUA/0128.

35. Francis E. Robinson, "Former President Hetzel Dies," *New Hampshire Alumnus* XXIV, no. 2 (October 1947): 3; Engelhardt, *History of the University of New Hampshire, 1866–1941*, 253, quoting from a 1921 editorial in *The Granite*; obituaries, various, sources unknown, in Vertical Files, University of New Hampshire Archives; *Biographic Survey of Centre County* (105).

36. Sackett, writing for the class of 1924, and Johnson 1956 (23).

37. Obituary, source unknown, in Ralph D. Hetzel, Vertical Files, University of New Hampshire Archives.

38. Ibid.

39. Lewis M. Branscomb, Fumio Kodama, and Richard Florida, eds., *Industrializing Knowledge: University-Industry Linkages in Japan and the United States* (Cambridge, MA: MIT Press, 1999); Eldon Lee Johnson,*From Turnip Patch to University: The University of New Hampshire at Durham* (Newcomen Address, NY: Newcomen Society of North America, 1956).

40. At one point while at New Hampshire, he arranged for a year's leave of absence so that he could learn more about the administration of higher education at the University of Chicago. They turned out not to have the courses he wanted, and they instead asked if he might come and teach them; he declined, and cancelled his leave (Sackett, *New Hampshire's University*, 94). On the systems view of the learning organization, see P. M. Senge, *The Fifth Discipline: The Art and Practice of the Learning Organization* (New York: Doubleday, 1990).

41. Address—Seventy-fifth Anniversary of the Signing of the Charter of the Farmers High School, February 22, 1930. Penn State was founded as Farmers High School in 1850.
42. One example relates to a major cooperative agreement with PA Grade Crude Oil Association (Letter, Hetzel to Fletcher, September 28, 1932).
43. Inauguration, 26.
44. Bezilla, *Penn State*.
45. Inaugural, 19–20
46. 75th anniversary address, 2–3. Hetzel affixed his signature to this.
47. The integrated leadership model and supporting citations that served as the theoretical framework for this last section evaluating Hetzel as a leader is contained in the earlier version of this paper given at the conference where these papers were first presented, June 2011. It is available from the author at jane.robbins@email.arizona.edu.

Part V

Universities and the Land-Grant Mission since 1930

Introduction

Roger L. Geiger

In 2009, forty-one land-grant universities each performed more than $100 million of research, and eleven of them, more than $500 million. To put this into perspective, seven land grants could be regarded as research universities in the mid-1920s (Part IV, Table 2), and twice this number had joined these ranks by the mid-1960s, including Arizona, Florida, Maryland, Purdue, NC State, Michigan State, and Texas A&M. By 2009, this had doubled again. Although one can only speak loosely of generations, most of this last cohort grew and transformed themselves into research universities in the 1960s and 1970s. Many of these institutions more than tripled their enrollments from 1960 to 1974—the "State" universities of Colorado, Louisiana, Mississippi, New Mexico, and Washington; the universities of Hawaii, Kentucky, Massachusetts, Missouri, Tennessee, and West Virginia; and Clemson and Virginia Tech.[1] Many of these former A&Ms (only the Texas Aggies still find this label endearing) evolved to resemble regular universities: Enrollments expanded less in agriculture and engineering than in arts and sciences, but especially in education, business, and social sciences, raising the question: What remained of the land-grant mission in these modern universities?

The three articles in this final section supply one emphatic answer—the spirit and the mission of the original Morrill Act has been embraced and perpetuated in Colleges of Agriculture; and one equivocal answer—inspiration to transpose the kind of relationships developed in agriculture to other forms of service to society.

Perspectives on the History of Higher Education 30 (2013): 277–283
© 2013. ISBN: 978-1-4128-5147-3

In a sense, the underlying vision of the Morrill Act was finally realized after 1914, when the Smith–Lever Act created the agricultural extension service. Thus, in meaningful ways, the land-grant institutions fulfilled the venerable triad of education, research, and service. Education was provided by the college of agriculture in both degree and nondegree programs. From 1905 to 1915, students in four-year degree programs had increased six-fold, to more than 15,000. Although enrollments declined in the 1920s as the agricultural depression deepened, the colleges maintained a solid base of undergraduate and graduate students. Furthermore, they educated far more people in nondegree courses: Short courses of less than one semester alone enrolled 32,000 in 1927–1928. Agricultural research in the experiment stations received increases in federal support in 1906 and 1925, and widened to include social and economic investigations of rural life. This largesse was accompanied by stipulations that these funds could only be used for research related to the agricultural industry. The Smith–Lever Act provided matching federal funds to establish an extension agent in each county, who was jointly responsible to the college and the Cooperative Extension Service, to bring the fruits of agricultural science to local farming practices.[2] Smith–Lever also included Home Economics in extension and sought to ameliorate problems of the farm, home, and community. Agriculture now had a system of education–research–application that was more complete than nineteenth-century Grangers and Populists could have dreamt of. This system was relatively autonomous from the land-grant universities, with funding and stringent regulations from the federal government. At the grass roots level, the county extension agent was the key figure—not a scientist but a local figure who was educated in the college of agriculture, and dedicated to solving problems and enhancing the welfare of the farming community.

By the 1930s, the county extension agent was a trusted and valued figure in rural communities, and this trust allowed the federal government to utilize them to implement New Deal policy. This remarkable development is analyzed from a policy perspective in the article by Christopher Loss. The Agricultural Adjustment Act of 1933 was one of President Franklin D. Roosevelt's first pieces of New Deal legislation. It sought to raise prices of seven basic crops by offering farmers compensation for limiting production. Faced with the problem of achieving compliance from the nation's scattered and unorganized farmers, the government mobilized the extension agents whom it had created and supported through the Department of Agriculture. This practice was inherently controversial.

The head of the Pennsylvania Extension Service, for example, insisted that his county agents confine their activities to education, as intended in the Smith–Lever Act. However, Loss explains how the county agents achieved a high degree of compliance with the Agricultural Adjustment Act and subsequent legislation limiting production. In some ways, this cooperative effort by agents based at land-grant colleges solidified an "iron triangle" between agricultural interests, Congress, and the Extension Service and land-grant universities. The conspicuous success of the extension land-grant union, politically and functionally, had significant postwar ramifications. Support from both the federal and state sources was dramatically increased; and the success of the model inspired efforts to extend it to additional areas of social needs.

The study by Ethan Schrum uncovers how the land-grant paradigm shaped the original plans to have the Irvine campus of the University of California specialize in applied social science. Behind this plan was the vision of Clark Kerr, president of the University of California (UC) and a dedicated social scientist, who was committed not only to advancing the disciplines but also to employing them to further sociial and economic development. In Kerr's early career as director of the Institute of Industrial Relations and as Chancellor of the Berkeley campus, he had sought to propel the theoretical advancement of social science disciplines in departments and to mobilize this same expertise for external sponsors through centers and institutes, locally called "organized research units."[3] With the Irvine campus, Kerr explicitly invoked the land-grant tradition in seeking an enlargement of that mission.

UC Irvine may have been the most ambitious attempt to enlarge the land-grant mission, but it was not the first. Between 1959 and 1966, the Ford Foundation awarded $4.5 million to eight universities for "urban extension experiments." Each experiment was unique, but the programs were explicitly modeled on Cooperative Extension in that they sought to train "urban agents" who would bring the expertise of university specialists to address the manifold problems of cities. The largest grants went to the University of Wisconsin (UW) ($1,250,000), Rutgers ($1,250,000), and the University of Delaware ($775,000). All three institutions established Urban Affairs units: The Department at the UW branch in Milwaukee sought to train urban agents and field "urban teams"; the Rutgers Center did no teaching and focused on research and advice; and Delaware's Division of Urban Affairs fell between these two approaches, offering limited academic training. Most problematic was the grant to UC Berkeley ($198,000), which supported incompatible initiatives to advise Oakland City government and mobilize grass-roots organizations.[4] In general, the Foundation concluded that urban extension was rather different from agricultural extension: "the ills of the farm sector tend to be economic and technological" and could be addressed by "a land grant school"; "urban research, on the other hand, tends to be conceptual, explanatory, and exhortatory. There are no direct benefits . . . from even a first-rate research monograph. . . ." On the bright side, it noted that these "experiments" had helped prepare the urban guinea pigs in applying for federal aid through the new programs of the war on poverty, especially those which were intended for urban extension.[5]

In retrospect, the cautionary lessons from the Ford experiments were prescient. However, few cautions were heeded in the mid-1960s, when both confidence in the advancement of social science and the resolution of urban problems were at flood tide. Urban extension, for example, was included in Title I of the Higher Education Act of 1965 and even received some funding.[6] Thus, Kerr and UC Irvine can hardly be faulted for encompassing both strands of this zeitgeist in an enlarged land-grant mission. Schrum describes the disappointing result. The Public Policy Research Organization, in particular, never fulfilled its putative mission of duplicating agriculture's blending of teaching, research, and service. More than one reason accounts for this failure. As Ford had found, cities differed from early rural communities in already offering their citizens a wide range of services, and this made it difficult for urban experts to identify points of intervention. The situation, in fact, was almost the obverse of Christopher Loss' extension agents who implemented government policies on farmers: Urban extension implied the implementation of university-devised policies on local governments. Applied social science, whether urban affairs, decision science, or public policy, could not escape its academic proclivity toward theory. Colleges of agriculture had been forced to become relevant to farmers by the Hatch Act and its successors, and the homegrown county agents of Cooperative Extension. In contrast, urban researchers remained in the ivory tower, at one point complaining to Ford that "research needs of [government] agencies are not posed in researchable form to the community of scholars in the university." UC Irvine's PPRO saw itself as primarily a research shop, and its proposals, Schrum notes, aimed to "discover and formulate basic principles . . . predictive relationships, and methodology." Ironically, perhaps the greatest contribution to public policy theory came from a case study—Aaron Wildavsky's analysis of the inept federal demonstration programs in Oakland, which launched the field of implementation studies.[7]

The idea of urban extension lived on into the 1970s, largely because policy makers, social scientists, and university leaders wishfully hoped the concept would succeed. Kerr may have prolonged these hopes with a 1967 speech that called for the creation of sixty-seven urban-grant universities, "where the city itself and its problems would become the animating focus, as agriculture once was and to some extent still is of the land grant university."[8] However, by that time, the land-grant mission itself was subject to the opprobrium that was directed at American universities in general.

Considering the role that imagery has played in land-grant history, Scott Peters' essay provides a fitting conclusion to this volume. He notes that we make sense of the stuff of history by configuring stories, or narratives, that not only signify meaning, but also serve as a moral compass. The studies in this volume certainly bear this out. From the outset, the ambiguous wording of the first Morrill Act yielded divergent "stories" that rationalized different claims on the land-grant institutions. No doubt the shrillest narrative came from those interests that claimed the "agricultural colleges" as their own. Through the end of the nineteenth century, their story emphasized the failure of the colleges to fulfill what they defined as its mandate. Proponents of the American university, although ultimately triumphant, narrated a more sophisticated story that, if it sometimes lacked coherence, mirrored the compartmentalized institutions which they sought to characterize. In addition, as just seen, urban extension embodied a story that proved impossible to realize.

Peters' depiction of three contrasting stories of the land-grant mission focuses entirely on agriculture, which underlines the identification of agriculture and the land-grant mission noted earlier. The heroic metanarrative describes the fruits of agricultural research, that is, solving problems and enhancing the productivity and prosperity of American farmers. Conversely, a tragic counternarrative interpreted the modernization of agriculture as having imposed high social costs in terms of community destruction and environmental degradation. As a third alternative, Peters offers the prophetic narrative in which cultural and technological advancement empowered farming communities and gave birth to a higher form of rural civilization—in some ways, the ideal of cooperative extension. Of these three, the tragic counternarrative is most jarring to the predominantly positive image of land-grant history portrayed in this volume. It also provides an insight into the context of the land-grant movement circa 1970.

The seminal document in this counternarrative is the brilliantly titled *Hard Tomatoes, Hard Times* by Jim Hightower, which appeared in 1973.[9] The product of a public interest research organization called the Agribusiness Accountability Project, an avowed legacy of student radicalism in the 1960s, its central indictment is that the "land grant college complex" became entirely beholden to corporate agribusiness. In its headlong pursuit of mechanization and monoculture, it favored the aggrandizement of large-scale farming and the extinction of the small family farm. Although hostility to capitalism is evident throughout, *Hard Tomatoes* was not imagining the problems facing agriculture. From 1940 to 1970, one half of the country's six million farms had disappeared. The farm population dropped by half from 1940 to 1960 and continued falling through the 1960s. This brutal process of survival of the economically fittest seemed to be largely ignored by the land-grant complex. Certainly, if "the fundamental function of Smith–Lever extension education is *the development of rural people themselves*," it was failing.[10] The land-grant complex, on the other hand, was thriving on public money. During the years when the number of farms was halved, for example, the budget for Extension rose from $38 million to $332 million. No doubt complacency pervaded the complex, especially in the close relations of the beneficiaries—USDA, the Farm Bureau, agribusiness corporations, Extension, and the colleges of agriculture. *Hard Tomatoes* was particularly critical of land-grant research for devising and promoting farm equipment, chemical fertilizers, plant breeding, and marketing—all furthering capital intensive farming and agribusiness. Thus, the report puts a negative spin on the transformation of American agriculture by championing the victims and castigating the land-grant universities as facilitators, while ignoring the inevitability of this transformation for feeding the population. The report had a long-lived influence, including critical Senate hearings in 1978 and the literature cited by Peters.[11]

Peters' article underlines the contingency of interpretations of land-grant history and mission, but his conclusion suggests that this condition pertains to living institutions, serving vital functions in society, that are constantly being shaped, reshaped, and reinterpreted. Nevertheless, the intention of this volume has been to bring greater accuracy to the stories of the land-grant institutions, to bring disinterested historical scholarship to bear on the multiple facets of this venerable and tangled history. The foregoing studies have illuminated a number of meanings at particular points of time that actors attributed to the institutions launched by the Morrill Land Grant Act of 1862.

Notes

1. Research expenditures from the National Science Foundation; for research universities in the mid-1960s, Roger L. Geiger, *Research and Relevant Knowledge: American Research Universities Since World War II* (New Brunswick, NJ: Transaction Publisher, 2004 [1993]), 206–9; G. Lester Anderson, ed., *Land-grant Universities and Their Continuing Challenge* (East Lansing: Michigan State University Press, 1976), Appendix Table 2.
2. Arthur J. Klein, *Survey of Land-Grant Colleges and Universities*, 2 vols. (Washington, DC: GPO, 1930), I, 284–86; II, 435–42.
3. Ethan Schrum, "Clark Kerr's Early Career, Social Science, and the American University," *Perspectives on the History of Higher Education* 28 (2011): 193–222.
4. The Ford Report is unusually blunt: "[T]he University-Oakland Project sought to establish close ties to indigenous groups in the slum areas of Oakland and provide technical and organizing assistance. In the course of this activity, some students involved in the University-Oakland Project community action programs developed serious conflicts with local officials who have questioned the motives of students as going beyond the project's objectives and into such areas as U.S. foreign policy [i.e., the Vietnam War] and the stimulation of local protest groups": Ford Foundation, *Urban Extension: A Report on Experimental Programs Assisted by the Ford Foundation* (New York: 1966), quote on 26.
5. Ibid., quote on 6–7.
6. Hugh Davis Graham, *The Uncertain Triumph: Federal Education Policy in the Kennedy and Johnson Years* (Chapel Hill: University of North Carolina Press, 1984), 80.
7. Ibid., quote on 27; Jeffrey L. Pressman and Aaron Wildavsky, *Implementation: How Great Expectations in Washington are Dashed in Oakland : or, Why It's Amazing that Federal Programs Work at All, This Being a Saga of the Economic Development Administration as Told by Two Sympathetic Observers who Seek to Build Morals on a Foundation of Ruined Hopes* (Berkeley: University of California Press, 1973).
8. Clark Kerr, *The Urban-Grant University: A Model for the Future* (New York: City College, 1968), quote on 6. The Carnegie Commission on Higher Education, which Kerr chaired, similarly recommended a $10 million federal investment in an urban-grant program: *The Campus and the City: Maximizing Assets and Reducing Liabilities* (New York: McGraw-Hill, 1972).
9. Jim Hightower, *Hard Tomatoes, Hard Times* (Cambridge, MA: Schenkman, 1973, 1978). This was scarcely the first critique of extension; since the 1930s, critics had accused county agents of neglecting smaller farmers and favoring local businesses: Wesley S. Feight, "Roadside Education in the Garden Spot: the Early Years of Agricultural Education in Lancaster County, Pennsylvania" (Master's Paper, Higher Education, Pennsylvania State University, 2005), 51–53.
10. Klein, *Survey of Land Grant Colleges*, quote on II, 442.
11. Hightower, *Hard Tomatoes, Hard Times*: The 1978 Hearing of the Subcommittee on Agriculture of the House of Representatives is in the 1978 edition, 149–242; as well as a Forward by Harry M. Scoble linking the project with the "turbulent politics of the 1960s" and the movement "for popularly-directed political change," vii.

The Land-Grant Colleges, Cooperative Extension, and the New Deal

Christopher P. Loss*

With the centennial anniversary of the signing of the Morrill Land-Grant Act of 1862 in sight, President John F. Kennedy issued a proclamation to kick off what he anticipated would be a year-long commemoration of the legislation. It was only "fitting and proper," declared President Kennedy on August 25, 1961, that that the federal government "cooperate" with the land-grant institutions in celebrating "the historical and present close cooperative relationship of such institutions with the departments and establishments of the Government." His description of the relationship as "cooperative" indicated that the Harvard-educated Kennedy had done his homework: Over the course of the land grants' first century, cooperation with the federal government—as in cooperative agricultural extension—had been essential to both the growth of government and higher education. This article explores the history of cooperative agricultural extension, paying special attention to the crucial decade of the 1930s, when the relationship between the federal government and the land grants blossomed into its modern form.[1]

The Great Depression and the emergent New Deal order pushed the nation's land-grant colleges closer than ever to the center of American political life. After decades of remote relations, college officials and government leaders agreed that the painful realities of the worst financial crisis in US history obligated them to chart a new course away from their laissez-faire past. Even professors thought it was time to try a different

Perspectives on the History of Higher Education 30 (2013): 285–309
© 2013. ISBN: 978-1-4128-5147-3

tack: "The cuts contemplated this year are so cruel and destructive as to threaten seriously our whole educational system," wrote an anguished professor to a newly inaugurated President Roosevelt in March 1933. "I appeal to you in the name of downtrodden and oppressed teachers, will you not do something for us, the forgotten men and women of America?"[2]

Although scholars have forgotten it today, land-grant extension departments dutifully served the New Deal and that service contributed to the creation of an expansive centralized state in a political culture which was hostile to "big government." Existing scholarship has highlighted the academy's role in crafting New Deal socioeconomic policy.[3] However, the role that land-grant colleges played in delivering services and programs to rural citizens, in implementing many of the socioeconomic policies developed by its own faculty, the coterie of executive-level policy makers known as Roosevelt's "brains trust," has remained obscured. I argue that the land-grant colleges were crucial to the New Deal's achievement of national administrative capacity and to the "education" of rural Americans for life in a bureaucratic state.

This argument challenges the prevailing belief that the nation's higher education sector was inconsequential to national policy makers in the 1930s. According to the received view, the state-academic partnership remained cold during the 1920s, simmered on low in the 1930s, and rocketed to life in World War II.[4] The exigencies of total war and the introduction of cost-plus-a-fixed-fee and master contracts, which allotted scientists vast autonomy to do their work, persuaded academic administrators and scientists alike that the government could be trusted to sponsor research without corrupting either the research process or the tradition of decentralized federal-academic relations.[5] World War II, according to the standard account, marked the beginnings of the federal-academic partnership that was to plot the course of higher education through the twilight Cold War struggle, down to the present day.

This version of events is not so much incorrect as incomplete. In concentrating on elite scientists' anticipated partnership with the state in World War II, scholars have missed the real state-academic partnership that took root in the 1930s.[6] By and large, it occurred far removed from the nation's elite, private research universities, in the hinterlands of the academic estate occupied by the land-grant colleges of the Midwest and South. Throughout the 1930s, the architects of the New Deal state requested and received support from the land grants, and the land-grant colleges requested and received support from the government. That this mutually reinforcing relationship has remained hidden speaks to the scholarly fixation on the birth of "big science" in World War II, and to the profound difficulty of making sense of the Roosevelt administration's penchant for state building by proxy—of using third parties, such as the land-grant colleges, to connect with the American people.[7]

As other scholars have noted, the most grandiose reform initiatives of the New Deal regime were often undermined by a lack of sufficient state capacity. The New Deal's seemingly skeletal administrative framework, what historian David M. Kennedy has called its "puny capacity,"[8] stemmed from two interrelated sources: the American polity's traditional preference for a weak central state on the one hand, and the strength of the southern Democratic wing of the New Deal coalition on the other. "Dixiecrats," as this group of southern Democrats was known, occupied an inordinate number of prime congressional chairmanships that they wielded with impunity during the New Deal. No aggrandizement in federal power went unchecked, particularly if it threatened the South's segregated, antiunion socioeconomic order.[9]

The combined force of ideological and congressional antistatism forced New Deal state builders to use intermediary institutions—what some scholars call "parastates"—in order to exercise federal authority at the local level. As ever, during the 1930s, the most common intermediary was state- and local-level government, whose functionaries administered the vast majority of New Deal programs. Unemployment insurance and welfare programs were managed by local officials, and so too the New Deal's bevy of "workfare" and cultural uplift activities. Where Roosevelt's hand seemed too heavy or the government appeared too big—for instance, when he clumsily tried to "pack" the Supreme Court, or later, to consolidate the country's socio economic welfare programming under the National Resources Planning Board—the antistatist political tides turned against him.[10] The New Deal achieved more durable results when it buried regulation in arcane mechanisms such as the tax code or when it provided funding and coordination but handed program administration over to intermediary institutions at least once removed from the federal government's burgeoning family of Washington-based administrative agencies.[11]

I contend that the land-grant colleges, led by their extension departments, served as a predominant intermediary organization during the New Deal, paving the way for higher education's even greater support of the federal government during and after World War II. Building on political scientist Stephen Skowronek's foundational premise that "state building is most basically an exercise in reconstructing an already established organization of state power," this article shows how the Roosevelt administration used the land-grant colleges, and its vast agricultural extension network, to mediate relations with rural Americans at the grass roots level.[12] Geographically diffused with strong regional allegiances, the land-grant colleges assisted New Dealers in naturalizing relations with rural Americans who trusted their local land-grant college personnel at least as much as they did their distant government.

No member of the land-grant colleges was trusted more than the county agricultural agent, whose job it was to comb the countryside on behalf of agricultural adjustment in the 1930s. The nation's troop of county agents helped "educate" millions of farmers about all the benefits of the New Deal for the American farmer. The agent's multifaceted professional identity, which connected him to the US Department of Agriculture (USDA), the land-grant colleges, and local farm organizations, such as the American Farm Bureau Federation (AFBF), made him uniquely suited for this challenging pedagogical assignment. Supported by his fellow farmers because he was himself a farmer, and empowered by his land-grant-conferred pedigree and expertise, the county agent personalized the New Deal state just enough to win the support of some of the nation's most skeptical citizens.

****

In the late winter months of 1933, the Roosevelt administration inherited a farm economy that had been in steady decline for well more than a decade. Unlike the industrial sector downturn that dated back to the market crash of 1929, the agricultural depression had been ongoing since the end of the World War I. By 1932, farmers' gross income was $5.3 billion, $12 billion less than it had been in 1919, and their total debt burden exceeded $9 billion.[13] "Unless something is done for the American farmer," the president of the American Farm Bureau Federation warned Congress in January 1933, "we will have revolution in the countryside within less than twelve months."[14] The spontaneous formation of desperate "farmers' holiday" organizations across the Midwest, which threatened to withhold crops from markets until farmers could be guaranteed the cost of production, seemingly corroborated such claims. In Lemars, Iowa, for example, a farmer mob, aggrieved over rampant foreclosures and rock-bottom prices, "marched in and carried off a judge" with the intention of killing him. The judge's life was spared, but not before a standoff with a battalion of Iowa National Guardsmen resulted in seventy-nine arrests.[15]

The farm collapse, the presence of powerful agricultural interest groups, and a large agricultural workforce comprising 30 percent of the nation's total ensured that farm policy would be central to the administration's economic recovery program. However, the administration's commitment to agricultural adjustment was guided by more than interest-group capture.[16] There were legitimate, widely held economic rationales that privileged a sweeping federal overhaul of rural America. Leading New Dealers, including Henry A. Wallace, the secretary of agriculture, and his undersecretary, Rexford Tugwell, believed that the Great Depression had been caused by poor farming practices and the dramatic loss of farmers' purchasing power since the war.[17]

The duress in the farm sector resulted from systemic agricultural overproduction on the one hand, and the decline of consumers' incomes on the other. Moreover, farmers' inability to purchase everyday consumables, to say nothing of the expensive equipment required for modern mechanized farming, had dragged down the industrial sector and destabilized the nation's entire economic order. Readjusting farmers' purchasing power toward "parity"—the ratio between farm prices and costs during the period from 1909 to 1914, the supposed golden age of American agriculture—surfaced as the immediate objective of the Agricultural Adjustment Act, which was passed in May 1933, one month before the National Industrial Recovery Act. It was no coincidence that agricultural legislation preceded industrial legislation: New Dealers believed that a full and complete macroeconomic recovery of necessity depended first on the full and complete recovery of the agricultural economy.[18] "Millions of the unemployed in the cities lost their jobs because farm people lost their power to buy," declared a USDA official. "Restoring farm purchasing power will set men to work in the cities, making the things that farmers need and will buy if they can."[19]

The Agricultural Adjustment Administration (AAA) was established to implement the act. However, as a practical matter, the AAA and its chief administrator, George N. Peek, an Illinois farm equipment manufacturer, were subordinate to the USDA and its new secretary, Henry A. Wallace.[20] No one person wielded more influence over New Deal agricultural policy than did Wallace. An agricultural economist by training, a hybrid corn innovator, and publisher of *Wallace's Farmer*, a popular farming newspaper, his grasp of agricultural issues was unmatched. Wallace, whose father had served a frustrating term as secretary of agriculture in the Harding and Coolidge administrations, was determined to do what his father could not: organize farmers across the country by increasing federal support for agriculture through a controversial policy known as "voluntary domestic allotment." Conceived by William J. Spillman of the Bureau of Agricultural Economics and popularized by Milburn L. Wilson, an agricultural economist at Montana State College and a Roosevelt adviser, voluntary domestic allotment emerged as the remedy to the overproduction problem. The program disbursed cash payments to farmers, funded by processor taxes, in return for farmers agreeing to reduce, or to use the official terminology, adjust, their agricultural output.[21]

This effort was complicated by the fact that the countryside's fear of federal power cut deep. Though farm groups had sought help from the government throughout the 1920s, the idea of the government paying farmers not to farm—and slaughtering thousands of animals—particularly when so many Americans were going hungry was disturbing.[22] "To have to destroy a growing crop is a shocking commentary on our civilization," admitted Henry Wallace, in his book *New Frontiers*. "I could tolerate it only as a cleaning up of the wreckage of the old days of unbalanced production."[23] His undersecretary, Rexford Tugwell, agreed, but thought it was the only option available to the USDA "under the competitive and money economy."[24] Strong reservations were voiced in and outside Washington, in part, because nobody was sure whether the plan would actually work. Past efforts at agricultural coordination had invariably fractured along commodity, regional, racial, and class lines. Would domestic allotment be different? Even though no one knew the answer to this question, major farm organizations, led by the Farm Bureau, whose leadership recognized the AAA as a way to extend its policy-making influence and organizational jurisdiction beyond its Midwest stronghold and into the South, threw their support behind the allotment plan. There was no other choice. All farmers, save for a handful of agribusiness firms, were desperate for help and agreed to march alongside the AAA down what Roosevelt himself called a "new and untrod path . . . to rescue agriculture."[25]

Time was of the essence. With the spring-planting season already well underway, and the prospects of another year of uncontrolled agricultural output looming, the AAA's organizational challenges were nothing if not monumental. Rather than constructing a whole new bureau and hiring thousands of new bureaucrats, the savvy Wallace turned to the USDA Cooperative Extension Service and its force of county agricultural demonstration agents, more commonly known as "county agents," to implement the AAA—the lone New Deal program assigned to an existing government agency.[26] The web of institutions that constituted the USDA Extension Service reached far and wide, and included federal, state, and local government; the American Farm Bureau Federation; and the nation's sixty-seven land-grant colleges and universities.[27]

To be sure, Wallace's choice to partner with the publicly supported land-grant colleges, which comprised 5 percent of the nation's total number of colleges but enrolled nearly a quarter of all students, was that of a seasoned agricultural man who was keenly aware of the mutually constitutive partnership between and among the USDA, the Farm Bureau, and the agricultural colleges.[28] The creation of the USDA and the Morrill Land-Grant Act occurred nearly simultaneously, in 1862, during the Civil War. Over the next several decades, the USDA and the land-grant colleges competed with one another to fulfill their overlapping statutory mandate to produce and disseminate up-to-date information and education on farming techniques, home economics and household management, and agricultural marketing to farmers and farm families. Subsequent federal legislation made the de facto relationship legally binding. The 1887 Hatch Experiment-Station Act, passed one year after the USDA had achieved cabinet-level status, provided each of the state land grants with an annual appropriation of $15,000 in research support; later, the second Morrill Act of 1890 and the Adams Act of 1906 increased the federal government's largess. The secretary of agriculture supervised the experiment station program, and occasionally recommended research topics, but permitted station directors significant autonomy in conducting research and managing their own operations.[29]

Station directors quickly discovered that the production of new agricultural research was pointless if that research failed to find an audience. The USDA and the land-grant colleges responded to the need for greater contact with farmers by forming extension divisions to communicate new research findings and agricultural practices to farmers and to collect firsthand knowledge of emergent issues from the field. The land-grant colleges and the USDA differed over how best to do this—the former preferring to have farmers come to the faculty, the latter preferring to have faculty go to the farmers. Variations on both approaches were tried in the late nineteenth century. Faculty from the land-grant colleges and research stations convened mass-meeting farmer institutes and small-group short courses; they tried mailing bulletins and organizing correspondence classes to educate farmers. None of these traditional instructional techniques worked as well as the agricultural instructors had intended. Farmers had neither the time nor inclination to go to school; so, schools would have to go to the farmers. The USDA's direct-to-customer model, delivered by county agents using a pedagogical style known as the "demonstration method," emerged as the preferred educational technique.[30]

The demonstration method avoided bookish instruction and instead emphasized applied learning—"showing" rather than "telling" farmers what worked. This seemed especially appropriate, as many farmers in the South and Midwest, where extension proliferated, lacked formal education. Agents met with farmers to demonstrate preferred plowing, fertilizing, planting, and crop rotation techniques and practices. The method first achieved national acclaim in Terrell, Texas, in 1904. The USDA and the Rockefeller-endowed General Education Board had provided funds for the organization of community demonstration farms and to train county agents to help cotton farmers combat the invasion of the Mexican boll weevil. Dr. Seaman A. Knapp headed the Terrell, Texas, demonstration farm. Knapp was born in New York in 1833 and graduated from Union College in 1856. After spending the next decade as a teacher, minister, physician, and farmer, he and his family moved to Ames, Iowa, in 1866, where he again busily pursued all of these vocations and more. In addition to helping his wife run a school for the blind, he ministered, raised hogs, and served as the editor of a local farm paper. This final assignment introduced him to members of Ames' farming elite that, in turn, led to a faculty position and, later, to a brief stint as president of the Iowa State College of Agriculture from 1883 to 1884. It was a frustrating experience for the no-nonsense Knapp, who discovered that he disliked academic agriculture and the men who engaged in it. Not surprisingly, his biggest accomplishment in these years was a practical one: He drafted an early version of the bill that eventually became the Hatch Experiment-Station Act of 1887.[31]

Having grown tired of deskwork, Knapp jumped at the opportunity to again get his hands dirty. In 1885, Knapp headed south to Lake Charles, Louisiana. He spent a decade there in land reclamation and speculation, and in developing new techniques for large-scale rice cultivation. After having helped to turn Louisiana into the "rice milling center of the nation,"[32] Knapp joined the USDA as a special agent for the promotion of agriculture in the South in 1902. It was in this capacity that he began experimenting with demonstration farming in Texas and in placing responsibility for the method in the hands of roaming agricultural educators. The agent was not an entirely new social invention. The Farmers Alliance, which sprouted in Texas in the 1880s and 1890s, relied on "traveling lecturers" to spread its cooperative vision among producers in the South and Midwest. The "education" it disseminated alerted farmers throughout those regions to the possibilities of fluid currency finance, subtreasury credit systems, and organized political insurgency under the banner of the "People's Party." Using farmers to organize and educate other farmers was a trusted method and had been since the "Populist Moment."[33]

Knapp recruited his first team of agents from around Terrell. He paired each agent with a professor from the Texas Agricultural College, assigning them eight hundred miles of railroad to stump on behalf of demonstration, to persuade farmers to try new seeds, fertilizers, and plowing techniques so that others nearby might be compelled to do the same. He also asked them to identify a leading farmer in their territory to serve as a USDA county agent. Who was chosen for this role? The land-grant faculty was not chosen, as Knapp considered them too theoretical. He insisted on real farmers who understood what it really meant to live off the land.[34] A few years later, Knapp explained his agent selection process to Congress: "We take men who are the progressive farmers. We aim to get the best farmers in their own section, men whom their neighbors believe in, and they will listen to. . . . We find that these men are more influential than if they knew ten times as much about science, as they know what the farmer considers the best science in the world—and that is the science of winning out, of making a good crop and making money on the farm."[35]

Agents found the work difficult. The pay was meager, and the days were long. An early agent recalled traveling "on horseback, usually leaving home on Monday morning and returning about the end of the week."[36] However, the biggest challenge was that most farmers were suspicious of the county agents and had to be sold on the idea of demonstration. Knapp was aware of this, admitting that "sometimes farmers have peculiar views about agriculture." Let farmers believe what they want, Knapp instructed his agents, as long as farmers "faithfully try our methods." He implored his agents to "avoid discussing politics or churches. Never put on airs. Be a plain man, with an abundance of good practical sense."[37]

An agent in the Mississippi Delta closely followed Knapp's advice, and to good effect. The most important thing, recalled the agent, was "to interest [farmers] and gain their confidence." He did this by requesting "from the experiment station specimens of cotton boll weevil and other weevils often mistaken for the cotton pest," which he carried in his pocket, into the field, for demonstration. "I stopped at . . . all the places where I could see farmers meeting or loafing, giving my little show, and enlisting farmers willing to receive information through visits, correspondence, bulletins, etc. I listed them as cooperators and tried to convince them that I had no axe to grind, no ambition in politics and that no cost was attached to this work, undertaken by the federal government."[38] For agents and farmers alike, the demonstration method was nothing less than a revelation. "Under [Knapp's] organization," gushed an awestruck agent, "all formerly dry agricultural principles became alive and potent as did the dry bones in Ezekiel's Valley when the spirit of the Lord brought bone to bone and clothed them with miraculous flesh and sinew."[39]

Knapp's county agent demonstration model brought agricultural education to the masses. The passage of the 1914 Smith–Lever Act, which created the USDA Cooperative Extension Service, extended it to all states. The act harmonized relations between the USDA and the land-grant colleges by merging the land grants' research and extension functions and channeling both into the person of the county agent. Both the colleges and the USDA got what they wanted. The colleges received new funding in exchange for adopting the USDA's county agent-led demonstration method; the USDA, in turn, agreed in principle that future agents would be land-grant graduates with professional ties to the colleges of agriculture.[40] To augment the funding of this cooperative enterprise, the act authorized "matching grants" in which the local match could derive from a combination of "public" and "private" sources. Cost sharing of this sort built support for the program and helped the land grants quickly ramp up their extension operations. In the four years after the passage of the Smith–Lever Act, the force of county agents climbed from 929 to 2,435. The combined impact of the Smith–Hughes Vocational Education Act of 1917 and the US entry into World War I had a lot to do with that, relying as they did on county agents to help with rural vocational education and to rally farmers on behalf of the war effort. Agent numbers held steady during the 1920s before climbing to 3,300 by 1935—enough to assign at least one agent to every county in the country. This growth was made possible, because the USDA Cooperative Extension Service developed its administrative capacity at the local level: Out of a total workforce of 8,400 personnel, a mere sixty-one employees worked in the Extension Service headquarters in Washington, DC.[41]

The Extension Service also discovered tangible political and bureaucratic advantages in sharing power with other stakeholders, in particular the American Farm Bureau Federation, arguably the most powerful farm organization of the twentieth century. The Smith–Lever Act's "private" matching-grant provision paved the way for the Farm Bureau's critical administrative role.[42] Private county "farm bureaus" comprising local farmers and businessmen grew in tandem with the Extension Service, eventually becoming a reliable "matching grant" contributor to the program and to county agents' salaries. An informal version of this relationship dated to the founding of the agent system under Dr. Seaman Knapp but did not crystallize until World War I when local farm bureaus formed a federated national network whose membership and geographic reach exceeded that of all other farm groups combined. This arrangement was encouraged by the Extension Service and the land-grant colleges, who viewed their partnership with the Farm Bureau as an expedient way to legitimize agricultural extension activities at the grass roots level.[43]

The Farm Bureau had multiple agendas, and from the beginning imagined using county agents for political as well as educational purposes. This posed something of a dilemma, and in 1921, the secretary of agriculture attempted to sever the county agent's systems ties to the Farm Bureau, ruling that county agents were supposed to be educators, not interest group agitators. No such clear delineation of agent duties and responsibilities was ever achieved, however, and by the dawn of the New Deal, the interdependent relationship among the Extension Service and land-grant colleges, the Farm Bureau, and key legislatures had hardened into an "iron triangle."[44] Wallace knew this better than anyone, and his decision to link the AAA to the Extension Service and its legion of "semi-governmental employees," county agents, was, thus, shrewd.[45] By activating local interests and minimizing the visible presence of the federal government, Wallace and the AAA achieved administrative capacity and a critical mass of built-in rural support while expending minimal political capital. As Wallace later mused, in 1935, "Fortunately, we had the extension services with their corps of . . . county agricultural agents and a background of 20 years of experience with which to contact farmers."[46]

The AAA's early production control sign-up campaigns by most accounts went smoothly. Agents collaborated with local advisory committees to introduce production controls on seven of the nation's basic agricultural commodities—wheat, cotton, corn, hogs, rice, tobacco, and milk and milk by-products. Some farmers complained of strong-armed sign-up tactics, but most others embraced the county agents with open arms. Indeed, corn-hog and wheat farmers in the Midwest and cotton and tobacco farmers in the South, the two main regional recipients of AAA largesse in 1933 and 1934, agreed to reduce acreage and curtail production at an astounding rate. The vast majority of growers signed up 75 percent of cotton growers; 95 percent of flue-cured tobacco producers; and upward of 95 percent of corn and wheat growers in the farm belt in the Midwest and Great Plains. In Madison County, Mississippi, 1,863 cotton reduction contracts were accepted, and a scant 25 were refused.[47]

As the "front line forces" of the AAA, county agents used every possible resource available to them to contact farmers and to personalize the expanding New Deal state. Agents primarily relied on timeworn retail methods. Agent R. E. Hughes of Bacon County, Georgia, devoted eighty-one straight days to his cotton reduction sign-up campaign; during that stretch, he made ninety-seven farm visits, received seven hundred office calls, wrote fifty-six letters, mailed out seven different circulars, wrote two news articles, and held eight meetings. In his annual report, agent Hughes credited himself with making the sign-up campaign a success: "The cotton reduction program was received with out stretched arms and open hands."[48] Hughes' dogged effort was mirrored by countless agents across the country who went about their business determining allotments and securing contracts often "without pay other than perhaps a mileage allowance."[49] In Iowa, for instance, agents held an estimated two thousand corn-hog meetings over a five-week stretch. Nationwide, the Extension Service reported that, in 1934, office calls from farmers jumped from 8 to 21 million, and that 3.5 million telephone calls were logged, which was more than double the number tallied the previous year.[50]

Given the amount of responsibility foisted on agents, controversy not surprisingly followed them into the field. Their alleged transformation from nonpartisan educators "into a tool for politicians . . . a rural ward-healer," as one critic put it, invigorated debates about higher education's relationship to the federal government and about the appropriate role of academic experts in American politics.[51] The Association of Land Grant Colleges and Universities approved of the AAA, because the promotional work required only a "minimum amount of activity." Some extension leaders in the upper Midwest and Northeast remained unconvinced. In Pennsylvania and New York—the regional stronghold of the National Grange of Patrons of Husbandry, the Farm Bureau's chief rival—extension officials resisted the AAA for a number of reasons. They insisted that the AAA subverted the educational intentions of the Smith–Lever Act and cited anecdotal evidence of agent malfeasance to support this claim. In 1939, the *Washington Daily News* reported that a county agent in Perry County, Alabama, had mailed an extension-franked letter to farmers in his county to let them know their government checks had arrived. The agent also urged his farmers to "express their gratitude and assure themselves of continued payments by joining the county farm bureau." Another agent devised a similar plan in Nebraska when he recommended that farmers allocate a portion of their government checks to cover their Farm Bureau membership dues.[52] Duplicity of this sort fueled the conspiracy theory that agents really were pawns of an all-powerful "Farm Bureau-Extension Axis."[53]

The other reason that some farmers disparaged the AAA and its agent emissaries was that some regions and commodity groups benefited more than others. In Pennsylvania and New York, and throughout the dairy farming mid-Atlantic and Northeast, farmers and extension officials correctly surmised that they were being hurt by commodity programs in the Midwest.[54] The AAA's wheat and corn programs had increased the cost of the feed grains needed by dairy farmers to produce their milk. "The farmers of the east," wrote the director of extension in New York State, "believe, and probably justly so, that the program of the Agricultural Adjustment Administration has been more harmful than helpful to them."[55] Then and later, most farmers' complaints usually subsided when government payments were increased.

Some farmers were more difficult to placate. In Pennsylvania, resistance to the AAA and to subsequent agricultural action programs was particularly fierce. This was partly a dollar-and-cents issue. Pennsylvania's well-diversified agricultural economy, a leader in dairy, eggs, chicken, mushrooms, peaches, and plums, was not devastated by the Great Depression. Farmers' total income more than doubled between 1932 and 1935 with only a miniscule percentage of the recovery deriving from federal payments. In 1935, Pennsylvania farmers collected a mere $1.6 million from the AAA out of a total federal outlay of nearly $180 million—among the very lowest amounts recovered by any of the country's major agricultural states.[56]

Pennsylvania farmers' opposition to the New Deal was also political. Milton McDowell, the director of agricultural extension at Pennsylvania State University from 1913 to 1942 and a dyed-in-the-wool Republican, forbade county agents from participating in New Deal action programs. He deemed those programs "noneducational" and, hence, in conflict with his understanding of county agents' terms of service as defined in the Smith–Lever Act. Farm groups and Penn State's Board of Trustees joined McDowell in his policy of noncooperation, and in 1937, the trustees barred extension personnel from engaging in New Deal programs that were "promotional, regulatory, or administrative in nature."[57] McDowell's opposition hardened, and the impasse dragged into the early 1940s even though the USDA threatened to withhold all extension funds from the college as a penalty for its noncompliance. The USDA never acted on its warning, and the college continued to refuse to administer any action programs well into the late 1940s—years past the heyday of the New Deal and long after Pennsylvania's mandatory retirement law had obliged McDowell to step down as head of extension at the end of 1941.[58]

The situation in Pennsylvania was extreme, and in most schools, extension officials defended agents' service as a logical outgrowth of their role as itinerant agricultural educators and as distantly affiliated members of the academic profession. Officials sought to inoculate their agents against charges of corruption and of private cooptation by reminding challengers of agents' multifaceted professional pedigree. They mounted a three-pronged defense that turned on agents' unique social role as a mediator of state-society relations with ties to both higher education and government. They reminded critics that a farming background and graduation from an agricultural college remained prerequisites for the agent position, and that working with the state land grant was an agent's primary professional affiliation. They also argued that the agricultural depression was a national emergency that required the organization and support of every branch of government, even those branches with tertiary relationships to the central government. Finally, they claimed that the definition of "education" in the Smith–Lever Act—which covered the diffusion of "useful and practical information"—was so broadly conceived as to encompass practically any activity undertaken by an agent.[59] A county agent from New York, Earl Flansburgh, defended this view in a 1933 radio interview. Education, as far as Flansburgh was concerned, was about encouraging "the production and prevention of change"—to encourage farmers to do what they were already doing, if that was best, or to do something new, if that was judged better. This definition of education was fluid if not "abstract," Flansburgh admitted, because education itself was "abstract." "In the broadest sense, man is an educator in every act that changes another man"; education "is a continuous and ever alive process."[60]

Most agents felt the same way. They subscribed to a wide-ranging definition of education that allowed them simultaneously to serve the

AAA, the Farm Bureau, the land-grant extension offices, and the farm families in their respective counties without hesitation. A county agent from Georgia, who devoted nearly all of his time to the AAA cotton reduction plan, carefully described that work as "an educational program." Even less charitable agents located outside the South thought the AAA possessed some educational merits. A county agent in Wood County, Wisconsin, grumbled that his AAA duties had cut into the time he could spend on other things and complained of the embarrassment caused by "delays in inquiries and in getting materials from Washington." This agent, nevertheless, concluded that the AAA "has served a very definite purpose in bringing about a greater confidence in farmers" and "will directly influence producers in keeping better records . . . and any agricultural statistics that they are called upon to give." In the end, agents supported the AAA, because it represented a continuation of the same local educational and interest group activities and services they had always provided. As one Louisiana agent recalled late in his life, during the Great Depression, agents did whatever they could to help "farm and rural families . . . to increase their efficiency and [raise] their standards of living."[61] In the 1930s, no doubt the increased cultural and political authority derived from their relationship with the Farm Bureau and the land-grant colleges greatly assisted county agents' efforts. In stark contrast to the failed organizing efforts of the past, agents' multifaceted institutional base and proven commitment to the countryside strengthened their purchase among farmers, a population not easily won over to coordinated intervention, especially if that intervention emanated from the federal government.[62]

Agents' thorough penetration of the countryside begot unexpected policy outcomes for both the state and higher education. This was ironic, as President Roosevelt initially did not view the land-grant system as an obvious administrative response to the federal government's lack of administrative capacity. In 1933, during a round of cost-cutting measures, he signed an executive order that slashed federal support to the land grants by 25 percent. Protests from Henry Wallace and the Farm Bureau, to say nothing of countless "educators, state officials and representatives of agricultural interests," as one senator put it, persuaded Roosevelt to rescind his order. After the Extension Service's virtuoso delivery of the AAA production-control program, the White House's opinion of the land-grant institutions changed completely. By 1934, Roosevelt and his fellow Democrats, at the urging of the Farm Bureau and the land-grant colleges, began lobbying to permanently increase the

Extension Service's federal appropriation and to grow its bureaucratic infrastructure.[63]

Southern Democrats held the key to increasing the Extension Service's funding and to mooring the land-grant system's bureaucratic structure to the New Deal state. Democrats had regained the House in 1931, the entire Congress in 1933, and no region benefited more from the Democratic restoration than the noncompetitive, one-party South. Its long-serving congressmen collected key committee chairmanships in both houses: Between 1933 and 1952, they controlled nearly one half of chairs and ranking minority posts in Congress, including coveted slots on the House Ways and Means Committee and the Senate Finance Committee. They used these posts to their advantage by killing all legislation that threatened their racially segregated, antiunion political culture while they fast-tracked agricultural policies of every stripe. In sum, virtually all New Deal policy making—but especially agricultural policy making—was southern policy making.[64]

Senator John H. Bankhead II (D-AL) spearheaded efforts to increase the Extension Service's funding. Born into prosperity near Old Moscow, Alabama, in 1872, Bankhead practiced law and helped run his family's coal properties before entering politics in 1930, when he was elected to the Senate, where he remained until his death in 1946.[65] Similarly to virtually all southern politicians at the time, in addition to defending Jim Crow, Bankhead, according to his biographer, "based his political future on a close alliance with farmers . . . and began his senatorial career as a spokesman for cotton farmers." During his Senate career, he talked about little else.[66] He supported the AAA and domestic allotment in 1933, and later drafted and sponsored several of the New Deal's most important agricultural policies, including the Bankhead Cotton Control Act of 1934, which mandated cotton producers' participation in domestic allotment; the Soil Conservation and Domestic Allotment Act of 1936, which continued the programs of the AAA after it was ruled unconstitutional, later superseded by the Agricultural Adjustment Act of 1938; and the Bankhead-Jones Farm Tenant Act of 1937, the largely unsuccessful program to help tenants and sharecroppers finance the purchase of their own land. As long as the legislation raised farm prices and in some way improved farmers' lot, or at least held out the possibility of doing so, Bankhead supported it.[67]

The same practical politics guided his sponsorship of increased agricultural extension funding. The Bankhead–Jones Act of 1935— cosponsored by Representative Marvin Jones (D-TX), chairman of the Committee on Agriculture—increased the federal government's supplementary funding for cooperative extension by $8 million in 1935, nearly doubling its annual appropriation.[68] Southern states and their land-grant colleges benefited disproportionately from the legislation, which covered more than county agent work, though that was its primary focus.[69] By 1940, the federal government's annual contribution for extension activities was $20 million, or nearly 60 percent of the nation's total cooperative extension budget.[70] The increase in extension funds was not lost on agents in the field. "The new Bankhead-Jones funds," reported the New York State extension director, in 1935, "have enabled us to do many things and to perform many services which we have long wanted to do and which have been asked of us and which were impossible without additional funds."[71]

Even with the magnanimity of the Bankhead–Jones Act, however, the total federal commitment to cooperative extension was relatively small compared with the size of the appropriations provided to other New Deal ventures. However, the significance of the act should be measured using more than a financial yardstick: The Bankhead–Jones Act solidified the relationship among the New Deal, the Farm Bureau, and the land-grant extension units created to organize and manage the AAA at the local level.[72] According to one scholar, the Bankhead–Jones Act was passed with the implicit understanding that the land-grant extension divisions would thereafter carry out educational, informational, and administrative work for all federal agencies without any request for additional funds.[73] The Soil Conservation Service, the Farm Credit Administration, the Rural Electrification Administration, the Tennessee Valley Authority, and the Works Progress Administration, among other New Deal action agencies, deployed their own representatives along with those from the extension bureaucracy to deliver services. That work, in turn, "educated" millions of farmers about the value of federally sponsored programs, easing acceptance and silencing charges of "big government." It is difficult to explain how some of the nation's most skeptical citizens ultimately embraced a landmark extension—so to speak—of national authority, especially in the South, without understanding the mechanisms by which that authority was infused into America's supposedly antistatist soil. The Advisory Committee on Education, appointed by Roosevelt in 1936, did not exaggerate when it concluded, "The Extension Service has developed into one of the major educational agencies in the United States."[74]

Not all parties approved of this. Two years later, the battle over the Extension Service and the county agent's dual role as educator and interest group operative came to a head. In 1938, H. R. Tolley, the head of the AAA, finalized the Mount Weather Agreement, which broke up the land-grant college and UDSA's monopoly of New Deal agricultural programs by empowering a range of emergent action agencies and their attendant client groups. Agitation among anti-Farm Bureau forces certainly contributed to this development, but it mostly resulted from the rapid growth of the New Deal state and its proliferation of new agricultural programs. According to one expert on the subject, "The relative unity of farm program administration during the first AAA, with authority concentrated in the USDA and executed through the Extension Service, broke down under the weight of increasing government complexity."[75] The rise of mission-driven agricultural agencies dedicated to conservation and modernization, land reclamation and relocation, marketing and price supports, among others, previewed the pluralist future of the agricultural welfare state. In a pattern that would be repeated with increasing frequency in other policy areas in the next few decades—from defense research and healthcare to welfare and education—the New Deal "broker state" dispersed the administration of agricultural policy among a host of agricultural agencies and their allied interests after the execution of the Mount Weather Agreement. Though the Extension Service and the land-grant colleges maintained their leadership roles in the state and county agricultural planning committees that were organized, from then on, their power was shared with personnel from other agricultural agencies.[76]

The thinning jurisdiction of the land-grant colleges and the Extension Service's command over agricultural policy after 1938 does not diminish the importance of what preceded it. Between 1933 and 1938, county agents scoured the countryside on behalf of agricultural adjustment, changing farmers' relationship to the state. "The hand of the federal unit reaches every family," observed sociologist Paul Landis of the State College of Washington, in 1936. Even though most farmers did not understand the theoretical underpinnings of agricultural adjustment, "when he gets his check for fifty dollars as a result of letting some of his acreage lie fallow, he feels that government is a real part of his life."[77] Having succeeded at aggregating and addressing millions of individual farmer's demands, county agents made the Extension Service, the land-grant colleges, and farmers themselves key players in the New Deal state. "By decentralizing the responsibility . . . and using the full facilities of the Cooperative Agricultural Extension Service," remarked Secretary Wallace before the US Senate Committee on Agriculture and

Forestry, in the late 1930s, "it has been found practical to carry through operations involving from hundreds to millions of individual farmers."[78] Hundreds to millions of individual farmers, Wallace might have added, who remained deeply suspicious of "big government."

Conclusion

The land-grant colleges helped the New Deal achieve administrative capacity in a political culture uncomfortable with a powerful national bureaucracy. New Dealers turned to the land-grant colleges—and their force of county agents—to deliver federal programs and services to farmers and their families. The agents naturalized the New Deal's expanded authority and made it politically palatable to average Americans and to southern politicians committed, above all else, to preserving Jim Crow. As the years passed and the New Deal matured, however, it became increasingly apparent that the polity supported an activist state most when that state operated through providers at least once removed from the federal government's immediate network of bureaucratic agencies. The land-grant colleges served as one of those providers.

Historians have for too long neglected this story, and the sesquicentennial commemoration of the Morrill Land-Grant Act is an appropriate time to acknowledge the contribution of publicly supported land grants to the nation's welfare. This article has demonstrated that the land-grant colleges played a vital role in bridging the divide between higher education and the state, and between the state and its rural citizens, thus setting the stage for far greater federal involvement in academic life later on. By focusing on the role of county agents as they traversed the countryside in the name of agricultural adjustment during the New Deal, this article reminds us that one of the defining features of the land-grant system was its readiness to serve the government and the American people. The land grants delivered on this dual mandate during the 1930s when New Dealers turned to the agricultural colleges to readjust the American countryside and its rural inhabitants to the realities of a new and more powerful central government.

After the New Deal, the land-grant system grew increasingly powerful, extending itself deep into the nation's social and intellectual soil, educating from thousands to hundreds of thousands of students and commanding from millions to billions of dollars in external research support. All the while, the land grants and their corps of itinerant county agents continued to comb the countryside, dispensing up-to-date research discoveries and plain common sense to farmers and their families.

Both at home and around the world, the land-grant sector still relies on cooperative extension to fulfill its mission. The federal government and the land grants, to say nothing of millions of Americans, have continued to benefit from the cooperative partnership that was sowed during the darkest days of the Great Depression.

Notes

*   Thanks to Roger Geiger for his intellectual generosity and for organizing *The Legacy and the Promise* conference; to Bruce McPheron, dean of Penn State University's College of Agriculture, for his valuable insights and questions; to my fellow authors for their stimulating explorations of the land-grant university; and to my great uncle Enos J. Perry (1891–1983), Penn State Class of 1916, county agent, professor of dairy husbandry at Rutgers University, and member of the National Agricultural Hall of Fame, whose book *Among the Danish Farmers* (Danville, IL: Interstate, 1939) first piqued my interest in agricultural history. A portion of this article is from Christopher P. Loss, *Between Citizens and the State: The Politics of American Higher Education in the 20th Century* (Princeton, NJ: Princeton University Press, 2012) and appears here with permission.

1.   Kennedy's proclamation in Henry S. Brunner, *Land-Grant Colleges and Universities, 1862–1962* (Washington, DC: GPO, 1962), v.

2.   Letter to FDR, March 19, 1933, Education: January–September 1933 file, box 1, Official File 107, FDR Library (Hyde Park, NY).

3.   See, for example, Martin J. Finkelstein, *The American Academic Profession: A Synthesis of Social Scientific Inquiry since World War II* (Columbus: Ohio State University Press, 1984), 26–27; William E. Leuchtenburg, *Franklin D. Roosevelt and the New Deal, 1932–1940* (New York: Harper and Row, 1963); Alan Brinkley, *The End of Reform: New Deal Liberalism in Recession and War* (New York: Knopf, 1995); and Barry Dean Karl, *Executive Reorganization and Reform in the New Deal* (1963; repr. Chicago, IL: University of Chicago Press, 1979). For a revisionist intellectual history, see Edward S. Shapiro, "Decentralist Intellectuals and the New Deal," *Journal of American History* 58 (March 1972): 938–57.

4.   See, for example, Robert Kargon and Elizabeth Hodes, "Karl Compton, Isaiah Bowman, and the Politics of Science in the Great Depression," *ISIS* 76 (1985): 301–18; Larry Owens, "MIT and the Federal 'Angel': Academic R&D and Federal-Private Cooperation before World War II," *ISIS* 81 (1990): 188–213; Daniel J. Kevles, *The Physicists: The History of a Scientific Community in Modern America* (New York: Knopf, 1978); Rebecca S. Lowen, *Creating the Cold War University: The Transformation of Stanford* (Berkeley: University of California Press, 1997), 17–42; and Roger L. Geiger, *Research and Relevant Knowledge: American Research Universities since World War Two* (New York: Oxford University Press, 1993).

5.   On the emergence of these contracts, see Bartholomew H. Sparrow, *From the Outside In: World War II and the American State* (Princeton, NJ: Princeton University Press, 1996), 175–90.

6.   For one exception, see Ronald Story, "The New Deal and Higher Education," in *The New Deal and the Triumph of Liberalism*, ed. Sid Milkis and Jerome M. Mileur (Amherst: University of Massachusetts Press, 2002), 272–96. To make his case for the importance of the New Deal, Story conflates the New Deal and World War II by using Franklin Roosevelt's presidential tenure (1933–1945) as an organizing frame. Although this approach permits Story to showcase the depth of the Roosevelt administration's commitment to higher education policy making, it obscures the

real differences in motive and intent, and in political and interest group alignments that distinguished each period.

7. On New Deal state building, see Ellis W. Hawley, *The New Deal and the Problem of Monopoly: A Study in Economic Ambivalence* (1963; repr., Princeton, NJ: Princeton University Press, 1995); Gerald D. Nash, *The Crucial Era: The Great Depression and World War II, 1929–1945* (1979; repr., New York: Waveland Press, 1992); Barry Dean Karl, *The Uneasy State: The United States from 1915–1945* (Chicago, IL: University of Chicago Press, 1983); Steve Fraser and Gary Gerstle, ed., *The Rise and Fall of the New Deal Order, 1930–1980* (Princeton, NJ: Princeton University Press, 1989); James T. Patterson, *Congressional Conservatism and the New Deal: The Growth of the Conservative Coalition in Congress, 1933–1939* (Lexington: University of Kentucky Press, 1969); and Jason Scott Smith, *Building New Deal Liberalism: The Political Economy of Public Works, 1933–1956* (New York: Cambridge University Press, 2006). My thinking on the influence of America's laissez-faire tradition on New Deal state building has been shaped by Ellis W. Hawley, "The New Deal State and the Anti-Bureaucratic Tradition," in *The New Deal and Its Legacy: Critique and Reappraisal*, ed. Robert Eden (New York: Greenwood Press, 1989), 77–92.

8. David M. Kennedy, *Freedom from Fear: The American People in Depression and War, 1929-1945* (New York: Oxford University Press, 1999), 171.

9. See, for example, Bruce Schulman, *From Cotton Belt to Sunbelt: Federal Policy, Economic Development, and the Transformation of the South, 1938–1980* (New York: Oxford University Press, 1991); Ira Katznelson, *When Affirmative Action was White: The Untold History of Racial Inequality in Twentieth-Century America* (New York: W. W. Norton, 2005); and Patterson, *Congressional Conservatism and the New Deal.*

10. Brinkley, *End of Reform.*

11. On the role of intermediary institutions, what some scholars call "parastates," see Eldon J. Eisenach, *The Lost Promise of Progressivism* (Lawrence: University Press of Kansas, 1994), 18; Brian Balogh, *A Government Out of Sight: The Mystery of National Authority in Nineteenth-Century America* (New York: Cambridge University Press, 2009). Ellis Hawley has dubbed this an "associative order," stressing the role of intermediaries in the development of an expansive governing regime in the 1920s and 1930s. See Hawley's *New Deal and the Problem of Monopoly* and *Great War and the Search for Modern Order.* Hugh Heclo does not use the term, but described a similar phenomenon when he discussed the role of "intermediary organizations" in the operation of the post–World War II federal government, what he called "government by remote control." See Hugh Heclo, "Issue Networks and the Executive Establishment," in *The New American Political System*, ed. Anthony King (Washington, DC: American Enterprise Institute Press, 1978), 87–124, esp. 92–93.

12. Stephen Skowronek, *Building a New American State: The Expansion of National Administrative Capacities, 1877–1920* (1982; repr., New York: Cambridge University Press, 1987), ix.

13. Theodore Saloutos, *The American Farmer and the New Deal* (Ames: Iowa State University Press, 1982), 3–14, esp. 12–13; Anthony J. Badger, *The New Deal: The Depression Years, 1933–40* (London: Macmillan, 1989), 14–15.

14. Wayne D. Rasmussen and Gladys Baker, *The Department of Agriculture* (New York: Praeger, 1972), 22.

15. Philip Kinsley, "79 Farmers Held by Troops: Iowa Extends Martial Law," *Chicago Daily Tribune*, May 2, 1933, 5; James O. Babcock, "The Farm Revolt in Iowa," *Social Forces* 12 (March 1934): 369–73.

16. On the farm lobby, see John Mark Hansen, *Gaining Access: Congress and the Farm Lobby, 1919–1981* (Chicago, IL: University of Chicago Press, 1991).

17. Badger, *New Deal*, 150–52.

18. Ibid., 73–75; Wayne D. Rasmussen, Gladys L. Baker, and James S. Ward, *A Short History of Agricultural Adjustment, 1933–75* (Washington, DC: Economic Research Service, US Dept. of Agriculture, 1976), 1–2. The AAA was passed on May 12, 1933; the NIRA was passed on June 16, 1933. On the success of the Agricultural Adjustment Administration and the failure of the National Recovery Act, see Kenneth Finegold and Theda Skocpol, *State and Party in America's New Deal* (Madison: University of Wisconsin Press, 1995).

19. H. A. Wallace, "More Purchasing Power for Farmers," *Extension Service Review* 4 (May 1933): 33.

20. Hansen, *Gaining Access*, 39.

21. Jan Choate, *Disputed Ground: Farm Groups that Opposed the New Deal Agricultural Program* (Jefferson, NC: McFarland, 2002), 131–33; Badger, *New Deal*, 149–50. Peek and Wallace had a contested relationship; see Saloutos, *American Farmer and the New Deal*, 155. On Henry C. Wallace's futile quest for agricultural reform in the Harding administration, see Rasmussen and Baker, *Department of Agriculture*, 16–17.

22. On the failures of the 1920s, see Hansen, *Gaining Access*, 26–77. The USDA eventually created programs to redistribute agricultural surpluses to the neediest Americans; see Rachel Louise Moran, "Consuming Relief: Food Stamps and the New Welfare of the New Deal," *Journal of American History* 97 (March 2011): 1001–22.

23. Rasmussen and Baker, *Department of Agriculture*, 26.

24. Donald H. Grubbs, *Cry from the Cotton: The Southern Tenant Farmers' Union and the New Deal* (1971; repr., Fayetteville: University of Arkansas Press, 2000), 18.

25. Edmund S. Brunner and E. Hsin Pao Yang, *Rural America and the Extension Service: A History and Critique of the Cooperative Agricultural and Home Economics Extension Service* (New York: Bureau of Publications, Teachers College, Columbia University, 1949), 81.

26. Badger, *New Deal*, 155–57; Murray R. Benedict, *Can We Solve the Farm Problem? An Analysis of Federal Aid to Agriculture* (New York: Twentieth Century Fund, 1955), 90–91.

27. Rasmussen and Baker, *Department of Agriculture*, 27–28. On Wallace's decision, see William J. Block, "The Separation of the Farm Bureau and the Extension Service," *Illinois Studies in Social Sciences* 47 (1960): 15; Badger, *New Deal*, 157–58.

28. For the number of land-grant colleges and universities, which included seventeen all-black institutions, see Arthur J. Klein, *Survey of Land-Grant Colleges and Universities* (Washington, DC: GPO, 1930), v. Enrollment data in Arthur J. Klein, "The Rise of the Land-Grant Colleges and Universities," *School Life* 16 (January 1931): 83.

29. Wayne D. Rasmussen, *Taking the University to the People: Seventy-five Years of Cooperative Extension* (Ames: Iowa State University Press, 1989), 22–23; Rasmussen and Baker, *Department of Agriculture*, 3–20; Alice M. Rivlin, *The Role of the Federal Government in Financing Higher Education* (Washington, DC: Brookings Institution, 1961), 21–26. For an overview of the entire period, see Roger L. Williams, *The Origins of Federal Support for Higher Education: George W. Atherton and the Land-Grant College Movement* (University Park: Penn State University Press, 1991), esp. 87–198. Political scientist Dan Carpenter has persuasively argued that the USDA became a de facto "university" in the first two decades of the twentieth century; see Carpenter, *The Forging of Bureaucratic*

Autonomy: Reputations, Networks, and Policy Innovation in Executive Agencies, 1862–1928 (Princeton, NJ: Princeton University Press, 2001), 212–54. The USDA's relationship to higher education was further enhanced by the creation of the Graduate School of the Department of Agriculture in 1921. See Paul Kaufman, "The Graduate School of the Department of Agriculture," *Journal of Higher Education* 11 (June 1940): 287–92.

30. On the differences between the instructional techniques of the USDA and the land-grant colleges, see Roy V. Scott, *The Reluctant Farmer: The Rise of Agricultural Extension to 1914* (Chicago, IL: University of Chicago Press, 1970), 138–69.

31. Joseph Cannon Bailey, *Seaman A. Knapp: Schoolmaster of American Agriculture* (New York: Columbia University Press, 1945), 96; Scott, *Reluctant Farmer*, 208.

32. Bailey, *Seaman A. Knapp*, 132.

33. Lawrence Goodwyn, *The Populist Moment: A Short History of the Agrarian Revolt in America* (New York: Oxford University Press, 1978), 29–35.

34. On Knapp's agent preferences, see Scott, *Reluctant Farmer*, 213–16.

35. Bailey, *Seaman A. Knapp*, 177–78, quote on 202.

36. Ibid., 204–5.

37. Ibid., 213.

38. Ibid., 206.

39. Ibid., 211.

40. After Knapp's death in 1911, his son and successor at the USDA, Bradford Knapp, loosened the rules governing the selection of agents, which opened the door for land-grant graduates; see Scott, *Reluctant Farmer*, 227. On the particulars of the act, see ibid., 288–313, esp. 307–11.

41. Figures in Rasmussen, *Taking the University to the People*, 72; Gladys Baker, *The County Agent* (Chicago, IL: University of Chicago Press, 1939), 61; C. W. Warburton, "County Agents—Today and Tomorrow," *Extension Service Review* 6 (July 1935): 81.

42. On the role of interest groups in extending the USDA's political authority, see Carpenter, *Forging Bureaucratic Autonomy*, 291. For a more reductive view of the Farm Bureau as "captor" of the USDA and the land grants, and ultimately of all New Deal agricultural policy, see Grant McConnell, *The Decline of Agrarian Democracy* (Berkeley: University of California Press, 1953). For a comparative interpretation that challenges McConnell's thesis, see Adam D. Sheingate, *The Rise of the Agricultural Welfare State: Institutions and Interest Group Power in the United States, France, and Japan* (Princeton, NJ: Princeton University Press, 2001).

43. On the Farm Bureau, see Christiana McFadyen Campbell, *The Farm Bureau and the New Deal* (Urbana: University of Illinois Press, 1962), 3–13; Baker, *County Agent*, 15–24; Brunner and Yang, *Rural American and the Extension Service*, 68–71.

44. Rasmussen, *Taking the University to the People*, 77–80. On the early partnership between the county agent and the Farm Bureau, see M. C. Burritt, *The County Agent and the Farm Bureau* (New York: Harcourt Brace, 1922).

45. McConnell, *Decline of Agrarian Democracy*, 53.

46. "A Message to all County Agents," *Extension Service Review* 6 (July 1935): 97.

47. Badger, *New Deal*, 158–59; Saloutos, *American Farmer and the New Deal*, 67–68; A. A. Myers, "County Adjustment Campaigns," *Extension Services Review* 4 (March 1934): 125.

48. R. E. Hughes, 1933 Narrative Report, *Annual Narrative and Statistical Reports from State Offices and County Agents: Georgia* (Washington, DC: NARA, 1951), film, roll 58 of 149.

49. T. B. Manny, "The Conditions of Rural Life," *American Journal of Sociology* 40 (May 1935): 721.

50. Baker, *County Agent*, 70; Ralph K. Bliss, *History of Cooperative Agriculture and Home Economics Extension in Iowa—the First Fifty Years* (Ames: Iowa State University Press, 1960), 167. Contact data in C. W. Warburton, "County Agents—Today and Tomorrow," *Extension Services Review* 6 (July 1935): 96.

51. Theodore Saloutos and John D. Hicks, *Agricultural Discontent in the Middle West, 1900–1939* (Madison: University of Wisconsin Press, 1951), 491.

52. On these and other alleged county agent transgressions, see Campbell, *Farm Bureau and the New Deal*, 85–102; Block, "The Separation of the Farm Bureau and the Extension Service," 25–28; and Baker, *County Agent*, 100.

53. Saloutos and Hicks, *Agricultural Discontent in the Middle West*, 491.

54. Baker, *County Agent*, 94–97; Campbell, *Farm Bureau and the New Deal*, 70–76.

55. 1935 Director's Report, Narrative Report, *Annual Narrative and Statistical Reports from State Offices and County Agents: New York* (Washington, DC: NARA, 1951), film, roll 51 of 90.

56. Michael Bezilla, *The College of Agriculture at Penn State: A Tradition of Excellence* (University Park: Penn State University Press, 1987), 205–6.

57. Ibid., 206–16, quote on 206.

58. Ibid.

59. Baker, *County Agent*, 38.

60. Brunner and Yang, *Rural America and the Extension Service*, 133–34; Earl A. Flansburgh, "What is a Farm Bureau," in 1935 Narrative Report, *Annual Narrative and Statistical Reports from State Offices and County Agents: New York* (Washington, DC: NARA, 1951), film, roll 51 of 90. On an agent's affiliation with the land grant, see H. C. Sanders, *The Memoirs of a County Agent* (Baton Rouge: Louisiana State University Printing Office, 1983), 1.

61. N. D. McRainey, 1934 Narrative Report, *Annual Narrative and Statistical Reports from State Offices and County Agents: Georgia* (Washington, DC: NARA, 1951), film, roll 69 of 149; George M. Briggs, 1934 Narrative Report, *Annual Narrative and Statistical Reports from State Offices and County Agents: Wisconsin* (Washington, DC: NARA, 1951), film, roll 23 of 49; Sanders, *Memoirs of a County Agent*, 1.

62. On the failed efforts of the 1880s and 1890s, see Goodwyn, *Populist Moment*.

63. On Roosevelt's decision making, see assorted items in Land Grants 1933–1937 file, box 1, Official File 381, FDR Library; Senator quote in Letter to FDR, April 21, 1933, ibid; and Story, "New Deal and Higher Education," in *New Deal and the Triumph of Liberalism*, 276. On New Deal funding for the Extension Service, see Baker, *County Agent*, 79–81, esp. 80n14; and Brunner and Yang, *Rural America and the Extension Service*, 202. On the Farm Bureau's influence and the land-grant colleges' support of it, see McConnell, *Decline of Agrarian Democracy*, 82, 164–65.

64. Julian E. Zelizer, *On Capitol Hill: The Struggle to Reform Congress and Its Consequences, 1948–2000* (New York: Cambridge University Press, 2004), 22–25; Ira Katznelson, "Limiting Liberalism: The Southern Veto in Congress, 1933-1950," *Political Science Quarterly* 108 (Summer 1993): 283–306.

65. On the Bankhead family, see Jack B. Key, "John H. Bankhead, Jr. of Alabama: The Conservative as Reformer" (PhD diss., Johns Hopkins University, 1966); and the congressional biographies available at http://bioguide.congress.gov.

66. Key, "John H. Bankhead, Jr., of Alabama," 1–3.

67. Ibid; Saloutos, *American Farmer and the New Deal*, 126, 164–65, 176–77, 196–97; *Memorial Services for John Hollis Bankhead*, 72–77; Hal Steed, "Cotton Country Pins Hopes on New Measure of Control," *New York Times*, April 22, 1934, XX3.

68. For the legislative history of the Bankhead–Jones Act, see Brunner, *Land-Grant Colleges and Universities*, 65–66.
69. By 1941, Texas was the top grantee at more than a million dollars annually, with North Carolina, Georgia, and Bankhead's home state of Alabama following closely behind. Overall, eight of the top ten largest appropriations went to southern states; only Pennsylvania, ranked eighth, and Ohio, ranked tenth, managed to crack the top ten. Funding data in US Congress, Senate, Committee on Agriculture and Forestry, *Authorize Additional Appropriations to Provide for the Further Development of Cooperative Extension Work*, 77th Cong., 1st sess., March 31, 1941, 1–3.
70. Rivlin, *Role of the Federal Government in Financing Higher Education*, 63–64; Baker, *County Agent*, 145–50; Brunner and Yang, *Rural America and the Extension Service*, 202; Walter J. Greenleaf, "The Colleges," *School Life* 21 (September 1935): 22; US Congress, Senate, Committee on Agriculture and Forestry, *Hearings on S. 2228*, 74th Cong., 1st sess., March 28–29, 1935, 30, 41–42.
71. Extension Director, 1935 Narrative Report, *Annual Narrative and Statistical Reports from State Offices and County Agents: New York* (Washington, DC: NARA, 1951), film, roll 51 of 90.
72. McConnell, *Decline of Agrarian Democracy*, 82.
73. Baker, *County Agent*, 82.
74. Floyd W. Reeves et al., *The Advisory Committee on Education: Report of the Committee* (Washington, DC: GPO, 1938), 146.
75. Sheingate, *Rise of the Agricultural Welfare State*, 115.
76. On the "broker state," see Hawley, *New Deal and Problem of Monopoly*; and, for a similar argument that examines the New Deal's role in the "redistribution of power" to new "groups," see Samuel H. Beers, "In Search of a New Public Philosophy," in *New American Political System*, ed. Anthony King (Washington, DC: American Enterprise Institute Press, 1978), 9–13. On the continued importance of county agents on the planning committees, see Dale Clark, "The Farmer as Co-Administrator," *Public Opinion Quarterly* 3 (July 1939): 488. On the rise of the agricultural welfare state during the 1930s and its eventual retrenchment in the 1990s, see Sheingate, *Rise of the Agricultural Welfare State*, 181–238.
77. Paul H. Landis, "The New Deal and Rural Life," *American Sociological Review* 1 (August 1936): 600.
78. E. R. McIntyre, *Fifty Years of Cooperative Extension in Wisconsin, 1912–1962* (Madison: University of Wisconsin Press, 1962), 133–34.

Social Science over Agriculture:
Reimagining the Land-Grant Mission at the
University of California-Irvine in the 1960s

Ethan Schrum

As an army helicopter bearing President Lyndon Baines Johnson hovered over massive piles of dirt just off the Pacific coast in Orange County, California, on June 20, 1964, one of the less-noticed symbolic meetings of that symbolism-laden decade prepared to mark history.[1] Johnson had arrived to dedicate the site for the Irvine campus of the University of California, one of the three new campuses that America's largest university built mostly from scratch in the 1960s.

Joining Johnson on the platform at Irvine before 12,000 spectators was America's best-known educational administrator Clark Kerr, who was the president of the University of California. The national spotlight would shine on him even more brightly, albeit ominously, several months later during the Free Speech Movement at UC Berkeley, the first major student uprising of the 1960s. Kerr had graced the cover of *Time* in 1960 as the "Master Planner" in recognition of his efforts in crafting the landmark California Master Plan for Higher Education, which guided the development of campuses such as UC Irvine and won international acclaim.[2] Kerr gained further renown with *The Uses of the University* in 1963, which among several major points argued that the nation's universities had become essential instruments for achieving economic growth.[3]

As much as Kerr the administrator and political figure grabbed the limelight, there was another, perhaps more fundamental side to him. Kerr

Perspectives on the History of Higher Education 30 (2013): 311–333
© 2013. ISBN: 978-1-4128-5147-3

was a social scientist who loved grand theory. His powerful speculative mind drove one of the great "big social science" projects of the postwar era, the Inter-University Study of Labor Problems in Economic Development, which consciously aimed at constructing such a grand theory that challenged those of Karl Marx and Alfred Marshall, yet would also have practical implications for stimulating economic development. Indeed, Kerr and his colleagues went on a round-the-world trip to brief leaders of several countries on the implications of their ideas. Kerr's belief in the connection between social science theory and practical programs for economic development led him to think that UC Irvine could be a new kind of land-grant institution—still committed to furthering California's economic growth, but through social science rather than agriculture. A study of UC Irvine, thus, enables us to explore a thoughtful attempt to enlarge the land-grant tradition.

Kerr set the overall focus for UC Irvine when he determined that it should be a "general campus" of the university. The primary mission of every general campus was to offer liberal education in the arts and sciences. However, Kerr decided that Irvine should also, in particular, aim at redefining and fulfilling the role of a land-grant university for the late twentieth century.[4] It is important to understand this decision in the context of the University of California's history. The university started in 1868 from a merger between the College of California and the land-grant Agricultural, Mining, and Mechanical Arts College. The new land-grant UC began with a single campus in Berkeley and added a "southern branch" at Los Angeles in 1919, later known as UCLA.[5] Each was considered a "general campus," because it offered a wide array of degree programs in the arts, sciences, and professions. The university also started other branches: the Medical Department at San Francisco (1873), the University Farm at Davis (1905), the Citrus Experiment Station at Riverside (1907), and the Scripps Institution of Oceanography at La Jolla (1912). Davis and Riverside were particularly tied to the UC's mission as a land-grant institution, because they carried out research on specific problems that were important to the farmers and growers who constituted California's economic backbone and made it the top state for agricultural production.

The 1950s witnessed dramatic changes in the University of California that were related to massive demographic and economic shifts in the state. Davis and Riverside added undergraduate liberal arts colleges early in the decade, and Kerr elevated them to general campuses in 1959. The University had taken over Santa Barbara State Teachers College in

1944 and transitioned it to a liberal arts college; it too became a general campus, UC Santa Barbara, in 1958. Meanwhile, as the Regents pondered how to handle the upcoming "tidal wave" of aspiring university students in the Baby Boom, they decided at the same October 1957 meeting where they elected Kerr as president to authorize three new general campuses to open in the 1960s. After Kerr assumed responsibility for planning the campuses on his ascent to the presidency in 1958, each campus took on a particular theme. UC San Diego, built from the Scripps Institution, would harness that resource for a focus on research in the sciences. UC Santa Cruz would focus on innovative approaches to liberal arts undergraduate education. UC Irvine would attempt to redefine the land-grant tradition, especially by incorporating the social sciences.[6]

Kerr understood that California's economy and its landscape had changed profoundly in the postwar period. Industry based on the physical sciences and engineering overshadowed agriculture, and suburbanization overtook former ranches and groves. For the university to fulfill its land-grant mission in this new environment, it would need to redefine that mission for a new era. Kerr believed that the new campus at Irvine offered a prime opportunity for carrying out this work. The location was also symbolic: the former Irvine Ranch, a massive piece of land that developers were turning into one of America's great experiments in planned suburbanism, the new city of Irvine.[7]

There was little question that Kerr intended the activities of the Irvine campus to focus on the economic development of its region. In the first announcement of its academic program, Kerr wrote that "Irvine will enroll its first students in September, 1965. These 'pioneers' will have an opportunity to share in the exciting beginning of a great new University campus, located in a part of the State that is growing rapidly in population and economic importance. The Irvine campus will be the focus for this region, serving many of its needs, and influencing its development."[8]

Among the fields that Kerr wanted to emphasize at Irvine were architecture and city planning. A 1961 document from his office suggested that "the new campus in Orange County should be given priority in future development in architecture and planning, which will probably be required in the late Sixties when the new campus is more fully developed. Students and researchers would profit from observing, and in some cases participating in the unique development of the campus and the entire Irvine Ranch area. The site could become a renowned center for these fields, similar in status to oceanography at La Jolla."[9] What is surprising is that these plans did not come to fruition. Although a UC-Irvine faculty committee to create a School of Architecture and Environmental Planning began in Fall 1967, and important faculty in the Graduate School of Administration and Public Policy Research Organization had city planning backgrounds, UC Irvine did not establish programs in architecture and city planning until 1992.[10]

Instead, the general idea that guided the early years of UC Irvine was that institutionalizing novel approaches to social science, including both theoretical and applied work, could spur economic development. Three related Irvine units institutionalized these hopes: the Division of Social Sciences, the Graduate School of Administration (GSA), and the Public Policy Research Organization (PPRO). All three of these units were in many ways substantial failures with regard to their goals, yet they reveal the power of a peculiar mindset that influenced many university leaders, including Kerr, in the postwar years.

These UC-Irvine programs overlapped with Kerr's intellectual commitments, even though Kerr played a direct part in only one of them, and even then more as a formality. In the first two Irvine projects—making social science interdisciplinary in order to bolster theory, and developing a general science of administration—Kerr had engaged in similar endeavors before Irvine started, yet contributed almost nothing directly to Irvine's initiatives. In the third project, PPRO, Kerr expressed great initial enthusiasm for the idea (though it was not his), but later failed to give sufficient backing to it, perhaps because other difficulties threatened his very position as president.

There are several possible explanations for why these Irvine programs overlapped with Kerr's intellectual commitments. The most obvious is that Kerr appointed Irvine's chancellor and approved the chancellor's selections for other top administrators. Another is that it suggests the intellectual homogeneity of postwar academic leaders, such that the candidate pool for Irvine administrators would largely share Kerr's worldview. Finally, the overlap might suggest that Kerr's innovative academic planning program for the University of California created an atmosphere that encouraged programs of a certain bent even if Kerr was not creating the programs directly.

Kerr's desire for UC Irvine to extend the land-grant tradition propelled his decision to appoint Daniel Aldrich as chancellor of the new campus in January 1962. Aldrich, a soil chemist, was statewide dean of agriculture for UC and thus thoroughly ensconced in the academic field most identified with the land-grant tradition. It would be his job to implement Kerr's dream of shaping that tradition to fit a new suburban area being built from scratch. Also important in that regard was the appointment of Ivan Hinderaker, a UCLA political science professor whose specialty was public administration, as vice chancellor of academic affairs at Irvine.

From the beginning of his chancellorship, Aldrich was thinking about specific programs that might characterize an updated land-grant university for economic development. Kerr had begun to create university-wide ten-year academic plans when he became president. Responding to a draft of a new plan being discussed in 1964, Aldrich suggested that a proposal be added: "One of the changing emphases in the next decade might well be the development of a means of bringing to the University scientists and engineers from industry for intellectual refreshment and renewal, a form of industrial sabbatical leave. Such periodic residency programs will do much to refurbish the intellectual equipment of our industry and enhance its position in the state's economy."[11] The most dramatic proposals actually enacted at Irvine, however, involved social sciences rather than physical sciences.

Indeed, a tremendous faith in the power of social science was a signature element in the common worldview of postwar academic leaders. In particular, there was a widespread belief that mathematical social science could provide certain knowledge about man and his behavior, and, thus, enable social control—a mode of thinking similar to what David Harvey and James Scott have called "high modernism."[12] This knowledge would enable efficient administration of organizations and expert-crafted policy that would lead the world into an American liberal-democratic capitalist golden age. The most important thinkers and institutions in developing and propagating this view were the polymath social scientist Herbert Simon, the Carnegie Institute of Technology Graduate School of Industrial Administration that he helped found, the RAND Corporation that he advised as a consultant, and the US Department of Defense.[13] Specific strands of this movement such as administrative science, the new organization theory, and systems analysis raised expectations for university research to solve social problems and shaped university structures and projects, nowhere more evidently than at Irvine.

RAND, a policy research organization founded after the war in Santa Monica, California, emerged from wartime research conducted by the Army Air Force on the efficacy of strategic bombing. Featuring "a certain style of mathematical-economic reasoning, an interest in organizational theory, and a commitment to what came to be known in political science as rational choice," RAND became the most influential institution for strategic thought in the postwar period. Systems analysis, a mode of reasoning that involved quantifying all possible elements of a situation and running multivariate equations to suggest the best course of action, became RAND's signature methodology.[14] Robert S. McNamara institutionalized this approach in the US Department of Defense after John F. Kennedy named him Secretary of Defense in 1961. McNamara hired Charles J. Hitch, chairman of RAND's Research Council, as Assistant Secretary of Defense and Comptroller. Together, they became known for the "McNamara-Hitch approach to public service," which involved an attempt to quantify whenever possible and to use the techniques of systems analysis for all decision making. They believed that this method would result in the most rational and scientific course of action and, thus, be best for the country. Their approach later became widely reviled, however, first by the military, then by opponents of the Vietnam War.

This set of high modern ideas shaped Irvine's program in social sciences. The key figure was James G. March, the first dean of social sciences at Irvine, who like Kerr worked in the behavioral science paradigm, but at its hardest, most scientistic edge emphasizing mathematical formalization above all. March came from the Graduate School of Industrial Administration at the Carnegie Institute of Technology in Pittsburgh, where he was a close colleague of Herbert Simon; together, they pioneered the new organization theory in the landmark book *Organizations* (1958). March wanted his Division of Social Sciences to be interdisciplinary and quantitative. He believed that it "should specialize by problem area rather than by traditional academic disciplines."[15] There would be no departments. He told Hinderaker that "the major subunits within the Division will be the Research Centers. Each Center will be comprised of a group of faculty and students interested in a specific problem area. New Centers will be added and old ones eliminated as interests, experiences, and opportunities change."[16] He believed this strategy could propel Irvine to national prominence. March's program realized a Kerrian vision for institutions to support integrated social science theory, even without Kerr's direct influence and while pursuing a more doggedly mathematical approach than Kerr used in his own work.

Irvine's Graduate School of Administration was a direct result of one strand of postwar behavioral science, the quest to create a general science of administration, which became institutionalized in the mid-1950s. Here, too, Herbert Simon was the leading thinker. He inspired the attempt to create a science of human decision making—sometimes called "decision science"—that its promoters thought would be at the center of a unified administrative science that could transcend the specific settings for which administration was usually taught, including business, public, educational, and hospital administration. In light of that belief, the UC-Irvine Graduate School of Administration offered a single degree, Master of Administration, rather than specific degrees such as the MBA. Kerr personally participated in the discussion of decision science, and expounded his views in a speech at the University of Pittsburgh in 1957, where he first began to connect it to emerging ideas about a knowledge economy and the university's role in relation to it. In light of these things, he probably believed that a focus on administrative science would be most appropriate for UC's new campus at Irvine.

Although Kerr helped create an atmosphere that was congenial to the development of administrative science, Ivan Hinderaker exerted more direct influence in establishing the Graduate School of Administration. Hinderaker included a Graduate School of Administration in the original academic plan for UC Irvine, which he wrote in December 1962.[17] He also thought deeply about the rationale behind this enterprise, and laid out his ideas in a 1963 article. He argued that "the core material for the study of administration . . . should include work in organizational theory, drawing primarily on research from such disciplines as sociology and psychology; in politics, where political science can make its most important contribution; in managerial economics; and in quantitative methods, not only because it is important to understand what quantification can be used for but to learn also its limits."[18] He also believed that "we should be giving more thought to the manner in which department boundaries can be lowered to facilitate an interdisciplinary attack on other problems which the world has every right to expect colleges and universities to deal with in a realistic and effective way."[19] Notions of how interdisciplinary social science could be harnessed to solve problems were central to the concept of a unified school of administration.

When Hinderaker left Irvine to become chancellor of UC Riverside in July 1964, he had not yet hired a dean for Irvine's Graduate School of Administration. His successor Jack Peltason, who later followed Aldrich as chancellor and eventually became UC president, hired Richard Snyder, the Benjamin Franklin Professor of Decision-Making and the chairman of political science at Northwestern University.[20] Snyder had previously taught at Columbia and Princeton, and was thoroughly immersed in the discipline of political science. Yet his scholarship focused on human decision making, which had cross-disciplinary appeal. His early book *Decision-Making as an Approach to the Study of International Politics*

(1954), reprinted as *Foreign Policy Decision-Making* (1962), became influential across a disciplinary spectrum. As colleagues remembered after his death, "For Snyder, the heart of politics is the making of human decisions that are embedded in cultural, social, and organizational settings. The hope of humanity lies in improving decision processes."[21] The implied attribution of such messianic powers to decision science was typical of its promoters. Snyder's emphasis on the study of decision making likely endeared him to Irvine leaders who sought a dean for a school whose existence was predicated on the possibility of creating some kind of unified science of human decision making.

Two of Snyder's earliest faculty appointments, Henry Fagin and Kenneth Kraemer, suggested a strong link between administrative science and city planning, two fields that rose to prominence in the American research university during the postwar period. Fagin and Kraemer worked on topics that drew on both fields and blurred the line between them. Fagin was a professional city planner, yet many of his scholarly papers were oriented toward concerns of administration.[22] After a one-year stint teaching city planning at Penn in the early 1950s, where he interacted with the intellectual leaders of the field, he led large-scale planning projects in New York and New Jersey for the next decade before returning to teaching at the University of Wisconsin. In 1958, he also served as a visiting professor in UC-Berkeley's political science department.[23] Kraemer earned his PhD in city planning at the University of Southern California, where the program was housed within the School of Public Administration. He was familiar with UC Irvine because of a consulting assignment with the Irvine Company in 1966, and the School of Administration concept attracted him. He admired Fagin's scholarship and was thrilled about Fagin's move to Irvine—so much so that he traveled to Wisconsin to implore Fagin to get him hired at Irvine.[24]

Despite the early energy and interest, the Graduate School of Administration at UC Irvine came unraveled after a few years, and it did not develop a unified science of administration and decision making. Snyder lasted just two years as dean. George W. Brown, a former RAND researcher who was developing a computer center at UCLA at that time, replaced him. Lyman Porter took over in 1972 and transformed the school into a pure business school, as reflected by name changes to the Graduate School of Management (1980) and the Paul Merage School of Business (2005). Although the early faculty had a strong leaning toward public administration, the number of students interested in public sector work soon dwindled, and many faculty members who were aligned with public administration departed.[25] There were constant tensions between the business and public cohorts of faculty. These factors led to Porter's dismantling of the GSA. Despite all its difficulties, the Graduate School of Administration was not the most substantial failure to meet expectations in UC Irvine's initial quiver of social science enterprises. This distinction belonged to the Public Policy Research Organization.

Out of all the endeavors that the University of California mounted in the 1960s, none was grander in concept and feebler in practice than the Public Policy Research Organization. Birthed by Berkeley's Institute of International Studies, and located at Irvine because of the campus' land-grant emphasis and its administration's lobbying with Kerr, the PPRO aimed at being the exemplar of a new genre: the university-affiliated policy research organization. The founders of PPRO adored the RAND Corporation, the leading policy think tank in the postwar era, and they wanted to bring RAND-style analysis of public problems into a university setting. They believed that doing so was essential for crafting the best public policy and for enriching the life of the university. The enthusiasm for PPRO reveals a significant manner in which academics at the University of California believed that the land-grant model could be updated for twentieth-century conditions by drawing on the social sciences. PPRO planners believed that by concentrating teams of researchers using rational scientific analysis on public problems around the world, the organization could help realize the promises of modernity. The PPRO was, in essence, meant to be the ultimate fulfillment of the dream for all public decisions to be guided by experts using university knowledge.

Ideas for a policy research organization came together in the spring of 1964, when Kerr appointed an all-university committee to study the proposition. The star-studded committee featured members from eight of the nine UC campuses (except Santa Cruz, which was still in preliminary stages), including Daniel Aldrich; eminent economist Seymour Harris (who had just arrived at UCSD from Harvard, where a year earlier he had introduced Kerr before the latter's *Uses of the University* lectures); and chairman Roger Revelle, the renowned oceanographer who was serving as UC's systemwide dean of research at the time. Kerr's letter to the committee proclaimed that he had "become increasingly aware of the opportunities and responsibilities of universities to provide expert advice on public choices between and among policy alternatives."[26] Ironically, the committee's first meeting was held on the day that

Lyndon Johnson dedicated the Irvine campus site, which meant that Aldrich missed the meeting.[27]

Another important figure in the founding of the PPRO was Albert Wohlstetter, one of the most famous American defense policy analysts of the postwar period, known for his strongly quantitative approach.[28] Before becoming a defense policy analyst, Wohlstetter worked for the National Housing Agency in 1946–1947, then worked several years for a company that tried unsuccessfully to mass produce the "Packaged House" designed by leading modernist architect Walter Gropius.[29] Wohlstetter gained his fame as a senior policy analyst at RAND, where he worked from 1951 until 1963, when RAND President Frank Collbohm fired him for allegedly mishandling a classified document.[30] Wohlstetter then landed a position as Ford Rotating Research Professor at UC Berkeley during 1963–1964.[31] Some evidence suggests that Wohlstetter was involved in the earliest PPRO discussions and that planners hoped the PPRO would hire Wohlstetter as one of its major stars, as suggested by various usages of cloaked language in the planning documents.[32] It appears that during that time Wohlstetter was weighing the options for his future, and some within the UC wanted to hire him as a senior scholar in the PPRO before another organization did.

A draft proposal of June 1964 formed the intellectual basis for establishing PPRO. The central goal was to improve the quality of policy research, which was presumed necessary for "the general public welfare." According to the proposal, policy research would reach its highest state only if located in the university, which had heretofore been hostile to it on the grounds that it did not fit with the university's central mission of teaching and basic research. Policy research in nonuniversity nonprofit organizations "had a problem in attaining and maintaining both independence and significance. In general, they do not have the stability to stand firm in the face of pressures from clients; pressures to do only work that comes up with conclusions supportive of the views or positions of the client and/or to do short-term rush projects to meet immediate needs." To solve this problem, both policy research and the university could change to embrace each other, to their mutual benefit. If the university could create a policy research organization "with a looser connection to the traditional university structure," it might allow "the significant minority of faculty members who wish to spend some of their time on policy-oriented work" to do so, and even attract top scholars from elsewhere who also sought such an opportunity, without conflicting with the central mission of the university.

A major purpose of the organization would be "significant research relevant to problems of American policy, particularly long term problems of international policy." The proposal clearly had RAND in mind as a model. It mentioned that RAND's statement of purpose had become the standard for similar entities, how RAND's handling of salaries and overhead might be a model, that the proposed organization might compete with RAND for personnel, and that "proximity to RAND and SDC [Systems Development Corporation] would be a possible advantage of a Los Angeles location."

One of the most interesting elements in the conceptualization of PPRO was the overt attempt to model it after endeavors that were considered great successes in the realm of "big science." PPRO, presumably, would be a leading model for a kind of "big social science" that its planners envisioned. One such way in which PPRO might resemble emblematic "big science" models was in its link to the university. "Perhaps the proposed organization may be most easily conceived of," the planners wrote, "if we consider the University of California, for this purpose, as a consortium of universities, something like the Associated Universities, Incorporated, which operates the Brookhaven National Laboratory and the Greenbank National Observatory for Radioastronomy."[33] Even more telling, however, was that the PPRO planning documents abounded with references to UC-Berkeley's Radiation Laboratory (popularly known as the "Rad Lab"). The Rad Lab, directed by Nobel laureate physicist Ernest Lawrence, inventor of the cyclotron, was the home of celebrated research in high-energy nuclear physics starting in the 1930s. This work was conducted by teams of researchers, and the Rad Lab was widely considered the initiator and exemplar of the new trend of "big science" that provided a template for wartime research activities and the postwar system of national labs, including Brookhaven.[34]

One measure of the scope envisioned for PPRO was the proposed level of funding. Planners hoped to secure from a foundation "a grant to establish the organization, that is, for the funds necessary for the physical plant, the core professional staff and supporting staff, and operating expenses. The minimum funds necessary would be something on the order of $500,000 for each of the first three years, and a reduced amount over an additional two years, with the expectation that other long-term grants and contracts could be negotiated within the first two years."[35] These numbers were sizeable for the social sciences and even comparable to some research organizations in the physical sciences.

Kathleen Archibald, the committee's executive secretary, made a thirteen-day trip to Washington, DC, and Cambridge, Massachusetts, in summer 1964 to meet top policy scholars—mainly to get their feedback on whether they saw such an organization as desirable, but also to discern whether any of them might be interested in moving west should the organization be established. She met with a number of luminaries. In Washington, her meetings included Robert Calkins, president of the Brookings Institution and a former dean at UC Berkeley; Charles Hitch and Henry Rowen at the Department of Defense; and Assistant Secretary of Commerce for Science and Technology J. Herbert Hollomon, who as the first incumbent of this new position launched an effort to involve American universities in economic development efforts. Her Cambridge meetings included two high-profile policy scholars: Carl Kaysen of Harvard, a RAND consultant and former Deputy Special Assistant to President Kennedy for National Security Affairs, and Max Millikan, director of MIT's Center for International Studies.[36] Her trip stirred some excitement among these policy thinkers. Calkins wrote to Kerr, "I am pleased to see that the multiversity is rapidly becoming a reality on varied patterns in California." He elaborated, "Word has reached me that you have appointed a committee to explore the question of establishing an institute of policy research. I have long thought that a 'Brookings of the West Coast' was desirable and eventually would need to be established. RAND is first-rate, but not broad enough in the scope of its work. The subject is a big one and there are special problems to consider. I am hoping to be in California about the first of October. If you wish to discuss the matter, I would be delighted to see you in Berkeley about that time."[37]

Archibald reported that in general, reactions to the proposal had been similar to those of Calkins: "We can be confident as to both the desirability and feasibility of such an organization from the point of view of national needs and Government interests." The interviewees told her that the proposed organization "could attract first-rate people . . . could easily become the ranking institution of its kind in the country, and . . . as a structural innovation, might well become a prototype followed by other universities." Archibald followed that summary with a caveat that she was "typically . . . more a negativist and 'wet blanket' than enthusiast, so it does reflect quite solid feelings of confidence."[38] Despite this alleged pessimism, the notion that PPRO was something unique and utterly important permeated the planning process.

The agenda and invitation list for a conference hosted by the ad hoc committee September 27–28, 1964 in the famous picturesque village of Sausalito at the northern terminus of the Golden Gate Bridge most clearly exhibited the intellectual proclivities of the proposed PPRO and its aspirations to grandeur. The conference's purpose was to "bring together four or five top people to act as consultants in drawing up the blueprint for an ideal setting for policy research and analysis. These should be people who could be seriously considered for appointments as senior staff members, and, in effect, we would be implicitly, though not too transparently, asking them what it would take to bring them to the new organization." The list of possible invitees read like a who's who of the policy thinkers who were then in vogue in government circles: Secretary Robert S. McNamara (a UC-Berkeley alum) and his lieutenants Hitch and Rowen from the Department of Defense; Wohlstetter and his competitor for top civilian nuclear strategist, Harvard's Thomas Schelling, a future Nobel laureate in economics; from MIT's Center for International Studies, Millikan and leading modernization theorist Walt W. Rostow, who was working for the State Department at the time; and Calkins and several others of less renown. Hitch, Rowen, Wohlstetter, Schelling, and several others actually attended the conference—including Richard Neustadt, who was just then in the midst of planning the new Kennedy School at Harvard.

While the UC central administration was planning PPRO in summer 1964, James March arrived at Irvine to begin his duties as dean of social sciences, and he and Aldrich got excited about the possibility of locating PPRO at UC Irvine, albeit for different reasons. For March, it would contribute to his social science program and raise UC-Irvine's overall prestige; for Aldrich, it might be the centerpiece of his program to plot a new course for the land-grant university. With Aldrich and March in key positions and a charge in place to extend the land-grant tradition, UC Irvine was disposed toward policy research before people at Berkeley proposed PPRO. Once Aldrich and March were physically together at Irvine and PPRO was on the table, the push to locate it at Irvine began.

Only weeks after his arrival, March wrote to Aldrich that "Irvine should make a major effort to get involved in policy research and policy activities as soon as possible and on a basis differentiated from the other campuses. If we are just one of the minor campuses tagging along with Berkeley, we will not make the kind of name for ourselves that we want to. We can, at present, move much more decisively and quickly than Berkeley or UCLA. I think we should propose to the [PPRO] group essentially that we will take charge." Aldrich wrote "AGREE" in huge capital letters next to this point (much larger than his other "agree" annotations on the same letter), and that is exactly what they did.[39] March not only got himself appointed to the ad hoc committee but also became its vice chairman.

Meanwhile, Aldrich was musing about how well the proposed PPRO fit within the framework of a land-grant institution. His marginal annotations on the PPRO proposal give us insight into his thought in a way that more formally prepared communications might not. In discussing the need to change the university's faculty incentive structure in order to promote policy research, the proposal noted that "in many cases success in applied research is actually given a negative valuation, and is interpreted as an index of, at best, lack of scientific respectability and, at worst, lack of creativity. Thus the incentives for doing interdisciplinary policy research are in most departments on most campuses at best absent and at worst negative." Aldrich jotted in the margin: "not in Agric[ultural] Exp[eriment] Station—perhaps AES should be used as model." When the proposal noted that "the distinctive nature of policy research means that it is both complementary to and in conflict with the main purposes of the University: teaching and basic research," Aldrich jotted: "Not the land-grant university."[40] To Aldrich, PPRO was exactly the kind of endeavor that a revamped land-grant university should pursue. He later elaborated, "There is considerable precedent within the Division of Agricultural Sciences for establishing a teaching, research, and public service capability envisioned by the Public Policy Research Organization . . . in many departments of the College of Agriculture are staff members holding appointment to the Agricultural Experiment Station only. They do no teaching, are hired to do basic and applied research, and are advanced in equivalent rank and pay but without professorial title for displaying appropriate competence in research . . . it should be possible, therefore, to set up a similar arrangement in every field of inquiry within the University."[41] This model became increasingly common in American research universities; as it did, the percentage of university resources allocated to people who were unconnected with any teaching department increased.

Aldrich's argument won the day with UC Dean of Academic Planning Robert D. Tschirgi. In a memo to Kerr summarizing the Sausalito meeting and suggesting how to move forward, Tschirgi wrote that "the proposed Institution [PPRO] would apply its resources to answering real-world questions generated by outside clients. This is most similar to the Agriculture Experiment Stations within the University . . . I am personally favorably disposed toward this philosophy as consonant with the increasing role of the University as an agency for direct public service."[42] In a separate letter to Kerr, Tschirgi wrote, "Although I can see virtues in establishing the first unit of such a University-wide Institution at Berkeley or UCLA, I believe that it might fit most appropriately at Irvine where similar concepts have already been considered." In the margin, Kerr wrote "favor Irvine" in his usual green pen.[43]

In the ensuing months, March wrote a modified version of the earlier proposal, which carried PPRO through approvals by various university entities that were necessary for establishing it. However, PPRO staggered out of the starting blocks. It barely had a staff for its first two years of existence. For a variety of reasons, the UC central administration did not adequately support the fledgling unit. To be sure, Kerr and his colleagues were distracted by the series of events from the Free Speech Movement at the time of PPRO's founding through Kerr's brief resignation the next spring to his firing in January 1967. The exorbitant salaries that were proposed to attract nationally renowned figures such as Albert Wohlstetter and Charles Hitch to PPRO also caused significant questioning among budget officials.[44] No director was in place until November 1967 when the statistician Alexander Mood arrived, fresh from serving as founding director of the US government's National Center for Educational Statistics, where he oversaw the famous "Coleman Report" on equality of educational opportunity.[45] However, even the advent of such a senior, pedigreed scholar as Mood did not launch PPRO to the heights originally envisioned. It did not develop a significant faculty of its own, and relied heavily on GSA faculty Fagin and Kraemer.

PPRO remained small and beset by continued self-criticism about its perceived failure into the 1970s, and never did the kind of foreign policy work that its planners envisioned. Moreover, none of the luminaries who planners targeted ended up joining PPRO. The planners still had Wohlstetter penciled in as their top senior scholar as of a November 1964 document, but he joined the University of Chicago's political science department shortly after that and stayed there until his retirement in 1980.[46] He headed PPRO's national advisory committee, but UC-Irvine officials disbanded it in the early 1970s because of perceived ineffectiveness.[47]

PPRO was not particularly successful in its grant proposals during its early years. It proposed seventy projects between April 1967 and April 1972, and only twenty of them were funded (two of which were extensions of an original grant). Only two of the twenty grants exceeded $67,000: $180,000 from combined Carnegie and Ford sources to Mood for a "Survey of Knowledge and Research Pertaining to Effective Use of Resources in Higher Education" and $123,852 from the US Public Health Service to Fagin as part of a joint project with the Orange County Health Planning Council (which received more than 80 percent of the total project funds). Many of the grants came from local agencies or other units of the university, with some funding coming from the National Institutes of Mental Health and the US Civil Service Commission. Eight of the rejected proposals exceeded $100,000, with some nearing $1 million, but many others were of a similar size to the accepted proposals. The largest number of rejected proposals went to the US Office of Education, probably in an attempt to take advantage of Mood's connections there, with topics such as "Peer Influence on Students' Achievement in School" and "Evaluation and Documentation of Experimental Schools Projects."[48]

PPRO also had two separate state appropriations: "General Support" and "General Research," annually beginning in 1966–1967 despite UC's early difficulties in funding. The General Support budget ranged from $43,300 to $69,006. The General Research budget hovered around $20,000 during most years. For the first three years (through 1968–1969), however, PPRO expended almost none of the General Research budget, perhaps because it was not conducting sufficient activity to require the money.[49]

One of the more interesting and revealing failed early proposals, especially with regard to the land-grant mission, suggested a project in the San Joaquin Valley. In early 1968, PPRO asked the Ford Foundation for $721,173 over twenty-eight months to launch this program. This proposal illustrated the all-university aspirations of PPRO, as it was made jointly with the West Side San Joaquin Valley Coordinating Council of the University of California Water Resources Center, a university-wide entity. The hypothetical overall project was typically grandiose, calling for individual scholars and groups on all nine UC campuses to organize the subprojects in a "significant collaborative program with a 25 to 50 year time horizon [that] will attract the energy and imagination of generations of graduate and post-doctoral students." This focus on involving students was unusual for PPRO, but it had a specific purpose: exposing budding researchers to interdisciplinary, organized work on development problems.

The proposal unabashedly employed the language of development that had so much currency in the 1960s, providing evidence of the heightened expectations for universities to stimulate development both abroad and at home during this period. Fagin, who chaired the Coordinating Council and hoped to be the principal investigator for the project, believed that "rapid development of a new type of urban-rural complex is about to occur" due to the completion of Interstate 5 running through the "heretofore relatively arid and remote West Side San Joaquin Valley" and the California Aqueduct, which was slated "to begin delivering millions of acre-feet of water" to the region by the early 1970s. The project would be "a case study of the resource development process" examining "the dynamics of the developmental process . . . to discover and formulate basic principles and relationships in this developmental process, including predictive relationships and methodology." It afforded "a unique opportunity for an interdisciplinary research-training program in an underdeveloped area immediately accessible to a major American university." As such, its planners believed that the project could sell a new generation of students on the importance of development work. They lamented that recent pioneering efforts in development, largely overseas, "were remote from large groups of students in American Universities [sic] and in consequence have left many students largely unaware of all the opportunities for career and service that lie in all the fields that comprise regional development." Highly visible activities in the West Side San Joaquin Valley would encourage extensive student participation.

The proposal expanded Fagin's comments about "a new type of urban-rural complex" into an argument for how the project might extend the land-grant tradition. It suggested that the valley's development "will call for the joint and concerted efforts of business, government, and the University," a kind of cooperation exemplified "for over one hundred years . . . in the rural areas of the country through the agricultural extension activities of the land grant colleges." More recently, "attempts have been made to apply the same principles through experiments in what has been called 'urban extension.'" The proposed UC program would be "still a further expansion of the 'extension' idea in a region having both agricultural and other industries and with both urban and rural types of development." The planners believed that "this region appears capable of evolving under proper leadership into a new regional structure that probably will be neither city nor country as we know them today." The UC, therefore, pledged to be "conscious of the challenge to be innovative in all the fields that contribute to the design, management, and utilization of the terrestrial environment."[50] Although the application to the Ford

Foundation failed, the UC Water Resources Center gave PPRO three grants totaling $78,564 to conduct a slice of the original project.[51]

The proposal's mention of urban extension merits further discussion, especially as it relates to new concepts of the land-grant university and Irvine continuing on a parallel track with Kerr even after the UC Regents fired him as president in January 1967. That October, Kerr delivered a lecture at the City College of New York that was widely reported in the popular press, "The Urban-Grant University: A Model for the Future." There, he extolled the land-grant concept as "one of the great ideas in the history of the United States and of higher education throughout the world."[52] He argued for its enlargement to something he called the urban-grant university, "which would have an aggressive approach to the problems of the city, where the city itself and its problems would become the animating focus, as agriculture once was and to some extent still is of the land-grant university." He boldly "propose[d] that we create, to stand beside the 67 land-grant universities, some 67 urban-grant universities, at least one for each city of over a quarter of a million and several for the very large cities." He believed that urban-grant universities would be "fully useful to the modern society" and that the federal government should aid these institutions.[53] "The urban-grant university might parallel the land-grant institution not only via city-oriented curricula and on-campus research studies but also by setting up experiment stations to work on the problems of the city as they once worked on the problems of the land, and by setting up intensified urban extension services such as agricultural extension."[54] Urban extension was an idea that had motivated some policies and programs since the late 1950s. Kerr was familiar with the Ford Foundation's urban extension program of 1959–1966, and Title I of the Higher Education Act of 1965 provided funding for urban extension. Kerr believed that the urban-grant university would be "a positive approach to some of the greatest of our national problems" and allow students to participate in "new approaches to our social problems."[55] As he had in the preliminary announcement for Irvine, Kerr continued to portray the university primarily as a problem-solving instrument.

PPRO revealed its engagement with this idea when it mentioned "urban extension" in its San Joaquin Valley proposal in January 1968. Moreover, Fagin and Kraemer were simultaneously developing a proposal for a PPRO Urban Affairs Program. "Typical Projects Contemplated" for this program included "Systems Analysis Applied to the Irvine Community" and "Systems Analysis Applied to Planning in Urban Government." One component of these projects would be "development of an on-going urban information system for the City of Irvine, the University of California and the Irvine Company." Fagin and Kraemer planned to "include before and after evaluation to test the hypothesis that a computerized information system results in better decision-making by government officials."[56] This vision led to a PPRO proposal to the US Department of Housing and Urban Development in August 1968, requesting nearly $600,000 for "Information Systems for New Communities: Prototype Design and Implementation in the Irvine Community." HUD denied funding. The Urban Affairs Program fizzled, as it proved unable to secure funding for other projects, such as the $150,726 it requested from HUD in September 1968 for "An Investigation of Alternatives for Governing New City-Scale Urban Communities with Special Emphasis on the Evolving Irvine Community as a Representative Case" and the $300,000 it requested from the California State Office of Planning in June 1969 for "The Governance of Developing New Areas."[57] The information technology aspect of the August 1968 proposal, however, augured a different future for PPRO.

In 1973, after several years of unsuccessful attempts at large-scale projects, PPRO changed course. Early in that year, it succeeded in two grant proposals related to information technology, totaling $180,000 for "Evaluation of Policy Related Research in Municipal Information Systems" and "Planning Grant for Evaluation of Urban Information Systems."[58] This success, along with an internal review of the organization, spurred it in a new direction, toward a tighter and primary focus on information technology policy. In the late 1970s, it also advertised focus areas in technology and public policy, environmental policy, administering public policy, and empirical research methods for policy studies.[59] In 1992, PPRO merged into an ORU that was solely dedicated to information technology policy.[60] This history suggests that frameworks from the land-grant tradition, despite the failure of the more grandiose projects they inspired, created a space in which the information technology emphasis that ultimately characterized UC-Irvine's policy research could flourish.

By 1973, UC Irvine had abandoned the bulk of its pioneering efforts to make social science the new heart of a land-grant university. March departed for Stanford in 1970, which led to a new dean and a revamped program for the social science division. The Graduate School of Administration became a more standard business school. PPRO abandoned its national and international aspirations and settled into a role as a minor player, specializing in local and regional policy and information technology issues. Considering the failure of these efforts, why should we attend to them today?

First, they suggest the power, vitality, and flexibility of the land-grant concept and tradition that captivated and inspired capacious thinkers such as Kerr to imagine how land-grant universities might move in new and more fruitful directions while exemplifying land-grant ideals. Second, the early programs at Irvine provide a window into a brief period in the 1960s when "high modern" ideas about relations between academic knowledge and social order reached their apex. The Irvine planners' overweening faith in mathematical social science was part of an important moment in American history, a hinge of massive cultural change, that we should continue to explore more deeply as a part of our attempt to understand this critical period that did so much to shape our current moment. Finally, the grand ambitions and meager results of UC-Irvine's initial programs provide a cautionary tale about the difficulties involved in effecting large-scale structural change in American universities and in using large-scale university programs to effect social change in the wider world.

Notes

1. Dick Turpin, "Former School Teacher Johnson Dedicates Vast Irvine UC Campus," *Los Angeles Times* (June 21, 1964): B; Claudia Anderson [LBJ Library archivist], email message to author, December 16, 2008.
2. On the Master Plan see John Aubrey Douglass, *The California Idea and American Higher Education: 1850 to the 1960 Master Plan* (Stanford, CA: Stanford University Press, 2000).
3. Clark Kerr, *The Uses of the University* (Cambridge: Harvard University Press, 1963).
4. Ivan Hinderaker, "A Provisional Academic Plan for the Irvine Campus, University of California, December 1962," Clark Kerr Personal and Professional Papers, CU-302, Carton 4, Folder 40, The Bancroft Library, University of California, Berkeley [hereafter BL].
5. During construction of the Berkeley campus buildings from 1869 to 1873, the university operated from the Oakland campus of the College of California.
6. On the history of the University of California, see Douglass, *California Idea*; Patricia A. Pelfrey, *A Brief History of the University of California*, 2nd ed. (Berkeley: University of California Press, 2004); Verne A. Stadtman, *The University of California 1868–1968* (New York: Mc-Graw Hill, 1970); Clark Kerr, *The Gold and the Blue: A Personal Memoir of the University of California*, 2 vol. (Berkeley: University of California Press, 2001, 2003).
7. Ann Forsyth, *Reforming Suburbia: The Planned Communities of Irvine, Columbia, and the Woodlands* (Berkeley: University of California Press, 2005); W. Benjamin Piggot, "The Irvine New Town, Orange County, and the Transformation of Suburban Political Culture" (PhD diss., University of Washington, 2009).

8. *Preliminary Announcement University of California, Irvine Academic Program 1965–1966* (Irvine: University of California, 1965).
9. Office of the President, "Need for Additional Facilities for Education in Architecture and Planning," May 12, 1961, Central Records Unit Records, AS-004, Box 65, Folder: Academic Planning, Irvine, 1961–1962, UCI Archives [hereafter UCI Central Records].
10. Records of UC-Irvine Academic Senate Committee on Preliminary Planning for a School of Architecture and Environmental Planning, Fall 1967, Representative Assembly of the Academic Senate, AS-005, Box 1, Folder: June–December 1967, UCI Archives.
11. [Daniel G. Aldrich], "Comments on the Academic Plan, 1964–1975, of the University of California dated September 1964," enclosure in letter to R. D. Tschirgi, October 5, 1964, UCI Central Records, Box 58, Folder: University Academic Plan 1965–1975 correspondence.
12. David Harvey, *The Condition of Postmodernity: An Enquiry into the Origins of Cultural Change* (Oxford: Blackwell, 1989); James C. Scott, *Seeing Like a State: How Certain Schemes to Improve the Human Condition Have Failed* (New Haven, CT: Yale University Press, 1998).
13. On Simon, see Hunter Crowther-Heyck, *Herbert A. Simon: The Bounds of Reason in Modern America* (Baltimore, MD: Johns Hopkins University Press, 2005); Stephen P. Waring, *Taylorism Transformed: Scientific Management Theory Since 1945* (Chapel Hill: University of North Carolina Press, 1991); Mie Augier and James G. March, ed., *Models of a Man: Essays in Memory of Herbert A. Simon* (Cambridge, MA: MIT Press, 2004); Herbert A. Simon, *Models of My Life* (New York: Basic Books, 1991).
14. Bruce Kuklick, *Blind Oracles: Intellectuals and War from Kennan to Kissinger* (Princeton, NJ: Princeton University Press, 2006) 23, 35–36.
15. James G. March to Ivan Hinderaker, November 1, 1963, Samuel C. McCulloch Oral Histories, AS-033, Box 5, Folder: James G. March, August 8, 1973, UCI Archives.
16. James G. March, "General Perspectives for the Social Science Division," enclosure in ibid.
17. Jan Erickson, *Transcription of an Oral History Interview with Ivan and Birk Hinderaker*, June 5, 1998, 32, http://www.ucrhistory.ucr.edu/pdf/hinderakeri.pdf (accessed November 10, 2008).
18. Ivan Hinderaker, "The Study of Administration: Interdisciplinary Dimensions," *Western Political Science Quarterly* 16, no. 3, Supplement (September 1963): 10.
19. Ibid., 11.
20. Samuel C. McCullough, *Instant University: The History of the University of California, Irvine, 1957–1993* (Irvine, CA: University of California-Irvine, 1996), 30.
21. Glenn D. Paige and James A. Robinson, "In Memoriam: Richard Carlton Snyder," *PS: Political Science and Politics* 31, no. 2 (June 1998): 240–43.
22. Interview with Kenneth L. Kraemer, January 8, 2008, Irvine, CA.
23. Henry Fagin, "Urban Transportation Criteria," *Annals of the American Academy of Political and Social Science* 352 (March 1964): 141.
24. Interview with Kenneth L. Kraemer, January 8, 2008, Irvine, CA.
25. Ibid.
26. Clark Kerr to Daniel G. Aldrich [same letter to several others], May 21, 1964, UCI Central Records, Box 128, Folder: Ad Hoc Committee on Public Policy Research Organization 1963–1965.

27. "Minutes of the Meeting of the Ad Hoc Committee on Policy Research, June 20, 1964, Hilton Inn, San Francisco International Airport," UCI Central Records, Box 128, Folder: Ad Hoc Committee on Public Policy Research Organization 1963–1965.

28. Kuklick, *Blind Oracles*, 60–64.

29. http://www.albertwohlstetter.com (accessed November 23, 2008).

30. Fred Kaplan, *The Wizards of Armageddon* (New York: Simon and Schuster, 1982), 348; Alex Abella, *Soldiers of Reason: The Rand Corporation and the Rise of American Empire* (Orlando: Harcourt, Inc., 2008), 196.

31. Richard N. Rosecrance, ed., *The Dispersion of Nuclear Weapons: Strategy and Politics* (New York: Columbia University Press, 1964).

32. Kathleen Archibald, "Institute vs. Institution," n.d. [likely late 1964], UCI Central Records, Box 128, Folder: Ad Hoc Committee on Public Policy Research Organization 1963–1965.

33. [Kathleen Archibald], "Draft Proposal for a University-wide Policy Research Organization," June 8, 1964, 8, 9–10, UCI Central Records, Box 128, Folder: Ad Hoc Committee on Public Policy Research Organization 1963–1965.

34. Peter Galison and Bruce Hevly, ed., *Big Science: The Growth of Large-Scale Research* (Stanford, CA: Stanford University Press, 1992).

35. [Archibald], "Draft Proposal for a University-wide Policy Research Organization."

36. Kathleen Archibald to Ad Hoc Committee on Policy Research, "Summary of Memorandum on Eastern Trip (June 21–July 3, Washington, DC–Cambridge, MA.)," UCI Central Records, Box 128, Folder: Ad Hoc Committee on Public Policy Research Organization 1963–1965.

37. Robert Calkins to Clark Kerr, August 12, 1964, Office of the President Records, CU-5 Series 5, Box 111, Folder 10, BL. It is not clear whether this proposed meeting ever happened, but three years later, Calkins was back in California for good as vice chancellor of the new UC Santa Cruz.

38. Archibald, "Summary of Memorandum on Eastern Trip."

39. James G. March to Daniel G. Aldrich, July 28, 1964, UCI Central Records, Box 128, Folder: Ad Hoc Committee on Public Policy Research Organization 1963–1965. Aldrich elaborated his agreement in a reply, telling March, "It is my hope that Irvine will plan immediately to develop policy research capability within the Division of Social Sciences and the Graduate School of Admin, and that the Irvine campus can become an example of how a campus of the U of C can respond to the opportunity described in the Policy Research Organization draft proposal." Daniel G. Aldrich to James G. March, August 11, 1964, UCI Central Records, Box 128, Folder: Ad Hoc Committee on Public Policy Research Organization 1963–1965.

40. [Archibald], "Draft Proposal for a University-wide Policy Research Organization."

41. Aldrich to March, August 11, 1964.

42. Quoted in Archibald, "Institute vs. Institution."

43. R. D. Tschirgi to Clark Kerr, September 29, 1964, Office of the President Records, CU-5 Series 5, Box 111, Folder 11, BL.

44. On concerns within the UC bureaucracy about proposed PPRO salaries, see Office of the Vice President to Clark Kerr, Analysis of 1966–1967 Target Budget Request Irvine Campus, n.d., Office of the President Records, CU-5 Series 5, Box 19, Folder 2, BL.

45. On Mood's career see Alexander M. Mood, "Miscellaneous Reminiscences," *Statistical Science* 5, no. 1 (February 1990): 35–43.

46. Daniel G. Aldrich to Clark Kerr, November 4, 1964, UCI Central Records, Box 128, Folder: Ad Hoc Committee on Public Policy Research Organization 1963–1965.

47. Daniel S. Appleton, Henry Fagin, Kenneth L. Kraemer, *Policy Research at UCI* (Irvine: University of California, 1973), iii.
48. Ibid., 65–70.
49. Ibid., 14.
50. Henry Fagin to William Felling, January 17, 1968, and West Side San Joaquin Valley Coordinating Council of the University of California Water Resources Center jointly with the Public Policy Research Organization, "Research Proposal to Ford Foundation for Support of a Graduate and Post-Doctoral Interdisciplinary Educational Program Oriented Around a Long-Term Case Study of Rapid Change in the West Side San Joaquin Valley under the Impact of Massive Public Investment in New Water and Transportation Facilities," ROX 570-10 URBIS-PPRO misc. papers, UCI Archives.
51. Appleton et al., *Policy Research at UCI*, 65–70.
52. Clark Kerr, *The Urban-Grant University: A Model for the Future* (New York: The City College, 1968), 5. Kerr delivered the lecture on October 18, 1967.
53. Ibid., 6.
54. Ibid., 7.
55. Ibid., 14, 9.
56. Urban Affairs Program of the Public Policy Research Organization, University of California, Irvine, revised April 17, 1968, ROX 570-10 URBIS-PPRO misc. papers, UCI Archives.
57. Appleton et al., *Policy Research at UCI*, 65–70.
58. Ibid.
59. Public Policy Research Organization, *Research Programs* (Irvine: UCI, 1978), UCI Central Records, Box 128.
60. Interview with Kenneth L. Kraemer, January 8, 2008, Irvine, CA.

Storying and Restorying
the Land-Grant System

Scott J. Peters

A few months after Senator Justin Smith Morrill's death in December of 1898, Representative William Wallace Grout of Vermont rose to speak on the floor of Congress about his legacy as a legislator. While noting Morrill's leading role in authoring legislation that created a new kind of college with grants of federal land, Grout asked:

> ... but who will measure the far-reaching influence of this galaxy of industrial colleges upon the future of the American people? Who will compute the result? The central purpose in founding them was to furnish the tiller of the soil such information and aid as would just a little lighten his burdens and if possible increase his profits, the former of which Mr. Morrill knew to be heavy and the latter small.[1]

Grout's assertion about the central founding purpose of the "galaxy of industrial colleges" that the Morrill Acts of 1862 and 1890 established and supported performs more than a descriptive function. Based on a particular way of understanding what many people refer to today as "the land-grant mission," it opens a path for a particular way of emplotting, narrating, or storying what we now call the land-grant system.

Over the years, historians, administrators, faculty members, students, elected officials, and various critics and supporters have storied and restoried the land-grant system in different ways, based on different conceptions of and claims about its public purposes and mission. This reflects an ancient human impulse. One of the main ways through which we make meaning of our lives and experiences, our society and its institutions,

Perspectives on the History of Higher Education 30 (2013): 335–353
© 2013. ISBN: 978-1-4128-5147-3

and the broader natural world we inhabit is by telling and interpreting stories about them. As the historian William Cronon has argued, stories are "our best and most compelling tool for searching out meaning in a conflicted and contradictory world."[2] By telling stories and constructing narratives, we reach beyond the simple recitation of facts and the chronicling of events. We *story* them. We situate them in a setting or scene, and in the unfolding of a plot with characters who act and react in particular ways. It is by storying and restorying facts, events, and actions that we come to know or assert or contest their meaning and significance.[3]

The sesquicentennial in 2012 of the first Morrill Act helps prompt a new awareness and assessment of the ways in which the land-grant system has been and still is being storied and restoried. In attending to this theme, we would be well advised to be mindful of an important reality. There is not and can never be just one objectively correct way for historians (or anyone else) to story the land-grant system. This is so for two main reasons. First, although history is scholarly work that is based on evidence, and historians are obligated to be fair and accurate in how they work with it, as William Cronin has pointed out, "it remains possible to narrate the same evidence in radically different ways."[4] This possibility hinges, in part, on how historians describe the setting or scene for the events and actions they narrate, and how they emplot and interpret events and actions. Second, historians must make judgments about what is important and what is not, and, therefore, what to include in and what to leave out of their work. Historians working on the same topic can and do make different judgments about these matters. Therefore, not only is it possible to tell different stories by using the same evidence; but it is also possible to tell different stories by using different evidence.

To be mindful of all this does not require us to adopt a soft epistemological relativism which holds that all ways of storying the land-grant system are equally good and valid. They are not. Rather, it calls on us to take up the task of telling different and more complicated stories in ways that are rigorously grounded in the fair and accurate treatment of reliable sources and credible evidence. My purpose in this article is to prompt and inform this task by identifying and briefly sketching and critiquing three different ways of storying and restorying the land-grant system. I have not only read but also heard these stories. I draw them from my personal experience in the land-grant system, as well as from my review of academic literatures and historical evidence. Interestingly, all three stories can be told in a way that features the same character: a man with the rather quaint-sounding name of Liberty Hyde Bailey.

A Heroic Metanarrative

Liberty Hyde Bailey was a groundbreaking and highly accomplished horticultural scientist who served on the faculty of Cornell University from 1888 to 1913. He also chaired President Theodore Roosevelt's Country Life Commission in 1908, and authored its final report.[5] There is a little story about something Bailey did in 1893 that Morris Bishop tells in his book, *A History of Cornell*. Bishop writes:

> The rich vineyards of Chautauqua County were attacked by disease. In 1893, Assemblyman S. F. Nixon of Chautauqua asked the Cornell Experiment Station to investigate. "No funds," said the station. Nevertheless, Liberty Hyde Bailey went to look, identified the disease as black rot, and devised a spray which saved the Assemblyman's vineyard. So delighted was he that he introduced in the Assembly in 1894, and carried through, a bill appropriating $8,000 for experimental work in his district. This was the initiation of extension work in New York State.[6]

This same story about Bailey, reduced to one sentence, also appears in an important passage in Frederick Rudolph's landmark history of American higher education, *The American College and University*. After noting farmers' skepticism about the value of land-grant colleges during the first few decades of their existence, Rudolph writes that what eventually changed their minds

> was evidence that scientific agriculture paid in larger crops, higher income, and a better chance to enjoy higher living standards—in other words, an opportunity to make frequent use of the Montgomery Ward or Sears Roebuck catalogue. Of primary importance were the pioneer efforts of natural scientists experimenting with seeds, livestock, and chemicals, who began to have something worth showing and saying to the farmers. Essential, too, was the Hatch Act of 1887, which provided federal funds for the creation of agricultural experiment stations which soon became extremely popular and effective instruments in winning farm support for the colleges. For the stations combined science and the solution of specific farm problems and helped to demonstrate to skeptical farmers that science could be a friend. Professor Liberty Hyde Bailey of Cornell investigated and cured black rot in the vineyards of a member of the state legislature who one day, as speaker of the assembly, would be of crucial help in gaining permanent state support for agricultural education at Cornell.[7]

This little story about Bailey curing a disease in a legislator's vine-yard is a heroic story about science-based service for economic ends. By itself, it is relatively trivial. It only becomes significant when it is placed within the context of a larger story. Both Bishop and Rudolph place it in the context of the story about how land-grant colleges won the support of skeptical farmers and legislators. The way they frame and tell this story, in turn, fits within an even larger story that I refer to as the land-grant system's *heroic metanarrative*.

In the heroic metanarrative, historical facts, events, and characters are selected and storied around an ascending plotline of steady progress through science-based service. I have heard and read the arc of this narrative many times over the past few decades in the speeches of administrators.[8] I have also found it many times in my historical research about the origins and evolution of the land-grant system's public purposes and work.[9] This includes Representative William Wallace Grout's speech commemorating Morrill on the floor of Congress in 1899.

According to Grout, the "central purpose" behind the founding of the land-grant system was "to furnish the tiller of the soil such information and aid as would just a little lighten his burdens and if possible increase his profits. . . ." This purpose, in essence, is the provision of science-based service for economic ends. With the addition after a comma of the phrase "the former of which Mr. Morrill knew to be heavy and the latter small," Grout sets an opening scene and suggests a plot: *Farmers were suffering from the burdens of hard work and low profits. Morrill knew this, so he acted by creating a new system of colleges. The new colleges hired scientists and offered courses and services that were all designed to help address the problems that are noted in the opening scene. And they were wildly successful, in ways that are beyond measurement and counting.* The whole history of the land-grant system and mission can be and often has been told from the vantage point of this plot. It has become the system's master narrative.

Some of the most elaborate examples I have found of the articulation of this heroic master or metanarrative were presented in November of 1931, on the eve of the seventieth anniversary of the first Morrill Act, at the forty-fifth annual convention of the Association of Land-Grant Colleges and Universities. The convention included four special addresses on the topic of "The Spirit of the Land-Grant Institutions." One was delivered by a sitting president (W. J. Kerr from Oregon Agricultural College, now named Oregon State University), two by emeritus presidents (W. O. Thompson from Ohio State University and E. A. Bryan from the State College of Washington, now named Washington State University), and one by an emeritus dean of a college of agriculture (Eugene Davenport from the University of Illinois).[10]

With the seventieth anniversary of the first Morrill Act in mind, the administrators who delivered these addresses spoke in depth—and in strikingly similar ways—about why and how the land-grant system was created, what its creation meant or signified, and what it had accomplished. At the time they spoke, the land-grant system included more than a set of colleges. It also included the agricultural experiment stations mentioned in the earlier quotation from Rudolph's book, as well as county-based extension offices that were established through the Smith–Lever Act of 1914.

The administrators set the opening scene of the story they told about the origins of the land-grant system within an early nineteenth-century society that was undergoing major economic, technical, cultural, and political transformation. In this context, they depicted a struggle between a backward, superstitious, ignorant, and uninformed mass of people and a bigoted and prejudiced aristocracy. They characterized the colleges that existed at the time as being modeled after England, with small and elitist student bodies, narrow and fixed classical curriculums, no connections to the common people, and neither the willingness nor the ability to meet the needs of an emerging industrial democracy. They spoke of growing demands for a new kind of college, and a few bold reformers who emerged with a vision of what it would do and how it could be established. The administrators described the vision these reformers held as one that marked a revolution in the means, methods, and purposes of higher education.

In the eyes of the four administrators, the successful establishment in 1862 of the new kind of college the visionaries had imagined represented a revolutionary overthrow of an antidemocratic aristocracy of education. It also marked the birth of a new spirit in American higher education. According to them, this new spirit turned out to be enormously productive and successful. Expressed through a distinctive public mission that combined science and service, it produced a fantastic array of accomplishments and results. In his address, for example, W. J. Kerr spoke of the

> great circles of helpful service that radiate from these centers—service that has changed deserts into gardens, redeemed abandoned lands, evolved new and more profitable crops, multiplied production, created new industries, conquered disease, destroyed pests and plagues, harnessed natural power and thereby increased human efficiency, guided agriculture and business, made science the handmaidens of the housewife as well as the captain of industry, revealed the processes of nature, and put into the hands of man the tools that enable him to work with natural law in shaping his own destiny and that of his country. The spirit that actuates this prodigious program and that arrives at such massive results, is the supreme and pervasive spirit of the land-grant institutions.[11]

The heroic metanarrative about the land-grant system and mission that we find in passages such as this has an ascending plotline of steady improvement and progress. It is built on a foundation of smaller heroic stories about the work of benevolent scientists and scholars. In agricultural examples of these heroic stories, such as Bishop's and Rudolph's story about Bailey, farmers are beset by technical problems they cannot understand, let alone solve. In the midst of their troubles, a scientific expert selflessly comes to the rescue. He or she diagnoses the problem, develops a solution (in the form of new knowledge and/or technologies), and applies it. The problem is solved. Efficiency and productivity are improved. Farmers' burdens are lightened, and their profits are enlarged. The interests and well-being of everyone—farmers and consumers, communities and states, and the nation as a whole—are simultaneously advanced.

In these heroic stories, farmers play relatively passive roles as needy and ultimately grateful clients or customers. They are mainly interested in raising their incomes so they can, as Rudolph put it, "make frequent use of the Montgomery Ward or Sears Roebuck catalogue." Land-grant faculty members, on the other hand, play active roles as unbiased scientific experts and responsive public servants. They are equally interested in advancing knowledge in their academic fields and in meeting the needs of farmers, consumers, states, and the nation. Their engagement in the world beyond the campus is portrayed as a means of pursuing both of these interests at the same time. It is, therefore, cast as being "mutually beneficial."

The heroic metanarrative stories the land-grant system in ways that are linked to other stories—stories of progress in agriculture and rural life, in science and technology, and in economic development. In addition, although it is rarely done now, the metanarrative used to be told in ways that also situate the land-grant system inside a story about the "democratization" of American higher education. As Arthur Klein put it in the first sentence of a two-volume survey of land-grant colleges and universities he edited, which was published in 1930 by the federal Office of Education, "The history of the land-grant institutions in the United States is the story of the growth of an idea—an idea centered in the democratization of higher learning."[12]

According to the metanarrative, land-grant colleges democratized higher education in three ways: first, by providing the common people with access to a college education, and thereby to opportunities for economic and social mobility; second, by expanding and equalizing the curriculum to make the professions of the common people (i.e., agriculture and the "mechanic arts") as worthy of study as the classics and the professions of elites; and third, by offering science-based service to the common people, a process that involved not only the development but also the active extension of new scientific knowledge, technologies, and expertise. Significantly, in the heroic metanarrative, each of these purposes is viewed as serving mainly (if not exclusively) technical, economic, and material ends.

As a master or metanarrative, the heroic story of the land-grant system and mission is positioned as the one "true" narrative that gives order and meaning to selected facts, events, and characters in land-grant history. There is some truth in this narrative. However, there are also several problems with it. Its depiction of existing colleges during the first half of the nineteenth century is inaccurate.[13] It flattens the meaning and significance of the land-grant system and mission to economics. It has a deterministic bias, as Roger L. Williams argues in his 1991 book, *The Origins of Federal Support for Higher Education*. In addition, as Williams also highlights in his book, it misses or obscures key realities about the founding and early development of the land-grant system: namely, that it was "rife with paradox, inconsistency, and ambiguity" and involved the "clash of competing ideas and interests" and "rough-and-tumble politics."[14]

A Tragic Counternarrative

In sharp contrast to the heroic metanarrative, various critics and scholars have offered what I refer to as a *tragic counternarrative* of the land-grant system and mission. The tragic counternarrative restories some of the same facts, events, and characters that are included in the metanarrative. It illuminates rather than obscures the clash of competing ideas and interests and a rough-and-tumble politics. In doing so, it offers a dramatically different assessment of the system's meaning and significance.

In the heroic metanarrative, the plot or storyline is about how the responsive provision of science-based service "democratized" higher education in ways that benefited—in relatively equal measure—the common people, communities, states, and the nation as a whole. A (if not the) signature achievement of the system, so the story goes, was a vast improvement of agricultural productivity and efficiency. In the counternarrative, the plot or storyline shifts. It becomes tragic rather than heroic.

As state institutions that receive considerable public funding, land-grant colleges and universities have played key roles in relation to agricultural productivity and efficiency through their contributions to the process of modernizing and industrializing agriculture. However, in the eyes of some critics and scholars, the state-supported process of modernization is not a story of steady progress and improvement, and it did not benefit everyone equally. It involved what historian Daniel T. Rodgers has called "a classic marriage of economic efficiency and unpaid social costs: cheap food at the expense of education, health, and ambition among its myriad small producers" (and also at the expense of the environment, as others argue).[15] Rather than a success story of steady progress, agricultural modernization in the United States and elsewhere can be viewed as a tragic story of technocratic colonization and cultural and environmental oppression and destruction—with land-grant faculty members and extension agents playing leading roles.

Interestingly, Liberty Hyde Bailey makes an appearance as a character in this narrative, too. However, this time, he is cast as a villain rather than a hero. We see this in the following passage from James C. Scott's important book, *Seeing Like A State*:

> The unspoken logic behind most of the state projects of agricultural modernization was one of consolidating the power of central institutions and diminishing the autonomy of cultivators and their communities vis-à-vis those institutions... For colonized farmers, the effect of such centralization and expertise was a radical de-skilling of the cultivators themselves. Even in the context of family farms and a liberal economy, this was in fact the utopian prospect held up by Liberty Hyde Bailey . . .

Scott goes on to condemn Bailey for being an oppressive technocrat who promoted a future rural society "organized almost entirely by a managerial elite."[16]

Drawing on the work of Scott and many other critics and scholars, a sketch of the tragic counternarrative about the land-grant system would go something like this:

> *In the early and mid nineteenth century, farmers' economic and material interests were not being met. This was not mainly due to their inability to understand and solve the technical problems they faced. It was a consequence of unjust political, economic, and cultural policies, structures, powers, and trends. In this story, scientific experts came on the scene not as heroes who advanced farmers' interests, but rather as villains who forced the modernization of agriculture in order to fuel the industrial economy with "cheap food." That was their main "public" purpose and mission. They sought to change farmers and other rural citizens in ways that (intentionally or not) privileged elite urban industrial interests over those of rural communities. Some farmers resisted. But through a process of rough-and-tumble politics and the workings and effects of markets they ultimately lost or gave up. Behaviors, methods, and views were changed, and agricultural productivity was improved to support*

a national "cheap food" policy, which benefited some, but not all, at least in the short term. In the long term, however, farmers, rural communities, the environment, consumers, and the nation as a whole were all worse off.[17]

Instead of the heroic metanarrative's ascending plotline of improvement and progress, the tragic counternarrative has a descending plotline of economic, political, cultural, and environmental destruction and loss. In Wendell Berry's version of this counternarrative, the plotline features the corruption of democratic and ecological principles and ideals, "the betrayal of a trust," and "the disintegration of intellectual and educational standards," all of which, he argues, inflicted a "degenerative influence" on farming communities.[18] In other versions, it is about a coercive process of discipline and control that was exerted on behalf of elite corporate and state interests.[19]

In its restorying of the land-grant system and mission, the tragic counternarrative shifts characters' roles. Instead of being heroes, land-grant faculty members and extension agents are cast as technocratic colonizers and oppressors who functioned as intermediaries for unjust market forces. Farmers either play roles as futile resistors or hapless victims, or as collaborators in an environmentally and culturally destructive colonial process. Cast in such roles, these characters are not engaged in a story about the "democratization" of higher learning, but rather its opposite.

For many, the tragic counternarrative I have roughly sketched here will likely be unconvincing or even preposterous. For example, I expect that many, if not most, people would view as preposterous the claim that farmers, rural communities, the environment, consumers, and the nation as a whole are all worse off as a result of the work of land-grant colleges. Yet this is exactly what is implied if not explicitly put forward in the writings of Wendell Berry and other critics. As another example, some (including me) would view as preposterous the implication of this counternarrative that land-grant history is nothing but a story of oppression and destruction, that it is only a tragedy.

Are there truths in this tragic counternarrative? In my view, yes. Are there problems with it? Again, yes. Whatever may be true or preposterous about it, we should not overlook a key fact: like all narratives, it is incomplete. It leaves events and characters out. Further, it stories and interprets evidence in ways that can be and are contested. Most importantly for me, by storying the land-grant system as a tragedy and nothing else, it not only misses but also ultimately erases positive democratic and democratizing characters and events in land-grant history.

A Prophetic Counternarrative

There is a second counternarrative about the land-grant system, one that helps illuminate what both the heroic and tragic narratives miss or obscure. The second counternarrative is prophetic rather than tragic. The person who has told it most eloquently and forcefully is none other than Liberty Hyde Bailey.

Bailey extensively engaged in agricultural extension work in the 1890s. During this period, he began writing about the need for the nation to pursue what he referred to as a "self-sustaining" agriculture.[20] Building on the philosophy of a long line of nineteenth-century agricultural "improvers" who were committed to what historian Stephen Stoll has referred to as an "ethic of permanence," Bailey viewed the pursuit of a "self-sustaining" agriculture as a multidimensional project that had technical, scientific, moral, economic, cultural, political, and even spiritual dimensions.[21] According to him, this project would both require and result in the development of a new rural civilization "worthy of the best American ideals."[22] Such a civilization would, in his mind, not only be worthy of the "American" ideal of material well-being for all. It would also be worthy of the democratic ideal (and practice) of self-rule, through which the common people, functioning as citizens, work as cooperative producers of the commonwealth, and the culture and politics of their own neighborhoods and communities.[23]

Although Bailey rejected the idea that a new rural civilization could or should be imposed from above by land-grant colleges of agriculture, he prophesied that these colleges would be the primary means for catalyzing the development of this kind of social world. "We are now beginning to be consciously concerned in the development of a thoroughly good and sound rural civilization," he announced in 1909. "The colleges of agriculture will be the most important agencies in this evolution."[24]

In Bailey's view, the aims of land-grant colleges of agriculture were not to be narrowly technical and economic, but broadly cultural and political. In an address delivered at the dedication ceremony for new buildings of the New York State College of Agriculture at Cornell in 1907, Bailey argued that land-grant colleges of agriculture "contribute to the public welfare in a very broad way, extending their influence far beyond the technique of agricultural trades."[25] Elaborating on this theme in 1909, he proclaimed:

> While the College of Agriculture is concerned directly with increasing the producing power of land, its activities cannot be limited narrowly to this field. It must stand

broadly for rural civilization. It must include within its activities such a range of subjects as will enable it to develop an entire philosophy or scheme of country life. All civilization develops out of industries and occupations; and so it comes that agriculture is properly a civilization rather than a congeries of crafts. The colleges of agriculture represent this civilization, in its material, business and human relations. Therefore, they are not class institutions, representing merely trades and occupations. The task before the colleges of agriculture is nothing less than to direct and to aid in developing the entire rural civilization; and this task places them within the realm of statesmanship.[26]

It is possible to interpret this passage as being consistent with James C. Scott's allegation that Bailey was a scheming technocrat who wanted land-grant colleges of agriculture to engineer a new rural civilization from above. However, Bailey was not a technocrat. He had strong democratic populist inclinations. He viewed the educational and scientific work of land-grant colleges as resources not only for the development of a "self-sustaining" agriculture, but also for the fulfillment of the common people's historical struggle for liberty. He once proclaimed that the Land-Grant Act of 1862 was "the most important single specific enactment ever made in the interest of education," because it represented the "final emancipation from formal, traditional, and aristocratic ideas."[27] He wrote,

Education was once exclusive; it is now in spirit inclusive. The agencies that have brought about this change of attitude are those associated with so-called industrial education, growing chiefly out of the forces set in motion by the Land-Grant Act of 1862. This Land-Grant is the Magna Charta of education: from it in this country we shall date our liberties.[28]

In "The Democratic Basis in Agriculture," a section of his most important book, *The Holy Earth*, Bailey positioned the story of the creation of land-grant colleges of agriculture within the larger story of the struggle for freedom and civic agency. He assumed a sweeping historical perspective on the human quest for liberty; his prose suffused with the high rhetoric of the era, full of parallelism and iteration. "For years without number," Bailey wrote,

for years that run into the centuries when men have slaughtered each other on many fields, thinking that they were on the fields of honor, when many awful despotisms have ground men into the dust, the despotisms thinking themselves divine—for all these years there have been men [sic] on the land wishing to see the light, trying to make mankind hear, hoping but never realizing. They have been the pawns on the great battlefields, men taken out of the peasantries to be hurled against other men they did not know and for no rewards except further enslavement. They may even have been developed to a high degree of manual or technical skill that they might better support governments to make conquests. They have been on the bottom, upholding the whole superstructure and pressed into the earth by the weight of it.[29]

In Bailey's view, the nineteenth century had brought a "parting of the ways" in the United States that foretold the end of this terrible history of oppression. During this time, farmers and others "at the bottom" started receiving recognition not only for the economic value of their work, but also—and according to Bailey most importantly—for their humanity, dignity, and agency, and for their standing as citizens. In his view, this multidimensional recognition was what inspired the creation of the US Department of Agriculture and land-grant colleges in 1862, agricultural experiment stations in 1887, and, finally, a national Cooperative Extension System in 1914. "A new agency has been created in the agricultural extension act which was signed by President Wilson on the 8th of May in 1914," Bailey wrote of the passage of the Smith–Lever Act that established the extension system. "A new instrumentality in the world has now received the sanction of a whole people . . . and it almost staggers one when one even partly comprehends the tremendous consequences that in all likelihood will come of it." Conceptualizing extension work in political rather than narrowly technical terms, he pointed to the problem of relating

> all this public work to the development of a democracy. I am not thinking so much of the development of a form of government as of a real democratic expression on the part of the people. Agriculture is our basic industry. As we organize its affairs, so to a great degree shall we secure the results in society in general.[30]

In Bailey's view, higher education's engagement with farmers needed to take the form of a democratic association that is deeply educative. For him, it was imperative that "education should result or function politically." With regard to the kind of education that should be provided by land-grant colleges of agriculture, he wrote,

> It is not sufficient to train technically in the trades and crafts and arts to the end of securing greater economic efficiency—this may be accomplished in a despotism and result in no self-action on the part of the people. Every democracy must reach far beyond what is commonly known as economic efficiency, and do everything it can to enable those in the backgrounds to maintain their standing and their pride and to partake in the making of political affairs.[31]

Bailey's broad, highly ambitious, and inherently political vision of the land-grant system and mission was not a momentary anomaly that no one else shared. It was embraced by many people and was incorporated into the rhetoric and culture of the national Cooperative Extension System during the first few decades of its existence. This can be seen in the opening paragraph of a book published in 1930 titled

The Agricultural Extension System, which was authored by two national extension leaders:

> There is a new leaven at work in rural America. It is stimulating to better endeavor in farming and home making, bringing rural people together in groups for social intercourse and study, solving community and neighborhood problems, fostering better relations and common endeavor between town and country, bringing recreation, debate, pageantry, the drama and art into the rural community, developing coopera- tion and enriching the life and broadening the vision of rural men and women. This new leaven is the cooperative extension work of the state agricultural colleges and the federal Department of Agriculture, which is being carried on in cooperation with the counties and rural people throughout the United States.[32]

This remarkable paragraph provides a tantalizing glimpse of a *prophetic counternarrative* of the land-grant system and mission. It tells the story of a collaborative, rather than oppressive, relationship between campus and community. Like the heroic metanarrative, this story has an ascending plotline. However, unlike it, the prophetic counternarra- tive is not mainly or only about economic productivity and efficiency and scientific progress. It is also and more centrally about the cultural and political promise of forwarding difficult struggles for freedom and sustainability. It reflects an embrace of the task that Liberty Hyde Bailey assigned to land-grant colleges of agriculture in 1909: to not only aid in developing the economy but also "to direct and to aid in developing the entire rural civilization." As he put it, such a task placed these colleges "within the realm of statesmanship." In other words, it placed them within the realm of politics. In this realm, farmers and others would take up roles as active and productive citizens rather than as passive and needy clients and customers. They would partner and collaborate with faculty members and extension agents who serve not only or mainly as infor- mation providers and problem solvers but also, and more importantly, as organizers of public work.

Rather than being a heroic story about the amazing results of science- based service, or a tragic story about the oppressive and destructive workings of power, the prophetic counternarrative is a hopeful story about the interrelated struggles for freedom and sustainability. It restories some of the same facts, events, and characters that are included in the other two narratives. It also adds different facts, events, and characters that the other narratives leave out.

By restorying the land-grant system around a struggle for freedom and sustainability, the prophetic counternarrative helps us see and appreciate positive political and cultural dimensions of land-grant history that are ignored or even denied in the other two narratives. However, the prophetic counternarrative poses its own difficulties. Cast in an uncritical and overly romantic and nostalgic manner, it can slight the importance of economic and material ends, as well as the value of technical expertise. It can also overlook the workings of power and harsh realities of racism, sexism, classism, and inequality. In short, similar to each of the other two narratives, it can be narrated in ways that are both incomplete and open to debate and disagreement.

Conclusion

In conclusion, I want to be clear about my perspective. As I see it, the history of the land-grant system is not just a heroic tale of science-based service for economic ends. It is not just a tragic tale of oppression and destruction, and it is not just a prophetic tale about the struggle for liberty and sustainability. It is, paradoxically, all of these at once. So in my view, the land-grant system not only can but also should be storied in ways that simultaneously attend to all three of these plots and perspectives.

To take up this task, historians and scholars of the land-grant system will need to develop a keen sensitivity to complexity and contradiction, and to the significance of values and perspective in shaping and guiding particular ways of setting scenes and emplotting and interpreting events and actions. They—or we, as I count myself among them—will need to learn to tell more complex stories that address erasures in previous works, incorporating new and different perspectives and neglected characters and events that enable us to see and care about the land-grant system in new ways. (This, of course, includes characters and events related to the "mechanic arts" or engineering, which I have not even mentioned in this article, as well as a myriad of other topics and themes.) We should do all this in ways that exhibit the highest standards of scholarly rigor, including the fair and accurate use and interpretation of reliable sources and credible evidence.[33]

Here, I want to offer a warning that further reveals my perspective. However much we may strive for objectivity, fairness, and accuracy, the craft of writing history has nonneutral and subjective aspects that we cannot escape. On this point, I agree with William Cronin. "Because stories concern the consequences of actions that are potentially valued in quite different ways, whether by agent, narrator, or audience," Cronin writes, "we can achieve no neutral objectivity in writing them."[34]

We should not see this as a license to abandon efforts to be objective, fair, and accurate, or to accept a relativist epistemology. We should see it instead as both an opportunity and a challenge. Storying historical events and actions in different ways, supported of course by evidence, offers opportunities for discovering new truths and meanings. There are two key challenges in pursuing these opportunities. The first has to do with the work of upholding standards of fairness and accuracy. The second has to do with the question of whether we are able and willing to hear and acknowledge the truths that new and different stories help reveal. For example, many of those who love the land-grant system will not want to hear that it has sometimes functioned in oppressive and destructive ways. However, evidence supports the claim that it has. Likewise, many who have condemned the land-grant system as an antidemocratic tragedy of colonialist oppression and environmental and cultural destruction will not believe that it has sometimes functioned in ways which were both democratic and democratizing. However, evidence supports the claim that it has (and still does).[35]

The latter of the two challenges named just now brings me to something we should not miss in the context of the sesquicentennial of the first Morrill Act. Those who work in and care about the land-grant system today are not simply looking backward. They—or we, as I also count myself among this group—are also looking forward. In doing so, we are not only wondering where we are going. We are also wondering what we should do.

One thing we should do is to listen to Alisdair MacIntyre. "I can only answer the question 'What am I to do?'" MacIntyre writes, "if I can answer the prior question 'Of what story or stories do I find myself a part?'"[36]

It makes a big difference how we answer what MacIntyre refers to as the previous question. To see why, let me again quote William Cronin, and in doing so, give him the last word: "Narratives remain our chief moral compass in the world. Because we use them to motivate and explain our actions, the stories we tell change the way we act in the world."[37]

Notes

1. "Address of Mr. Grout of Vermont," delivered on February 22, 1899, and published in *Memorial Addresses on the Life and Character of Justin S. Morrill Delivered in the Senate and House of Representatives* (Washington, DC: Government Printing Office, 1899), 95–96.
2. William Cronon, "A Place for Stories: Nature, History, and Narrative," *The Journal of American History* 78, no. 4 (1992): 1374.

3. There is a vast literature on the use of narrative in human discourse and academic research. Notable examples include Hayden White, *The Fiction of Narrative* (Baltimore, MD: The Johns Hopkins University Press, 2010); D. Jean Clandinin, ed., *Handbook of Narrative Inquiry: Mapping a Methodology* (Thousand Oaks, CA: Sage Publications, 2007); Mary Jo Maynes, Jennifer L. Pierce, and Barbara Laslett, *Telling Stories: The Use of Personal Narratives in the Social Sciences and History* (Ithaca, NY: Cornell University Press, 2008); and Catherine Kohler Riessman, *Narrative Methods for the Human Sciences* (Thousand Oaks, CA: Sage Publications, 2008).

4. Cronon, "A Place for Stories," 1370.

5. For accounts of Bailey's life and work, see Andrew D. Rodgers, *Liberty Hyde Bailey: A Story of American Plant Sciences* (Princeton, NJ: Princeton University Press, 1949); Philip Dorf, *Liberty Hyde Bailey: An Informal Biography* (Ithaca, NY: Cornell University Press, 1956). For a collection of Bailey's writings, see Zachary Michael Jack, ed., *Liberty Hyde Bailey: Essential Agrarian and Environmental Writings* (Ithaca, NY: Cornell University Press, 2008). On Bailey's role in the Country Life Commission, see Clayton S. Ellsworth, "Theodore Roosevelt's Country Life Commission," *Agricultural History* 34, no. 4 (October 1960): 155–72; Scott J. Peters and Paul A. Morgan, "The Country Life Commission: Reconsidering a Milestone in American Agricultural History," *Agricultural History* 78, no. 3 (Summer 2004): 289–316.

6. Morris Bishop, *A History of Cornell* (Ithaca, NY: Cornell University Press, 1962), 313.

7. Frederick Rudolph, *The American College and University: A History* (Athens, GA: The University of Georgia Press, 1962, 1990), 260–61.

8. For example, I have found the heroic metanarrative in many of the speeches I have read that were presented as a "Justin Smith Morrill Lecture" or "William H. Hatch Lecture" for USDA. To read some of these speeches, go to http://www.nifa.usda.gov/about/speeches/speeches.html (accessed April 1, 2012).

9. For examples of the heroic metanarrative of the land-grant system and mission in the academic literature, see especially F. B. Mumford, *The Land-Grant College Movement* (Columbia, MO: University of Missouri Agricultural Experiment Station, 1940); Earle D. Ross, *Democracy's College: The Land-Grant Movement in the Formative Stage* (Ames, IA: The Iowa State College Press, 1942); Edward Danforth Eddy, Jr., *Colleges for Our Land and Time: The Land-Grant Idea in American Education* (New York: Harper & Brothers, 1957); Alan Nevins, *The State Universities and Democracy* (Urbana, IL: University of Illinois Press, 1962); Patricia H. Crosson, *Public Service in Higher Education*; James B Edmond, *The Magnificent Charter: The Origin and Role of the Morrill Land-Grant Colleges and Universities* (Hicksville, NY: Exposition Press, 1978); Wayne D. Rasmussen, *Taking the University to the People: Seventy-Five Years of Cooperative Extension* (Ames, IA: Iowa State University Press, 1989); John R. Campbell, *Reclaiming a Lost Heritage: Land-Grant and Other Higher Education Initiatives for the Twenty-first Century* (Ames, IA: Iowa State University Press, 1995); and National Research Council, *Colleges of Agriculture at the Land-Grant Universities: Public Service and Public Policy* (Washington, DC: National Academy Press, 1996).

10. These special addresses were published together in *The Spirit of the Land-Grant Institutions: Addresses Delivered at the Forty-fifth Annual Convention of the Association of Land-Grant Colleges and Universities at Chicago, IL, November 16–18, 1931* (Washington, DC: Association of Land-Grant Colleges and Universities, 1931).

11. Ibid., 22.

12. Arthur J. Klein, ed., *Survey of Land-Grant Colleges and Universities* (Washington, DC: United States Department of the Interior, Office of Education, Bulletin No. 9, 1930), 1.

13. Roger Williams notes the inaccuracy of several scholars' portrayals of the nature of higher education during the early nineteenth century in his book, *The Origins of Federal Support for Higher Education*. Williams draws mainly on two studies: Stanley M. Guralnick, *Science and the Ante-Bellum American College* (Philadelphia, PA: The American Philosophical Society, 1975); Colin B. Burke, *American Collegiate Populations: A Test of the Traditional View* (New York: New York University Press, 1982). These and other studies question the accuracy of the "traditional" account of American higher education in the colonial and early national periods that Donald G. Tewksbury presented in his book, *The Founding of American Colleges and Universities before the Civil War* (New York: Teachers College, 1932). For more recent scholarship that challenges presumptions about and previous studies of the ante-bellum college, see Roger L. Geiger, ed., *The American College in the Nineteenth Century* (Nashville: Vanderbilt University Press, 2000).

14. Williams, *Origins of Federal Support for Higher Education*, 9.

15. Daniel T. Rodgers, *Atlantic Crossings: Social Politics in a Progressive Age* (Cambridge, MA: Belknap Press, 1998), 321.

16. James C. Scott, *Seeing Like A State: How Certain Schemes to Improve the Human Condition Have Failed* (New Haven, CT: Yale University Press, 1998), 286, 287.

17. The essence of the tragic counternarrative can be found in Jim Hightower, *Hard Tomatoes, Hard Times* (Cambridge, MA: Schenkman Publishing, 1973, 1978); Wendell Berry, *The Unsettling of America: Culture and Agriculture*, 3rd ed. (San Francisco, CA: Sierra Club Books, 1977, 1996). Also see Rachael Carson, *Silent Spring* (Boston, MA: Houghton Mifflin, 1962); David D. Danbom, *The Resisted Revolution: Urban America and the Industrialization of Agriculture, 1900–1930* (Ames, IA: Iowa State University Press, 1979); Katherine Jellison, *Entitled to Power: Farm Women and Technology, 1913–1963* (Chapel Hill, NC: The University of North Carolina Press, 1993); Mary Neth, *Preserving the Family Farm: Women, Community, and the Foundations of Agribusiness in the Midwest, 1900–1940* (Baltimore, MD: The Johns Hopkins University Press, 1995); Frieda Knobloch, *The Culture of Wilderness: Agriculture as Colonization in the American West* (Chapel Hill: University of North Carolina Press, 1996); Ronald R. Kline, *Consumers in the Country: Technology and Social Change in Rural America* (Baltimore, MD: The Johns Hopkins University Press, 2000); and Deborah Fitzgerald, *Every Farm A Factory: The Industrial Ideal in American Agriculture* (New Haven, CT: Yale University Press, 2003).

18. Berry, *Unsettling of America*, 155.

19. For example, Frieda Knobloch draws from Michele Faucault's works to sketch a tragic counternarrative about both the land-grant system and USDA in her book, *The Culture of Wilderness*. In another example, Gordon Gary Scoville draws on Antonio Gramsci's works in his full-scale elaboration of the allegedly antidemocratic nature of the land-grant system and mission, *Anti-Democracy's College: An Outline of the Corporatist Culture of Organized Social Machinery and the Leadership of the Land-Grant Agricultural Colleges in the "Progressive" Era* (Unpublished doctoral diss., Montana State University, 1990).

20. Liberty Hyde Bailey, *The Principles of Fruit Growing* (New York, NY: Macmillan, 1897), 26.

21. Steven Stoll, *Larding the Lean Earth: Soil and Society in Nineteenth-Century America* (New York, NY: Hill and Wang, 2002), 19–31. For a history of the idea

and ideal of a "permanent" and "self-sustaining" agriculture in the twentieth century, see Randal S. Beeman and James A. Pritchard, *A Green and Permanent Land: Ecology and Agriculture in the Twentieth Century* (Lawrence: University Press of Kansas, 2001).

22. Liberty Hyde Bailey, *The College of Agriculture and the State* (Ithaca, NY: New York State College of Agriculture, 1909), 1.

23. For more about Bailey's work and views on these matters, see Scott J. Peters, "Every Farmer Should be Awakened: Liberty Hyde Bailey's Vision of Agricultural Extension Work," *Agricultural History* 80, no. 2 (Spring 2006): 190–219; Paul A. Morgan and Scott J. Peters, "The Foundations of Planetary Agrarianism: Thomas Berry and Liberty Hyde Bailey," *Journal of Agricultural and Environmental Ethics* 19, no. 5 (August 2006): 443–68; and Ben A. Minteer, *The Landscape of Reform: Civic Pragmatism and Environmental Thought in America* (Cambridge: MIT Press, 2006).

24. Liberty Hyde Bailey, "The Better Preparation of Men for College and Station Work," in *Proceedings of the Twenty-Third Annual Convention of the Association of American Agricultural Colleges and Experiment Stations*, ed. Alfred C. True and William H. Beal (Washington, DC: Government Printing Office, 1910), 25–26.

25. Liberty Hyde Bailey, "The Outlook for the College of Agriculture," in *Addresses at the Dedication of the Buildings of the New York State College of Agriculture* (Ithaca, NY: Cornell University, 1907), 40.

26. Bailey, *College of Agriculture and the State*, 11–12.

27. Liberty Hyde Bailey, *Cyclopedia of American Agriculture*, vol. IV (New York, NY: Macmillan, 1909), 411.

28. Liberty Hyde Bailey "What Is Agricultural Education?" in *Cornell Nature Study Leaflets* (Albany, NY: J. B. Lyon Company, 1904), 53.

29. Liberty Hyde Bailey, *The Holy Earth* (New York, NY: Charles Scribner's Sons, 1915), 140–41.

30. Ibid., 140, 141, 142.

31. Ibid., 41.

32. C. B. Smith and M. C. Wilson, *The Agricultural Extension System of the United States* (New York, NY: John Wiley & Sons, 1930), 1.

33. For a recent work of history about the land-grant system that meets all these requirements, see Scott M. Gelber, *The University and the People: Envisioning American Higher Education in an Era of Populist Protest* (Madison: University of Wisconsin Press, 2011).

34. Cronon, "A Place for Stories," 1370. On the issue of objectivity in historical and other scholarship, see Peter Novick, *That Noble Dream: The "Objectivity Question" and the American Historical Profession* (New York: Cambridge University Press, 1988); Allan Megill, ed., *Rethinking Objectivity* (Durham, NC: Duke University Press, 1994); Joyce Appleby, Lynn Hunt, and Margaret Jacob, *Telling the Truth about History* (New York: W. W. Norton, 1994); Georg G. Iggers, *Historiography in the Twentieth Century: From Scientific Objectivity to the Postmodern Challenge* (Middletown, CT: Wesleyan University Press, 1997); Thomas Haskell, *Objectivity is Not Neutrality: Explanatory Schemes in History* (Baltimore, MD: The Johns Hopkins University Press, 1998); Naomi Scheman, "Epistemology Resuscitated: Objectivity as Trustworthiness," in *Engendering Rationalities*, ed. Nancy Tuana and Sandra Morgen (Albany, NY: SUNY Press, 2001), 23–52; and Lorraine J. Daston and Peter Galison, *Objectivity* (Brooklyn, NY: Zone Books, 2007).

35. On the democratizing functions, see Scott J. Peters et al., eds., *Engaging Campus and Community: The Practice of Public Scholarship in the State and Land-Grant University System* (Dayton, OH: Kettering Foundation Press, 2005); Scott J. Peters,

Democracy and Higher Education: Traditions and Stories of Civic Engagement (East Lansing: Michigan State University Press, 2010).

36. Alasdair MacIntyre, *After Virtue: A Study in Moral Theory* (Notre Dame: University of Notre Dame Press, 1981/1984), 216.

37. Cronon, "A Place for Stories," 1375.

List of Contributors

J. Gregory Behle is professor of Christian Education at The Master's College in Santa Clarita, California. His research focus is on student backgrounds, collegiate life, and postcollege attainments at the University of Illinois during its first twenty-five years.

Roger L. Geiger is distinguished professor of Higher Education, Pennsylvania State University, and editor of *Perspectives on the History of Higher Education*.

Scott Gelber is an assistant professor of Education and assistant professor of History (By Courtesy) at Wheaton College in Norton, Massachusetts. He has written *The University and the People: Envisioning American Higher Education in an Era of Populist Protest*, and his current research project examines the legal history of American higher education from 1860 to 1960.

Christopher P. Loss is assistant professor of Public Policy and Higher Education at Vanderbilt University and the author of *Between Citizens and the State: The Politics of American Higher Education in the 20th Century*. He will be a visiting fellow at the American Academy of Arts & Sciences in 2012–2013.

Peter L. Moran, J.D. is the assistant dean of Policy and Planning at Penn State Altoona and a PhD candidate in the higher education program at Penn State. His research focuses on legal issues in higher education.

Adam R. Nelson is professor of Educational Policy Studies and History at the University of Wisconsin-Madison. His chief publications include *Education and Democracy: The Meaning of Alexander Meiklejohn, 1872–1964*. He is currently writing a book titled *Empire of Knowledge: Nationalism, Internationalism, and Scholarship in the Early American Republic*.

Scott J. Peters is a professor in the Cultural Foundations of Education Department at Syracuse University, and Co-Director of Imagining America: Artists and Scholars in Public Life (imaginingamerica.org). His latest book is *Democracy and Higher Education: Traditions and Stories of Civic Engagement* (Michigan State University Press, 2010).

Susan Richardson is an independent scholar and principal of Education by the Numbers, LLC. She resides in Houston, TX.

Jane Robbins is senior lecturer, Innovation, Entrepreneurship, and Institutional Leadership in the McGuire Center for Entrepreneurship, Eller College of Management, University of Arizona. Her research interests include patent policy, conflict of interest, and institutional change in research universities.

Ethan Schrum is a postdoctoral fellow at the Institute for Advanced Studies in Culture at the University of Virginia, where he is writing a book on American research universities after World War II. He holds a PhD in history from the University of Pennsylvania and has published articles in *History of Education Quarterly* and *Perspectives on the History of Higher Education*.

Winton U. Solberg is professor emeritus at the University of Illinois, Urbana-Champaign. He has written extensively on the history of the University of Illinois, most recently, *Reforming Medical Education: The University of Illinois College of Medicine, 1880–1920.*

Nathan M. Sorber is assistant professor of Educational Leadership Studies at West Virginia University. His 2011 dissertation, *Farmers, Scientists, and "Officers of Industry": The Formation and Reformation of Land-Grant Colleges in the Northeastern United States, 1862–1906,* was honored with the Alumni Association Dissertation Award from Pennsylvania State University.

Roger L. Williams is executive director of the Penn State Alumni Association and associate affiliate professor of Education at Penn State. He is the author of *The Origins of Federal Support for Higher Education: George W. Atherton and the Land-Grant College Movement.*

Gregory R. Zieren is a professor of History at Austin Peay State University, where he has been teaching since 1991. He is currently working on a book about German impressions of the United States.